Bushels and Bales

Memoirs and Occasional Papers
Association for Diplomatic Studies and Training

In 2003, the Association for Diplomatic Studies and Training (ADST) created the Memoirs and Occasional Papers Series to preserve firsthand accounts and other informed observations on foreign affairs for scholars, journalists, and the general public. Sponsoring publication of the series is one of numerous ways in which ADST, a nonprofit organization founded in 1986, seeks to promote understanding of American diplomacy and those who conduct it. Together with the Foreign Affairs Oral History program and ADST's support for the training of foreign affairs personnel at the State Department's Foreign Service Institute, these efforts constitute the Association's fundamental purposes.

J. Chapman Chester
FROM FOGGY BOTTOM TO CAPITOL HILL
Exploits of a G.I., Diplomat, and Congressional Aide

Robert E. Gribbin
IN THE AFTERMATH OF GENOCIDE
The U.S. Role in Rwanda

Allen C. Hansen
NINE LIVES: A Foreign Service Odyssey

James R. Huntley
AN ARCHITECT OF DEMOCRACY
Building a Mosaic of Peace

John G. Kormann
ECHOES OF A DISTANT CLARION
Recollections of a Diplomat and Soldier

Armin Meyer
QUIET DIPLOMACY
From Cairo to Tokyo in the Twilight of Imperialism

William Morgan and Charles Stuart Kennedy, eds.
AMERICAN DIPLOMATS: The Foreign Service at Work

James M. Potts
FRENCH COVERT ACTION
IN THE AMERICAN REVOLUTION

Daniel Whitman
A HAITI CHRONICLE
The Undoing of a Latent Democracy

Bushels and Bales

A Food Soldier in the Cold War

Howard L. Steele

Association for Diplomatic Studies and Training
Memoirs and Occasional Papers Series

NAP NEW ACADEMIA PUBLISHING VELLUM

Washington, DC

The views and opinions in this book are solely those of the author and not necessarily those of the Association for Diplomatic Studies and Training or the United States government.

VELLUM/New Academia Publishing, 2008

Printed in the United States of America

Library of Congress Control Number: 2008931230
ISBN 978-0-9800814-9-7 paperback (alk. paper)

Contents

Preface

An earlier book called *Food Soldier,* privately published by Ravens Yard Publishing in April 2002, contained many of the incongruous confrontations, escapes, family problems, and often humorous experiences in my overseas life in developing countries from 1964 until my retirement from federal service with the Foreign Agricultural Service (FAS) of the United States Department of Agriculture (USDA) in 1997.

The manuscript for *Food Soldier* contained many anecdotes, experiences, and observational stories that were edited out by the publisher in the interest of shortening the book. I believe that the reader will enjoy those that were left out then but included here, and many more, written down before memory or facts go missing.

I have also corrected some misconceptions that crept into the original work. For example, the publisher, while properly indicating that I retired from the FAS, left the impression that I served with the FAS continuously from 1971 until retirement in 1997, twenty-six and a half years. In fact, I was hired by the small, independent agency of USDA called the Foreign Economic Development Service (FEDS) in January 1971. It worked primarily with United States Agency for International Development (USAID) contracts and funding, trying to improve the income, level of living, and well-being of people in the rural sectors of developing countries.

In 1972, FEDS was merged with the Economic Research Service (ERS) of USDA as the Foreign Development Division, when our administrator, Dr. Quentin West, was named administrator of ERS. With the change in the executive branch following the election of 1976, we were soon separated again and became the independent Office of International Cooperation and Development (OICD). Finally, we were merged back with the FAS in 1992, where we had been before 1968.

I mention these changes because being moved around to different agencies while serving overseas often created serious organizational and administrative problems for us technicians and our families. I discuss some of these restrictions and problems later in the text. But many of my experiences with the United States government had interesting antecedents in the private sector and academia. *Bushels and Bales* is primarily about the exceptionally interesting people I met and worked with in the various states and countries where I had the privilege to serve. In this new volume I have also recorded facts about my early life and education, plus interesting trips of a more touristy nature taken recently that I wanted to share.

But, let us begin!

Acknowledgments

A person accomplishes very little alone. The support and encouragement of family, friends and colleagues is catalytic. In my case, I owe much to many persons, but probably cannot properly acknowledge each person's contribution. Primary supporters of mine include my wife, Elaine Haddock Steele, who suffered ups and downs with me as *Food Soldier* and *Bushels and Bales: A Food Soldier in the Cold War* laboriously came to fruition and publication. She and my children—John, David, Pat, and Jen—always gave me encouragement and support, as did my stepsons, Matthew and David Haddock, for which I am most grateful.

My good friend and primary editor, Eric Rozenman, gave me the encouragement to begin to write down my experiences, many of which I related to him as we commuted home from work together on the Fairfax, Virginia CUE buses over a five-year period. He was also instrumental in editing my dull, pedagogical prose, helping make the text more readable and interesting; thanks for all your help and support, Eric. My attorney and friend Ralph Tener saw possibilities in my text, led me to the publisher of *Food Soldier*, Ravens Yard Publishing, Ltd., and has been helping me in many supportive ways as I complete *Bushels and Bales: A Food Soldier in the Cold War*. I am very grateful for his support and help.

Janet Hulstrand, through her firm Winged Words Editorial Services, has been of great help in giving me advice and editing my manuscript. I owe her a deep debt of gratitude for all the improvements she has helped me make in *Bushels and Bales*—thank you sincerely, Janet!

I am especially grateful to Margery Boichel Thompson, publishing director, and Kenneth L. Brown, president, of the Association of Diplomatic Studies and Training (ADST) for their support and assistance in publishing the book. Many thanks to both of you. Three ADST interns—Brian Moran, Rachel Jurkowski, and Iris Aikins-Afful—helped edit the manuscript under Margery Thompson's watchful eye, and I am most grateful to them all. Anna Lawton of New Academia Publishing, LLC put the manuscript into excellent book form, for which I am most grateful. Thanks, Anna.

My daughter Jen also helped select the pictures illustrating points in the text, using her grand photography skills. Thanks Jen. My parents Howard B. and Ruby L. Steele started it all back in 1928, and I would be remiss in not recognizing them for their educational and career support; their memory is precious. Sally Steele Farren and Jane Cornelius Steele suffered my "late night" writing proclivities in earlier years, and also supported my efforts, for which I owe them sincere thanks.

Howard L. Steele, Ph.D.
Fairfax, Virginia

Introduction

My interest in subsistence agriculture and the work of agriculturalists began as a preteen in the mid1930s as I traveled to rural areas of western Pennsylvania, eastern Ohio, and West Virginia with my father. Dad was secretary-manager of the Dairymen's Cooperative Sales Association, a bargaining co-operative that worked to bring better prices and incomes to farmers for their milk in the middle of the Great Depression. Hard-working small farmers and their families suffered many deprivations in those years, and I saw their poverty close up. My dad often said, "The farmers who need the help most are the ones who cannot get it." This made a deep impression on me, and I wondered why that was. That curiosity and those early years traveling around with my dad were the seeds from which my life's work grew.

When I moved to South Carolina to teach agricultural economics at Clemson University in the mid 1950s, I saw another type of poverty; it was caused by soils worn out from the repetitive planting of row crops such as tobacco and cotton. Poor farmers in this area of the rural South often lacked basic knowledge of improved agricultural practices, or alternative methods that could improve farming efficiency, reduce the drudgery of their labor, and raise their incomes. I decided I wanted to spend my professional life helping poor farmers increase their earning power and improve their quality of life. In a thirty-four year career that took me to forty-three different developing countries, I did just that.

It was an exciting career—often rewarding, sometimes frustrating, but always interesting. I believed then, and I believe now, that through this work we have the power to make a difference in the world. We can make a positive impact through our peaceful intervention in developing countries by exporting bales, bushels, and our agricultural expertise; not bullets or bombs. This book tells the story of my years as an enthusiastic "Food Soldier" during the years of the Cold War.

From 1960 to the present, the United States Agency for International Development (USAID), a program which began during the Kennedy Administration as part of the Alliance for Progress (but had its conceptual roots in Truman's Marshall Plan), funded agricultural and rural development programs in developing countries with the help of Department of Agriculture (USDA) technicians. The basic objectives of this work were to increase food production, improve food distribution and marketing, and help farmers earn better incomes and obtain higher levels of living. Did we who were serving in these countries and our foreign counterparts make a significant difference in the lives of these people? I think we did; but, unfortunately, not nearly as much as we had hoped for. In my opinion, the biggest contribution that we made in the "golden era" of country-to-country technical assistance from the 1950s to the 1980s was in the area of participant training, in which potential leaders from the developing countries were selected to study and observe agricultural activities in America or other developed countries. That part of our efforts has had clear and indisputable long-term benefits. Many of the participants of these programs are now in positions of significant influence in their home countries and have had a major, positive impact on agricultural practices in the developing world. These programs were immensely important in helping change local values and perspectives and in fostering cooperative international relations, regardless of whether the participants were on short-term observational trips or longer-term degree programs in U.S. universities.

USAID's development programs also helped strengthen the local universities in developing countries. My first overseas assignment was at the Agricultural College of the State of São Paulo, Brazil. The Ohio State University had been selected by the local university, the Superior College of Agriculture, and the Brazilian government to develop a graduate degree program there, using professors and graduate students from Ohio State University's College of Agriculture and Home Economics. In addition to training young professors in the United States, the program included exchanges of scientists and expanded agricultural research and extension of results to farmers and agricultural businessmen. This cooperative program of institutional development, which was funded by the United States from 1964 until 1994, involved significant exchanges of agricultural information; scientific collaboration continues between the two universities today.

Today, USAID (with sharply reduced funding from Congress) is involved in far fewer developing countries around the world than formerly, and cannot have the impact that it once did. Its programs now concentrate more on Africa and Middle Eastern countries such as Iraq, Afghanistan, Israel, Egypt and Jordan. Dramatically fewer USAID programs are active in developing countries in Asia and the Western hemisphere than before.

When I tell people that I spent most of my career working for the U.S. government in various foreign posts from 1971 through 1997, I am often asked if I was a spy. My negative response seems to disappoint many people. Of course, I did know and encounter quite a few spies during my years abroad; those who were not "under deep cover" were research analysts, usually gathering intelligence information that could take a number of forms. Though I was not a spy, as a civil service employee within the USDA during those years, it was necessary for me to obtain a "Top Secret" security clearance.

One humorous episode occurred when I received a telephone call from a former neighbor in Clemson. We had moved away some years earlier, and were not in frequent communication any longer, so I was surprised to hear from him. He began by chatting about some general things, telling me about the health of his family, asking me about mine. But I could tell he wanted to ask me something else that he was not getting to. Finally he blurted it out: "Howard, are you in some kind of legal trouble? There has been an FBI agent visiting the neighborhood and asking all kinds of questions about you." I laughed and explained that I was applying for a job with the USDA, and that because of travel overseas and work with USAID missions, I needed security clearance. Although my job was unspectacular—at least compared to the work of spies—during the Cold War, even an agricultural economist has moments of drama, such as the night I put top-secret classified documents under the mattress of my hotel bed rather than risk taking them to the U.S. Embassy through the mean streets of Tehran in the middle of the night!

Spending much of my professional career in developing countries has not only given me the opportunity to help make a difference through agriculture, it has also given me a privileged perspective on daily life in other parts of the world. I learned early on that the aspirations and hopes of the average citizen in developing countries are, not surprisingly, the same as they were in America in earlier times. The typical rural resident in these countries wants a higher level of living for his family: less drudgery in daily labor requirements, better education for their children, improved health care and housing, increased security from the unavoidable down cycles in farming, better markets for the sale of crops, peace and tranquility, and more free time to enjoy life.

It was a particular thrill for me to see the results of our work in Honduras between 1980 and 1982, when we taught peasant farmers how to raise perishable vegetables during the dry season. They earned outstanding incomes from it. Those campesinos had never been entrepreneurs before, but mere laborers for absentee owners and their overseers. Through our project, The Fresh Vegetable Export Project in the Comayagua Valley, they learned how to produce perishable vegetables for the export market using a high level of technology—drip irrigation—then harvested, packed and shipped them to the U.S. winter market in what became one of the first (and most successful) Caribbean Basin Initiative projects. When I returned to Honduras for a visit in 2001, I was able to see the result of that work in the form of expanded operations in that valley, most of them now owned by Honduran farmers and businessmen. That is one project I am very proud of having managed.

The principles of economic development for the poor rural sectors of underdeveloped countries are basically quite similar, although details differ from country to country. This can be extremely rewarding work. Because of the poverty in these countries, even small changes in agricultural practices can yield dramatic changes in the levels of living and well-being for the people. There were, of course, serious risks to contend with. Weather is always a capricious risk to farmers, as are disease and pest problems. Markets and price behavior are also beyond the average farmer's control.

There were of course many other obstacles to successful intervention in these countries. Often American consultants grappled with apathy on the part of their foreign counterparts, or a fatalistic "resignation"—an attitude that things could not get any better in the host country. Sometimes false pride or misplaced skepticism kept host officials from accepting innovations and new techniques, or wanting to change the older ones. But also, sometimes American technicians would forget that they were guests in the developing country, and as such needed to be extremely sensitive to local history, traditions, culture, and the pride of accomplishment people felt in their work and traditions. Finally, there was the problem of finding a sufficient number of well-educated and motivated leaders in the top echelons of the host country. Often the number was quite small, and there was a dearth of talent in the middle levels, where most development technicians must operate.

Did we make mistakes in our efforts to help developing countries "jump start" their rural sectors? Yes, we did. The most blatant of them were rooted in a lack of understanding of local economic and cultural traditions. Many development specialists tried to transfer American agricultural technology directly to the developing countries with little success, or without thoroughly thinking through the consequences. Sometimes the attempt to transfer very expensive capital goods to primitive rural areas was highly impractical, or even detrimental, to the farmers. Peasant agricultural societies on the edge of subsistence parameters cannot afford the costly mechanical planting, pest control, and harvesting inventions routinely used in developed countries. Additionally, for social and cultural reasons, farmers need to be gradually weaned away from traditional practices used for centuries in these societies—not shocked or forced into change. And in some cases, introducing certain technological advances may not have even been appropriate.

For example, how many American or other Western development specialists were familiar with the inexpensive, extremely low-tech, and extremely effective practice of intercropping in Central America? In intercropping, two basic food crops, for example beans and corn, are planted together, with the beans planted at the base of the corn plant. The beans can then use the corn stock as a "trellis" as the two plants mature together. In the mountainous rainforests of Mexico and Costa Rica, coffee and banana trees are planted together. The leaves that fall from the banana trees prevent the growth of weeds harmful to the coffee. In cases like these what is needed is not *replacement* of the cultural system, but an attempt to improve or maximize it. In other words, in order to make the most effective impact, sometimes Western development specialists have to change *their* thought processes.

When they did take the time and have the right mindset to build on already effective local agricultural practices, the result was a good one. In the case of intercropping, it was possible to double or even triple the output simply by introducing higher yielding seeds and an innovative fertilization program.

My first boss at USDA, Dr. Quentin West, often provided expert witness testimony to Congressional Committees in support of more foreign assistance funding for the executive departments, including USAID and USDA. I was often by his side as he testified, prepared to hand him statistics and other factual material to back him up. Dr. West's justifications for more Congressional funding for our programs and projects were very succinctly stated, and provided a good overall answer to the question of what we were aiming to do in our development work during those years of the Cold War: 1) we were in a geopolitical competition with the Soviet Union and Communist China for friends and their support, and our new friends needed our economic and military support; 2) we were humanitarians, and frequently came to our friends' assistance with food and financial support when natural disasters like earthquakes, droughts, floods, typhoons, and hurricanes struck. Having said that, however; 3) we acknowledged the fact that our goals were not completely altruistic. We hoped to help these underdeveloped countries grow and become economically stronger, and in so doing were developing them as future trading partners.

My graduate school training had taught me that development in agricultural and rural sectors in most developing countries is a powerful engine of total economic growth, a truth that was confirmed by my own personal observations through my work in these countries around the world. This is true because the added units of income earned by the rural poor are very quickly spent on other goods and services, having a "multiplier effect" throughout the economy. Since the rural poor in these countries have so many unsatisfied needs and wants, they will spend sixty percent or more of that added income. This creates demand for other goods and services in the economy, thus more jobs, incomes, and economic growth.[1] Seeing this principle in action, I was pleased to spend most of my career engaged in seeking to generate this kind of activity.

I am retired now, and as I have the time and leisure to look back on my career, I have found myself wondering how many young professionals (whether they are still in school, or are merely contemplating a change of career within the private sector) could benefit from reading about many of my experiences overseas in developing and developed countries. I had a lot of good experiences and also some not so good ones; I experienced both successes and failures. It occurred to me that my story might inspire young people contemplating a career in international development, and could also shed light on some of the pitfalls in overseas careers and how best they might be avoided.

The Cold War has been over for nearly twenty years now, and we are embarked on a new stage of international politics. The struggles that will shape the world for our children and grandchildren are not the same ones that we were grappling with in the last half of the twentieth century. On the other hand, many of today's struggles have common elements with those struggles of the past, and the work of Americans abroad is hardly less crucial, or controversial, than it has ever been. What do we owe the world? What does the rest of the world owe us? How can we export our American ideals to other countries and societies in a way that helps others, without insensitively and ineffectively imposing our values on other cultures? These are important questions that remain to be grappled with, and are more important than ever in our post 9/11 world.

Today American agriculturalists are at work in Africa, the Middle East and some Asian and Western hemisphere countries. What are the issues of importance to them today? What lessons can be drawn from the past? What do we need to be concerned about for our children, and for children around the world? How well are we advancing the cause of feeding the world? Where are we falling short, and what can we do about it? It is my hope that by telling my story and reflecting on my career and my times, there will be valuable lessons for the young Americans who today are already active in (or who are contemplating) international development work, and that they can gain from my experiences.

I also thought it would be to fun to share some of the more exciting situations I found myself in over the years—some humorous, some downright terrifying. I was fortunate to have survived a number of near-miss and hot water situations I found myself in during my years of Foreign Service. Sometimes I found myself in these situations through carelessness, and sometimes I was just plain unlucky. Hopefully, some of the tales I tell in these pages may serve as cautionary tales to young people following in a similar path, and may perhaps even save them from some danger or agony.

While I have no regrets, and regard my career as a very interesting and productive one, it is also true that life for the families of international development workers can be difficult in the poorest countries. In many places, there is a lack of reliable electric power and modern sanitation; there are the dangers of being exposed to diseases such as malaria or dysentery, and frequent food shortages to cope with. Language and cultural barriers must be overcome (repeatedly in most cases, as the family moves from assignment to assignment), and educational opportunities for the children may be poor at best.

On the other hand, there are so many benefits. The financial incentives then, as now, were often quite good. Housing and living costs are usually subsidized in developing countries, which are frequently classified as "hardship posts" by the State Department, and frequent "home leave" and "rest and recuperation" travel is provided. For those employed by the private sector, including the universities, there are tax advantages for international development work. Also, the exciting vacation locations and opportunities to experience other cultures at first hand draw many Americans and their families to this kind of work. Last, but hopefully not least, there is the chance to make a real difference in the lives of poor people around the world, while improving the image of America and Americans abroad.

I have been a most fortunate individual to have had three separate, but complementary, careers in my life: as a young executive in a privately owned dairy processing and distribution company in the Midwest; as a professor at several universities with teaching, research, and student counseling responsibilities; and as an international economic development specialist with the USDA for more than twenty-six years, much of that time spent working overseas. I want to share what I learned from all three of these careers with others, in the hopes that they will help others carry out international development work more effectively.

Finally, I have great pride and joy in my family. My children suffered much from my long absences, especially during their teenage years. I should like a chance to explain to all of them what I was doing during those absences. When they were teens it was not easy to describe to them what I was doing, or why I felt it was important enough to be away from them so often. Here is my chance to "fill in the record."

1

My Circuitous Route
to International Development

One Sunday in April 1989, while I was on a short-term assignment in North Yemen working on an agricultural marketing improvement project, I got myself into a very risky situation. A Consortium for International Development (CID) specialist living in Sanaa, the capital of the country, had invited one of my colleagues and me to take a ride to an oasis about twenty miles away for a picnic. He said it was a restful place with a big artesian spring. We all needed a little rest and recuperation in that hot desert country, and it sounded like a delightful idea. However, R&R was not what we were in for that day.

The ride out was uneventful, but as we went to get out of the car at the oasis, our host suddenly let out a long whistle and said, softly, with a very serious undertone, "Well, well, just look at our welcoming party." I looked up and saw five large pickup trucks loaded with Yemeni men wielding rifles. The first two trucks were outfitted with mounted machine guns. There was not a single smile as our friend greeted the Yemenis in their local Arabic dialect, and told them who we were and what we were doing there. Our host quickly gave the leader in the front truck all of our picnic supplies to "share" with his men. Then, after we had gotten back into the car, as we sped back toward the highway, he explained that we had been ordered to return to Sanaa immediately, as we were trespassing on a powerful warlord's personal oasis. Another narrow escape!

This is only one of the many close calls I managed to get into in my thirty-four-year career overseas. Somehow, I survived every time, and I have lived to tell the tales. How did I, a boy from suburban Pittsburgh, come to have all these amazing international adventures? Well, it was a long and winding road, and it had its roots in rural Pennsylvania.

My early years were spent in Mt. Lebanon Township, Pennsylvania, which is a pleasant suburb seven miles southwest of Pittsburgh.

My mother and father moved into a new house there in the summer of 1931, when I was two and a half years old. My father was then the secretary/manager of a dairy farmers' bargaining cooperative called the Dairymen's Cooperative Sales Association (DCSA). The association's headquarters were on Seventh Street in downtown Pittsburgh, not far from the Allegheny River; they also had offices in Cleveland, Ohio, and in Wheeling and Charleston, West Virginia. Dad traveled a lot, meeting with dairy farmers in eastern Ohio, western Pennsylvania, and throughout West Virginia.

As a youngster I accompanied my father on what were, for me, interesting and entertaining trips. It was on these trips that I became intimately acquainted with farmers, their lives, and their families. This was during the Great Depression, and while dairy farmers fared better than many of their neighbors—at least they had plenty of food—the prices they received for their milk (and consequently the returns for their very hard labor on those farms) were marginal. These were mostly small, family-run dairy farms, perhaps a few hundred acres in size. They had maybe fifteen to twenty dairy cows that needed to be milked every morning and evening, seven days a week, 365 days a year. I learned early in my life that dairy cows take no vacations, and consequently, taking vacations is hard for dairy farmers too.

In 1932, Governor Gifford Pinchot, President Teddy Roosevelt's first Chief of the Forest Service and a famous conservationist, appointed my father to the first Pennsylvania Milk Control Commission in Harrisburg, the state capital. Dad also helped write the first Pennsylvania Milk Control Legislation, which brought some stability to milk prices and conditions in the industry. Later, after he had entered the dairy processing and distribution business, his knowledge of Pennsylvania dairy law was helpful to his company.

My formative years were spent during the Great Depression. Like many parents, mine attempted to shield me from the frightening aspects of that terrible time. Later, when I was in college and learned that 25 percent of the labor force in America had been out of work, I wondered why we had not suffered a violent revolution. Fortunately for America, President Franklin D. Roosevelt and his advisors believed wholeheartedly in our democracy and republican form of government, and did all they could to save it from the more radical elements in the country.

Pittsburgh—with its many steel mills, aluminum industry, and copper, coal, and coke companies—was the industrial capital of America, and was particularly hard hit. Many of our relatives in the coal or steel industries were out of work, and often stayed with us for a time when they were down on their luck. Several of my dad's brothers had made lots of money in coal and steel, until the Depression hit. Then they were either out of work or had greatly reduced income. Dad had chosen to go into agriculture because, as he explained to me, he knew that everybody had to eat every day. "I figured that meant steady work for me," he told me, "though not a high salary." I paid attention to Dad's philosophy; it seemed to me that he had chosen a good career, and I felt that agriculture and the food industry were what I would also select as a career.

My parents tried hard to protect me from negative experiences. I remember witnessing only one shocking Depression-era experience, from which my mother tried, unsuccessfully, to shield me. One day when I was nine years old, in front of Kaufmann's Department Store in downtown Pittsburgh, I saw one man stab another man to death while our #38 streetcar was stopped by the crowd that had gathered as the two men fought over a space on the corner to sell apples.

Mother carefully explained to me what had happened, assured me that we were in no danger, and said the man who had committed the murder would surely be tried and would either spend his life in jail or be executed for taking another person's life. I remember that horrible scene (and how frightening it was) today as if it had occurred yesterday. This was an era of suicides, robberies, fights and murders, as desperate, unemployed men would do almost anything to provide for their families—or just to survive. Later, when we were safely back home and talking at our dinner table about what we had witnessed, Mom and Dad tried to explain the economics of the Depression and its social implications to me. They talked about speculators driving up the prices of goods and gambling in the stock market, people running on the banks because they were afraid their money was losing its value, and the problems caused by an oversupply of goods that either nobody wanted or could not afford.

From around the same time, I have a vivid memory of the only time in my life I was both hungry and frightened. My father was traveling somewhere in West Virginia, probably negotiating with farmers to take less money for their milk in order to keep their purchaser from having to declare bankruptcy. Dad and the others were supposed to have returned home by Thursday afternoon; when they did not, my mother panicked. She had a few staples, such as sugar and flour in the kitchen, but nothing else for us to eat. We had finished the large pot of vegetable soup she had made earlier in the week, and she had been counting on Dad to bring home some cheese, butter, meat and other produce, as he always did after his visits to farmers.

Friday morning she called the DCSA's main office in downtown Pittsburgh. She asked what they knew about Dad's whereabouts. They knew nothing, but promised to telephone Mom the minute they heard something.

At that point, my mother turned to me and said, "Howard, I have 10 cents. Walk up to the store in Mt. Lebanon [a mile and a half away] and buy a quart of milk [for five cents] and a half loaf of bread [also 5 cents], and we will have milk toast to eat for dinner tonight." I did what she asked, wondering and fearing all the way to the store and back what had happened to my father and what my mother and I would do after the milk and bread were gone. By the time I returned with the groceries, Mom had heard from the cooperative that the men had been delayed, but would be back in Pittsburgh by Saturday morning.

When Dad finally got home that Saturday morning, his car was loaded with fresh produce, canned meats of all kinds, butter, cheeses, and other food given to him by the grateful members of the cooperative. The three of us literally danced around the living room with our newfound largess! This experience gave me an appreciation for how lucky I was, and I never forgot the fear I had felt when it seemed that our luck could run out.

My parents tried to shield me from hardship, but they did not spoil me. I received no allowance, but earned money selling magazines—the *Saturday Evening Post, Ladies Home Journal,* and *American*—door to door, starting at the age of eleven. Like the proverbial postman, I made my rounds to my customers in rain, snow, sleet and hail, not to mention blazing sun. Later, when I was about thirteen, I had a Pittsburgh Sun Telegraph daily newspaper route. I also mowed lawns for elderly neighbors in the summer time and shoveled snow in the winter. My parents taught me the value of a dollar early in life and I have been thankful for that knowledge ever since.

Fortunately for our family, Dad was always fully employed, though he had to absorb cutbacks in his salary in order to keep his job, and he worked hard, six days a week. In 1933 the DCSA board of directors told him they would have to cut his salary in half—from $4,000 a year to $2,000. They did offer him a deal, however; they told him that if he would agree to serve as the secretary of the Pittsburgh District Dairy Council, a public relations nonprofit organization for dairy farmers, they would restore $1,000 of his salary. Dad agreed. This meant that his travel itinerary was doubled. For me, that meant that I got to take more trips with him!

Around this time, my father enrolled in night school at the University of Pittsburgh's Graduate School of Business

Administration, and he got his masters of business administration in the summer of 1937. I was there to see him be awarded his diploma, and I remember it was a very proud moment for us all.

In 1936, Dad was also called to the Agricultural Adjustment Administration in Washington, D.C., under President Franklin D. Roosevelt's New Deal, to help write federal milk marketing orders for selected cities. My father hated this work because he and his cooperative did not want the federal government establishing milk prices. They felt the cooperatives already had a good system in place working through the various state milk control commissions or boards. He also resented the politics of the left wing lawyers of the U.S. Department of Agriculture (USDA), and their attempts to dictate what the farmers and dairy processing firms should do. His service in Washington, D.C. meant that Mom and I enjoyed a number of trips to our nation's capital (as we had earlier to Harrisburg) to visit Dad, see new sights, and meet interesting people. Consequently, my taste for travel developed early in my life.

In the summer of 1942, when I was thirteen years old, my parents thought it would be good if I went to a military type summer camp to learn some regimentation, in case I had to serve in the armed forces later. World War II was raging, the attack on Pearl Harbor had taken place the previous year, American forces had been whipped by the Japanese in the Pacific, and we were about to take on the Nazis in Europe. Off I went for a month of training at Camp Sha-Mi-Del-Eca on the Greenbrier River in West Virginia.

The camp was run by the Greenbrier Military Academy. We were drilled in physical fitness, rifle use and maintenance, life-saving, boating, canoeing, horseback riding, saddlery, mountain camping, and so on. I returned for a second session in the summer of 1943 and took more advanced courses in the same subjects.

During this time, because many of the young men had volunteered or been drafted for military service, there were good job opportunities open to me as a fourteen year old. I started working at Mandell's Drug Store in Mt. Lebanon, and sometimes at Anderson's Food Market after school and on weekends. These jobs only paid about twenty-five cents an hour, but were good work experiences for me.

In the summer of 1944, at the age of fifteen, I went to work on W. W. Bullard's dairy farm near Andover, Ohio, about one hundred miles northwest of Pittsburgh. Dad helped me find the job. Mr. Bullard was a leader in the DCSA, and he and my dad were good friends. There I learned the realities of agricultural life. We milked about forty dairy cows at five o'clock every morning, fed the dairy stock, pigs, horses and poultry, and then worked in the fields all day until milking time again at five in the afternoon.

That summer I learned how to harness a team of horses, drive the team, operate a tractor, and many more agricultural chores—some of them merely tedious, others quite difficult. Yes, we did have Saturday nights free after the chores were done, and Sunday after church and Sunday dinner—until it was milking time again. Our schedule revolved around the cows' unvarying need to be milked twice daily; they could not adjust their needs for our convenience!

What was I paid for this summer of hard work? In addition to free food, laundry, and a bed to sleep in, I received a grand total of sixty dollars for my labors. When I returned to Pittsburgh at the end of the summer, my father asked me how I liked dairying and farm work.

"Dad," I said, "If I never see the south end of a dairy cow from the north end the rest of my life, it will be too soon!"

"Son," my father replied, "I was twenty-two years old before I made that decision, and went on to Penn State to find out more about the world at large. I think you've learned some good, basic lessons about work and income, a little bit ahead of me." My father had done me a real favor by sending me to Bullard's that summer!

The following summer, I became an engineer's assistant for Pennsylvania Bell Telephone Company. This turned out to be another interesting and formative educational experience. The work consisted of tapping and drilling telephone poles to see if they were rotten, checking on the safety of guy wires and connections, and so on.

Howard Cornelius, the engineer I worked for, was past retirement age. Since the younger men that Bell Telephone would have replaced him and other aging engineers with were serving in the military, they kept him on to do the thinking, and hired teenagers like me to do the physical work. Mr. Cornelius drove the car and marked all the changes needed on the blueprints for the telephone lines, poles, and services for the area, which were to be implemented by others at some future time. I did the running and climbing. This system worked well.

This job paid well enough that I was able to pursue my first love, without telling my parents what I was doing. That summer I started taking flying lessons at the grass airstrip at Bridgeville, Pennsylvania, not far from our home. I would ride my bicycle to the airfield after work and take a half-hour lesson from the owner, a pilot and Certified Flight Instructor who had been wounded in World War I. He had two Piper J-3 Cubs, and I flew in these for two dollars per lesson. I was determined to become an Army Air Corps pilot like two of my cousins and a neighbor I admired.

Eventually, I had logged about ten hours dual time with my instructor and was about to solo. The Piper J-3 Cub had a ninety horsepower engine, flew at about seventy miles per hour, and stalled at about thirty-five miles per hour. I remember one gusty, windy day when my instructor and I probably should not have been flying. I came down very slowly on the final approach, with a strong wind directly on my nose, gusting to greater than our stall speed; when I looked down it seemed like we were stationary in the air, or even going backwards and sideways.

"What should I do?!" I yelled to my instructor.

"Open the throttle and go around!" he shouted back. "You can't land in this headwind. Maybe it will calm down on your next approach."

I did what he said, but the second time was not much better, so he took over for me and landed that little plane beautifully on our third approach. Even so, I had to jump out on landing and hold the wing on the right side to steady the plane, as the wind had shifted with another hard gust and would have tipped it over otherwise.

One evening, one of the planes was down for a one hundred hour inspection and I had to wait for my lesson. When I finally got home that night my mom was in the kitchen preparing dinner and asked where I had been. It was nearly dark and she had been worried about me. I did not want to lie to her, so as I passed through the kitchen I answered, in as casual a tone as I could muster, "Oh, I was at Bridgeville, taking a flying lesson."

She said, "Oh, that's nice, you were taking a … you were taking a WHAT?!"

I told her about my furtive flying expeditions, and that grounded me for a number of years. This was the summer of 1945, and World War II ended with the Japanese surrender in August. The military was discharging thousands of pilots, including my cousins and neighbor, and they would not need me. However, by then I had the flying bug and I would never lose it.

In January 1946, during my senior year at Mt. Lebanon High School, Dad left the dairy farmers at DCSA and invested with a partner, T. H. Sappie, in a small dairy processing business on the north side of Pittsburgh called Beverly Farms, Inc. The company had been awarded a single service paper milk carton franchise by the American Can Company for "bottling" milk, probably the first in the greater Pittsburgh area. Those disposable milk cartons were preferred by many consumers to the heavy, hard-to-clean glass milk bottles that had been used for years by the industry. Therefore,

Beverly Farms had a merchandising tool that it advertised heavily and used to expand its business to supermarkets and other stores. The company did not deliver to homes at that time; it was strictly a wholesale business.

My father's knowledge about where to find reliable raw milk supplies and how to negotiate purchasing contracts was needed by Beverly Farms as its processing and distribution business grew rapidly. He was soon named executive vice president of the company, and there was a spin-off advantage for me—I soon found myself working at the dairy plant at good hourly wages. I did all kinds of menial labor: puttying windows, painting, cleaning coolers, loading and unloading freight and dairy delivery trucks. Soon I began driving the supply truck to pick up sugar, chocolate powder, butter, and empty paper milk containers at warehouses all over the Pittsburgh area.

My parents had gone into debt to buy their share of the corporation. They remortgaged our home and borrowed on all of Dad's insurance policies. This meant I would have to pay a significant portion of the cost of my college education myself. The work at the dairy during vacations and summers helped me do so.

When I grew up there, Mt. Lebanon Township had an excellent school system. My school was rated in the top one hundred high schools in the country. This was a good thing for me, since my grades were less than stellar. My real interests were in extracurricular activities: varsity track; the school radio station, where I worked as the head announcer; band (I played the clarinet); student government; drama and musicals in theater. Because of the school's solid reputation—and perhaps my winning smile—the Washington & Lee admissions officers overlooked my C+ average and accepted me. I was on my way!

I did not know it then, but this was the first big step toward that oasis in Sanaa, and to all of the other adventures I experienced in my career in international development.

2

South Carolina's Blanket of Green

Perhaps we should first track this somewhat convoluted path that eventually took me to Brazil and other international experiences beyond. I was twenty years old and taking summer courses at Penn State University (PSU) between my junior and senior years at Washington & Lee University (W&L). I needed credit for a course in business law if I was to graduate at the end of my senior year at W&L (in June of 1950) with a degree in business administration and commerce. As I had an opportunity to go into the dairy processing business with Beverly Farms, Inc. in Pittsburgh, Pennsylvania, it seemed logical to also take a course in the College of Agriculture at PSU, to see if I wanted to go there for graduate study in dairy marketing and dairy manufacturing after W&L. In other words, would I like being an "aggie"?

I registered for an intensive six week summer session in July-August 1949, signing up for both the business law course and one in dairy husbandry. The first day of class in Dairy Husbandry I (DH I) gave me a shock. The professor, Mr. Swope, read out the names of the students who had presented their attendance permission cards upon entering the classroom. When he came to my card and read my name, I responded, "Present sir". He paused, then looked at me for what seemed a long time, and said: "Mr. Steele, please stay after class as I want to talk with you." I thought: "What the heck have I done wrong? I've just entered the classroom, answered my name, and get called down for some reason to stay after class. Am I going to like this dairy husbandry caper?"

Following that first lecture I went up to Mr. Swope. After the other students' questions had been answered and they left the two of us alone, he looked at me and asked, "Are you the only Howard Steele in Pennsylvania?" I answered, "No sir, my father is also named Howard Steele." "I thought so" he answered. "Is your father in the dairy business and was he a graduate of PSU back in the mid 1920s?" "Yes sir", was my quick response.

"Well I'll be darned", said Mr. Swope, "I taught your dad here in dairy husbandry in 1925 when I arrived as a young instructor; how is your dad, and where is he now?" he continued. That conversation was friendly and positive. The next day in class, after reading our names, he asked me to stay after class again. This time he asked me, "Howard, would you like to earn some money this summer?" Paying for all my class costs, plus room in the Pollock Dormitories, meals, and expenses for my 1947 Dodge car put a financial burden on the old bank account, so I answered with a quick YES!

Mr. Swope told me to report to Mrs. Foltz, secretary to the head of the Dairy Science Department, Dr. Josephson, the next afternoon. I did, and she also remembered my dad when he was a dairy husbandry major there from 1922–25. To test my work ethic, she assigned me to clean and wax all of Dr. Josephson's chairs and large conference table in his office. There had been heavy construction work earlier in the summer in Borland Hall where his office was located, and everything was covered with dust and dirt from that activity. Apparently I passed the test.

The next day, she led me to one of the dairy laboratories and storage rooms where there were about twenty cream separators torn down into hundreds of pieces. Each piece was heavily covered with dirt and dust from the construction. My job was to scrub and rinse every part, dry it, and assemble each set of stainless steel parts into a complete cream separator ready for use. This task took several days. Again, I passed inspection!

Dr. Davy, the laboratory instructor in my dairy husbandry class, then asked if I would set up one of the laboratories for the short course students who were coming for instruction in another week. He showed me how each lab position, of which there were thirty in the room, should be stocked with various sizes of glass pipettes, a Bunsen burner, flasks, calipers for measuring, filter papers, agar dishes, and microscopes. This was very interesting since my class colleagues and I in DH-I only recently learned how to use this lab equipment. We were learning how to conduct Babcock tests to determine the butterfat content of milk samples, take samples for bacteria contamination, develop bacterial cluster growth in agar dishes, count bacteria under the microscopes, and the use of lactometers to test for water contamination in milk.

Then Mr. Swope kept me after class lecture another day to explain that he was going on vacation, and Dr. Davy (who was going to take over the lecture series) wanted me to be the laboratory instructor for the short course students due at PSU the next week. I was floored!

"But Mr. Swope," I said, "I just learned these laboratory techniques last week myself—they're very new to me." "Right" said Mr. Swope, "They are very fresh in your mind and you should be able to do a smashing job with the new students!" End of discussion.

The following week, with Dr. Davy's laboratory manual in hand and dressed in the required long white laboratory coat, I met the new short course students in my lab class! Half of them looked old enough to be my father! They came from all over Pennsylvania, some from New Jersey and Maryland, and were anxious to learn these new (to them) dairy science laboratory techniques. I felt nervous, with a keen sense of caution in my instruction, yet was very proud of my new activity. We got along very well together. Need I tell you that because I was teaching the subject to others I aced the course myself with an A+? What a marvelous experience, and I got paid too. Plus, I earned a B+ in business law! This probably contributed to my decision to leave the dairy processing business in western Pennsylvania in 1956 and join the faculty at Clemson University to conduct research and teach agricultural economics subjects. I felt sure I would enjoy academia and working with students through research and teaching.

My First Experiences in a "Developing Economy": South Carolina in the 1950s

Following the completion of my Master's Degree at PSU in March of 1952, I became Sales Manager of Beverly Farm's Greenville Dairy Company in Greenville, Pennsylvania, which was about ninety miles northwest of Pittsburgh. My high school girlfriend, Sally Funk, and I married in June of 1952. She had been teaching music in the Mercer County, Pennsylvania schools since August of 1951, having graduated from Westminster (Pennsylvania) College's Conservatory of Music in June of that year. Since Mercer was only fifteen miles from Greenville, we rented an apartment in Mercer, and I commuted by car to my work while she walked to the Mercer schools.

After four years at Greenville Dairy Company, fighting the International Brotherhood of Teamsters—which represented all our employees at Greenville Dairy, including my deliverymen and salesmen—I had it with the dairy business. International Vice President James R. Hoffa, operating out of Teamster's Detroit, Michigan territory, and International Vice President Harry Tevis, operating out of Teamster's Pittsburgh territory, were fighting for the presidency of the union. My employees were caught in the middle. Additionally, I did not like the management structure in my company, or the lopsided competitive battles I had to fight in the sales territories that were my responsibility. Therefore, when my former fellow student for the Master's degree at PSU, Ernest Evan Brown, wrote to me about the great opportunities in our field in South Carolina and the southeast, I became very interested.

In spring of 1956, Sally, oldest son John (three years old), and I took a vacation to Clemson to visit the college and the Browns. When I met Dr. George H. Aull, famous head of the department of agricultural economics and rural sociology at Clemson, he offered me a job as assistant agricultural economist beginning in September of 1956. Evan Brown had "greased the wheels", and I was excited. I talked the situation over with my parents. Dad was an official of Beverly Farms and Greenville Dairies, and I did not want to compromise his relations in the companies. He said, "If you do not want to stay in the dairy processing business, I can understand, and your leaving will not affect my position or retirement plans. By all means, go and do what you think you will like best." He continued, "That is what I did when I left our farm, moved to Pittsburgh, and worked with the dairy farmers in western Pennsylvania, eastern Ohio and West Virginia. Go with our blessings!"

So I accepted Dr. Aull's offer at Clemson, resigned from my position at Greenville Dairy Company, and we moved to Clemson, South Carolina over Labor Day of 1956. Talk about cultural adjustment—please pay attention to some of this Pennsylvania Yankee's experiences in the mid-1950s.

Our moving van was waiting for us at the nice home we had rented in Clemson on Fort Rutledge Road when we arrived the Sunday before Labor Day. I told Sally I would spend the whole Labor Day unpacking boxes, moving furniture, and putting things away. On the trip down from Pennsylvania through West Virginia, Sally was nauseous constantly. Later medical tests confirmed that sons John, three and a half, and David, one and a half, would have a sibling, so Sally needed my help. When I reported for work the Tuesday after Labor Day Monday, Dr. Aull said he heard we were in town. I explained what I was doing on Labor Day. In his high-pitched laugh he said, "Howard, we don't recognize Labor Day as a holiday here in South Carolina. We do recognize General Robert E. Lee's birthday, however!" I was really embarrassed to be AWOL on the first day of my new job. He found it amusing.

Later that first week Dr. Aull introduced me to the department faculty at their weekly meeting. He was quite gracious, and kidded me some more in his light manner. "Howard comes to us from Pennsylvania up there in Yankee country. I told him that didn't matter, after all he had no control over where he was born, but he sure did have a choice as to where he wanted to live, and he wants to live with us here in South Carolina!" This brought a howl of laughter from the other faculty. Then Dr. Aull said: "Howard told me that he was a Methodist, and I told him I didn't think one HAD to be a southern Baptist to get into heaven, but it sure would help." Again more laughter: I think I was accepted in the group, thanks in great measure to Dr. Aull's humorous words.

Then I had an appointment to see the department's famous full professor and teacher of economic theory at Clemson for many years, Dr. James Marvin Stepp. This was a required protocol, to call on South Carolina's famous economist. He invited me into his office and after some polite chitchat about my family and experiences, he asked: "Steele, do you know what Clemson A. & M. College stands for?" I responded, "Yes sir, I believe that it stands for Clemson Agricultural and Mechanical College." "Wrong, Steele; it stands for 'Clemson athletic and military college' and we got rid of the military (meaning mandatory Reserve Officers Training Corps) two years ago, in 1954." He let out a guffaw that could be heard all over the building. Jim Stepp was a fine gentleman and a great teacher, as I soon found out, and it did not hurt our relationship when he found out I was a Methodist just like him and his family.

We Will Cover South Carolina with a Blanket of Green

That was the theme of South Carolina's agricultural and rural development programs in the 1950s and 1960s. The state had nearly recovered from the devastating "reconstruction" after the Civil War, including too many years of occupation by northern military troops, carpetbaggers, and bad government. That period was followed by World War I, the Great Depression, and then the many shortages of resources during World War II. However, World War II also brought new military bases and other economic activity to the major cities of Charleston, Columbia and Greenville-Spartanburg. But rural South Carolina was still suffering from underemployment in row crop cultures that had depleted soils and output for generations. For example, the reliance on short staple cotton, corn, and tobacco production for generations had worn out the nutrients in the soil, led to serious erosion of land, and caused the development of an underemployed, poor generation of both white and African American citizens. The welfare programs started by President Franklin Roosevelt's "New Deal" gave subsidies to these farmers, encouraging them to keep farming, even if incomes continued to be marginal. Small cotton farmers were given government production quotas, which soon became capitalized in the land values, and helped keep them farming. Short staple cotton was actually a drag on the market, ending up in government warehouses, and producers and their children were being perpetuated in poverty via government welfare programs.

So the push in rural South Carolina was to replace worn out soils by planting grasses and legumes, and planting trees where topography led to erosion if planted with row crops. Grasses and legumes meant an expansion of the cattle industry, which thrives on pastures. Thus, dairy, beef cattle, and sheep were introduced to many new livestock farmers in South Carolina. Trees became the base for rapidly expanding saw timber, paper pulp, and tree fruit enterprises.

But what was the research base upon which county extension agents could rely in making recommendations and guiding these new farmers? What were the appropriate agricultural practices to be used? At what costs and returns? Where were the best markets for these expanding enterprises? We in agricultural economics and rural sociology had lots of research to do to provide scientific answers as we worked with our colleagues in dairy science, animal husbandry, agronomy, forestry, and horticulture.

We Initiate the First Grade-A Dairy Production Cost Study in the State's History

Dr. Aull teamed me up with a fine farm management specialist who had also recently joined the department, Dr. Hooper C. Spurlock, who was originally from eastern Tennessee. Hooper and I soon became close personal friends as well as co-research partners. First we had to analyze the size of the South Carolina Grade-A dairy industry (pronounced "deery industry or deerying" in South Carolina). There was a fledgling Grade A Dairy Commission in the state capital at Columbia headed by a young executive director named James E. Cushman. Jimmy was most cooperative and was willing to let my colleague Clyde Woodall and I analyze the statistics he had on licensed dairy farms in every district and county of the state. From the dairy commission data, we randomly selected a representative sample of dairy farms to be studied and classified by size and geographical areas. Then we developed a farm management questionnaire, pre-tested it, and turned a team of interviewers (including Hooper and me) loose on the dairy farmers.[2] Of all the places I could start to interview these farmers, I chose the lower coastal plain near Charleston. Not a wise decision for a Yankee with the thick Pennsylvania accent I had at that time, but the Clemson College identification card helped, plus my ability to talk "deerying"!

Here is one memorable example. When I finally located a large Guernsey cattle dairy farm in upper Dorchester County one hot summer afternoon, I was ushered into the owner's office on the side of the cow stable to await his arrival. I had already learned that no employee on the premises, white or African American, would answer any questions about the operation in the owner's absence; they would only talk about the heat, the mosquitoes, and the need for rainfall.

The owner arrived. His first question was: "What you want, Boy? I'm a very busy man!" I explained our "deery" production cost study and that all data was confidential, and would only be grouped with that of other "deery farms." Thus, each cooperating farmer's situation would be protected, and they could compare his or her operation with the averages for all similar farms in the size and geographic groups in which the farm belonged. Now he squinted at me from under his large straw hat. "Whatcha gonna do with these results, Boy?" he asked. "Lower the price we get for our milk and hard-earned labor?" I said, "No way, Sir—from what I've been seeing in this study, it may call for raising the price of milk to the farmer, especially for high butterfat content milk like you produce from this beautiful herd of purebred Guernsey cows! But that would be up to the South Carolina Dairy Commission. We at Clemson are just trying to get more reliable facts which will permit them to make better policy decisions."

Now I saw a bit of a smile on his face. "You ever plow a mule, Boy? You ever work on a 'deery' farm, Son?" he asked. I said, "No sir, I've never 'plowed a mule,' but I've worked a team of Percheron horses and I know the south end of a 'deery cow' from the north end. I worked on a 'deery farm' in Ohio where we milked sixty head during World War II." His next response was: "You worked horses and milked cows and you're from Clemson, Boy—I think you're alright. Now what information can I give you for this survey?" I passed the test, yet at first I thought I was going to be tossed off his farm. We had lots of similar experiences, but finished a very detailed and beneficial study in about a year. It was published and received a lot of attention.

Now We Become "the White Milk Boys from Up North"

One of the problems the South Carolina dairy industry was having at this time, as were dairy industries in other states, was declining per capita consumption of milk and dairy products by consumers. South Carolina's decline was steeper than that for states in the northeast, midwest, and far west. What was the problem? Of special concern, why was per capita consumption for fluid milk by consumers in such a steep decline? For one thing, the nutrition and medical professions were concerned about the rising incidence of bad cholesterol in the American consumers' diets. Animal fats, including milk fat, were suspected. We at Clemson were suspicious that the laws governing what could be sold as "beverage milk" in the state were also causative. The minimum butterfat content of milk that could be sold as beverage milk in the state was 3.8 percent, while that in the three major urban areas was even higher, 4.0 percent butterfat. This was much higher than in the major dairy producing states, including Pennsylvania, which were between 3.0 percent and 3.2 percent. Furthermore, a milk product of growing demand by consumers elsewhere in the country, low-fat and nonfat milk, was illegal for sale in South Carolina at that time.

The dairy herds in South Carolina included predominantly high butterfat producing cows, breeds like Jerseys and Guernseys. The purebred breed associations were strongly organized to the extent that they could powerfully influence state policies through the state legislature and dairy commission. Those of us who had studied dairy marketing in the north, as I had at Penn State, and had been involved in the dairy processing and distribution business in Pennsylvania, Ohio and West Virginia, knew that consumers were moving toward lower butterfat products such as skim milk or low-fat milk, which were not available to South Carolina consumers at that time. What did South Carolina consumers prefer? How could we research this variable scientifically? We gave it a good shot,[3] and in the process became known as "the white milk boys from up north," meaning people thought we would be promoting Holstein-Friesian cows and their milk, which is much lower in average butterfat than that of the dominate herds in South Carolina. Actually, we wanted our objective dairy research to benefit both consumers and producers, and as research scientists we would let our results speak for themselves. It is perfectly feasible to produce high quality low-fat or skim milk from Guernsey and Jersey milk too; it is simply a matter of standardizing at the processing plants.

So with the help of the dairy science department at Clemson, especially that of Dr. Jack Janzen, the agricultural economics and rural sociology department conducted a controlled milk tasting experiment with more than 9,000 persons. Nine pairs of beverage milk were prepared for tasting. Variations in butterfat and total milk solids were included in each pairing. Consumers tasted a pair of these milk samples and evaluated each product. They were then asked to pick the sample they liked best and explain why. The results of the study were conclusive. Two groups of South Carolina consumers preferred different types of beverage milks. Adults always indicated a preference for a sample product containing at least a one percent higher level of total solids than any alternate product sampled. The youth group, on the other hand, expressed a preference for a product having less fat and a higher solid nonfat content than the beverage milk then available in the state. The dairy industry would be well advised, it seemed, to diversify their product line and permit the sale of lower butterfat beverage milk or a solids added product to reach both youth and adult consumers.

Some Innovative Marketing Research Gets Requests for Speeches and Travel

Dr. Aull supported my desire to complete graduate study for the Ph.D. By Clemson rules I could take up to six graduate credits per semester without losing any salary. I moved back into graduate work slowly in 1957 and took courses in experimental designs, advanced farm management, and intermediate economic theory (both micro and macro) under Dr. James Stepp. Later, I also took a course in agricultural policy. The University of Kentucky accepted all of my Penn State graduate credits for the Masters degree, and those from Clemson. In September of 1958, Sally, John, David, and Pat, who was born in Anderson Hospital on April 30, 1957, moved with me to Della Drive in Lexington, Kentucky as I began my heavy class load in agricultural economics toward the Ph.D. The graduate school at Kentucky also allowed me a double minor in economic theory and social psychology. The latter subject was of particular help because of my new interest in consumer buying behavior.

My great interest at this time in my career, and the subject of my doctoral dissertation research, was the use of projective techniques in interviewing food consumers about buying behavior. This was an effort to improve the accuracy and reliability of consumers' responses about food and food purchase variables by having them project their values onto others in hypothetical, neutral situations. The goal was to eliminate the many stereotypical responses often given to interviewers by those being questioned. We experimented with indirect interviewing techniques, such as the Rosensweig Picture Frustration Cartoons. Then the researcher/interviewer performed other structured tests using indirect stimuli to verify the interviewee's personal values about the subject, or carefully crafted direct or semi-direct questions. The researcher then tried to discern the actual quantitative use of the product by household members, including the homemaker.

It required two and a half years after our return from Kentucky in late 1959 to complete the dissertation research work and write the results for presentation and defense with the University of Kentucky faculty. Sometimes my research required that I work in my office at Clemson, or that I travel back to Lexington, Kentucky to work on the IBM-650 main frame computer at the University of Kentucky over holidays such as Thanksgiving and Christmas in the wee hours of the mornings—the only time graduate students from out of state could access time on that monster.

Fortunately, Clemson was a member of Southern Marketing Research Technical Committee 13, a regional research project, whose members were also interested in the subject I had chosen. Soon I was traveling to one or more of the eight cooperating southern states as Clemson's marketing economist on the technical committee. Marketing economists like me were teamed up with home economists in each state for fuller coverage of the research variables. In South Carolina, this meant that Clemson would need to develop a closer working relationship with Winthrop College at Rock Hill and South Carolina State College at Orangeburg, South Carolina, where the state's home economists were trained and conducted research.

My Ph.D. Degree Completed and Dissertation Defended in Early Spring of 1962

The Technical Committee 13 members elected me chairman for the year 1962–63. I was soon asked to speak about my research and that of other members of the committee at various fora, including the Southern Association of Agricultural Workers, which met annually, and at an American Dairy Association Symposium on Improving Dairy Marketing Research at Chicago. In October of 1962, we had a full Technical Committee 13 meeting at Clemson. I will never forget the night Sally and I had all the members and some invited speakers to our new home on Willow Street for a buffet dinner. All day long, and especially that night, we heard low-flying airplanes of the United State Air Force crossing above our house on the way to Florida and elsewhere in the southeast. This was the famous Cuban-Soviet missile crisis, about which we all know much more now than we did then. President John F. Kennedy had ordered a full military alert and muster in our southern states, especially in Florida, in case it was necessary to invade Cuba to prevent an atomic missile strike at the United States. We went on with our program of speakers over the next few days as if nothing would deter our research efforts into consumer values and buying behavior.

Exciting Research, Speechmaking, and Recruitment by Ohio State University

The most innovative and surprising research I directed at Clemson had to do with egg yolk color preferences. We solicited consumer preferences with both direct and indirect questions at homes using trained interviewers. Later, we followed up using a Latin square design with a rotation of sales and price treatments in a Winn Dixie supermarket for nine weeks. The catalyst for the study was that poultry scientists had perfected a way to pelletize Coastal Bermuda grass for use in hen egg laying rations, substituting it for expensive, imported, dehydrated alfalfa meal. But the Bermuda grass contained significant pigments that turned the egg yolks darker in color. How much Bermuda grass should be substituted in South Carolina hen rations? How dark would consumers in the state tolerate egg yolk color? Did egg yolk color matter?

Trained interviewers completed questionnaires with a representative sample of 662 South Carolina consumers in their homes. Home economists from Winthrop and South Carolina State College conducted the interviews about a number of foods. Homemakers did care about egg yolk color. Darker yolk eggs, preferred for baking, were often referred to as "yard eggs," or local eggs. Native-born South Carolinians referred to eggs with very light yellow yolk color, often preferred by consumers who had moved to South Carolina from the northern states, as "shipped eggs."

Here was the big surprise: consumers said they would pay an average of four cents per dozen more if they could always get eggs with the color of yolks they preferred. We researchers at Clemson had our doubts.

The poultry science department at Clemson placed three groups of laying hens on special diets so test eggs with three standardized levels of yolk pigmentation could be furnished to a sample of consumers previously interviewed. Analysis of 270 usable responses from the 300 consumers revisited and furnished with eggs (four eggs each marked with the letters R, S or T on the shells[4]) showed that they would pay two cents more per dozen if they could get eggs with the yolk color of their choice. Winn Dixie Supermarkets was interested in the experiment, and allowed Clemson researchers to use one of their Greenville, South Carolina stores in a Latin square price and egg yolk color experiment using their brand. Again, Clemson's poultry science department produced standardized yolk colors, pictured on the egg display board, along with a picture of the usual range of yolk colors in the typical Winn Dixie egg case.[5] Consumers did indeed pay an average of two cents more per dozen to obtain the egg yolk color they preferred. The researchers were dumbfounded!

As word about the consumer preference research studies at Clemson spread, I was invited to make presentations about our egg yolk preference study and our milk butterfat, total solids-not-fat studies to different fora around the south and midwest. While on vacation in Pennsylvania during the summer of 1963, Dr. Aull called me from Clemson and asked if I would represent Clemson and the department at the annual meeting of the American Institute of Cooperation at Ohio State University in Columbus, Ohio at Clemson's expense. I agreed. While there, Dr. Mervin G. Smith, Chairman of OSU's Department of Agricultural Economics and Rural Sociology, called and interviewed me. He had heard from two faculty members about my exciting research reports, and said he would like to talk to me in the coming year about joining OSU's faculty. I was delighted.

Nothing much happened until early 1964 when the Batelle Memorial Institute, which adjoins the OSU campus but is in no way related to the university, invited me to fly from Clemson to Columbus at their expense to interview for a job as an agricultural economist. I checked the Institute's reputation, which was excellent, and accepted. However, during the interview I could not get the other agricultural economists to talk about opportunities for advancement or salary levels there. I called my two friends at OSU, Dr. Elmer Baumer and Dr. Ray Bailey, and asked them what they knew about Batelle's salary scale and advancement opportunities. They both asked me if Mervin Smith knew I was in town interviewing at Batelle. I said no. They said he was in Washington, D.C. signing a PASA contract with USAID to send OSU professors to São Paulo, Brazil, and had indicated he wanted to hire me. Both said, "Don't accept a job at Batelle until you have had a chance to talk to Mervin!"

I reached Mervin Smith the following Monday from my office at Clemson, and he asked if I would come back up to Columbus the next weekend at OSU's expense to interview for a job. I said yes. After having met and interviewed with the senior faculty at OSU, the dean of agriculture, the director of the extension service, the director of student instruction, and then flying to Wooster, where the director of the experiment station (called The Ohio Agricultural Research and Development Center) also wanted to interview me, Mervin made me an offer. I will never forget this: we were flying back to Columbus from Wooster in an OSU twin-engine executive plane, and Mervin said, "Howard, I'm authorized to offer you one of three jobs at the annual salary of $13,000. A fifty-fifty job as a teacher and researcher in dairy marketing economics, a fifty-fifty job as a researcher and extension specialist in dairy marketing economics, or a general agricultural development economist teaching and conducting research in Brazil on our new contract with USAID." We discussed the pros and cons of each job.

As we made our final approach to land at OSU's airport, I asked him, "Mervin, what would you do if you were me?" He said quickly and loudly with enthusiasm, "Howard: I would go to Brazil. It pays a ten percent bonus on your base salary, plus the first $70,000 of overseas salaries is federal income tax free. (I didn't have to worry about the upper limit!) Also, OSU gives you free housing, educational allowances, and many other benefits." I responded, "Let me go home and talk to my family about moving to Brazil. I'll call you in two days with our answer!" I accepted within three days. Next, I resigned from my position at Clemson, effective September 1, 1964, and got ready to go to OSU at Columbus, Ohio to begin teaching and studying Portuguese in preparation for the departure of my family and me to Piracicaba, São Paulo, Brazil in October of 1964.

3

A New World: Brazil

To earn my salary at OSU while the paperwork was being completed for our move to Piracicaba, I taught agricultural marketing principles to a group of visiting Brazilian bankers and agribusiness leaders from the state of Minas Gerais. The department had facilities for simultaneous translation, and the Department of State sent Portuguese interpreters for the group. While working with this group, I started to pick up some Portuguese vocabulary and phrases. It was a good thing I did, since I had to start teaching in Brazil in three short months, and the only language training I would be provided with was six weeks in Piracicaba right before I began teaching!

While I was teaching in Ohio, Sally was on the home front in Clemson, preparing for our move. We sold our house and began packing. I helped as much as I could when I was home on weekends. Ohio State arranged for a moving company to pack and ship our major sea and air freight, and to store our furniture.

Finally, in October, the day of our departure arrived. At this time, my family and I were anything but seasoned international travelers. In fact, our total previous international experience consisted of going into Canada on a few fishing trips and once over the border into Juarez, Mexico for perhaps an hour. There I was, about to take my wife—who had real reservations about leaving the States and her family and friends behind—two young sons (John, 11, and Dave, 9) and a 7-year old-daughter, Pat, and head into the wild South American interior. It was the height of the Cold War, Brazil had just three months earlier suffered a full-blown revolution and thrown out a communist government, none of us spoke Portuguese, and I was to begin teaching economic subjects at the university level, in Portuguese, within forty-five days of arriving. What was I thinking?

However, at the time I was more focused on the immediate risks I was taking than on the relatively long-term ones. Suffice it to say that the demise of Pan American Airlines nearly thirty years later would not surprise me. Flying down to Brazil on that first trip, I found both management and the work force disorganized, incompetent, frustrated, and frustrating!

We were told in Columbus that our Pan Am flight from Miami — on a Boeing 707, the "gem of air travel" at the time — would fly first to Puerto Rico, then to Caracas, Venezuela, then nonstop to the new jetport at São Paulo, called Veracopas. But that is not exactly what happened. The night before our flight we stayed overnight at the Miami Airport Hotel. We had driven our new Ford Country Sedan down from Clemson and turned it over for shipment by sea to Brazil the day before. When I casually inquired at the airport if I could check in the fourteen pieces of luggage for our morning flight to Veracopas the next day, a surly Pan Am clerk responded, "Of course, you can check in at the counter beginning at 8 a.m. tomorrow." Then she asked to see our tickets. "Oh, this is wrong," she said, sounding the first note in a series of confusing information that would come to characterize our trip to Brazil. "That flight goes to Rio de Janeiro. You'll have to take a shuttle from Rio to São Paulo; and all shuttles go to the other airport, Congonhas, which is downtown."

Panic set in immediately. I knew that my chief of party was going to be at Veracopas Airport to meet us. I had no idea where that was, but I now knew we were going someplace else. There were no cell phones in those days, and I did not know how to reach my chief of party, John Sitterley, by international telephone. I fired off a short telegram announcing the change of our arrival location; that was expensive, but I thought it was worth it. Again, this did not exactly turn out to be true. The telegram finally arrived in Piracicaba two weeks after we did!

A short while later, airborne over the azure Caribbean Sea, all five Steeles were finally enroute to our new adventure. Without being able to do anything more about our fate, I began to relax. The flight attendants brought us a delicious lunch, and all was peace and tranquility — at least until I asked one of the flight attendants if it was true that the final destination of this flight would be Rio. She said she did not know, but that the head steward would get the answer for me. She added "The whole crew is leaving this plane in San Juan; you'll have two more crews before you arrive in Brazil." Okay, that was fair enough. Or so I thought.

After lunch and more beverages, a ruddy-faced steward came by and asked, "Who wants to know the final destination of this flight?" I held up my hand. "Young man, the last I checked, this flight terminates in Veracopas — but check with the next crew, which gets on in San Juan; you see, we're revising all our schedules in the next two weeks."

Oh great, I thought. You are going to dump a family of five in the middle of nowhere at 2 a.m. with fourteen pieces of luggage. We do not speak the language, and my chief of party, because of the telegram I sent him, will be looking for us frantically at some other airport. But I smiled and thanked him, as I felt my knees begin to shake. Of course I hid my fear as well as I could; like anyone in a similar position, I did not want my family to know that at this point I was asking myself why I had ever decided to do any of this.

We stopped in San Juan for an hour. Once we were airborne again, I learned that the second crew did not know where the plane was terminating any more than the previous one had. They were all getting off in Caracas and flying right back to Miami later that night. They understood my problem and asked the captain to radio ahead to Pan Am Operations in Caracas for an answer. "Of course we understand your concern," they said. "Everything will work out O.K. for you and your family," they assured me. Never mind all that, I thought to myself, just tell me where we are going to land!

As we approached the Caracas International Airport, a flight attendant told me that a ground representative would be there to meet my family at the airport and answer my question. We landed, and for the first time in my life (but not the last), my family and I found ourselves staring into the muzzles of automatic weapons.

"What's this?" I whispered to the Pan Am ground representative who had sought me out as we got off the plane. "Are you having a revolution?" "Oh no," she responded, "This is just Airport Security; they're here to protect you!" At this point my wife began to feel nauseated (and this time it was not due to pregnancy). She headed with Pat to the door marked "*Damas.*"

As in many developing countries, the army controlled all public facilities. In time, we learned to be blasé about this kind of thing, but this was the first time for us, and it was pretty intimidating. The fuzzy-faced kid holding a rifle aimed at my heart actually kept his finger on the trigger the whole time he was "protecting me" on the bus from the plane to the in-transit terminal as we bounced across the tarmac! As he did so, I wondered how many tourists accidentally died of "lead poisoning" every year as a result of that system of protection.

After safely arriving in the transit lounge, I went back to worrying about our original quandary: where we were going to land in Brazil. Quite candidly the Pan Am rep told me, "Yesterday this flight flew nonstop from Caracas to the new International Airport at Veracopas. But our company said there is some problem with the runway instruments being installed there, so they may be diverted to Rio—your crew will announce the final destination during your flight. Have a nice trip, and I'm glad I could be of help to you." Then she added, with a winning smile, "Thank you for flying Pan American World Air Lines!"

We flew for a long time over the Amazon River Basin and down the northeast coast of Brazil, through lunch and dinner, and into the night. By now I figured I was powerless to do anything but roll with Pan Am's punches; I even managed to doze off and relax a bit. Just before our final approach, the captain announced that we would be landing in Rio that night, and added that all the São Paulo passengers would be ushered into a waiting DC-6 of Pan Agra Air Lines for the forty minute hop to Congonhas Airport in downtown São Paulo. Okay, I thought—but where will my chief of party be? Where will we sleep? Where will our bags end up? By this time, any ability to control the details of our fate was gone. I felt quite philosophical about it all. This turned out to be good on-the-job training for an international career.

It was now nearly twenty-four hours since we had left the Miami Airport, though it seemed a lifetime. As the Pan Agra DC-6 opened its door at Congonhas Airport, a voice on the loudspeaker asked the Steele family to identify itself. Once off the plane, we were met with a reassuring message from John Sitterley, my chief of party, and his wife, Lucille. "Howard, Sally, and kids—don't worry; we know where you're landing tonight. We have a driver, a vehicle, and a reservation for you at the Real Hotel, and we'll see you as soon as you clear customs. Tomorrow, after you've had a good night's rest and we've done some paperwork at the U.S. Consulate, we'll drive to Piracicaba." What a welcome message that was. For the first time since we had left Miami I truly relaxed!

I will give Pan Am credit for one thing: all fourteen pieces of our luggage arrived in the same place we did—quite a feat considering all the uncertainty along the way about our destination. Of course getting it past the Brazilian customs official, even with the help of a bilingual Pan Am representative, was a hassle. We were told in Columbus that the team in Piracicaba needed insecticides, so we had filled up the top of one suitcase with about twelve big cans of the stuff. The customs officer, with glasses as thick as Coca Cola bottle bottoms, immediately went for them after I had opened all fourteen suitcases for her inspection. Much Portuguese conversation went back and forth with the Pan Am rep. I did not understand it, but the heated gestures back and forth were frightening.

Later it came out that the customs officer had suspected the cans of bug spray were disguised bombs. Finally it became evident that in order to go through all fourteen of our suitcases, being an underpaid and tired civil servant, the customs officer needed a financial incentive. In Brazil this was called "*da jeito*," which means, literally, to "find the way" (or to get the job done now). I assume Pan Am took care of this; I did not know what was going on and at that time would never have paid a bribe to a public servant; certainly not in plain view anyway. Through necessity, I loosened up a little about this as time went on, but I never liked it, and I tried to avoid it everywhere I went in my travels. However, it was evident that developing country's governments did not pay their civil servants livable wages, and this was one result.

It was great to see the Sitterleys waiting for us outside of customs at Congonhas Airport when we arrived there at 2 a.m. Brazilian time. They had two drivers, Aristedes and his brother Getulio, and two jeeps. They loaded all our baggage into one of the jeeps and what we needed just for the night into the other, and we left for the Hotel Real.

Typical Brazilian hotels in the major cities at that time were family-run affairs, many only three or four floors high, and open to the streets. São Paulo then had a population of about six million, and was a cacophony of noise all night long. We got into bed by about 4 a.m. Though I was completely exhausted by the trip, I did not sleep much that night as I was "entertained" by the music of samba and bossa nova bands from nearby clubs.

About 9 a.m. the next morning, Lucille Sitterley knocked on our door and announced that *cafe de manha* (breakfast) was being served. The waiter in bow tie and white jacket entered with a sumptuous tray filled with fruit of all shapes and sizes—I recognized only the bananas—*cafe com leite* (coffee with boiling milk), *pão* (breads of all shapes and sizes) with *manteiga* (butter) and *geleias* (jellies). Lucille told us that the funny fruit with the round black seeds was papaya. "Here it's called *mamão*, which means mammary, or mother's milk," she told us. "Scrape the seeds off, and squeeze some orange and lemon juices on it. I think you'll like it!" I certainly did, and ever since that day I have never been able to have enough papaya.

The countryside of central Brazil was lush, green, and beautiful, with sugar cane, coffee, fruit trees, woods, mountains, and rivers that run down to the Atlantic Ocean. The next day, as we headed northwest toward Piracicaba, the country became rolling agricultural land with rich red soil. The cattle were various crosses of native beef types brought originally from Portugal and the Indian Brahma, loosely called Zebu. Dairy cattle were red Holstein types imported from Holland and some black-and-white Holstein-Frisians from North America. We passed through many small towns and villages in the three and a half hour ride; most of the people had shining black hair and dark brown eyes. Suddenly, in one town, I looked out the window and saw nothing but blond, blue-eyed kids and adults. "What is this?" I asked. "It's Americana," I was told. Here families from Mississippi, Louisiana, Alabama, and Georgia had moved to Brazil after the South's defeat in the Civil War, and had lived and prospered there ever since. Later, in Piracicaba, we had two Brazilian secretaries from Americana who spoke American English with lovely southern accents, even though it was their great-grandparents who had last lived in the Old South.

We were the sixth of the eventual twelve Ohio State University families who would be in Piracicaba helping establish a graduate program at the Master of Science level in agricultural disciplines at the University of São Paulo. A second goal was to select potentially outstanding young leaders to go to the States for advanced degrees. Thirdly, we hoped to help the Brazilian faculty increase their research and extension work, thereby helping farmers and agribusinesses in the region, including the development of marketing cooperatives. That was the plan for our work, but first we had to get settled.

"Will we have a thatched roof? A hard mud floor?" Those were some of the first questions Sally had asked me back when I first told her Ohio State had invited me to go to Brazil for two years. All we knew about Piracicaba before we got there was that it was a city of about 140,000 in the interior of the state of São Paulo, some 130 miles to the northwest of the capital city of São Paulo. Though we had no idea what the living conditions were like, we had read about how the U.S. Peace Corps volunteers were living, and were prepared to accept the most basic housing. However, the administration at Ohio State assured us that the contract with USAID/Brazil called for rental housing similar to what the faculty members at ESALQ had, and that the house would be furnished. They gave us a list of things to ship by air freight, which would arrive soon after we did, and also what to ship by sea freight, including our car. Ohio State had much experience in USAID institutional building contracts and faculty needs from their ten years of similar work in India, in the Punjab and Hyderabad, where they helped develop agricultural colleges.

The name of the agricultural school we taught at was the Escola Superior de Agricultura Luiz de Queiroz, or the Luiz de Quiroz [the name of its founder] Superior College of Agriculture, which we all called ESALQ for short. When we arrived in Piracicaba that October day in 1964, accompanied by the Sitterleys, we were pleasantly surprised to see the house they had rented for us. It was on Rua Dr. Alvim in the Jardin Europa suburb, quite close to ESALQ. It had four bedrooms, a full bath, a small living room and dining room, an ample kitchen, and a servant's apartment in the rear. We used the latter as a storage area and playroom for the kids when inclement weather kept them indoors. We used one bedroom as a game room and communications room, where we kept our shortwave radio to listen to the Voice of America and the Armed Forces Network. This was our closest link to the U.S.A. Here we could listen to news from home and American sports games. Usually these games were replays, but that did not make any difference to us, as it made us feel closer to home. We had no telephone; of the twelve OSU families there, only the Sitterleys had a private phone. Telephones and telephone lines were very scarce in the interior of Brazil at that time.

We didn't hire a live-in maid, as some of the other American families did. We had heard stories about problems with "live-ins" from Americans we had talked to before moving there. However, one day a young woman appeared at our house, and clapped at the front gate. (There were no doorbells in Piracicaba—people would just come to your front gate and clap their hands to indicate they wanted to talk to you). Sally went outside, and there encountered a lady named Cinira. With the help of a neighbor who spoke English, Cinira explained she had been a maid at the dean of the university's house for a number of years, but had temporarily retired to have two sons. Now she was ready to go back to work, and had heard that the new *Norte Americanos* were looking for day help, which is what she wanted to do. We took her name, and our Brazilian neighbors helped us check up on her reputation. We learned that her husband Jose was the number one driver at the university, and that the couple was honest and dependable, so we decided to hire her.

Next we negotiated the terms of our arrangement. You would not believe what the standard wage was for day maids in Piracicaba! Cinira arrived at 7 a.m. every day, with fresh papaya, mangos, and other fruit brought from her garden. She worked like a Trojan every day until 5:30 p.m. and then went home to take care of her own family. Her pay?—the equivalent of U.S. $1.10 per day. We were amazed. Yet even at that low rate, the Brazilian *damas* complained that we *Norte Americanos* were ruining the labor market for maids in Piracicaba by paying them too much!

Incredibly, we could not even get Cinira to sit down for lunch; she just kept working. Eventually we offered her the option of either coming with us for a free round trip to the United States at the end of our tour or an automatic washing machine, so it would be easier to take in university students' laundry (something she had been doing by hand between her maid jobs, while raising her two infant sons). We felt this would partially compensate her for the two years of marvelous work she did for us at the low local pay. Need I say that her work ethic was exemplary? When the time came, she chose the washing machine. When I returned to Brazil several years later in the summer of 1967 as a consultant and had a chance to visit Piracicaba, I saw that her husband had built a small addition to their modest house to protect her precious washing machine. At that time they had no hot water in their house, so they either used cold water or water heated on a stove and poured it into the washer! Again I was reminded that we Americans take a lot of creature comforts for granted.

"Howard, what is this funny bowl in the bathroom?" Sally asked me as we explored the house. I took a look. Yes, there was a commode, a bathtub with shower, and then a funny little hourglass-shaped bowl with spigots. I said, "Well, it must be a foot washing gadget or something. It sure looks funny!!" Neither Sally nor I had ever seen or heard of a bidet before, so we did not know how it was used. Bidets were not big in Pennsylvania or South Carolina in the 1960s, although we both knew what a two-holer outhouse was. Cinira knew what the bidet was for, but she used it to soak my shirt collars and cuffs before putting them in the washer!

We got hot water to the shower in that house through an electronic gizmo—220 volts—that was hooked onto the shower head, which heated the water as it flowed through. We had to turn a lever to make an electric connection after climbing into the tub. Supposedly the connection was grounded to prevent the user of this gizmo from getting a shock: but, knowing what I knew about the uneven competency of Brazilian workers, it always made me a little bit nervous. All I could think of every time I turned the lever was the newspaper headline that I imagined might announce my demise: "American Professor Electrocutes Self in Local Shower."

Most Americans are familiar with the land-grant university systems in each of our fifty states where teaching-research-extension activities habitually go hand-in-hand, but that was not the norm at universities in Brazil or much of Latin America in the 1960s, as I found out later. University education was mostly theoretical, based on the old European system from which it derived. The big task for university students in this system was to pass the entrance exams. After that, the average student put in his or her time, stayed out of trouble, honored their professors, and collected their diplomas.

The average age of the student body at ESALQ, which granted only the equivalent of our bachelor's degree, was twenty-four years when we arrived, instead of the nineteen to twenty years at a typical U.S. university. Few of the students and faculty we met in 1964 came from the rural areas; most were from the city and knew very little about agriculture. Only a small percentage of the student body had ever lived and worked on farms. Some of the wealthier students knew a few facts about livestock or coffee because their families had large land holdings, even though the children had grown up in the big cities and only spent holidays on their family *fazendas* (farms). There was a significant population of Japanese Brazilians in the state of São Paulo, and many of these students had grown up on working farms. Their average age was lower since they studied diligently to pass the the agricultural college's entrance exam on their first try (at age eighteen or nineteen). They usually scored high and were admitted. One evening early in my time there, after I had learned a decent amount of Portuguese, I was invited to a student meeting. As we passed the men's dormitory, my Brazilian student colleagues pointed to the few lights on and said, "Look at the lights on in the dorm—those are Japanese students studying! They study at night!"

Today, Brazilian universities have changed a great deal, as has the whole country in many ways. But old patterns were slow to change; during those days in the 1960s, we saw some very interesting contrasts with the U.S. higher education system. For example, I could not ever get my distinguished counterpart professor to go with me to interview agribusiness and cooperative managers. He always supported the idea in theory, but then discovered some last-minute conflict that prevented him from coming with me. I soon discovered that this was a face-saving strategy on his part; he had never interviewed a working farmer, marketer, or agribusinessman in his life, even though he was a full professor of agricultural economics. His knowledge was from the textbook scholars of Brazil and Europe. Trying to apply the theory he had built his career upon in the field might embarrass him, and he was smart enough to know that without having to learn the hard way! I am convinced that one of the most successful activities that USAID promoted and financed was sending developing country participants to look at our educational and agricultural institutions and to talk, meet, and work with our farmers and private sector agribusinesses. There is simply no substitute for the kind of practical knowledge that comes from such exposure and interaction with people in the field.

Speaking of learning the hard way, mastering a new language by the immersion approach under a strict time constraint—and being a bit thick headed when it came to languages anyway—led me into some interesting experiences. I had to deliver my first economics lectures at ESALQ at the start of the new term, which was six weeks after my arrival in-country. Though I had studied German for four years, I had never had one lesson in a Romance language. I literally had to start from scratch with Portuguese.

Fortunately, the Brazilian minister at the Piracicaba Methodist Church, a fine man named Gerson Vega (who had just returned to Brazil after earning a Ph.D. from Northwestern University), enlisted the teachers at a missionary language training center in Campinas to teach all of the Ohio State professors. Our intensive training lasted six hours each day. I came home dead tired in the late afternoon—then there was a mass of homework: grammar exercises, readings, and so on, at night.

Later that same autumn, some new Ohio State families arrived after just a smattering of training in Portuguese at Columbus. With my new knowledge of Portuguese, I helped them order their meals as we had dinner at the ocean near Santos during a trip to São Paulo. All went well until we got to dessert. I managed to convey all of their orders to the waiter, and then he asked me if I would like dessert. Very quickly I responded, *"Si, quero um prato de cerveja, por favor."* This threw the waiter into a quandary; he did not want to offend his international visitors or lose a tip, so he very politely replied in Portuguese: "Excuse me, sir; we have glasses of beer and we have bottles of beer, but I'm sorry to have to tell you we have no plates of beer. Please forgive us. May I get you a glass or a bottle of beer?" Suddenly it dawned on me: at that early period in my study of the language, the words *cerveja* and *sorvete* sounded the same to me. However, one meant beer and the other meant ice cream! I had asked for a plate of beer!

About a year later, as I traveled alone by jeep in the mountains of Minas Gerais interviewing small farmers' co-operative managers, I began to feel pretty good about my Portuguese. After an hour of interviewing and filling out my questionnaire, the president of the little cooperative asked me in Portuguese where I was from. He told me he was confused. My shoes and clothes were different and I was blond and green eyed, so he did not think I was Brazilian. "Where do you think I'm from?" I asked him, and immediately he said, *"Alemana"* (Germany). When he told me I spoke Portuguese with a German accent, I broke up laughing. I told him about my early language training, and was pleased that he had not identified me as a "gringo." I felt I had come a long way in a short time!

Our Brazilian counterparts lost no time in showing us around Piracicaba. One essential stop was at the then-famous restaurant called O Mirante, at the waterfalls of the Piracicaba River. This restaurant was built on a promontory nearly over the waterfalls. As soon as you entered the restaurant and were seated out in the open (where the spray from the falls quite often fell on your table), a waiter arrived with ripe olives, cheese squares, toothpicks, a bowl of olive oil, and freshly baked hard-crusted white bread. You dipped the cheese and bread chunks into the olive oil and chewed the ripe olives away from their seeds while contemplating the menu of the day. These were large, brown olives about the size of plum tomatoes—not the small black olives we are sold as "ripe olives" here in the United States.

The featured entrée was Dorado grilled fish. This freshwater fish was two to three feet in length, weighing anywhere from ten to thirty pounds Little Brazilian boys waded in the river pools at different levels of the cascading falls to catch them with their bare hands as the fish tried to jump up the falls to spawn further upstream. The restaurant grilled the fish on skewers and served them with French fried potatoes and salads. You could also have the fish fried or broiled. It was a tender white meat that was, when served with the proper sauces, quite delicious. Other meats were also available.

Northern Italian immigrants had founded the state of São Paulo, and it soon became the financial and industrial capital of Brazil. When we arrived in 1964, the economic statistics showed that São Paulo state accounted for about twenty-five percent of Brazil's total gross national product. At that time, the country had about 90 million people, two-thirds of whom lived within one hundred miles of the Atlantic Ocean. The major industry in the Piracicaba area was sugar cane production. The major employers in Piracicaba were a steel mill and a sugar cane processing equipment-manufacturing plant owned by the Dedinni family. My counterpart at ESALQ was Alcides Zagatto. These were second and third generation Brazilians of Italian descent. One of the Dedinni's sons was married to an American he had met while studying in the United States. We OSU families were the beneficiaries of the Dedinni's kindness, as we were frequently invited to parties at their country estate on the Piracicaba River. These usually included sumptuous barbeques, music (the Dedinni son preferred playing his guitar to working in his father's business), fishing, horseback riding and other sports.

Despite the linguistic and cultural challenges, teaching at ESALQ went well for the most part. However, there were less pleasant moments. Once in a while, a mimeographed cartoon would be clandestinely slipped under the door of my classroom at night. I was always pictured as a dog with big, floppy ears smoking a pipe, which I did back then. Not only was the cartoon a bit unflattering, but the text was usually worse. I believe this was partly due to my struggle with the Portuguese language those first few classes at ESALQ, as well as being a "gringo" from North America, not dearly loved in many parts of Latin America at that time.

When we arrived in Brazil, it was only a few months after the military had thrown a communist government out of power in a revolution. During the years 1956–1961, the Kubitschek government had built Brasilia 400 miles in the interior by a massive printing of currency, kicking off runaway inflation, which neither the Quadros nor Goulart communist governments could lower. Power shortages, shortages of food, and breakdowns in mail delivery and in transportation, had brought Brazilian housewives into the streets of the major cities in the summer of 1964. They banged their pots and pans in an appeal to the military to take over the federal government, restore control to the economy, and bring back order to society. Very few people were killed during this revolution—it was almost a bloodless coup d'etat. But inflation was still 160 percent per year at the time we arrived, and there were still many shortages during our first year there.

We were there under the auspices of the USAID/Brazil development program to help Brazil's economy and society recover from years of bad government and political infighting between various factions within the country. However, we were not welcomed by everyone. We were told in our security briefings that many communist sympathizers were probably still hidden under the guise of being university students, so we had to be careful of who we talked to and what we said. This helped explain why the average age of college students at ESALQ when we arrived was twenty-four years—there were left-wing activists hiding in the student body as "professional students" in the interim.

However, the majority of Brazilian students in my classes was kind and gave me a lot of slack. They were patient with my budding Portuguese and often helped me deal with the students I soon discerned were troublemakers. Quite often, one of those troublemakers would ask a question about some economic concept we were discussing and would continue on and on, making a speech with thinly disguised political overtones. Sometimes the other students would boo or shout the student down. My best ploy was to listen carefully at first, then say in Portuguese, "I was listening to your wonderful discourse so closely that I forgot—what was your specific question?" The other students loved this approach and gave me great support. It really paid off to respond with humor, not rancor.

I mentioned how kind the Dedinni family was to the OSU families at ESALQ, but they were not the only true friends we had in the state of São Paulo. Ellen Bromfield Geld and her husband

Carson had their home and *fazenda* open to guests constantly. It was near Tiate, a small town about forty miles from Piracicaba. Ellen was one of two daughters of the famous author and expatriate Louis Bromfield. Louis and his wife had lived in France in the 1920s and early 1930s, where he had established a model farm in France and named it after his home farm in Ohio. He and his family had escaped the Nazi occupation of France, returning in 1940 to his family's farm, Malibar, in Ohio, which was being held in estate by a local bank following the death of his parents. The Hollywood crowd kept Malibar Farm busy, according to Ellen. It was, among other events, the location of the marriage between actors Lauren Bacall and Humphrey Bogart, who appeared together in many Hollywood movies either written or scripted by Louis.

Ellen went to Cornell University, where she met Carson Geld from New York City, who was studying agronomy. They soon began dating regularly, and Ellen took Carson home to Ohio to meet her parents. Carson was so nervous on that visit, he backed Louis Bromfield's car into a barn beam when he tried to take Ellen to the movies. Louis, although normally possessed of a bad temper, found Carson's nervousness so endearing that he and Carson became friends that first visit. After they had graduated from Cornell, Louis asked Carson and Ellen to move to Brazil where he was trying to establish a show farm, Malibar do Brasil. That operation soon went bankrupt due to low world prices for coffee, Brazil's marginal beef cattle industry, and a dishonest business manager who handled Bromfield's assets.

Louis promoted "natural farming," as he had witnessed it being practiced in France. That is, he was a bit of an environmental guru ahead of his time. "Don't poison the soils with industrial chemicals and fertilizers," he wrote. "Rotate pastures and crops without using weed-killing chemicals. Let cattle graze on lush pastures and legumes and do not coop them up in unhealthy stanchions and stalls," and so on. But Ellen let us in on a bit of a secret about her father. She emphasized that he was good at fiction writing, and suggested that people should do what he said, perhaps not exactly as he did, at least when it came to farming.

Ellen and Carson loved Brazil so much that they bought a small coffee farm near Tiete and began a well-organized renovation. They toiled long hours until their improved coffee bushes began to pay good dividends. Then they started a modest pasture program for feeding beef cattle, which was also successful. Their third enterprise was the production of sterile pigs raised under tightly controlled environmental housing for use by a pharmaceutical company producing vaccines. Finally, the business proclivity of these two transplanted Americans led them to start a fast-food chain, which they began in the city of Campinas. I believe it was called *Frango Assado* (baked chicken), and it was patterned after the newly popular Kentucky Fried Chicken restaurants in America.

With their financial success at Tiete, Ellen and Carson built a beautiful home patterned after the early fazenda manors of old Brazil. It had a large open patio in the center of the structure, and most of the bedrooms were heated with huge wood-burning fireplaces. Few homes in Brazil at that time had central heat, so fireplaces and supplemental heat from kerosene or electric space heaters were required in the colder rainy season. On their birthdays and those of their children, their wedding anniversary, and American holidays like Thanksgiving and the Fourth of July, all of us from OSU at ESALQ were invited by Ellen and Carson to stay overnight and enjoy their hospitality and the animated conversations that took place there. The only way we could reciprocate was to bring American goodies from our commissary, which they thoroughly enjoyed. You seldom find such a marvelous host and hostess. Discussions about agriculture, Brazilian and American politics, and other events of the day held sway into the wee hours of the morning at the Gelds' lovely fazenda.

Before leaving Ohio, we had been advised to pack electric space heaters and electric blankets for the colder rainy season in São Paulo, when the nighttime temperatures could dip quite low. Kerosene heaters could be obtained on the local market, but not the more efficient electric space heaters or electric blankets. The city of São Paulo was at the top of a mountain plateau several thousand feet above sea level. I remember staying there in the Cambridge "ex Claridge" Hotel in the cold, wet, rainy season and thinking I would surely get the flu. The thick stone walls supporting that hotel radiated cold all day and all night long. I recall a number of occasions calling room service for more blankets to keep my body temperature close to normal. There was no escaping that cold!

In our house on Rua, Dr. Alvim we had marvelous electric blankets on our double bed for warmth at night after turning off the electric space heaters and kerosene stoves. One fine feature of our modern American electric blankets was that they had dual controls: one for him and one for her. How efficient! However, there could be complications. One night I started to get chilled under my blanket, so I turned my control up to warmer in the dark. Soon I got even colder. I moved the control again. Now my wife awakened and said, "I'm burning up; what is wrong with this blanket?" I said, "I don't know. I've been freezing and turning the control up to warmer, but I keep getting colder." Sally said, "Well, I'm trying to turn it down to cooler, but it's not working." We turned the lights on, and discovered that Cinira had somehow reversed the controls while making the bed that day. Mystery solved!

Reverend Gerson Vega did all he could to help us acculturate into Brazilian society and life. He was the president of the Piracicabana School, a boarding and day school for grades 1–12 that had originally been founded by American Methodist missionaries in 1910. He suggested that our children enroll there, and he arranged for bilingual teachers from his church to teach our wives several mornings a week and tutor our children so they could be taught in Portuguese. The school taught only half days, so it was not long until our grade school kids were going to the Piracicabana School in the mornings and our junior high kids in the afternoons. The other half of the day, OSU mothers would take turns teaching them American subjects from the Calvert Correspondence School of Baltimore, Maryland. Therefore, our children studied Brazilian subjects in Portuguese for a half day, then American subjects in English the other half of the day.

Reverend Vega also organized an English language church service for us (and those Brazilian members of the Methodist church who were interested) at an earlier time than his regular Portuguese service each Sunday. Finally, to help make our education of the Brazilian culture complete, he organized trips for us to the *favelas* (slums) of São Paulo to see the poverty and to meet our Brazilian and American missionaries struggling to help those unfortunate souls escape their miserable situation. He and his wife, one of those blond, blue-eyed, bilingual secretaries from the southern town of Americana, were such good, kind friends to all the Americans from OSU.

As we grew more comfortable with the language, and our children settled into their new school, Piracicaba was beginning to feel like home.

4

Our Life and Work in Brazil

The area around the town of São José do Rio Preto, in the far
northwestern part of the state of São Paulo and 280 miles from
Piracicaba, was an area fairly new to agricultural use. There was
a leading *fazendeiro* (farmer) there named Dr. Labiano Mendoça,
a thoracic surgeon who had bought a coffee *fazenda* and was also
raising corn and cattle near his hometown of São José. Dr. Mendoça
had become so incensed at the poor marketing of his products,
the low prices he and his neighbors were paid, and the exorbitant
prices they were charged for their supplies (feed rations, fertilizer,
pesticides, and seeds) that he decided to start a cooperative. News
of his leadership in that rural area spread quickly, and he was
elected president of the new organization as it expanded to several
thousand members.

Dr. Mendoça soon began visiting the offices of USAID in the
city of São Paulo and later at its headquarters in Rio de Janeiro,
soliciting help in developing his farmers' cooperative.

He had heard about, and seen during his travels to other
countries, farm service centers with their bulk storage facilities
for grains, elevators for moving grains, scales for weighing trucks
and their cargos, bagging equipment for grains, and feed ration
mixing equipment. There were even more complete centers with
warehouses for storing seeds, fertilizers, pesticides, and driers for
reducing the moisture content and protecting the quality of stored
grains. He thought it was time to bring such advantages to Brazilian
farmers.

USAID had several sets of farm service equipment in storage at
the port in Rio de Janeiro. They began to help Dr. Mendoça plan
a basic center for his cooperative at São José de Rio Preto, with
options for expansion as volume grew. As the marketing specialist
on the OSU team in Piracicaba, I was assigned to work with Dr.
Mendoça and his employees at the cooperative on a regular basis.

This required my taking a number of trips to São José, sometimes in an OSU jeep and sometimes by train. I loved traveling there by train. It was a passenger train that made one round trip to and from São Paulo city each day—overnight to São Paulo each night and a daylight trip back to São José do Rio Preto each morning. The train consisted of a diesel locomotive, six or eight rickety coaches, a dining car with plastic tablecloths and flowers, a few boxcars, and one modern, air-conditioned Budd stainless steel sleeping car. Dr. Mendoça had enough political influence with the railroad that he was able to get me a roomette in that last car when I returned to São Paulo on the overnight train, as I frequently did. It was a bumpy, swinging ride on that ancient rail bed! I loved it, and soon knew all the crewmembers. The food in the dining car was pretty good too.

Driving an OSU jeep, although on a new two-lane asphalt highway, was much duller than the trip by train, as there were no *postos* for rest and coffee on that 280 mile stretch of highway. It was also a bit dangerous driving alone, so when I drove I usually took one of our graduate students with me. I also carried a licensed pistol with me in case we encountered bandits, but I am not sure if I would ever have been able to use it. I preferred to use caution as my main defense—I certainly was not going to pick up anybody waving for me to stop for them along the side of that lonely highway!

The cooperative soon had some bulk grain storage bins erected in São José. They began to move grain in bulk by truck, and they now had a protected warehouse for storing supplies and some small feed mixing and bagging equipment. This was a real boon to the cooperative's members. Previously, they had moved their corn and other grains to São Paulo in sacks and then had to backhaul feed rations for their poultry, hog, dairy, or beef: a double transportation cost that was not necessary any longer. The word spread as cooperative members' patronage dividends grew each month, and Dr. Mendoça's cooperative membership numbers grew rapidly. By the time I left Brazil for OSU in the fall of 1966, the cooperative was negotiating with USAID to install a continuous grain drying system at the farm service center. The members were also benefiting from the ability of the co-op to purchase fertilizers, pesticides, and other farm inputs in bulk at much lower costs than before. The last I heard, the cooperative is still going strong and is the major agricultural business in the area.

Today Brazil has many good farm centers run by producers' associations at various locations around the country. Brazilians are quick learners and hard workers, and Brazil is now an outstanding producer and exporter of soybeans, rice, citrus and tropical fruits, and vegetables, along with their more traditional agricultural products: coffee, sugar, chocolate, and livestock. It gives me no small measure of satisfaction to have been a part of the large team of American and Brazilian experts who worked together in the 1960s to make this diversification and greater agricultural productivity a reality for Brazilian farmers.

We Hire Antonio to Guard Our House

A few nights after our arrival in Piracicaba, our neighbor, Zilmar Marcos, came over to our house and said, "Howard, Sally, there are no city or university police patrolling the streets here, but we in our block, as well as other families in adjoining blocks, do have night guards. Ours is an elderly gentleman named Antonio. He used to work for my mother and father. He asked someone the other morning if the new family across the street from us would be paying him to continue guarding the property at night."

I asked Zilmar what the cost was. When he told me how many cruzeiros each family paid the night guard per month, I had trouble believing it was so little. I asked how many hours he put in guarding, and learned that Antonio was there all night long, seven nights a week, every month. "He carries an old antique gun," Zilmar said. "I don't know if it works or if he knows how to use it. But you will hear the whistle that he carries and blows frequently. We're not sure whether this is just his way of letting his patrons know he is on the job, a way of keeping up his courage, or if he is letting any would-be robbers know where he is so that he won't be mugged or hurt if he suddenly came upon them as they were trying to break into a home." He went on to say that Antonio was a nice fellow and really needed the money. "It could be that he sleeps a lot in the wee hours of the morning when we are all asleep, but look at it this way: he is one less person to worry about robbing you!" Disarmed by Zilmar's logic and his practical nature, I agreed, and we hired old Antonio. He came by to thank us, but since Zilmar collected all the money to pay him, I think we only saw him once or twice in our two years there. However, we did hear his whistle nearly every night after dark.

One night, after we had been there for a few months, Sally awakened me with a start and whispered into my ear, "I hear somebody outside our bedroom window, inside the wall! What shall we do? Are we going to be robbed?" With fear and trembling, I located my flashlight and slowly lifted one strip in our Venetian blinds to try to see something without being seen myself. Just as I was about to turn on my flashlight, about fifteen sweet voices began singing Christmas carols in Portuguese right outside our bedroom window. It was the youth and young adults from the Piracicaba Methodist church who had come to give us a Christmas welcome, Brazilian style! Later we learned they had talked to Antonio about their plan to serenade us, and he let them in through our front gate. We tried to offer them hot chocolate, coffee, or tea, but they said they had other Ohio State families to serenade and were soon on their way. We went back to sleep that night feeling happy and safe.

Our 1964 Ford Country Sedan finally cleared customs in April 1965. Now we could start exploring the Brazilian countryside. In addition to visiting the Atlantic Ocean beaches as often as we could, we made our first trip to the new Brazilian capital of Brasilia. However, first we drove to Belo Horizonte, the capital of the state of Minas Gerais. We had been invited by our friends Maria de Cunia and Antonio de Silva, who we knew from my first teaching experience with Brazilians back in Columbus and who both worked in the agricultural credit section of a large bank in Belo, to visit them. Now we finally could.

The Portuguese meaning of Minas Gerais is "General Mines". While the state has beautiful mountains and agricultural land—it reminded us of West Virginia—it also has much mineral wealth. Some of the purest iron ore deposits are located in this state, as well as manganese, bauxite, nickel, silver, and other minerals. We visited Cristalina and Ouro Preto, two places famous for their precious and semiprecious stones. Here one could buy beautiful topazes of all shades, sizes, and cuts, marvelous aquamarines, garnets, rubies, and other precious stones, as well as all types of gold and silver settings. Interestingly, the Brazilians at that time preferred a soft gold, an assay of eighteen, while Americans prefer an assay of fourteen or harder. But Brazilian jewelry setters would make any kind of setting you wanted with any type of gold, silver, or platinum.

Later, in my travels back and forth to Brazil as a consultant, I found it prudent to buy only the cut and polished unset stones. At that time, United States Customs laws had a much higher import duty on set jewelry than on unset stones, so I got more bang for my buck that way. I thought I was in trouble at John F. Kennedy Airport in New York City early one morning after arriving nonstop from Rio de Janeiro. I had bought my maximum import quota of cut, polished stones at one of my favorite lapidary shops in an arcade in São Paulo. The owner of the shop, Seu Antonio, had wrapped each smoky topaz in tissue paper and placed them in small, tied leather pouches; he did the same with the yellow and brown topazes and the various shades of aquamarines he sold me.

The young United States Customs Officer I encountered that morning asked the usual question, "Did you declare everything you bought while in Brazil?" When I told him all I had purchased were some cut, polished, semiprecious stones, he wanted to know where they were and if I had an invoice for them. I showed him the invoice, converted from the Brazilian cruzeiro currency to U.S dollars at the current exchange rate. Then he asked to see each stone. You can imagine the loud groans from the people behind me in the customs line as I untied each leather pouch and unwrapped each stone from its tissue! Finally the officer said, "Wait here while I check these stones out." More groans from behind me in the line. After what seemed an eternity, he returned with my stones and invoice and smiled for the first time. "My supervisor said that you got a good buy there in São Paulo, Mr. Steele. Congratulations! Those are the first semiprecious stones I've seen here on the job. I just started my job two weeks ago."

We left Belo Horizonte after a delightful two-day visit with Maria and Antonio. It was a long, hot drive across the *sertão*, or inland plain, to the new Distrito Federal and the city of Brasilia. The high, barren plain of the Sertão reminded me of parts of Texas and New Mexico. There was very little vegetation, just the occasional Zebu cattle trying to survive on cactus and brush, and little green. But then one would come over a hill, and looking down from the top of the hill there would be a verdant, green valley with houses, barns, tree crops, dairy cattle, and beef cattle grazing in lush pastures. Upon later inquiry, we learned that those verdant spots were long-term land development concessions given by the Brazilian government to Japanese and Dutch immigrants to settle and develop. Those immigrants, carefully selected by their own governments, were very good agronomists who took great efforts to locate and protect water supplies in that arid land for proper use on crops and pastures.

We finally arrived at Brasilia and stayed at the new Presidential Hotel, beyond the Presidential Palace and the Congressional buildings. Brasilia, which was designed by the communist architect Oscar Neimeyer, was laid out in the shape of a large jet airplane, with the "wings" running from north to south and the "fuselage" from east to west. Government workers' apartments were found in the north and south zones, along with playgrounds, small parks, churches, and small shopping centers. The government ministry offices, near the Congressional buildings, were in the western part of the "fuselage," as were the Presidential Palace and the ornate Ministry of Foreign Relations, called Itamarate. Later, a large lake would be built further west of the Presidential Palace for individual residences. Movie theaters, large shopping centers, banks, restaurants, and other commercial enterprises were located in the eastern side of the "fuselage" beyond the "wings" of apartments.

The architecture was concrete, steel, glass and stone, all new and modern. While it was quite a unique place to visit for the first time in 1965, it was still primitive. The Cathedral, designed by an architect who was a communist and therefore most likely an agnostic or atheist, is one of the most inspiring buildings I have ever seen. It wasn't finished when we made our visit there as a family in 1965, but I had the opportunity to visit it in 1970, and I was amazed at the power and beauty of this steel and glass creation.

When we were there in 1965, dust and dirt were everywhere as construction was in full force, and the thousands of construction workers lived in shantytowns and shacks all around the edge of the city. Nevertheless, we enjoyed touring this new city carved in the interior of the country. Many experts said it would be an expensive flop as no Brazilian worker living in the beauty of Rio de Janeiro and its suburbs would ever move to Brasilia. The government had a plan to attract workers, however, and by the time I last visited Brasilia in the summer of 1970, a great transformation had taken place. It did not look like the same city. The military government of Brazil at that time had ordered all civilian government workers, their families, and supervisors to move to Brasilia. As an incentive, the government issued many free round trip airline tickets to Rio de Janeiro and the other major cities from which the employees had come. Unfortunately, this incentive also added to the runaway inflation Brazil was suffering at the time.

Back at Piracicaba, the OSU team was having trouble getting approval for its newly proposed graduate program from ESALQ's chair professors. We later learned that there had been a lot of infighting within the faculty, due to the fact that there were several departments of agricultural engineering, as well as several departments of agronomic subjects and agricultural chemistry. If memory serves me correctly, there were twenty-two different departments there when the OSU professors arrived, and students had to take courses in each of the twenty-two departments before earning their agricultural engineering degree! The fact that no livestock subjects were taught at ESALQ and were only taught at specialized veterinary universities created even more confusion within the agricultural education system in Brazil.

A story told by my friend and neighbor, Zilmar Marcos, who was an agricultural engineer, illustrates the kind of problem that resulted from this system. After four or five years successfully taking courses in those twenty-two departments, Zilmar's big day, graduation from ESALQ, arrived. The Dean placed a crown on his head and slipped a big *engenheiro* ring on his finger. Zilmar and his fellow graduates were now officially agricultural experts, entitled to be addressed with the respectful words, "O Doctor." Of course Zilmar was very proud of his accomplishment, and he had been hired as an agronomist by an American company, Anderson-Clayton, which had a significant quantity of farmland in the interior of São Paulo. On his first day on the job, he was greeted by the farm manager, a grand man of the soil, but without the benefit of a college education.

"O Doctor, please ride with me to our eastern field and tell me what is killing our crop there," the manager said, so they drove off to the eastern field. Zilmar got out of the jeep and walked into the middle of the crop with the farm manager. Then the manager asked him the critical question, "Doctor, what is wrong here?" At this point, Zilmar panicked. "I asked myself, 'What kind of a crop is this?' I had never seen these plants before in my life! But I could tell from their color that they were obviously sick." Zilmar realized right then and there that his education was far from complete. A smart and honest man, he confessed to the farm manager on the spot that he didn't know this crop. The manager said, "These are peanuts to be crushed into peanut oil, but they are diseased!" Zilmar kept his cool, suggested they cut a representative sample of the diseased plants, and said he would drive to the plant pathology laboratory run by the Secretariat of Agriculture in Campinas to find out what was wrong and how to cure it. Shortly afterward, Zilmar decided to go to the United States for a Master of Science degree at an agricultural university. He knew that the theoretical education he had received in Brazil was insufficient training for what he had been hired to do.

Dr. Erica la Rocha Nobre, my chair professor in the department of agricultural economics and a native of Manaus in the Amazon territory, was a bear of a man: very large and heavy by Brazilian standards. He towered over all his Brazilian colleagues. Dr. Nobre had fought hard to get several of his chair professor colleagues to allow American professors onto the faculty to help Brazil recover from the dire economic consequences of the malfeasance of prior federal and state governments. He and I got along royally.

Dr. Nobre usually gave the eulogies when one of the ESALQ faculty passed away, and there were a number of faculty deaths in the two years I was there. The standard format was to have the distinguished faculty member laid out in the main hall of the ESALQ administration building, where members of the faculty, the administration, and family members would gather to hear the eulogy before the remains were carried in the coffin to the cathedral, where a formal mass would be held. Once, when a chair professor who was dearly beloved by the whole ESALQ family had passed away, all of us, Brazilians and Americans, gathered in the main hall to hear Dr. Nobre's eulogy. I listened as hard and as carefully as I could, but I could not make any sense out of what he was saying. Finally, I whispered to my friend Zilmar, who was standing next to me, "What is he saying?" Zilmar whispered back, "I don't understand it either, but isn't the Portuguese he's using beautiful?" Since my native Brazilian colleague could not understand it either but was happy to enjoy the beautiful sound of the words, I decided to do the same.

Dr. Nobre always supported the OSU team as we worked together with the Brazilians to develop a Master of Science curriculum for ESALQ, but we had a lot of trouble getting the concept of specialization accepted by our Brazilian counterparts. (They called it diversification). However, it was finally adopted by adding a fifth year to the student's program for the *engenheiro agrônomo* degree. We thought this unfair since most masters degrees in the United States and other developed countries can be earned in a year to eighteen months following a four-year bachelors program. The Brazilians convinced us this could be the first year of a two-year Master of Science degree program.

Around the time all these variables were being debated, I was invited to the home of the Director of Agricultural Economics Research for the Secretariat of Agriculture of the State of São Paulo, Dr. Ruben Araujo Dias. At that time, the Secretariat was a more professional organization than the federal Ministry of Agriculture. The director was a graduate of ESALQ and was very loyal to his alma mater. He also strongly supported the OSU group and wanted to see progressive change at ESALQ. He was soon named the new Secretary of Agriculture of São Paulo, so it is clear that his peers held him in high esteem. One night he had invited a number of other alumni of ESALQ, now influential in both the private sector and the government, to his home to hear directly from Professor Steele what the OSU team of twelve professors had proposed to the ESALQ faculty, what the objections of the Brazilian professors and chair professors were, and to discuss the pros and cons with them. (I believe he chose me for this honor because I was the only OSU professor in town at that time). Fortunately, I was well versed in our proposal, having made a number of contributions to it myself, so I was able to rise to the occasion.

The evening started with Scotch and appetizers, served in the drawing room of the director's lovely home in a suburb of São Paulo.

At that time, I had never tasted Scotch whiskey before in my life, and because of the embargo on imported products designed to protect Brazil's recovering domestic industries, this was a domestically produced Brazilian Scotch. Not knowing the strength of the stuff, I ordered a Scotch and water on the rocks. They all looked at me as if I was a bit of a wimp, but this was not an event I wanted to blow by looking foolish from drinking too much. It was a good thing I took a watered-down version, since I did not know the strength of the stuff. To this day, I cannot take a drink of even a very good, smooth Scotch whiskey without having that startling taste sensation come back to me with full force. It tasted like wet cardboard! The dinner, however, which was served by the Director's wife and servants, was elegant. From the comments the ESALQ alumni shared with me that evening, I was able to return to our team in Piracicaba and say, "I think the alumni will force the chair professors to accept most of what we are proposing." Indeed, that soon came to pass, albeit with a few minor, acceptable, modifications.

At that time in the mid-1960s, the major American agricultural universities represented in Brazil in the field of rural development included: OSU (in São Paulo state), Purdue (in Minas Gerais), Wisconsin (in Porto Allegro), Arizona (in Fortaleza), and Michigan State (which was working in various parts of the country). After a while, we got our collective heads together and asked: "Why don't the agricultural economists and rural sociologists have a professional association in Brazil, the way we do in the United States?" Our idea was an organization in which Brazilian professionals could share their experiences and the results of their research, discuss the problems they were encountering, and maybe even work on Brazil's problems together. It was obvious to us that because of the competitive atmosphere between the various Brazilian faculties, the professors were reluctant to meet with each other and share their results and other matters of common interest, and that this lack of professional collaboration and cooperation was inhibiting progress toward their common goals.

Again, Dr. Nobre supported our idea. But when we suggested that he travel with us to the University of São Paulo (ESALQ was technically a part of the state university) to meet with the economics faculty there, he hesitated. Working through Dr. Araujo Dias, the Director of Economia Rural, we arranged an invitation for Dr. Nobre from the Head of the Department of Economics at the University of São Paulo, Dr. Antonio del Fin Netto. Dr. del Fin Netto was soon to be Brazil's foremost economist and head of the Ministério de Fazenda (which is like our Department of the Treasury and Department of Commerce combined into one agency)—very prestigious and very powerful! Our strategy worked, and as a result, the infant Assoçiaçăo de Economistas Rurais was born in 1965. It is now a very strong organization throughout South America, and we OSU and other American professors who helped it in its embryonic development are quite proud of our role in its creation.

One evening, Sally and I went to the main movie theater in downtown Piracicaba to see an American movie starring Ethel Merman. I had never heard of the movie before, nor for that matter have I heard much about it since. It was what we would call a "Grade-B flick." But since the ads on the marquee said that the soundtrack was in English, with Portuguese subtitles, we decided to go see it. It was a simple love story about a young American couple down on their luck, but not on their love for each other, set on the left bank in Paris. The owner of a French café, played by Ethel Merman, befriends the couple. Now this is all quite innocent in itself, but serious linguistic and gesturing problems arose in the translation. Hundreds of times during this film, actors used the "O. K." sign, formed with the thumb and index finger, that we Americans use so frequently but which has a totally different, salacious meaning in Brazil. In addition, each time the name of the Ethel Merman character was mentioned, Madame Coco, the Brazilian audience went into hysterics because that word in Brazilian, pronounced the way it was in the movie, refers to barnyard excrement! We could not even hear most of the dialogue because the constant, uproarious laughter of the audience kept drowning it out. As we left the theater that night, we felt quite conspicuous as we noticed Brazilians cupping their mouths and laughing at our embarrassment. Need I say that serious linguistic and cultural training is an important step before sending Americans to work overseas? You even need to study all the common gestures in order to stay out of trouble!

Our sons, John and David, had brought their American football along with them to Piracicaba. One day they were out on our street, passing and kicking the ball to each other. The young Brazilian kids in the block started to laugh at this crazy looking ball, not at all like their round soccer ball, which they called a "futebol." Of course, when they tried to kick our ball, it took all sorts of crazy turns and bounces, and this threw them into fits of laughter. They called it the *"bola norteamericana loco"* (the crazy North American ball). John and David called for me to come out and show the Brazilian boys how far an American adult could kick a football, and I obliged. The first kick was a beauty; unfortunately, on the second kick the ball went off the side of my foot, hit the telephone wire, and snapped it right in two. The two broken ends fell to the ground right in front of our house.

The Brazilian boys hooted and broke into even more hysterical laughter. I had to contact my neighbor, Zilmar, in great embarrassment. "How can we get that wire fixed?" I asked. "That's easy," Zilmar assured me. "I know the installers at the telephone company." Within an hour, a man came and spliced the wire back together and refused my offer to pay for the repairs. He thought what I had accomplished with one swift kick of an American-style football was quite humorous!

Our Brazilian friends may have learned about football from us, but we learned about fruit from them. A banana is a banana, is it not? It is that six to eight-inch long, bright, yellow-skinned fruit that every supermarket in the United States sells, right? Well, yes—and no. That is what the major banana marketing firms have trained us to demand and to call a banana. The United Fruit Company, Standard Fruit Company, Del Monte, and all the rest cultivated those particular varieties which ship well from Central and South America and advertised them until American consumers believed that is the only banana we should consider buying. In Honduras, these bananas are fried and used by campesinos in their meals much like their close cousins, plantains, are.

My family and I were surprised to find out in Brazil that there are about 150 different varieties of bananas in the tropical world! Many of them cannot be shipped long distances because of their delicate skins and juicy internal fruit, which bruises and decays rapidly if not properly refrigerated or consumed quickly. My favorite was the *banana ouro*, followed by the *banana maça* and the *banana nectar*. The ouro (gold banana) was sold in bunches, called "hands," about the size of a large farmer's hand. It had dark yellow-orange skin, and the individual bananas were about the size of my middle finger. Those bananas literally melted in your mouth, they were so sweet and juicy. The *maça* (apple banana) that we ate in São Paulo had a red skin, was bigger than the *ouro*, and perhaps three-quarters the size of typical bananas marketed in the United States. It also was much sweeter and juicier than what we are used to in the United States; the *nectar* was much like the Cavendish variety perfected by the English in Malaya.

I could go on at length about other varieties of bananas, but we also discovered untold riches and complexities in the varieties of citrus fruit available during our stay in Brazil. First: oranges. Oranges that grow in groves in the United States are orange, are they not?—again, yes and no. Nearly all the oranges sold to us in our American supermarkets have had orange coloring added when they are packed for shipment. This is true of Navels, Valencias, and other varieties as well. Imagine my surprise at the open *feira* (market) in Piracicaba the first time Zilmar took me there. I picked up a round green-skinned fruit and asked him what it was. He laughed heartily and said, "Howard, don't you recognize an orange when you see one?" Then he whipped out his pocketknife and cut it into two halves; to my surprise, the flesh inside was red. He said, "Here, taste a typical São Paulo *laranja*." I had to admit that it tasted like any other orange, although it was a bit more acidic than my favorite variety in the United States Then he picked up another round fruit about the same size, this one with a red skin. He cut that one into two halves also, and the fruit on the inside of this one was green. That orange was really sour, but Zilmar told me it was excellent to eat along with papaya. Before that day, I had no idea there were so many varieties of oranges.

In the next two years, we ate all kinds of citrus fruit that were not anything like what we have here in the United States. What the Brazilians call a *limão* (lemon) is very sweet and not at all acidic, although you can also find *limões ácidos* (sour lemons) for sale. Their *lima* (lime) is very sweet as well. But whenever a Brazilian mentioned how much he liked his native *toranja* (grapefruit), I had to respectfully beg to differ in my opinion. Almost all of the grapefruits I ate in Brazil were so sour and acidic that I could never finish them. The Brazilians put lots of salt and sugar on them to create the taste they liked. As with oranges and bananas, there must have been one hundred or more different varieties and colors of grapefruit, in many different combinations of skin and fruit colors.

My favorite Brazilian fruits were *mamão* (papaya), *manga* (mango), *jabuticaba*, and *carimbola* (star fruit). After my first taste of papaya on the very first morning in Brazil, at the Hotel Real in São Paulo, I was permanently hooked on that fruit and have never been able to get enough papaya. As Lucille Sitterley had instructed us that first day, we would always squeeze a little orange juice or lime juice on it to bring out the papaya flavor. I got into the habit of having fresh papaya nearly every morning for breakfast when our maid, Cinira, brought it to us from her large garden.

The first mangos I ate in Brazil, on the other hand, were quite stringy. One had to use floss or toothpicks after eating them. Great progress has since been made in selective breeding to minimize the stringy quality of mangos, and they are still delicious. My sons used to fight for the "bone" as they called it, the large flat seed in the middle of the mango that still had succulent juice and flesh to be savored. Brazilians who had been to the United States told us that mangos were the tropic's answer to ripe peaches in northern climates. There are hundreds of varieties of mangos too; the really good ones must be eaten when fully ripe over a plate or sink because they are so full of sweet juice.

The *jabuticaba*, for which there is no English translation, is like no other fruit I have seen in the world. The tree grows up with limbs that run nearly parallel to the ground. Growing directly out of the bark of those limbs is a large black-skinned fruit about the size of one of our small purple plums. The skin slips off easily, and inside is a sweet, white flesh with a flavor uniquely its own. Each fruit has a black, oblong seed in the middle. It was fun to watch Brazilian boys scramble up the limbs of those *jabuticaba* trees in their bare feet, scraping the fruit off the bark as they climbed from limb to limb. Then their pals on the ground would gather the beautiful black fruit into boxes or bags.

Nowadays, star fruit (*carimbola*) is pretty well known in the United States, at least on the East Coast. At that time, it was a novelty to us. It is slightly acidic, with a lovely flavor all its own. I could write much more about the various tropical fruits we "discovered" at the various posts I held in tropical countries during my international career; suffice it to say that consuming fresh, tropical fruit is one of the great pleasures of living in developing countries on or near the equatorial belt.

In May 1966, my chairman at Ohio State University, Dr. Mervin Smith, came to Brazil for a visit and announced that he and my Dean were very impressed with my work. When Dean Roy Kottman arrived for a review of our program, he told me that if I signed on for another two-year term at Piracicaba, my full professorship would be assured. I was also one of the top candidates to replace Dr. Sitterley as chief of party for OSU in Brazil when Sitterley decided to retire. I was elated! This was what I had been working toward professionally, and what we as a family had been sacrificing ourselves for, all these years. It represented professional recognition for my work, and offered wonderful opportunities for our future—at least that is how I saw it.

However, when I returned to Piracicaba from Rio, where I had met with Dean Kottman and Dr. Smith, to share the good news and discuss their offer with my family, I was in for a shock. Sally wanted to return home; she said that she had been away from her mother for two years, and that was long enough. I could not believe what I was hearing.

In time, I came to believe that Sally's mother had always held it against me that her youngest child, the apple of her eye, had given up a potential singing career to marry me.

I tried to reason with Sally. I pointed out that she had made great sacrifices for me and my career, helping me finish my Ph.D.

at Kentucky by raising three little Steele kids in a cramped house in Lexington while I was largely absent, studying so hard. Now was the time for us to reap the payoff: prestige, higher pay, more fringe benefits, even a private telephone in Brazil—all these were to be ours!

Sally was not buying my arguments. I did not know what to do. Dean Kottman came to Piracicaba to look at our projects a few days later and asked me if I had made a decision. I said I needed a few more days to discuss things with my family. I begged Sally and the kids to see what a wonderful opportunity this was for us, and to support me in accepting the offer. But the kids agreed with Sally; our oldest son, John (who was then 13), came to me on his own and asked if we could not go back to Columbus. He said he missed Boy Scouts, Little League baseball, and American schools. Now I was really in deep water!

Within a few days, I had to go back to São Paulo for final meetings with Dr. Smith and the USAID people there to give them my answer. After staying awake all night long, evaluating the consequences of each of the options, I finally decided, reluctantly, to turn the offer down. I said I would take my chances integrating into the OSU faculty in Columbus and earning my full professorship some other way. I felt that the psychological scars the kids might suffer if I insisted on staying in Brazil against their will was not worth the job satisfaction and career advancement that staying in Brazil meant for me. Also, I still thought that Sally and I would be able to resolve our differences.

It was late August 1966 when we headed up the western coast of South America, meandering on our way back to the United States. We had eleven days of vacation time to use before we entered the United States, and we wanted to protect our income tax-free status by staying out of the United States for a minimum of 510 days during any eighteen-month period. So we had a nice, slow, touristy trip back home, flying to various points and stopping along the way. We had to sell our car to the U.S. Embassy Automobile Committee, a new requirement that precluded Americans from earning additional profits with their duty-free cars.

We spent several days in Lima, Peru, courtesy of Braniff International Airlines who, because they had no direct daily flights to the United States, put us up at a Lima hotel. Then we visited Bogota, Colombia, the Panama Canal, and Mexico City. As we were passing through U.S. Customs at San Antonio, Texas, my kids all spotted a water fountain. They asked if they could drink directly from it (forbidden in Latin America in those days because most water in fountains was contaminated). When we told them they could, each of the kids spent about ten minutes elatedly slurping the first clean, safe water they had been able to drink directly (not boiled or filtered) in two years. They were happy to be home again!

Back in Columbus, I worked hard at integrating into the OSU faculty, but I never was able to do so fully. I chose not to join any of the departmental political cliques, declined to trash the department chairman who had hired me, and refused to participate in a mutiny to replace him. I naively thought that my future promotion and position would be based on the merits of my teaching, my research, my counseling with students, and my committee efforts. I was wrong about that. We got a new department chairman who did not particularly believe in international development work. Obviously, I disagreed with his position and with several of his other policies. This was not conducive to my being promoted to full professor. Unfortunately, my relationships with my mother-in-law and my wife did not grow any warmer either.

5

Back to Brazil with the Cooperative League of the USA

During the first few years following the takeover of Brazil by its military in 1964, the United States government was pouring about 500 million dollars a year into the country, an amount equal to about 3 billion dollars a year in today's currency. This money went to Brazil as direct aid and technical assistance in the form of appropriated foreign assistance funds approved by Congress. This was a very competitive period of the Cold War, and the U.S. government did not want Fidel Castro and the other communist agitators in the region, such as Che Guevara in Bolivia or Salvador Allende of Chile, to gain strong footholds in Latin America.

My good friend, Dr. Richard Newberg, was still the head of USAID/Brazil's agricultural and rural development office in Rio de Janeiro at that time. Since the rural poor were a serious problem for Brazil as they flooded into the major coastal cities looking for work, a large part of the technical assistance funds provided by the United States were directed at agriculture and helping the rural poor. It was hoped that USAID/Brazil and the North American technicians they sent could help the Brazilians improve the efficiency of production and output for the average farmer, improve their overall agricultural marketing system, and lower its costs.

One day in the spring of 1967, when I was at my OSU office in Columbus, I received a telephone call from Dr. Newberg. He asked me to join an agricultural cooperative marketing improvement team he was putting together to continue and expand the type of work I had been doing with Dr. Mendoça's cooperative, at São José do Rio Preto. They were now looking to include the state of Minas Gerais in their plans for developing cooperatives. He said he had two outstanding, experienced cooperative developers from the FELCO Cooperative of Fort Dodge, Iowa lined up for the team and knew that they could benefit from my expertise and knowledge of agricultural issues in São Paulo state. He wanted me to travel through Brazil with them for about six weeks that summer. After obtaining the approval of my department chair, I called Dr. Newberg back and agreed to participate in the project.

Dr. Newberg told me that Donald Daughters of the Cooperative League of the United States, a consulting firm that worked in developing countries primarily with cooperatives funded by USAID or the Department of State, would be the logistical member of the team. He would put our contracts together and spend the first several weeks with us in Brazil. One of the FELCO experts was a finance specialist, and the other, Bill Davidson, was a management specialist. The Cooperative League would pay us for our services. This sounded like a good plan to me; I started corresponding right away with Bill Davidson, answering his many questions about the cooperative movement (or lack thereof) in the states of São Paulo and Minas Gerais. I also had several preparatory meetings with Don Daughters in Washington, D.C. and Columbus, as he put the team's contract terms and paperwork together. The four of us were never all together in one place until the night we flew to Rio. We met at LaGuardia Airport, and Don Daughters had us sign our contracts. He put them in the mail, and we got into a New York Helicopter Co. chopper to fly to Kennedy, where we would catch our international flight to Rio.

Things started out quite badly for us on that trip. After we arrived at Kennedy, as the helicopter that had brought us there lifted off to return to LaGuardia, Don Daughters suddenly realized that one of his three attaché cases was missing. He panicked and told us in confidence that the missing attaché had classified documents in it that he was taking to the U.S. Embassy in Rio. "We cannot leave until I have that in my hands," he insisted. "I cannot believe that they didn't offload that at the helipad!"

As I was mulling this over, Don Daughters was dealing with VARIG airlines officials, trying to get back the missing attaché case. Apparently he showed them his diplomatic credentials, and they started a search for the missing case inside their warehouse and in the hold of the Boeing 707 jet we were to fly in to Rio. They located all of our suitcases and the two other attaché cases that Don had checked through, but not the one he intended to carry on and keep with him under his seat.

After about two hours of frantic phone calls to New York Helicopters, inquiries with ground personnel at Kennedy, and intense, persuasive talks with VARIG airlines officials who were angry about holding up the departure of their plane (which was full of angry passengers), the problem was finally solved. New York Helicopters found the locked, missing attaché case at the side of their heliport at LaGuardia and flew it directly to VARIG's terminal area, where Don Daughters received it with sweaty hands and would not let it go of it, even for a second, as we finally entered the plane and took our seats. About 130 passengers gave us extremely dirty looks and irritated frowns as we strapped into our seats, but we were finally on our way. I truly believe the other passengers were angry not so much because of our late departure—Brazilians are generally quite blasé about schedules—but because the captain had not allowed them to smoke during the long delay. Also, they were more than ready for their pre-dinner cocktails, and to tell you the truth, I could use a stiff one right about then myself!

The tension of our delayed departure and the brand-new knowledge that neither of my two colleagues from FELCO, with whom I would be working day and night for the next six weeks, spoke one word of Portuguese, had put me in a pretty bad mood. I realized that on top of sharing my knowledge of agricultural marketing and my other technical and cultural knowledge, I was going to be in the unofficial (and unpaid) position of translator.

The VARIG cabin crew tried to make up for the late departure with marvelous service. Perhaps the captain of the flight had told them about the diplomatic problem caused by New York Helicopters, I do not know. However, I do know that they kept our glasses full and served an outstanding dinner as they always did on every flight I took on VARIG Airlines in those days. Eventually, everybody mellowed out. The dinner was over at about 2 a.m. Eastern Standard Time, I answered the last questions posed by my FELCO colleagues by about 3 a.m., and then fell fast asleep until the VARIG cabin crew started serving breakfast around 6 a.m. the next morning somewhere north of Rio. Donald Daughters was in the first class section of the jet while Bill Davidson, the finance officer, and I were in coach. I have a feeling that Don fell asleep immediately after takeoff with that attaché case strapped to his arm; he had really been through the wringer that day.

We landed at Galeão International Airport in Rio, cleared customs, and were met by a United States Embassy representative, driver, and car. At the embassy, we were welcomed by Dr. Newberg. We completed some paperwork, had an embassy security briefing with Don Daughters, who was managing several projects for the Cooperative League in Brazil, and then proceeded to the offices of USAID/Brazil. There we met the USAID/Brazil Mission Director, William Ellis, in a courtesy call. After a short interview, he wished us well in our work and then called for Dr. Newberg to come up to his office and take charge.

We spent the rest of the day with Dick and his staff hearing about their hopes and objectives, listening to what they wanted help with, taking notes, and getting lots of reports for our late-night reading while we were there. Our headquarters would be in the city of São Paulo, where we would be working with the Mogiana Group of newly organized agricultural cooperatives that was under the dynamic leadership of Gilberto Borges, who I had met while at Piracicaba. Gilberto was highly respected in agricultural circles in Brazil. He came from a working-*fazenda* owned by his family, received an economics degree from the University of São Paulo, and was helping organize farmers' producer associations and cooperatives.

The next day, we flew on to São Paulo. We had reservations at my favorite hotel in the center of town, the small Hotel Cambridge, where I had often stayed. This hotel was very close to the downtown junction of major streets. The main thoroughfare, Avenida Nove de Julio, and the famous Ponte de Cha were within walking distance of the Cambridge, as were hundreds of restaurants, arcades, and shops. Taxis were plentiful and cheap. The offices of the Mogiana Group were in a quiet suburb of São Paulo, perhaps fifteen minutes away by taxi from our hotel.

We were given small offices at the Mogiana Group and were quickly introduced to the resident specialists there. The Mogiana Group had received some support from the Food and Agricultural Organization of the United Nations (FAO), the Inter-American Development Bank (IDB), and the World Bank. Most of that funding paid for cooperative organization and rural development specialists from other countries. There was a resident agribusiness specialist from France, a rural sociologist from Colombia, a rural credit specialist from Argentina, and so on. Each specialist, including the resident Brazilian college graduates, had ongoing projects that they reviewed with us.

It soon became clear that although there were a number of badly needed and potentially good development projects being implemented, there was no cohesive development plan which would incorporate them into an overall plan. Rather, each specialist was going off on his or her own. This did not bode well for the long-term success or efficiency of the venture. We discussed these concerns with each other when we were away from the Mogiana offices at our hotel in the evenings. We felt that our first priority was to put together a comprehensive, integrated development plan, incorporating the best of these individual projects for the complete development of the Mogiana program.

Fairly early in our stay, Gilberto Borges had planned a long trip through the agricultural regions of the states of São Paulo and Minas Gerais for us. We would meet the managers of small, struggling farmers' cooperatives, as well as the managers of some large, successful ones, including Dr. Mendoça's co-op in São José do Rio Preto. We were also going to look at possible assembly market locations for soybeans, corn, fruits, and vegetables that we thought could provide good storage and marketing centers within Brazil.

However, first I insisted that we visit the central agricultural market in São Paulo. At that time, there was no modern facility for perishable produce, which arrived daily in the city from thousands of points in the interior to feed the six to eight million residents. There was a modern central market for perishables on the drawing boards, but it had not been completed in 1967. The historic market place was along one of São Paulo's rivers, which often flooded in the rainy season. It was dirty, with limited sanitation and water facilities and very little protection from the elements. It was very dusty in the dry season and muddy in the wet season. I wanted the Iowa specialists to see that there was no formal system of grades and standards for agricultural products such as those in the United States. At that time, only the Japanese-Brazilian cooperative, COTIA, was trying to grade their fruit and tomatoes to quality standards.

One morning around 4 a.m., a Mogiana driver took us to the marketplace. The Iowa men had never seen such chaos. There were hundreds of trucks with horns blaring, thousands of pushcarts moving about everywhere, and thousands of *corregedores* (human runners) carrying boxes or bags on their heads, pushing through the melee. Imagine the damage inflicted on the produce! Imagine the waste in quality and value!

I suggested that we go to a warehouse COTIA had built to receive their farmers' fruits and vegetables. At that time, COTIA specialized in handling tomatoes, onions, peaches, apples, cherries, and grapes. They were trying, with quite a bit of success, to develop a superior brand that would command the highest prices in the market. I had been there before and knew the resident Japanese-Brazilian manager, who also spoke English. I knew this would be helpful to my non-Portuguese-speaking colleagues from Iowa and me.

We found the manager in the middle of the warehouse, near several truckloads of boxes of tomatoes that had been shipped by his members in rural São Paulo. He greeted us with a big smile as I introduced my Iowan cooperative specialists. This manager and I had been together in marketing meetings and elsewhere, and I had visited him in his warehouse on several occasions before. On this particular morning, we interrupted him as he was ordering several employees to locate wooden boxes of tomatoes in the center of each truckload and to place them on the floor in front of him. We noticed that the tomatoes on the top of each box were beautiful specimens. Then, to our surprise, the manager dug down to the middle rows of each box, took out some tomatoes, and displayed them on newspapers spread out on the floor. These tomatoes were clearly of sub standard quality, not in compliance with the written guidelines COTIA had distributed to their farmer-members. Some were not red-ripe, some were misshapen, and some had evidence of disease. The manager pointed out these violations to each of the truck drivers who had delivered the tomatoes. Then he rejected the whole truckload of tomatoes that contained sub standard fruit.

When I told the Iowa specialists what the manager had just told the truck driver, they were quite shocked. They asked, "Won't the other members, the ones whose fruit was good, be angry? Won't they try to have the manager fired?" When we repeated this question to the manager, he just smiled an even broader smile. His answer was, "These are all neighbors. When the members who tried to ship only fruit meeting our standards find out about their neighbors trying to cheat, they will be furious with them—not with me. We worked these standards out together, and they all voted to only ship fruit that meets those standards. They know I've gotten them superior prices. They know I cannot sell boxes with inferior quality tomatoes hidden in the middle. They will make their neighbors either shape up, or leave the cooperative." The two Iowa specialists whistled and shook their heads up and down knowingly. This was basic agricultural marketing grading to quality standards in the embryonic stage!

Soon Gilberto had us travel to the interior of São Paulo state and Minas Gerais, where we visited individual cooperatives in his loosely federated Mogiana Group. USAID/Brazil had also assigned one of their specialists in agronomy and a contract person in agribusiness to travel with us. I was happy about this. One of the two men I knew from my earlier work in Brazil, and I knew the other by reputation; I knew that he had knowledge and experience in Brazil that went beyond mine. These two men were George Coonrod, an agronomist with USAID, and Stan Bednarzic, an agribusiness specialist.

Stan Bednarzic had worked for American cooperative federations for many years before moving to Brazil. He had a neat way of introducing himself to Brazilian business managers and breaking the ice with them. He always carried one of the original Polaroid instant cameras and lots of film with him. At that time, most Brazilians in the interior had never heard of a Polaroid camera, let alone seen one. Stan would line them up outside the cooperative offices and, with the manager in front, take their picture. The "ooohs" and "aaaahs" when they saw the picture instantly appear were inevitably followed by smiles and warm welcomes. We all agreed this was a great door opener, and it helped get us off to a good start.

We began our travels in the area around Ribeirão Preto, in São Paulo state. There we heard a story regarding a number of rice producers and their struggling cooperatives that had become targets for purchase by brokers in the cities of São Paulo and Rio de Janeiro. The military government of Brazil started an investigation after hearing a number of complaints and concerns and discovered that the brokers had been hired to buy these struggling cooperative businesses by an American capitalist corporation. The name of the principal owner of the American corporate finance company was the August Busch Brewing Company. The Brazilian military government, trying to protect domestic businesses until Brazil's economic recovery from ten years of communist policies, tried to stop the process.

When the senior president of the company, August Busch, heard about this, it is alleged that he flew directly to Brasilia in his corporate jet and asked for a private audience with the president of the country, General Castelo Branco. Busch convinced the president that he needed the Grade 3 rice for his new beer brewery in Jacksonville, Florida. That grade of rice was of poor length, bad color, and contained many broken kernels. The Brazilian cooperatives were practically giving Grade 3 rice away to farmers as animal feed or were burning or dumping it. Busch promised the president that he would clean up the domestic rice business in Brazil by improving quality controls on the Grade 1 and Grade 2 varieties, help them improve packaging, and would then be able to lower costs to consumers while paying better prices to farmers, if they allowed him to export all the Grade 3 rice at a fair price to his new brewery in Florida. The Brazilian government eventually approved Busch's plan after studying the details, and the rice industry in that area of the country benefited from that decision.

But our team was not dealing with rice. Nor were we interested in coffee, which was well graded and marketed. The Brazilian Coffee Institute had done an excellent job over the years working with farmers to improve varieties, cultural practices, storage, marketing, and exporting. Coffee was Brazil's number one export and, in a very competitive world market, was earning foreign exchange for many years. If the grading and marketing system for coffee was so advanced, why could that advanced marketing system not also be used for corn, soybeans, wheat, fruits, and vegetables? We knew that Brazilians were intelligent, hard-working people; and Brazilian businessmen now had access to new sources of credit and financing. So why was the domestic marketing system for nonexport commodities not efficient and profitable like that of the coffee industry? We figured that a lack of competition, insufficient incentives, and lethargy were the main culprits. Dr. Mendoça had proven to his neighbors that with a little initiative, a little capital, and dedicated management the system could be improved, and farmer members' incomes could benefit. We needed to find a way to make this kind of success more widespread in Brazil.

We traveled to São José do Rio Preto, to numerous little towns on the border between São Paulo state and Minas Gerais. Later we spent time around the area of Sete Lagoas in Minas Gerais and eventually visited all fifteen of the member cooperatives of the Mogiana Group. By the end of the second long trip across rugged roads, with red dust coating us, our baggage, and the jeeps, and suffering from that exhausting Brazilian interior heat and humidity, Gilberto Borges gave us a break to help rescue our sanity. We arrived at a hot springs resort hotel called Poços de Caldas, high in the mountains of Minas Gerais. There the mineral water of the springs was invigorating yet very relaxing. We followed our immersion in the hot springs with cold showers in the resort hotel. The food and beverages at the hotel spa were unsurpassed, as was the service and hospitality. Under these circumstances, we quickly regained our happiness and friendly comportments again.

After our exploratory travels, we five American technicians, along with our Brazilian, FAO, IDB, and World Bank colleagues, began to put together a comprehensive organizational and development plan for the Mogiana Group, which included adopting the COTIA system of grading and standardizing for fruits and vegetables. The team also developed a proposal to study corn, soybeans, and other small grain scientific standards by the São Paulo Secretariat of Agriculture, using university experts from ESALQ and Viçosa. When accepted by the scientific community, the agribusiness firms, and farmers, it would be incorporated into the Mogiana development plan. The team also proposed a series of interior assembly market centers and farm service centers, with satellites for the smaller cooperatives until they grew large enough in membership and volume of produce handled to justify their own centers.

Another significant part of the proposal we put together for Gilberto Borges and his Mogiana executives involved funding to send selected present or future farm service managers to study our agricultural cooperatives in the United States. This would not just be theoretical training at the universities and USDA, although some of that was needed too. Rather, the emphasis would be on hands-on management training. The Brazilian managers selected to travel and study in the United States would be expected, after some introductory training and English comprehension testing, to work side by side with American cooperative farm service center managers in the field for an extended period of time. We felt this was the best way for Brazilians to learn financial controls, personnel management, competitive forces, management of facility equipment, costs and returns, and other aspects of managing agricultural cooperatives. That aspect of our plan for the Mogiana local cooperatives worked very well. Eventually, about a dozen young potential farm service managers came to the United States and received this training. They returned to Brazil, became excellent cooperative management leaders, and were essential in creating a much more diversified, productive agricultural industry there. This is one aspect of the USAID work in Brazil about which the team could feel very proud.

I wish I could say that the organizational and financial structures our team designed for the Mogiana group were also accepted and adopted, but I cannot. At that time in Brazil's history, none of the local cooperative managers wanted to give up their sovereignty to an untried federation, as we were proposing they do. While all fifteen of the cooperative presidents and managers agreed that the plan we presented made sense and was the correct way to go, each of them also felt strongly that he should be the new federation president. They could not accept the fact that our proposal called for agreement and compromise on finance proposals, constitution and bylaws approval, and then an election to determine who would be the new officers of the federation. Each wanted to be named up front as the new president. The organizational proposal failed because of this short-sighted and self-serving attitude, even though various other parts and pieces of our scheme were adopted.

Our work was completed in August, and we returned to our homes. It had been a grand experience working with the FELCO executives, George Coonrod, and Stan Bednarzic. Although we regretted that we had not been able to convince the local cooperative leaders to accept our organizational and financial plan, we still felt we had made good headway, and time would prove us right. Besides, only Brazilians would be able to solve the interpersonality problems of these strong farm leaders.

I earned enough money on that contract to be able to return to Columbus and buy a second car for our family. We bought a fairly new Volkswagen Squareback, a small station wagon that ran for days on a little bit of gasoline. Soon, John, our oldest son, had his driving learner's permit and then his license. He loved that little Volkswagen with a passion and took good care of it.

6

Ohio State, and My Book
Comercialização Agricola

Of the several marketing courses I taught at both the undergraduate and graduate levels at OSU, my undergraduate course in agricultural marketing principles gave me the most pleasure. I asked my students to subscribe to the *Wall Street Journal*, and then we started following the agricultural commodity market prices and movements together as a class. Later in the term, I had the students divide up into small groups and form one of several hypothetical companies or cooperatives, such as a flour-milling concern, a feed mixing company, or a farmers' co-op grain storage operation. They were then "given" a hypothetical capital infusion of ten thousand dollars and were told they were free to take market actions with it (such as investing the money in their commodity, buying advertising, or hedging with it), keeping track of each transaction carefully, and then making weekly reports to me and the rest of the class about their progress, based on what they saw reported in the *Wall Street Journal*.

The students preferred this approach to studying the agricultural marketing system, organized commodity markets (such as the Chicago Mercantile Exchange), and the pros and cons of risk-taking and risk-aversion to the more traditional format of lectures and quizzes. One term, I had a senior who was so excited with the coursework that he called the President of the Chicago Mercantile Exchange to ask him some questions. When I first heard this, I wondered if both he and I would get into some kind of trouble. It was not easy for him to get through to the president, but he finally succeeded. As it turned out, the president was so impressed with this student's enthusiasm and initiative that he invited him to come to Chicago, arranged for him to meet with some of the Exchange's junior executives, and offered him a special tour of the Exchange. Later I found out this student was offered a job at the Mercantile Exchange after graduation.

Word spread about the approach I was using in class, and soon the acting chairman asked if I would help organize an International Agricultural Marketing Training Center for participants from other countries within the department, a companion program to the already established International Agricultural Finance Training Center. The Finance Training Center received ten to twenty international participants every term from developing countries. The Center was set up with simultaneous interpretation booths and headsets for translation into any one of four different languages. Most classes were simultaneously translated into Spanish, French, Portuguese, and sometimes one other language, depending on where the participants came from. We decided we would establish the International Agricultural Marketing Training Center using a similar format. The students would spend about half of the term studying various aspects of the American agricultural credit system. We invited guest lecturers, including representatives of agricultural credit institutions, bank managers, and agricultural cooperative finance officers, to come and speak to them. The second half of the term, we took the students on field trips to visit farmers, local agribusiness leaders, and bankers.

The USAID mission in the participant's country usually paid the costs for these programs. Sometimes we received participants whose programs were paid for by the FAO of the United Nations or by one of the development banks. It took one semester for several of us in agricultural marketing within our department to develop the curriculum, line up guest speakers, and plan field trips.

The program's long field trip was near the end of the term. We traveled across Ohio and Indiana and ended up in Illinois. Along the way, we visited outstanding farmers' co-operatives of all sizes—some big, some small. We also visited various commodity processing and storage facilities, such as ketchup and meatpacking plants, grain storage facilities, and supermarket warehouses. In Chicago, we visited the Chicago Livestock Market, the Chicago Terminal Produce Market, and the Chicago Mercantile Exchange. Usually we traveled by OSU bus, but on several occasions, when we had a smaller number of students, we flew in OSU aircraft and rented station wagons to get around locally. After returning from this extended field trip and summarizing what we had done during the whole term, we arranged a nice graduation ceremony for the students with a dinner at the OSU Faculty Club, the awarding of a certificate of completion, and a picture with one of the deans attending. This made the participants feel like "alumni of OSU" and was very well received.

One term, we had a group of international students from India and Africa. They all got along well together and we had a great field trip across the Corn Belt. When it came time for their graduation dinner and awards program at the Faculty Club, we made sure to order chicken for the Hindus from India and beefsteaks for the Africans. ("No bovine meat please," the Chief of the Indian group had specifically requested, adding, as if he needed to explain, "The cow is sacred in our religion.") We had a larger turnout of faculty than we had expected that night, so my technical officer Chan Connelly and I were eating our dinner in a room adjoining the private dining room where our sixteen participants and the teachers were seated.

At one point, the head waitress came out of the kitchen with a number of plates of chicken and vegetables and asked us which participants were to have the chicken. Chan and I answered in unison, "The Indian gentlemen, just inside the partition to the left of the door." The head waitress said, "But they are all eating steak!" We said, "That cannot be—they're Hindus and do not eat beef; it's against their religion." She said, "Go look for yourselves!" So Chan and I entered the room together, and sure enough, there was the Indian chief of party just placing a large chunk of steak in his mouth. Surprised, Chan said, "Govan, what are you doing eating that meat? You all ordered chicken, remember?" With a very satisfied smile, Govan answered, "Mr. Connelly, Dr. Steele, this is the best chicken any of us have ever eaten!" His Indian colleagues all nodded their heads in approval. All we could do was ask the chef to put the chicken in the warmer and cook up more steak for the Africans.

None of those who witnessed the first moon landing in the summer of 1969 is likely to ever forget it. One of my OSU colleagues and his wife graciously invited the faculty and their spouses to an all-day barbecue to watch the attempt to land on the moon. They had set up large television screens at strategic places on their patio and in various rooms of their home, so everyone could closely follow the pictures being relayed by NASA from outer space. What a thrill it was that summer evening, just at dusk, to see Neil Armstrong make that historic "one small step for man, one giant leap for mankind."

The following week, we were taking a group of students from the Kikuyu tribe of Kenya on a field trip through Ohio. They all were fairly small men—all, that is, but their tribal chief. He was a giant by comparison. He towered over all of them and probably weighed more than 250 pounds, while his tribesmen weighed about a hundred pounds each. While all of the men spoke English, which was one of the official languages of Kenya, they also frequently spoke with the chief in Swahili or in another indigenous dialect. The chief wore a large U.S. Army Korean War winter hat with large ear fobs that could tie under his chin. Where he got that hat and what its significance to him was, I do not know, but he wore it all summer and fall when he was with us. Usually he had the ear fobs tied up on top of the hat, as we were in the heat of an Ohio summer.

The chief was a kind man. He kept his countrymen on schedule and allowed them to ask all kinds of question of our professors and the resource people we visited in the field. He had one curious habit: when he talked, he placed the heel of one of his very large hands on the side of his face, and the rest of his hand, the palm and his extremely long fingers, would go up over the top of his head and the Korean War hat and down the other temple. One day on the bus, we were discussing the moon landing. When I asked the chief what he and his men thought about it and if they had seen the television coverage and the pictures, up went his right hand—up and over his head, and down on his left temple—fingers drumming.

He started shaking his head no, no, no from side to side. Then he said to me in English, "Professor, that film was made in Hollywood. Nobody could go way up there to the moon. No, no, no. This is a Hollywood 'fool the world' trick." I tried to convince him that it was real, that it had happened. I told him that the scientists had perfected large enough rocket engines and navigation controls to make it happen, after much trial and error. He was not buying it for one minute. I then asked him what his men thought. He relayed my question in English to the men into the microphone and over the loudspeakers. There was a lot of discussion in Swahili and local dialects. Finally, he fingered the microphone again and said in English, "It's not possible for a man to go to the moon, is it, men?" In unison they all answered in English, "Oh no, no, no—no man can go to the moon, chief!!" That ended that discussion. The chief always had the last word with his men. While he could not comprehend the advanced rocket and electronic technology that made the trip to the moon possible, he was in tune with advanced American agricultural marketing technology and wanted his men to see it and understand it. He knew that making improvements in the system in Kenya would pay dividends. These were trained agriculturalists; most had grown up in rural villages and farms. They knew the hardships of production agriculture and many of the companion marketing problems in Kenya, but they did not know or understand rocket science, physics, and compulsion.

Later, when Ray Hancock, Deputy Administrator of the National Agricultural Statistics Service of USDA, and I visited Kenya in the spring of 1989, we were impressed with the levels of education being completed by both Kenyan men and women. These trained Kenyans were making great improvements in their farming and marketing practices and in rural development, despite significant corruption in government.

Back in the fall of 1966, as I was about to leave Brazil, the chief of the rural development office of USAID/Brazil, Dr. Richard Newberg, asked me if USAID could publish my class workbook, notes, and cases in agricultural marketing. I had spent two years putting this material together with the help of my senior students, and it was a very useful teaching tool. However, I told Dr. Newberg that it was not in shape to be published as a book and would require quite a bit of fleshing out and improvement. He said he wanted to help get it published as a textbook, because such a text was badly needed by Brazilian students. He told me to work on it back at OSU, to keep him informed of my progress, and that he would try to protect the book publishing funds he had put aside for such a project. I was most grateful and vowed to finish it as soon as my workload would allow.

On May 5, 1970, the Ohio State University campus was closed by the Ohio State Police and the Ohio National Guard. It was feared that more demonstrations against the Vietnam War and rioting, like that which happened earlier in the week at Kent State University, would erupt on the OSU campus. Several fires were set in classroom buildings at OSU that afternoon. The 50,000 undergraduate students did not have photo identification cards, so outsiders could enter campus at will.

I had been working on the manuscript of *Comercialização Agricola* in my office on campus most nights, but that night I was told by the OSU police to go home and to take my precious manuscript with me. They had no idea how long the campus might be closed.

The details regarding financing and completing the trip back to Brazil to finish up the book, provide a clean copy of it in Portuguese, another in English, and a bona fide publishing contract to USAID/Brazil were presented in *Food Soldier*.[6] While completing that task, I had some more unusual experiences, one of which occurred in a plane over Brazil. That year, Brazil was favored to win the World Cup in soccer (called *futebol* in Brazil and most other places in the world, except the United States and Canada). The cup was taking place in Mexico the first month I was in Brazil. When Brazil is playing a World Cup *futebol* game, all work stops in the whole country. On the day Brazil was playing Yugoslavia, I was flying a

VASP Lockheed Electra flight back to Brasilia from São Paulo. The captain of the plane (one of the largest of the four-engine propjets at that time) was a true Brazilian fan.

He had tuned his Automatic Direction Finder (ADF) radio to a powerful local broadcast station and patched it into all the loudspeakers in the plane's cabins. We all gathered around the speakers to hear the play-by-play. Imagine my surprise when Brazil's Pele scored the first goal, and the captain dived that giant plane several hundred feet, then regained his altitude in steep, climbing S-turns! I could not believe it but, at that point, I had to grab onto a seat back with both hands to keep from falling, rather than try to rationalize his behavior! I asked the steward, who was hanging onto the seat next to me as we both tried not to fall down, "Is anybody flying this airplane?"

His answer: "*Si, penso e Deus!*" (Yes, I believe God is!) Now, how can you get mad at Brazilians who constantly demonstrate all that enthusiasm? My concern was soon for the integrity of the plane's superstructure and my safe arrival in Brasilia, as the captain continued his aerobatics with every Brazilian goal. The reader may recall that Brazil defeated Italy in the finals of that 1970 World Cup.

Pele and Carlos Alberto Ride with Me in a Boeing 737

One morning, three weeks after Brazil had won the World Cup in 1970, I was scheduled to fly on a VARIG Airlines Boeing 737 from Congonhas Airport in downtown São Paulo back to Brasilia. I had taken this flight several times as I shuttled back and forth to Rio, then São Paulo negotiating with USAID/Brazil, and then Editora Atlas, S.A., the publishing company that was interested in printing and distributing *Comerialização Agricola*. The 8:30 a.m. departure was usually delayed fifteen or twenty minutes until the ground fog, common at Congonhas that time of year, lifted. This particular morning, the fog had disappeared, the plane was only half full of passengers, and we continued to sit at the gate. Finally the captain came on the radio and apologized for our late departure, but said he thought we would be pleased. "We are privileged to have as fellow passengers the Santos Futebol Team this morning," he said. Everyone in the plane cheered: Santos was the home team of the great Pele and Brazil's World Champion team captain Carlos Alberto.

The Santos team was scheduled to play an exhibition game against the Goias team in Goiania, the only stop on our flight from São Paulo to Brasilia. Soon the whole Santos team filed into the airplane. All of the players were in sports clothes except for Pele, Carlos Alberto, the Santos team president, and the vice president, who were in suits and ties. I was sitting in the front row on the right side of the plane in an aisle seat, and a Brazilian man occupied the window seat. The middle seat was empty, and who sat down in it but Carlos Alberto himself! Alberto told the two of us he hated flying and was a nervous wreck from takeoff until successful landing. I told him in Portuguese that I was a licensed pilot from the United States and would explain all the plane's noises and maneuvers. I reassured him he had no reason to fear and that it would be a beautiful day weather-wise, so he should not worry. Carlos Alberto was not buying it. He was sweating and was a nervous wreck.

Pele had entered the plane surrounded by his bodyguards, several of who went with him everywhere he went. He had been named a national treasure by the military government and they didn't want to take any chances with his safety. He and his bodyguards sat in the rear of the plane. I asked Carlos Alberto why he, Pele, and the other two men were in business suits and the rest of the team's players were dressed casually. He told me that Pele, he, and the Santos executives were going to fly on to Brasilia the day after the exhibition game with Goiania to meet the president of the country and members of his cabinet. Their objective was to discuss equitable ways to tax professional athletes who only have a limited time in professional careers due to the physical demands of professional sports. Even though they earn big money annually when they are young and healthy, that money has to last them many years after their short careers are over.

I thought this a very enlightened point of view. I had also just heard that when we published our book, the Brazilian government would take 50 percent of any royalties I made as "income tax at the source" (meaning that the publishing company would take the money out of my royalties before submitting a check to me for the remainder). I felt that my situation was a bit nasty: the Brazilian government only took 25 percent out of my coauthor Francisco Vera's share of the royalties. He was a Brazilian native; Bob Welsh, my other coauthor, and I were foreigners, and I guess the government was "protecting the domestic industry and population".

As we approached Goiania, they brought Pele and the two Santos officials up to the front of the plane. They opened the cockpit door and I heard all the radio communication — there was a problem. Some thirty thousand fans had broken down the restraining fences lining the runway and were racing up and down the landing area. The plane obviously could not land with all those people out of control and storming the runway. The captain did not help the situation at first; he kept circling the field, and as he did so, the fans waved their banners and shouted their congratulations even more. Finally, logic prevailed. The captain said he was going to fly away from the airport until they got another one hundred or so policemen, firemen, and Guarda Civil military men, and the people were back behind all the barriers, which would also have to be strengthened. Then the officials of the Santos team and Pele's bodyguards said they wanted two fire trucks to pull up to the exit stairs of the Boeing as soon as it stopped. From these trucks Pele and Carlos would be somewhat protected, with police help, and could then sign autographs for a period of time.

By this time Pele was standing next to my seat. He and I started a bit of a conversation as the captain flew the plane away from the airport for about fifteen minutes. Pele was interested to hear what I was doing in Brazil, obviously an American with my clothes, blond hair, and accent. I told him I had two sons, aged seventeen and fifteen, who had helped start soccer at their high schools in Columbus, Ohio after our return from two years in Brazil at Piracicaba. He was very interested in this bit of news. Then I asked him and Carlos Alberto if they would sign autographs for my boys. They both agreed. Pele signed his to John and David with his given name above, Nelson Naciamento, and in big, bold letters below: PELE. Carlos Alberto just signed his name. I thanked them both sincerely and told them how impressed I was with the subject they were going to present to President Medici.

Finally the radio squawked that all the fans were behind fences lining the airport runway, and more police, firemen, and soldiers were present to restrain any attempts to rush the plane. Pele complained to all of us when they mentioned that the fire trucks were also ready for him and Carlos Alberto. "*Meu Deus em ceu; um outro caminhao de bombeiros em minha vida. Ninguem tem um omnibus cobrido para me?*" (My God in heaven: another fire truck in my life. Doesn't anyone have a covered bus for me?) You could tell by looking at Pele's eyes that he had been awake too many hours, signing too many autographs and getting too little sleep since Brazil won the World Cup. Yet when that plane came to a stop and he and Carlos each exited into those fire trucks to sign autographs, they smiled and waved to their audiences and stayed there signing by that airplane for another hour. Naturally, this was one time I wished that I had my camera in my attaché case and not in the suitcase stored below the plane where I could not get it! However, I gave the autographs to my boys when I got back to Columbus; they have been framed and are interesting possessions of theirs.

Arguably, Pele is the best soccer player of all time. I remember going to the small soccer stadium in Piracicaba while living there in the 1964–1966 period whenever Santos came to play the local team, named *Quinze de Novembro* (Fifteenth of November, a national holiday). Pele was the Santos' star. Santos would put him into the game early, he would score about three goals literally all by himself in his first few minutes of play, and the manager would take him out. Nobody on the Quinze team was fast enough to guard him. Similarly, when Pele came to the United States to promote soccer in the early 1970s and played for the Washington, D.C. team in Robert F. Kennedy Stadium, I went to see him play. Again, he was an exhibition player and was kept on the field for a limited amount of time. Nevertheless, his U.S. tour promoting soccer with youth groups was quite successful.

Standing next to Pele in the aisle of that VARIG Airlines Boeing 737 near Goiania, Goias, waiting for the police and firemen to move the fans back behind the barriers at the airport, I was surprised to see how short he was. Though Pele probably was not much taller than five feet, eight inches, seeing him in a soccer uniform was quite impressive. The thighs and calves of Pele's legs were easily twice as big as mine and were extremely muscular and strong. Furthermore, he seemed to have eyes in the back of his head the way he saw both defenders and his own attacking players. He could avoid the former by quickly changing direction without losing the ball or his stride. He could also place perfect kicks at the correct angles and distances to permit his own players a good shot at the opposing goals—in the vernacular, awesome.

July 4th Celebrations at All U.S. Embassies

No matter what country you find yourself in on July 4th, if you can, wend your way to the U.S. Embassy or nearest Consulate. That holiday is the biggest, most festive occasion of the year for all American citizens at home and especially for Americans abroad. The one I attended in Brasilia in 1970 at the new U.S. embassy was typical. The festivities started early in the morning with games and contests for the younger children, including lots of prizes. Then there were contests for the teenagers, such as two-legged sack races with two people's legs in the gunnysack racing around a course. Next, there were the usual softball games between teams of Foreign Service Officers, spouses, local hire employees, and marine guards. While all this was going on, a group had fired up the charcoal grills and was beginning to prepare grilled chicken, hot dogs, hamburgers, and all the goodies that Americans can think to cook or barbeque. Later, all this was consumed with lots of potato salad and coleslaw.

The food and activities continued all day long, through lunch, late afternoon, and finally the dinner hour. As soon as it got dark, everybody gathered in their favorite spot for the upcoming fireworks display. Sometime before this finale, the ambassador or deputy chief of the mission made a welcoming speech sprinkled with patriotic overtones. It was indeed a very festive occasion. It also helps remove the stigma of being away from home, relatives, and friends for a few hours. The 4th of July in Brasilia in 1970 did just that for me.

Clearing the Book Publishing Hurdles in Brazil

Francisco Vera Filho, my former graduate student working toward his master's degree at OSU, had gone to North Carolina State University and completed his doctorate degree in agricultural economics. He then returned to Brazil and was appointed Director of the Office of Economics and Statistics in the Brazilian Ministry of Agriculture. Francisco was trying to transform that office into a strong, professional organization. Unfortunately, he was having a very difficult time since he had inherited nine hundred political appointees spread out all over Brazil. Also, he could only get approval his first year in office to hire thirty-five new professionally trained economists. One might characterize the majority of his inherited employees as "political hacks".

Francisco had said he fully supported publication of my book, *Comerçializacão Agricola*, voted for it in the bilateral Brazilian-American Book Publishing Committee of USAID, and would help me with updated cases for each chapter. He said by telephone from Brasilia that if USAID removed support for the book, he would have it published by the Ministry of Agriculture. I told him he would be my coauthor for all this help. He finally accepted and made it possible for me to travel to Brasilia in May 1970. He kindly had me stay in his government apartment with his wife, Norma, a sister, two kids and a live-in maid. I insisted that he and I locate an apartment or hotel room for me as soon as possible. Francisco had a plan, however, which I described in detail in *Food Soldier*.[7] I stayed in the vacant apartment adjoining the consular office of the Austrian Minister Consul, Alfredo Gastner, and answered his phones at night after his staff had left for the evening. Francisco sent his ministry vehicle and driver to the apartment for me at 8 a.m. every morning to drive me to his office.

One day, Francisco called me into his office at the ministry in Brasilia to hear a discussion with his six associate directors about the organization's budget situation. This was in the middle of June, halfway through Brazil's fiscal year. He asked each associate director how much of his annual budget had been spent, then repeated the figures for each of them from his notes and told the percentage of the annual that each figure represented. In nearly every division, far less than the fifty percent one would expect to have been spent halfway through the fiscal year was recorded. Most divisions' calculations fell between ten and twenty percent of the amounts budgeted and approved.

Francisco next went around the room asking what type of accelerated expenditures they could accomplish and for what purposes in their approved budgets. This was a most embarrassing discussion.

One associate director proposed buying hundreds of prepaid airline tickets to all the major cities in the country, with heavy emphasis on many trips to Rio de Janeiro. Francisco inquired how this would advance the division's program of research into improving agricultural marketing facilities and the use of uniform grades and standards to facilitate trade and its efficiency. The associate director had no answer except that his proposal would use up a lot of his budgeted funds in a short amount of time. Francisco's temper flared after going around the room and receiving a number of other half baked schemes to spend the budgeted money. In effect, he told the men to get their people out of their chairs and offices. "Get the technicians into the field to help Brazilian farmers, processing firms, cooperatives, and other agricultural enterprises and try to accomplish what they were supposed to as a part of this ministry," he said. Francisco continued, "The money that is not used for these legitimate purposes by the end of the current fiscal year will be taken away and returned to the Brazilian treasury, and your jobs may very well be in jeopardy."

I was the beneficiary, in one sense of the word, of Francisco's employees' malfeasance. Francisco provided me with many round trip airplane tickets from Brasilia to Rio de Janeiro, to negotiate with USAID officials, and to São Paulo, where the major publishing firms had their offices (including Editora Atlas, S.A., the firm that did publish our book). I questioned Francisco how he could justify these costs. He said that the content of the book was so germane to Brazilian agriculture's need to improve the efficiency of its agricultural marketing system that his superiors had agreed it was in the interest of the ministry of agriculture to support my work with funds and clerical help. Francisco had also gained their approval to publish the book if USAID/Brazil pulled its funds from underwriting the fixed cost of the book with the publisher.

I mentioned in *Food Soldier* that Francisco asked his uncle, Estanislo Vera, a respected lawyer in São Paulo, to help me negotiate a contract for publishing the book in Brazil.[8] Estanislo introduced me to the president of Editora Atlas, S.A., one of the premier publishing firms in the country. With the English manuscript I showed the president and his staff, plus the letters of commitment from USAID/Brazil (which I finally obtained after my arrival), plus a couple of chapters already translated into excellent Portuguese, our negotiations proceeded quickly. Estanislo represented us authors at no cost, only accepting payment for travel and other expenses. This included a number of round trips between Brasilia and São Paulo and between São Paulo and Rio.

The hardest part of the negotiations occurred within the USAID/Brazil Book Publishing Committee, Francisco told me later in the summer. He had to do a lot of political arm twisting with the Brazilian members of the committee to get my book approved. This was before I named Francisco as my coauthor. He said that Michigan State University and Purdue University faculty working in Brazil did not want to see Ohio State University's name on the first full agricultural marketing text published in Portuguese from beginning to end. I had trouble as well with my new department chair back at OSU over traveling to Brazil and finishing the book. I had to go over his head to the dean of the college of agriculture, who supported me. This made the new chairman furious, and I knew that he and I would never meld with mutual admiration. I found out later that he, a Michigan State graduate, was pulling for his former faculty members who were also interested in writing a marketing book.

More Interesting Encounters in Brasilia

Francisco and I agreed one thing that would help sell our manuscript to a reputable publishing company, such as Editora Atlas, S.A., was perfect Portuguese style and grammar. After all, Francisco, Bob Welsh (my other coauthor), and I had taken a technical subject — agricultural marketing, with all of its specialized terms — and converted it from English to Portuguese. Even Francisco said, "My Portuguese is probably contaminated with English since I've spent so much time studying the subject in English in graduate schools in the United States; I don't know what a professional translator here in Brazil will think." He located for us the number one interpreter/translator in the Brazilian Congress, Sra. Yvette Pinto de Almeida.

Yvette had been the administrative assistant at the U.S. Consulate in Recife, Brazil for many years before moving to Brasilia. She spoke American English better than I did. She had trained a large number of American consular officers about Brazil, the Brazilian culture, and Portuguese in the Recife office for many years. We met with Yvette, showed her several chapters we had completed in both English and our translations in Portuguese. She studied them for several days and then called us for a meeting. She said she could do the job after her work at the Brazilian Congress every day, beginning at 4:30 p.m. She would charge a fixed amount of money per page of editing and reserved the right to call me or Francisco in the evenings for more detailed explanations of marketing terms she could not comprehend in either language. We signed a contract with her within forty-eight hours!

One of the reasons she was willing to work at night on our manuscript was that she had a teenage daughter who was so bright that she had been accepted to attend university in France. However, the cost would be quite high for Yvette, and our editing job at the rate she was charging (a bargain for us in reality) would help get her daughter to Europe and into college the next fall. We both won. It was an educational experience working with Yvette in another language, as my experience at Piracicaba had also been with those marvelous secretaries from the São Paulo town of Americana.

I can remember several specific questions that Yvette called and asked me about. In discussing the organized commodity market behavior regarding price movements, we talked in that chapter about "Bulls" and "Bears." Obviously those words exist in Portuguese, "*Torros* e *Ursos*," but these are only the names of animals and do not explain the marketing behavior meant in an organized commodity exchange setting. After my explanation to Yvette (that Bulls buy at a price expecting the price of the commodity to rise and to be able to sell at a profit; Bears sell at a given price expecting prices to fall and intend to buy it back at a lower price, making a profit), she made the simple expedient of using the terms in quotations in Portuguese followed by a detailed explanatory footnote.

Another time she called me and said, "Howard, please explain what this concept of a 'backward sloping demand curve' is all about. My education just won't serve in getting the concept across so I can put it in the right phraseology in Portuguese." There were many more telephone calls, and she often wanted me to go to her apartment to read the way she had translated certain terms and concepts into Portuguese. There were times when I had to take her proposed language back to the ministry the next day for Francisco to read and approve or reject. When it was finally done, sometime in early July

1970, I took a number of the finished chapters to Editora Atlas in São Paulo for their editor to look at, and we received accolades and encouragement to continue full speed ahead. Yvette did a superb job for us, and the Editora Atlas editor printed the manuscript with very few changes. Near the end of our time together in Brasilia, I invited Yvette and her charming daughter out for dinner at their favorite restaurant as another way of thanking them.

The book manuscripts, in both Portuguese and English, were accepted by Editora Atlas, S.A. in São Paulo the second week of July 1970. *Comerçializacão Agricola* was published in April 1971 and became very popular. But now it is time to leave Brazil. What a great country it is, and the people are a total joy to know!

After my near escape from death at the hands of that inebriated pilot flying from Belo Horizonte to Viçosa and the Purdue group, I followed through on my personal promise to earn all the pilot's credentials I could at OSU's excellent Department of Aviation. I started accelerated pilot training in the fall of 1967, earned my private pilot's license in 1968, and attained the coveted instrument rating in 1970.

7

Goodbye Ohio, Hello Taiwan and Asia

In addition to my work at OSU, I went to USDA in Washington on occasion to help counsel international participants who were suffering from culture shock. In my case, these were usually Brazilian students or their wives and families. I would meet them and take them to one of the great Brazilian restaurants in the Washington area with their specialties such as "*arroz e feijão*" (rice and beans, as only Brazilians can prepare them), *cashasa* (a mixed drink with sugar cane alcohol, lemon, sugar, and cinnamon), and other favorites, and we would talk for hours while listening to Brazilian performers play sambas and bossa novas.

Many times, the problems were simple, and the solutions were easily accomplished the next day at USDA. In any event, USDA paid me well. (OSU encouraged consulting—up to one day per week without salary penalty, under the theory that it kept teachers up with current events and changes in their disciplines). Each time I went to USDA as a consultant, officials there asked me to move down and join the agency, specifically the Foreign Economic Development Service (FEDS) at that time. Plus, they kept increasing the potential salary as an incentive. However, I had a full platter of research, teaching and committee assignments, and a good group of graduate students at OSU, and I felt I could not bolt then.

Meanwhile, in Columbus, a new department chairman was hired to replace the man who had hired me, who became assistant dean of the College of Agricultural and Home Economics for International Programs. The new chairman was trained in econometrics— mathematics and statistics applied to economics. I soon discerned that he only wanted to hire new professors who were trained exactly as he had been. Furthermore, the new chairman did not seem interested in international development. It seemed to me that he did not understand what we as a faculty were trying to do, and further, that it would be difficult for me to receive my full professorship from him. I watched as he began to pull financial support from our international training programs.

My loyalties were torn. I tried hard—with some success—to get excited about Ohio apples, tomatoes, cucumbers, green house produce and grapes, but I kept gravitating to the international students and our programs with them.

Finally, the chairman and I had a confrontation over my marketing textbook and my need to go to Brazil to finish it. I went over his head to Dean Kottman for funding to finish the book in Brazil in May 1970, and I knew from the chairman's reactions that he and I would never mesh, so I would have to go. Earlier that term, he had suggested that I switch my interest to agricultural finance, a scheme I fully resisted.

On the way back from Brazil in July 1970, I accepted the feds' invitation to stop in Washington, D.C. for a discussion. I was soon talking to my family about moving to suburban Washington. This culminated in my request for a year's leave-of-absence from OSU, without pay, to test the waters of federal government employment.

USDA wanted me to come to Washington by September 1, 1970, at the latest. However, I had a full schedule of courses to teach in the fall, three master's degree candidates who needed help finishing theses and degrees, and three Ph.D. candidates to assist. January 1971 was the earliest I could begin at USDA. I also had been asked by the Agricultural Development Council in New York City to go (at their expense) to Taiwan in August to help one of my doctoral candidates, Dick Tseng, kick off his Ph.D. dissertation research.

That date, January 1971, caused another problem. All three Steele kids were in school at Columbus; John, the oldest, was in his senior year at Upper Arlington High School. We voted on moving and changing schools in the middle of the winter. I lost! The vote was one for moving and five against (including Duke the dog). So I reported to work on January 4, 1971 at USDA in Washington, having rented a small efficiency apartment within walking distance of the agency. Every weekend, I commuted (by car, which was all I could afford) the four hundred and twenty miles to Columbus on Friday night, then back to Washington on Sunday night. Determined to help my graduate students finish their degrees, I worked with them every Saturday.

The Federal Government Has an Exception for Everything

Since these were your tax dollars that I spent (some were mine too, especially the cash I sent to the Internal Revenue Service the ten years I was in the dairy business and the nearly sixteen years I taught college), I think it only fair to let you in on a little secret: You can do nearly anything you want in the federal government. The operations and contracting manuals make a pile about as high as a three-story house, but I found that for nearly every rule, there can be an exception—a waiver can be granted, extenuating circumstances make the rule moot, and so on to the point that real people can do what needs to be done.

During the negotiations to accept the USDA job in the summer of 1970, I did a little research and found that the cost of living in the greater Washington, D.C. area averaged about $2,000 per year higher than in neighborhoods like the one we enjoyed in Upper Arlington, just northwest of Columbus. Furthermore, why should I not give myself a raise for making the move?

The salary they offered me was GS-15, Step 1 on the General Services Salary Scale of the Civil Service. As I recall, this was $18,500 annually. I was earning $16,000 as an associate professor at Ohio State University, so the Step 1 salary at USDA they were offering would take care of the difference in cost of living but did not provide for my personal promotion. I told them by telephone that I was sorry, but I could not come for that salary and would accept only a GS-15, Step 2.

The answer was, "Oh that's impossible—you must start at the beginning of the Grade Scale!" I told them I was very sorry. They said, "Well, don't turn us completely down yet; USAID is paying for this work—you are to be deputy director in charge of a world-wide agricultural marketing study in developing countries. We'll review your concern with USAID and get back to you tomorrow, O.K.?" I agreed and waited.

A day or two later, I was informed that if I rewrote my Standard Form 171 (the federal government's old, omnipresent hiring information form required of all job applicants), emphasizing my overseas work and accomplishments up front, they felt they could justify the GS-15, Step 2 salary. It worked. This was an early example of a lesson I later confirmed: When dealing with foreign governments, all serious negotiations must be somewhat fluid.

Next I had a conversation with the fellow who was soon to be my director. "I'm delighted that we've been able to work out the salary condition and am looking forward to coming to Washington to work with you," I enthused. "Whom do I contact about paying for my moving expenses and making arrangements for my family's move in January?" "Oh my goodness," he replied, "you are not a federal employee being transferred back to Washington, so we do not pay new hires' moving costs!"

"You must be kidding, sir; I do not have $1,600 to move my household furnishings, three teenage kids, and a wife to Washington," I said. I was serious—my oldest son was leaving for Miami University in Coral Gables, Florida in September 1971, and that was not an inexpensive school.

This new negotiation was protracted, but it was finally agreed upon that USDA would pay for our move to northern Virginia in the summer of 1971. In return, I had to agree that if I left the job before a calendar year from my starting date of Jan. 4, 1971, I would repay the federal government what they had paid for my move.

Then came the sweetener. Before USDA sent me my final contract, President Nixon gave all civilian federal employees a large cost-of-living pay raise effective in January 1971. I ended up with a $3,000 pay raise, a $2,000 adjustment for the difference in cost of living between the two cities, and reimbursement for my moving expenses. I was ready to jump into my work at USDA with enthusiasm.

However, the tension in my marriage was growing. Looking back, I believe my wife Sally feared that I was enjoying my international work too much and that some day I would spring on her a desire for all of us to move back overseas for another resident assignment.

The strains on both of us—plus raising three energetic teenagers—caused more than a little friction in our marital life. Also, my wife's mother kept throwing curve balls. For example, she returned every gift we had ever given to her and to my father-in-law—rewrapped carefully in the original gift wrappings—when they moved from Pittsburgh to Indiana, Pennsylvania. With the spurned gifts came the statement, "You can have these back. We had no use for them; you might some day." Sally was crushed, and her tears flowed. I was furious but powerless to do anything, except go for a long walk and cool down. My wife was torn between her mother's demands and our marriage and overseas life.

My First Look at Asia

After returning to Brazil to complete my textbook in the summer of 1970, I knew that my marriage faced a turning point, especially if I went to Taiwan and left Sally and the kids for another extended period. In my own somewhat weak and half-hearted way, I decided that I must do something to try to save our marriage, while simultaneously advancing my career. Sally agreed to go to Taiwan, and we worked an arrangement out. A colleague came to live with our three teenagers while we were gone, and we boarded a Trans

World Airline (TWA) Boeing 707 in Columbus to head for Taipei, Taiwan in August 1970.

Asia is not just big; it is diverse. When you take an aggie from Pennsylvania, whose total international experience had been in Canada and Brazil, and send him to Asia, watch out! Such a character may adjust and make successful inroads, or he may fall flat.

In the autumn of 1970, when OSU sent me to Taiwan, the island was struggling to regain its equilibrium and join the successful developing middle-income countries in the third world. The fall of mainland China to Mao Tse-tung and his communist army in 1949 and the escape of General Chiang Kai-shek and his Nationalists to the island of Taiwan with about 4.5 million Chinese from the mainland, doubling the population on this Colorado-sized island, is a well-known story. Imagine the problems the United States would have if our population doubled in two years! The strain on the whole social and institutional structure, especially the food system, is unimaginable. But that is exactly what happened in Taiwan.

Of course, this happened in the early years of the Cold War with the Soviet Union and Communist China, and the United States had drawn a line beyond which we declared we would not let communism advance. In Asia, that line ran to the northwest of Taiwan in the China Sea, up and across the 38th parallel on the Korean peninsula, and west of the Japanese islands. The United States and its allies gave massive quantities of military and economic assistance to Chiang Kai-shek to arm his bastion against the communists across the Taiwan Straits.

The U.S. government provided vast amounts of money and technical assistance to a program called the Joint Commission for Rural Reconstruction (JCRR). The goal was to help jump-start Taiwan's rural sector, especially its food production, to feed the newly doubled population with domestic output—especially with rice, pork and poultry—as soon as possible.

The Republic of China (Taiwan) did not allow its students working toward their doctorates in various disciplines outside of China to bring their families with them. My graduate student Dick Tseng's program was a five-year one, and that is a long time to be away from a wife and children. The Republic of China used this as leverage to insure that students granted visas to study abroad would indeed return home, thus reducing the brain drain in Taiwan.

The JCRR experience in Taiwan between 1950 and 1970 was one of the most successful country development programs ever recorded. It is still a classic case studied in all development work.

The Japanese Imperial Army and Navy and Japanese civil servants had occupied Taiwan and run all its institutions from the early days of its war with China, beginning in 1937. All industry was nationalized, and surplus production of rice, other crops, and manufactured goods was all exported to Japan. Add to that the end of World War II with Japan in 1945, the Communist/Nationalist civil war on the Chinese mainland, and Chiang Kai-shek's escape to the island of Taiwan in 1949 with millions of people, and it's clear the island was in a tough situation.

Taiwanese managers and capital in the former nationalized industries of Taiwan, which had been controlled by the Japanese military occupation, were about to escape to other parts of Asia. The Nationalists faced two challenges: Keep this managerial skill and capital on the island to build a new institutional base and double food production quickly.

The Nationalist government developed the JCRR plan with help and financial assistance from the U.S and other allied governments. The program was two-fold. First, compensate the native Taiwanese entrepreneurs and keep them on the island by giving them either stock in the former Japanese nationalized businesses or Republic of China bonds for their financial interest, with the hope that they would use this capital in new enterprises (such as fertilizer processing plants, improved seed businesses, or container manufacturing). Secondly, use the educated specialists who had emigrated from the mainland, who were underemployed in Taiwan, to teach Taiwanese peasant farmers how to raise rice with improved yields. This would launch new, alternative enterprises and develop strong farmers' marketing associations.

The JCRR program was a resounding success. Most of the native Taiwanese businessmen took their capital, reinvested it, and helped develop new light industries on the island. The cadre of trained mainland Chinese worked long hours with the peasant farmers, teaching them to use improved varieties of rice and other agricultural products, and to adopt improved technologies of all types. When peasant farmers were reluctant to invest their earnings in fertilizer for the next crop, for example, the farmers' associations paid them for part of their rice harvest in fertilizers, which the improved varieties required for expanded yields. Further, the farmers' associations' trained field men were present on each farm to assure that the fertilizers were applied to the peasant's fields in the right quantities and at the correct time in the growing cycles.

The rice harvests increased beyond expectations, and the farmers began to experiment with alternative crops and enterprises, and soon became believing, small private entrepreneurs in their own right. The Taiwan experience is quoted often in the literature about ways to kick start less-than-developed economies.

The upshot of this activity, in addition to benefiting Taiwan's food supply, was that as peasant farmers' incomes increased, so did their demand for consumer goods. They were no longer in a barter-subsistence situation. They would want to spend sixty to seventy percent of each additional yuan available for clothing, shoes, better housing, and education. Thus the program created a consumer demand that spurred the whole Taiwanese economy. The old entrepreneur class saw opportunities for more profitable activities and formed the necessary enterprises and businesses to meet those rising demands. This led to the early growth of Taiwan's economy, its diversification, and finally to the Asian success story of its many light industries.

A New Cultural Experience in Taiwan

TWA had advertised the Trans World Airline name for years following World War II, but unlike Pan Am World Air Lines, it never actually flew around the world until the summer of 1970, when Sally and I headed for Taiwan. TWA's approved routing took it across the central and then south Pacific Ocean (almost at the equator)—the longest way to Asia. We stopped at some small airports where a limited number of passengers loaded: Guam; Papua, New Guinea; Manila; Okinawa; and finally Taipei. TWA did not keep that cross-Pacific route running long.

We arrived at Taipei one morning, quite tired from the long trip. As we came down the portable stairs to the tarmac at the airport, we heard loud voices from the observation deck of the terminal yelling in English: "Hi Dr. and Mrs. Steele—Welcome to Taiwan!" Every one of the Republic of China students that I had ever taught was there—about ten in number, plus their families—from all over the island of Taiwan. They had come, some over long distances, as a welcoming party. I nearly cried.

My Ph.D. student informed me on the way to the hotel suite they had reserved for us in Taichung, halfway down the west side of the island from Taipei, that I would be asked by the president and dean of the university to give a few informal lectures on basic agricultural marketing economics. Dick explained, "With such a distinguished OSU professor on our campus, we had to give you the opportunity to address our students!" I started to get suspicious.

Fortunately for me, I guess, a typhoon hit the island the next day. With the flooding and damage done to the university and the city, I was able to stay quietly in my hotel and hurriedly write some notes in a quickie primer on the principles of the economics of agricultural marketing as practiced in the United States. That typhoon saved my skin—and the reputation of professors from OSU.

"Look at the size of those cockroaches! They're as big as silver dollars!" Sally screamed in the middle of the night on our second evening in the hotel. The typhoon rains had begun to flood into the sewage pipes, and these giant cockroaches were trying to escape. Somehow they found their way single file up the downspout just outside our hotel bedroom window, out onto a small ledge, and discovered a crack between the window frame and the side of the building: Miraculously, for them, they found a dry room—ours!

I awakened to find something scratching all across my chest and ribs on both sides. I turned on the reading lamp next to my bed to find a long line of the largest cockroaches I had ever seen. They were slowly marching single file across the inside of our bedroom window ledge, down the wall, across the floor, up the side of the bed (mine, of course), across my bare chest, down my left side, then making a right turn down to the bottom of the bed (luckily avoiding my wife), across the floor, and out under the crack in the door.

The fact that they did not crawl across Sally's body did not stop her from letting out the most blood-curdling yell I ever heard from her in nearly twenty-five years of marriage! I picked up the phone and called the front desk right away, but night maids heard Sally's scream, and the house detective was on his way before the desk downstairs could react.

They moved us to another room immediately, at Sally's insistence, and as we were moving out, the hotel's resident exterminators already had arrived with the insecticide bombs and masks. I believe they had seen those giant suckers on their premises before because they knew exactly what to do. The next day, they moved our belongings to the new suite and then fumigated our old rooms. The manager of the hotel kept calling our room and visiting to apologize—he even sent flowers to us, as I recall.

I had seen a small barbershop on the corner by the hotel, so I told Sally after lunch the next day that I would get a haircut to look my best. I computed the price advertised in yuan and found that it was equivalent to twenty-five cents U.S.; I could not go wrong at that price, I thought.

I entered the barbershop knowing about ten words of Mandarin. For all I knew, it was a Taiwanese-speaking shop, but with gestures I should be able to communicate—not exactly. The first thing the staff did was run and get some dog-eared English-language girlie magazines for me to read. Then they put on a tape of some Western rock and roll music. Next, a lovely young woman appeared in the door opening to a back room at the rear of the barbershop, one of those entrances hung with strings of beads so you could not see in.

The young lady beckoned to me to come back and follow her through the door. I shook my head vigorously, trying to signal, "No, thank you, I'm not interested in what I think you have to offer—I just want a haircut." The gentleman stationed at the first chair, who I took to be the proprietor, left his customer and gestured for me to go with the girl. I kept shaking my head no, but was not communicating. Finally I started pointing to my wedding ring, pulled out a picture of my wife, and pointed to the hotel sounding out its name.

The three barbers and their seated male customers all shook their heads knowingly. The proprietor then took me by the arm and led me to the beaded door. He threw back the beads and pointed to the young woman, nearly in tears, who was standing by a washbasin. At last it was clear to me: for twenty-five cents you first get your hair washed by the young lady, then you get it dried, and finally the barbers will cut it. Such service—was I ever embarrassed!

Dick Tseng had indeed told me a little white lie. It turned out that I did not give just a few lectures on marketing economics to one of the classes, as Dick Tseng had implied, but to the whole senior class of the university! In the main auditorium of the university, the president gave me a long, flowery introduction in front of about five hundred students and professors. It was so hot in there with the tropical sun beating down after the typhoon that I began to sweat profusely. They took pity on me, and someone brought two large fans to the dais, but my summer suit was already drenched with perspiration. A woman next to me simultaneously translated my speech into Mandarin Chinese. She and I played cat and mouse with my phraseology. With the American marketing terms I was using (such as a "bear" or a "bull" in our commodity futures trading markets), she had to stop the proceedings and ask me to explain the terms to her in English. What a show!

The formal part was over in three days, and I was exhausted. I must say that the half hour we left after every formal period for questions and answers was the most fun. Surprisingly, when the period in the auditorium ended, those who did not have to run to their next classes stayed behind with more questions and discussion. Some even followed Dick Tseng and me to our offices, where the discussions continued for another hour. For me as an educator, this was a fulfilling and memorable experience.

"The president invites you and Mrs. Steele to a banquet."

Near the end of my first week in Taichung, Dick informed me that the president of the university was inviting my wife and me to a banquet. "Tell me how this works, Dick; we don't have any formal evening wear, I have just a business suit, and my wife has a few good dresses."

"No sweat," replied Dick. "The formal invitations to you and the deans who are also invited will say 'Informal Dress.'"

He also informed me, "The president's banquet will be big; in China, if you have a formal dinner between friends, you have as many courses as you have people at the table. I think our president will have eight guests including deans, department heads, and their wives; plus me and my wife, you and Mrs. Steele, and him and his wife. Dinner will be fourteen courses!"

"Next week, the dean of the college will host a dinner for you and Mrs. Steele. He will probably have twelve people and a twelve-course meal (it's not good to have more than the president had at his dinner for you, you understand?). At the end of next week, the department chairman wants to have a nice dinner for you and Mrs. Steele—he will probably have ten people; this means a ten course meal. Mrs. Tseng and I also want to have a dinner for you; maybe with six persons. We do not have as big of an income as others, so will have a more modest dinner; you understand?"

"Dick," I asked, nonplussed, "do Mrs. Steele and I need to think of repaying all these wonderful officials by hosting reciprocal dinners for them?"

"Oh no Dr. Steele—you are not expected to entertain them here in my country; you came to help me with my research for my Ph.D. degree, you are my major professor at Ohio State University, and you gave wonderful lectures to the whole senior class at my university for no charge! Thank you for coming to our university. You understand?"

The Day of the University President's Dinner for Us

The afternoon before the president's banquet arrived. Dick Tseng assured me that he and his wife would sit next to Sally and me to explain each course, which sounded like a good arrangement to me. Dick also asked if Sally and I ate with chopsticks. Fortunately, both of us did, so that social stigma was out of the way.

When I say we both used chopsticks, I am not saying we were proficient with them. I remember watching in horror as those delicious little button-shaped mushrooms cooked in oil shot out of my chopsticks, across my plate, and out onto the tablecloth. Early on, rice was also a problem, until I saw how natives ate it. They either lifted the bowl and shoveled the rice into their mouth, as is quite customary in Japan and Indochina, or moved other goodies into the rice bowl, which could be grasped along with the rice. All of this came later in our "training," however.

As I was sitting in the lobby that afternoon, one wall of which was a lovely salt water aquarium full of exotic fish from the China Sea and the Straits of Taiwan, reading and relaxing, when a white suited chef in his tall chef's hat appeared at the top of the aquarium. He was holding a hand fish net. Curious, I observed. He dipped down and captured some lovely looking, small tuna-type fish one at a time. Then he brought up a couple of crabs and some indescribable looking critters from the bottom.

I turned away, then, hearing splashing water and thrashing, I looked back up to see him wrestling with one of the ugliest looking eels I had ever seen. I thought to myself, "Well somebody is going to have an eel meal here today." It reminded me of rattlesnake, which I had never eaten but had heard was served in the Southwestern United States. That and the thought of that big eel the chef just wrestled out gave me goose bumps. "Oh well—to each his own," I mused.

"You must drink bottoms up Dr. Steele—ching-ching!"

Those were my instructions from Dick Tseng after we had been seated, following introductions all around the round dinner table, which had rotating carousels in the middle on which the serving dishes were later placed. At each place was a small thimble-sized glass. Hot sake soon filled all fourteen glasses around the table.

The president stood and toasted our two great countries—the United States of America and the Republic of China. All took small sips out of their cups, except the president and me. He said, "Ching-ching," drained his cup, and added, "Bottoms up!"

Dick whispered to me, "Now you say 'Ching-ching' and empty your cup in honor of his toast." I did.

Then I reciprocated with a small toast in honor of the president and his wife and thanked them on behalf of Sally and me for this marvelous dinner. "Ching-ching, bottoms up!!"

Again, a waiter filled my empty glass and that of the president. Next, the dean of the college of agriculture was on his feet, saying, "Let me propose a toast to our two great universities, Taichung Provincial University in Taiwan, and The Ohio State University in the United States of America! Ching-ching, bottoms up!"

Oh boy, here we go again. "How long does this keep up?" I asked myself, and "When does the food arrive?"

Well, you have the picture now. I had to "Ching-ching, bottoms up," for every toast given, and then for my return toast. They sipped if they hadn't proposed the toast. A man could get plastered pretty quickly with this routine. Thank goodness for me at Taichung the cups were modest, almost thimble sized. When Sally and I got to Taipei, at the end of the month-long trip, and were entertained by the JCRR economists, several of whom were Ph.D. graduates of my Department of Agricultural Economics and Rural Sociology at OSU, the sake cups were twice as big! Sally came to my rescue that night, and we walked around the block of our hotel for about an hour until Taipei City quit spinning!

About halfway through the fourteen course meal, which was absolutely delicious, one delicacy arrived, and I leaned over to ask, "What am I eating now Dick?"

"That is 'crap,' Dr. Steele."

"Spell that for me please, Dick."

He spelled very slowly, "C-R-A-B, CRAP."

Thank goodness it was just a pronunciation difficulty. Another serving from the lazy Susan was a delightfully light tan, delicate-flavored meat in light soybean oil, accompanied with yet another type of delicious Chinese mushroom.

"What in the world am I eating here, some kind of young chicken meat?" I asked.

"No, no Dr. Steele, that is lamprey eel—very good, very expensive, a favorite at holidays."

So now I knew why the cook had struggled to get that giant in his net earlier while I watched; it was part of our supper. I have got to admit it had a fine taste too—but prior knowledge might have spoiled it!

Now all the duck, pork, chicken, beef, seafood, and the marvelous vegetables and sauces all hit the gastronomic spot with me, except three dishes. I would caution you to think twice before ordering them, unless your stomach is more iron-clad than mine. First, sea slug—it is oily, and as fishy-oily as anything I have ever tasted. Second, sea cucumber—truly, it is even worse. Finally, a dish I thought had the consistency of (and was about as palatable as) chewing rubber bands—nothing less than jellyfish tentacles. They are considered a delicacy in some Chinese quarters. For me, you may keep them! But overall, the food was incredible—we never came away from a Chinese dinner hungry, believe me.

Well, we had four more dinners, hosted by the dean of agriculture (ten participants, ten courses), the chairman of the department of economics (eight participants, eight courses), the academic dean (again, eight participants and eight courses), and finally by Dick Tseng and his wife (just the four of us and four courses). They were all such friendly, courteous people.

In all of our conversations the main theme was this: "We Republic of China Nationalists love America and Americans; please don't abandon us to the communists because we will never survive." As I write these lines many years later, the mainland Chinese communists are calling Taiwan "the renegade province" and are threatening to invade it once again.

The Work and Research of My Former Taiwanese Students

One of my participants for a quarter at OSU had been a fine Taiwanese agricultural marketing student, William Chiang, who worked for a large banana, pineapple, and lichee fruit production and marketing cooperative on the southern tip of Taiwan, near the port city of Kaohsiung. He was one of the group that had traveled to Taipei to greet Sally and me on our arrival nearly a month before. Before he left the airport that day, he invited us to visit his co-operative and packing facilities, which he had help develop since returning from OSU two years ago.

In virtually all of our field trips at OSU, Chiang was always late returning to our bus. We would find him holed up with a banana buyer, merchandiser, ripening manager, or packer, completely oblivious to the time. Hence, he got the name of "Bananas Chiang," authorized by his fellow students! He loved the name and always referred to himself that way when he introduced himself to others.

Well, "Bananas" was extremely proud of the packing facilities that he had established in the banana plantations of the cooperative farmer members. He also had converted the packing process so that "hands," what we call bunches but really are only sections of a full bunch of bananas, were placed in coated cardboard boxes with his cooperative's name and a "Product of Taiwan" label on each box. This was common with fruit shipped from Central and Latin America to the United States at the time, and he had studied all aspects of it so as to include it within Taiwan's industry. He also had established a lichee packing facility for fresh lichees and a small canning operation for both lichees and pineapples. He just beamed with pride as he took us around and we sampled the various fruits.

Then we went to the main offices of the cooperative at the port of Kaohsiung. There we saw boxes of his green, ripening bananas being loaded onto ships for transportation to Japan, one of his biggest customers. While touring the port facilities, "Bananas" was urgently called away. He was gone quite a while. When he returned, a dejected look on his face replacing his typical smile, he carried a box of hands of his green bananas. He came to me and asked, "Dr. Steele, you know bananas—do these look overripe to you?"

I took a look and broke one hand; they were still in the starchy stage, just right for a seven to ten day trip under controlled conditions aboard ship. At least that was my judgment, although I did not claim to be an expert.

"What's the problem, Bananas?" I asked.

"The Japanese inspector is rejecting truckload after truckload of my beautiful bananas and calling them 'overripe'—my cooperative will be ruined!"

"Why do you think he is doing this?" I asked. He explained, "Japanese traders just made a big contract with Ecuador during our typhoon, thinking that we would have our banana plantations flattened and not be able to fulfill our contract, despite all of our telegrammed assurances to them as we inspected our damages. They will ruin us financially."

"What can I do?"

We sat sympathizing with Chiang and his junior officers. My only suggestion was for him to telephone his minister of agriculture and try to get some help from the government in Taipei.

We felt sorry for Bananas and his cooperative, but I had seen this type of sharp trading by Japanese buyers before—very impersonal, and often cutthroat.

Dick Tseng's Doctoral Research Project

Even though the soybean plant is native to China, Taiwan did not produce it as a major crop, especially after the Nationalists flooded onto the island in 1949–1950 and all effort was made to double rice output, the basic food of the populace. However, the humble soybean is such a versatile product. It has a high oil content, and when crushed yields this oil, which is used for making cooking oils and margarine, in baking, and in many other processed food products for a number of purposes. Further, after the oil is extracted, a joint product remains that is highly competitive in animal feeds mixing. For example, a mixture of soybean meal and cake is used in poultry, pig and dairy rations.

The Agricultural Development Council was interested in what was happening in the domestic Taiwanese soybean production and processing industry. We knew that the domestic producers were only supplying about ten percent of the total product used on the island; the rest was being imported as beans, principally from the United States. As I remember the figures, Taiwan produced approximately seventy thousand metric tons of soybeans per year and imported about seven hundred thousand metric tons, all to be crushed on the island. Dick Tseng was to study the annual growth in native production and how it compared with the growth in total demand for the two by-products, soybean oil and soybean cake/meal.

Dick and I had developed a research outline before either of us left Columbus, and Dick's special research committee in OSU's Department of Agricultural Economics and Rural Sociology, with me serving as chairman, helped Dick revise it until approved. While I was in Brazil earlier in the summer of 1970, Dick returned to Taiwan and began to collect basic production, import, and use statistics from secondary sources (mostly from the JCRR economists and publications in Taipei). When I arrived, Dick had a serious problem.

He could easily reconcile his historic data for about ten years, which allowed him to project future trends for local production changes, import changes, and the dramatic growth in the use of soybean cake and meal in Taiwan's growing livestock industry. However, he could not reconcile where the oil, as a joint product of the local soybean crushing industries on the island, was ending up.

The local crushers were what we would call "batch crushers." They used physical crushing machines, which did not yield as much oil as more advanced chemical extracting machinery. The chemical extractors were expensive, whereas local batch crushing machines were much smaller and cheaper. Their use led to a more or less cottage oil extraction industry in Taiwan. However, the soybean cake and meal, resulting as a joint product, was richer in oil or energy for the animal rations, as well as full of fiber as roughage the animals needed.

We were in a quandary. We could not account for about half of the oil that should have resulted from crushing approximately seven hundred and seventy thousand metric tons of soybeans every year. The local margarine industry took some of the oil, and some low-grade oil was exported to other countries, but the mayonnaise and other users' purchases just did not add up to the totals we needed to reconcile our data. I suggested that Dick pull a representative sample of the crushers in the country and also sample the wholesale grocery middlemen, and we developed a questionnaire for interviewing purposes.

"Oh my, Dr. Steele—the owner doesn't speak Mandarin Chinese!" Dick told me as we visited a small soybean crusher's operation less than ten miles outside of Taichung. Now Dick had grown up in Taiwan and lived there for twenty years by 1970, but he, like many of his countrymen from the mainland who had arrived during the 1949–1950 period, had never learned to speak Taiwanese. We had to get the owner's daughter to come in as our translator. There were a few times when my question went to Dick in English, who translated it into Mandarin Chinese for the owner's daughter, who in turn translated it to her father in Taiwanese. This, of course, made for a slow afternoon.

However, that crusher's factory, and two others we visited in the vicinity, plus a grocery wholesaler's office, yielded the information that led us to solve the missing soybean oil mystery. They told us that the absolute favorite cooking oil of the Taiwan housewife, chef, baker, or cook was peanut oil. Peanut oil was one of the most expensive oils at that time.

Our interviewees claimed one could substitute up to eighty percent of a quantity of peanut oil with cheaper oils, such as soybean oil, and the average person could not tell that there had been a substitution. The product still looks, smells, and tastes like peanut oil, they claimed. When Dick entered the eighty percent substitution factor in his computer data about peanut cooking oil sold in Taiwan, he accounted for nearly all the missing megatons of soybean oils crushed on the island. I must add that there were no labeling laws in Taiwan at that time, so the substitution of soybean oil in peanut oil for cooking was perfectly legal.

Dick Tseng did such a fine job analyzing and writing up his data for his doctoral dissertation, he had no trouble defending his work and his projections with multiple regression analysis back at OSU in the 1971–1972 term. I remember coming back to OSU for Dick's defense of his dissertation in early 1972. He brought his wife and small children to Columbus and was a proud graduate when he received the coveted Ph.D. diploma in 1972.

8

A Case of Mistaken Identity

I began work at USDA on January 4, 1971. The family stayed home in Upper Arlington, Ohio to finish the kids' school years, especially my oldest son John's senior year and graduation. I rented an efficiency apartment within walking distance of USDA and went to work writing a definitive work for USAID, with their financing, which was published within the year. It was entitled *Improving Agricultural Marketing in Developing Countries—An Approach to Identifying Problems and Strengthening Technical Assistance.* It became very popular, was translated into Spanish, and was reprinted many times in the next ten years. Friday evenings, I would drive home to Columbus, Ohio, work with my graduate students on Saturday mornings, and be with the family until I drove back to Washington, DC on Sunday evenings, an eight-hour drive in good weather.

In September 1971, I was asked by USDA's director of international training to take fifteen Brazilian diplomats around the United States and down to Mexico to look at agricultural operations and agribusinesses. My Portuguese was still sharp, and even though we had official Department of State simultaneous interpreters traveling with us, they only worked eight or nine hour days. So I would get a call, sometimes at 6 a.m., from one of the diplomats asking how he could get a maid to find his laundry, as he had no clean shirts. Or they would call me and speak to me in Portuguese (since their English was very sketchy) late at night and tell me that Jose or Marcos lost his travelers checks while out visiting some nightclub. Sometimes their adventures were more risky than that, but fortunately I never had to go get them out of jail.

To the diplomat who lost his travelers checks, cash, and wallet, probably in less-than-presentable circumstances, I just said, "How unfortunate for you; do you have a record of the numbers of the checks so we can order replacements?" Of course the papers for the travelers' checks were in the wallet, which was stolen. Maintaining a calm, diplomatic exterior (yes, I have been known to do this at times, but it is not the norm), we placed a call to Washington, D.C. the next day, and his embassy arranged to wire more travelers checks ahead to our next major city. Meanwhile, we floated him a loan to get him through until the new checks arrived. These situations are known as: "U.S. Government official performs other duties not specifically assigned."

My two months traveling with the Brazilians did not involve typical agricultural education. We had basic orientation in Washington, D.C., at USDA, and then headed for North Carolina State University at Raleigh, N.C. We went up into the Blue Ridge Mountains and observed an integrated small-farm vegetable production project for processing baby foods. The objective was to get small mountain farmers out of the production of burley tobacco, which had been carried on for generations on the steep topography of the mountains and is very soil depleting. The North Carolina Extension Service was teaching them how to grow carrots, beans, sweet corn, squash, sweet peas, and other vegetables that like cool, moist weather. With the proper crop rotation, these enterprises also enriched the depleted soils and helped control erosion.

Soon the production exceeded local demand for fresh vegetables at the newly established State Farmers' Markets, and the university people convinced a major U.S. baby-foods processor to locate a plant in the area. Vegetables began to be produced by the local farmers under contract to the processing plant. It was an innovative arrangement of great interest to the Brazilian agriculture directors who had not seen a project that integrated the private sector, a university, the county government, and state agricultural extension service specialists.

Next, we flew to Indiana to see another type of American agriculture. The Corn Belt featured corn, soybeans, hogs, pork production, and other livestock. What impressed the Brazilians most was that one farm family in Indiana, or any other Corn Belt state, could be farming as many as one thousand acres of intensive crop production. The family's capital investment in tractors, planting and harvesting equipment, buildings, and trucks was enormous by Brazilian standards, but the family's output and income were the real eye-openers for these Brazilian government officials.

Does it surprise you to know that Latinos set their own time schedules while we Americans try to keep to a planned schedule? This was my biggest problem early in the trip. I could not impress on the Brazilians that keeping to the schedule and starting at the time specified were mandatory and that buses, airlines, and busy executives would not, and could not, rearrange their schedules to meet those of the Brazilians.

I knew these Latin habits from my own culture shock when I first visited, then lived in, Latin America. If you are invited to come for dinner, and the host and hostess say "Come at 7 p.m.," we North Americans will arrive at 7 p.m. Forget it! You will be embarrassed to find the host or hostess in the shower or in some state of casual dress. The dinner really is not intended to start until later.

The biggest problem with Latinos on a North American schedule, of course, is the morning starting time. When the itinerary says we leave for the Eli Lilly research and experiment station promptly at 8 a.m. from the front of the hotel, with breakfast, with all baggage, and checked out of your rooms, we mean just that.

I had been fighting a late sleeper all the way from Washington, D.C. Every day, at almost every stop, the guy was not on time to go to the next scheduled event. I lectured him privately. It went in one ear and out the other. I diplomatically discussed the problem with him and the head of the delegation together. This worked magic for about two days, but then he was back to his old pattern. Three more admonitions followed, the last shaming him in front of his colleagues. Finally, I told him in public that next time he failed to show up, we would leave without him, and he could find his own way to the next stop on our itinerary.

Sure enough, the Greyhound bus I had chartered to take us to the Eli Lilly facilities and then to the Indianapolis Airport for our flight to St. Louis—under a very tight schedule—was waiting at our hotel at 7:30 a.m. as planned, but "Mr. Night Owl" did not show. I sent one of the other Brazilians to check on him.

The other fourteen Brazilians, plus the two interpreters, were all there and checked out, with breakfast, and baggage. The investigator came back to the bus to announce to me and the head of the delegation that Mr. Night Owl was enjoying his "early morning shower and said he would be with us as soon as he got dressed and had his breakfast!" I said to myself, "This is it, Howard—he has got to learn a lesson."

I informed the head of the delegation, "We are leaving without Senhor X; he will have to either catch us at Eli Lilly, at the airport, or in St. Louis. He has our detailed itinerary with addresses and telephone numbers."

He responded in Portuguese, "*Parabens*! (Congratulations!) You have spent too much patience on him already." Then he announced over the bus' loudspeaker system in Portuguese what was going to happen, and all the Brazilians broke into applause! I should mention that Mr. Night Owl joined us at Eli Lilly in a private taxi, which I am sure he paid dearly for. He apologized to all of us and was ready on time from then on.

It was in Texas that our problems really got serious. We had some proud agriculturalists with us from Brazil. They were good students and knowledgeable about their own agricultural enterprises. However, some had trouble accepting our institutions and our productivity and output, as shown to them in written materials or in verbal conversations. This was particularly true of the Brazilians from the livestock states of Goias and Mato Grosso. The traditional livestock enterprise at that time in Brazil was much like our Texas Longhorn cattle days of the 1800s where cows and calves roamed wild on the sagebrush land, eating whatever natural vegetation they could digest, until rounded up, placed on grass for a little fattening, then driven to market.

This practice was still the rule in the high, arid plains of Brazil's major cattle states of Mato Grosso and Goias, where the Brahma cattle of India had been crossed with the criolla cattle originally imported from Portugal, and loosely called Zebu. They would roam the arid plains for years, and then be driven to grassland to fatten up.

The Brazilian cattlemen would not accept the age and weight data given about our grade cattle, which were fed high energy and high roughage rations under controlled conditions, going to market at perhaps eighteen months of age, weighing around a thousand pounds. One director of agriculture was so convinced this was a CIA plot of lies that he publicly accused me and Texas A&M University professors of falsifying every bit of information we gave them.

This gentleman left our team but showed up later in Mexico City. He had independently gathered U.S. cattle growth information on his own, as he spoke enough English to accomplish the task. He publicly apologized to me, the head of the delegation, and all his colleagues. Nevertheless, his actions in Texas put a damper on my enthusiasm for the trip. I must admit it was a shock, even to me, to see how much high technology was being practiced by these Texas entrepreneurs. A few examples will demonstrate my point.

"Where Are The Cowboys? Where Are Their Horses?"

These questions were common at first. We drove the group in a fleet of station wagons from Texas A&M in east central Texas to a large ranch operation west of Dallas and Fort Worth. The remaining fourteen Brazilian directors of agriculture were very eager to see some purebred cattle, and here were some of the finest in Texas, owned by a Santa Gertrudas cow-and-calf operation located on a range of plush, improved pastures. We arrived to see approximately one thousand cows and calves grazing. The manager had promised the Brazilians to see how American cowboys herded cattle, moving them from one field to another, cutting out small groups.

When we arrived, there were no cowboys and no horses. The manager got out his two-way radio (this was the top communication technology for American agriculturists before our space program's spin-offs created the explosion of personal computers and cellular phones) and started talking. Soon we saw a long tractor-trailer coming out to meet us. It had ten beautiful mustang horses in it, all saddled up. There was a wrangler with them, who was also the driver of the rig, but no other cowboys.

One Brazilian asked, "Where are the other *vaqueiros* (cowboys)?" The manager pointed up in the sky at a small twin-engine airplane approaching the pasture we were standing in. Sure enough, the plane landed, and out stepped the rest of the cowboys, including the pilot, all dressed in the proper attire! They mounted their mustangs and put on a show that none of us will ever forget: cutting, whooping, and hollering; roping calves and herding brood cows and calves into a quickly erected fenced-in area. The Brazilians shouted, "*Nossa Senhora!*" which loosely translated means "Good Gracious in Heavens Above!" (i.e., we have never seen anything like this before!). Truthfully, neither had I.

The Brazilians also wanted to see the American high technology rice production system in Texas, including its aerial planting, fertilizing, and pest control, plus irrigated and mechanically harvested practices. We leased a Beechcraft Model 99 propjet from Rio Air Lines to fly us from Dallas to Beaumont, where the center of Texas rice production was, then overnight in Beumont and fly us back to Dallas for departure to California the next morning.

When leasing the plane I informed the ground personnel that I was a licensed, instrument- rated pilot and would like to fly up front with the crew. "No sweat," responded the airline manager.

So we loaded up a few days later for the trip (I made these arrangements while the Brazilians were touring the great Texas State Fair in Dallas with the State Department interpreters) and the crew invited me to sit in a little jump seat up front. They asked me to check their weight and balance calculations on their flight plan document. When I looked at it and the plane's manifest for the flight to Beaumont, I saw my name listed as "stewardess." When I pointed this out to the captain and first officer, they broke out laughing and said they loved to have fun with other pilots flying with them.

Two days later, I had the last laugh. We had a full day in the rice fields and operations and got to bed quite late. All of us were up bright and early for a sunrise departure for Love Field, Dallas, where we were scheduled to take an American Air Lines Boeing 747 Jumbo jet to San Francisco; the Brazilians and I were quite excited about this since none of us had flown in this new giant of the sky, which was just going into frequent commercial service in 1971.

This time, I helped the crew go through the flight check list and soon started monitoring the FAA Automatic Terminal Information System (ATIS) for Dallas, which gave weather, active runway, wind direction and velocity, temperature, and barometric pressure information crucial to all incoming flights. About twenty minutes into the flight, the ATIS gave an update on weather at Dallas Love Field, and I heard loud and clear: "13:00 HOURS ZULU (Greenwich Mean Time, or 7 a.m. Texas time) DALLAS LOVE FIELD IS CLOSED TO ALL COMMERCIAL AIR TRAFFIC BECAUSE OF GROUND FOG, CEILING ZERO, RUNWAY VISUAL RANGE ZERO. EXPECT FURTHER INFORMATION AND UPDATE AT 13:15 ZULU." Now I got the crew's attention and asked them to tune in to that frequency. Next began a flurry of communications with Air Traffic Control to arrange for alternatives for our flight.

Finally, after being held circling some fifty miles southwest of Dallas, we were given an alternate airport to land at while Air Traffic Control tried to unclog the logjam at Love Field as the fog began to rise. We were told to divert to the old Fort Worth airport and to expect an instrument approach to runway 16 Left. Now the "stewardess" suddenly became quite useful.

The Rio pilots were busy with their holding pattern, and I had been given the book of approach plates, which was full of standard landing procedures for each and every runway in the United States, and was asked to pull out the approach plate for an Instrument Landing System (ILS) to runway 16 Left at Fort Worth.

All maneuvers of the aircraft during the final ten miles to each ILS runway are rigidly specified, and no aircraft can deviate from them without declaring an emergency. The approach plates also specify the correct altitudes to maintain during different phases of the approach through the clouds (or fog, in this case), radio fixes by discreet frequencies, the locator beacon that tells the pilot if he is left or right of the center line on the runway, his angle, and the rate of descent. There are also outer and middle marker radio beacons, which light up in different colors on the instrument panel of the aircraft and emit a specific Morse code identifying signal, orally indicating passing an important location on the ground.

In the case of our tired old Rio Air Lines Beech-craft Model 99, some of the radio and navigation equipment on board wasn't functioning to our satisfaction when the pilots tested it. We reported that to air traffic control and the controllers assigned us a new instrument approach, not as precise as the ILS (called a VOR approach). This meant we had a higher minimum descent altitude, below which we could not descend further unless we had the runway clearly in sight. This also meant we had to go into a holding pattern until the fog lifted a few hundred feet higher, so it was goodbye jumbo jet to San Francisco. I knew this was true because I had been monitoring Love Field's tower frequency. I actually heard them clear our American Airlines Boeing 747 flight to San Francisco for take off. I would have my hands full when we finally got on the ground in Ft. Worth. Meanwhile, the two pilots of our plane were glad they had an instrument qualified "stewardess" named Howard Steele on board as we struggled to get all the important information for a safe landing in the fog at Ft. Worth!

As soon as we stopped at the terminal in Ft. Worth, I was on the telephone with American Airlines at Love Field and then arranged for ground transportation for the twenty miles to Love Field for eighteen people and their thirty-eight pieces of luggage. I also called our international coordinator at the University of California at Davis, Linda Childress, who already had a small bus and several station wagons on the way to San Francisco International Airport to meet us. The original plan called for us to go from San Francisco directly to Sacramento to meet California's commissioner of agriculture. I was a nervous wreck, but Linda, in that relaxed California attitude, said, "Not to worry Howard; I can call the vehicles back. Just call and tell me where you will be landing and when; I can quickly reschedule our meeting with the commissioner and we'll come and get you."

So it was off to Love Field with fifteen disappointed Brazilian diplomats who wanted very badly to have their first ride in a Boeing 747 jumbo jet. That was the least of my worries. However, American Air Lines already had reservations for us on another of their flights to Las Vegas, which connected there with a Hughes Air West flight to Sacramento about forty-five minutes later. Great!

"Find your missing Brazilians or this plane leaves without them!" Those were the words of the Hughes Air West gate supervisor in Las Vegas, where my diplomats took off to play the airport slot machines while we waited for our flight to Sacramento to be called. Well, the flight was called — then its final call was issued — and I was still missing two of my charges. I told the gate supervisor that these were all diplomats, and the flight would not leave without them or we would have a serious diplomatic incident to report to the FAA. Of course I had no right to say this, but I was exhausted and again in a near state of panic, given everything else that had already happened that day.

Fifteen minutes after the departure call, the Hughes Air West captain came out of the plane madder than a bull elk in the rut. "Who is holding up this flight?" he demanded to know. I identified myself and gave him some serious line about diplomats.

He said, "If they're not here in five minutes, we close the door and are on our way—do you understand?"

I said, "If you leave without all my diplomats, we will call the Department of State, who will call the Federal Aviation Administration, and you will have to answer to your company."

The gate supervisor handed me the microphone after asking me if I could call the Brazilians by their names over the airport loudspeaker system in Portuguese. I did that, and the captain informed me he was leaving just as the two wayward gamblers came running up to the gate all out of breath!

When we arrived at Sacramento, the captain had the last laugh; only two of our thirty-eight pieces of luggage were unloaded from the Boeing 737—he took the rest to San Francisco, I think just to show me who was really the boss of that flight. So I wasted time filling out forms, using my diplomats speech, and praying that I could get their luggage shipped to Davis, where we would spend the next several days at the University of California before traveling again.

Linda Childress had to reschedule our meeting with the commissioner of agriculture, but she did it with a smile, and we left for Davis in the bus and station wagons, which then had been on the road almost all day. At 11 p.m. that night, a Greyhound bus arrived in Davis with all thirty-six pieces of luggage, graduate students hauled them from the bus station to our motel, and I relaxed for the first time in twenty-four hours.

"We must see Disneyland before leaving America, Dr. Steele!" I was told by the Brazilian second in command. I should have expected that—the boy seems to stick in the man, no matter how old we get. We had a lot of traveling and agricultural items yet to see in the Sacramento and San Francisco areas, as well as in Los Angeles and Riverside. To make matters worse, somebody had fouled up in Washington, D.C. and four of my fifteen charges were flying back to Washington, then to Mexico City. The rest of us were to go directly from Los Angeles to Mexico City. Those four did not have visas to enter Mexico, having expected to get them in Washington.

Now I had to convince the Mexican consular officer in Sacramento to break up his weekend and come in to his office just to issue visas to four Brazilian diplomats. He questioned the story being told to him in pretty shaky Spanish over the telephone by this "Norte Americano." Finally, trying to convince him of its legitimacy, I asked if he would prefer that I have the assistant secretary of state for Inter-American affairs call his ambassador in Washington, D.C. to authorize him to do this on Saturday morning. (I had seen the sign on the door that said: "Office Hours—Monday to Friday, 9 a.m. to 3 p.m.; Saturday 9 a.m. to Noon;" when I found the doors locked on Saturday at 10 a.m., he tried to tell me over the phone that they were closed on Saturdays.) I called his bluff, but he made me wait until late afternoon; I was probably messing up his golf or sailing date. But we got the visas.

Off we went to San Francisco by way of the Port of Sacramento and some specialized farms en route. In San Francisco, Linda Childress and the UC professors had some interesting visits and experiences lined up for the Brazilians. I got to camp out at the offices of VARIG Brazilian Airlines, trying to get the four tickets changed from Los Angeles/Washington, D.C./Mexico City/Rio de Janeiro to simply Los Angeles/Mexico City/Rio de Janeiro. Obviously, the Brazilian travel agency did not want to endorse the tickets over for a much shorter flight and less revenue.

However, I insisted and again "pulled out all the chestnuts" I could think of as telegrams flew back and forth from the San Francisco office of VARIG to its headquarters in Rio. Fortunately for me, there were several fine Brazilian employees of VARIG in San Francisco, or I would have been lost. We finally scored, and off we went to the Riverside Experiment Station of UC, then to Disneyland, and finally to Mexico City.

One of our visits near Riverside was at a gigantic beef cattle feed lot—about 50,000 steers being fed out to slaughter weights by one firm owned by four brothers, who used computers to control everything. Another one of the Brazilians, who considered himself an expert on Zebu cattle, could not believe (as his colleague who left us earlier could not) that the cattle he was seeing were between twelve and eighteen months old and already weighed 1,000–1,200 pounds. Further, he accused us of doctoring the data and records and left the delegation. I guess the shock of seeing how far behind Brazilian cattle fattening programs were compared with the U.S. programs was too much for these Brazilian livestock men. Undoubtedly, they had bragged to their Brazilian colleagues about how great the cattle programs were in Brazil under their leadership. He, like his colleague I mentioned earlier, somehow did independent research and reappeared in Mexico City, also apologizing to me and his colleagues.

In Riverside, we also saw experiments on irrigating citrus orchards by drip irrigation, which was so new that none of us had seen it before. The Israelis get credit for this technological breakthrough. The system is excellent in arid areas since it: 1) conserves scarce water; 2) applies only what is needed by each tree; 3) avoids the useless evaporation that spray and flood irrigation systems are guilty of. The systems we saw were experiments by agricultural engineers and horticulturists measuring which automatic timing methods were best, checking evaporation rates during hot days and humid nights, and monitoring the health and yields of the various citrus fruit trees being tested (oranges, grapefruit and lemons).

In Mexico, we went to the International Corn and Wheat Research Center (CYMMT) near Chapingo (outside Mexico City) and had a great briefing and tour of the new miracle varieties being developed that were increasing yields all over the developing and developed world. We also saw marvelous research being conducted at Mexico's National Agricultural Experiment Station in Chapingo. Here, they were working with several hundred varieties of edible beans, the staple of the Latin American diet, as well as cooperating with the scientists at CYMMT on corn research; corn is another staple in the diet of all Americans in the hemisphere.

When a small group travels together for two months—even with the inevitable problems and personality difficulties—lasting friendships tend to form. This was the case with us. We missed airplanes, lost luggage, had wallets stolen, lacked visas, needed to replace travelers' checks, and renegotiated tickets. We got bone tired together. But we also relaxed and played together, including watching our first bull fight. The Brazilians felt as I did about that experience; "*luta de sangue horrivel!*" they called it (a horrible blood fight), and neither they nor I cared if we ever saw another one, though this was an "educational" experience.

Our last morning together in Mexico City, before they were to return to Brazil and I to Washington, I could not get anybody to agree to go to dinner with me. I was really depressed! At about 4 p.m., the head of the delegation found me in the hotel and asked me to go to dinner with him. I was so relieved. At 8 p.m., he took me to one of the fanciest hotels in Mexico City, and when we entered the restaurant, the headwaiter ushered us to a private banquet room. There they all were, honoring me with a surprise party. I was nearly speechless. Many hours later, after good food, many speeches, toasts, and camaraderie, they presented me with a silver plaque engraved with very nice compliments and all of their names. It is one "award" I have always cherished, and will forever!

Off to India and Nepal

I had not been back in Washington two months from the trip with the Brazilians, working again in USDA's International Agricultural Development Center, when I received a call from New Delhi, India—it was my old friend Dr. Dick Newberg. He wanted me to go to Nepal, a lovely, mountainous kingdom (bordering China and Tibet, on the top of the Himalayan Mountains), the highest in the world, to participate in the first National Symposium on Improving Agricultural Marketing, put on by USAID. Dick had recommended me as a keynote speaker to Dr. Raymond Forte, who was in charge of the agricultural marketing seminar and USAID's technical assistance and training portfolio in Nepal. Dr. Ronald Pollock, another old friend from my Ohio State days, was also working in India with Dr. Newberg. I looked forward to stopping in New Delhi with those two friends.

Now I am either naive about wars and domestic disturbances, or poorly briefed. In any case, I walked right into another international hotspot. This time it was the bloody civil war between East and West Pakistan. The Indian government was strongly supporting East Pakistan because of the Hindu Indians' fear of a powerful Muslim West Pakistani military. India supported the Bengali Muslim Easterners, who later formed the new country of Bangladesh. The United States supported the West Pakistanis. I, unfortunately, had not been paying enough attention.

There I was, blithely flying to Bombay and New Delhi on an official United States government passport on the Air India Boeing 747, called the Ashoka. Now that was a thrill in itself—the jumbo Boeing 747 was new to the international airways, and this one was a jewel. We were scheduled to leave New York's John F. Kennedy International Airport at 8 p.m. On the way across the Atlantic from London earlier, somebody had failed to turn on a necessary heating element, or one failed, and a faucet in one of the rear toilets froze and burst. This messed up the entire sanitation system, and the captain refused to leave New York without repairs.

Now why is it that in one of the largest airports in the world, one can quickly find a jet engine, an airplane wheel, airplane tires, and hydraulic systems and can repair almost anything on a jet in a short time, but one cannot find a $14.50 faucet? We sat on the tarmac for hours while all the maintenance people searched for a Boeing 747 toilet faucet

Finally, at 10 p.m., an important decision was made. Since the maintenance crew could not locate a faucet, they would search for a plumber with a blow torch, braze that pipe, mark that bathroom closed, the water system would work again without leaking, and we could fire this plane up and head for London, Rome, and Bombay. We took off about three hours late. Perhaps as compensation, there were only about one hundred passengers on board this gigantic airplane (which holds 400–525 people, depending on how it is configured), with a cabin and flight crew numbering thirty-three; we were going to have some good service.

Indeed we did! Outstanding curries, rice, vegetables, nahn bread, all washed down with copious quantities of beverages. One young flight attendant spent a lot of time in conversation with me because: 1) he did not have much to do on that flight—he only had to serve three passengers instead of ten to twelve on a fully occupied flight; and 2) when I found out he was from Goa, the former Portuguese colony on the southwest coast of India, I started speaking Portuguese with him, and we had fun. Further, when he found out that I was a licensed pilot with an instrument rating, we got right into flying. He was going for a commercial license and wanted to be a crop dusting pilot in Brazil some day. The daily double! We talked into the wee hours of the morning.

Sometime around 6 a.m., my flight attendant friend awakened me out of a semi-slumber (the seats in that Air India 747 were most comfortable, unlike what one finds on so many jet planes today.) He said that we were stacked up over the Atlantic about an hour from Heathrow Airport in London, which was closed because of fog. Further, this newest of Boeing 747s had the capability and the trained crew to make a zero-zero landing, which is accomplished completely by instruments and computers when pilots cannot see the ground. The captain had invited me to go up and sit in the jump seat if I would like to watch. Would I? Of course I would since I had only read about these landings in my flying magazines.

So after some juice, coffee, and a sweet roll, I walked upstairs to the gigantic flight deck of this monster of the commercial sky; it was very impressive, especially as seen for the first time. After introductions all around and some discussion of backgrounds and experiences, the crew of the Ashoka got its clearance from British air traffic control to start its zero-zero approach. That was impressive to watch. The captain always had his thumb on the override control button in case things were not right and we had to do a missed approach and go around at the last minute using the printed procedures. The other two pilots were reading out loud the radar altimeter heights above the surface, air speeds, and distances to touchdown while the captain monitored his flight instruments.

That landing was as smooth as silk, all done by the bank of computers properly programmed to the correct frequencies on the ground guidance system. The computers even controlled the engine power, reversed the thrust as a breaking device, used the wheel brakes, dumped the spoilers on the wings, and then brought the gigantic plane to a complete stop on the center of the runway! I was impressed; few of my landings in small airplanes were as smooth as that one—ah, modern technology.

"Now what do we do, ground control?—can't see the lights on our wing tips." The calm ground controller said to stand by; he would see if his ground radar would be operational. (The weather radars in the flight deck of the plane cannot be used on the ground, for example, to locate the terminal. There is too much interference or clutter.) Soon the ground controller informed us to stay where we were; his ground radar guidance system was not working properly, and he would send a vehicle with flashing strobe lights out for us to follow in. Back to basic, old-fashioned technology again! We made it there in about fifteen minutes. Of course, now we were about five hours behind our scheduled arrival times. Oh, well, relax and enjoy the trip. There will always be another flight I can catch in Bombay to get to New Delhi tonight, right?—(probably not). I had never traveled by air in India before.

In the war between West Pakistan and East Pakistan, with complications about which one India supported and which one my country supported, I was about to become an innocent pawn in the hands of minor government officials. In London, we nearly filled up that big jumbo jet with returning Indian citizens. From Rome, we arrived in Bombay sometime in the middle of the afternoon. As I went through immigration, the official looked at my official U.S. government passport and called a Sikh Indian Army sergeant over and spoke to him in Hindi, all the time waving my passport.

Apprehension in the pit of my stomach told me that something was not right. Sure enough, the Sikh officer informed me that I must accompany him to the office, "just a few steps away—this will only take a few minutes."

"What's wrong?" I asked. I told him I was due in New Delhi that day, was already five hours late, had to locate another flight, and had to get going.

The immigration officer said, "Oh not to worry—this can all be worked out; you see, sir, the visa in your passport is not valid."

"Not valid? It was put in there by your embassy in Washington, D.C.—Of course it is valid!"

"I'm terribly sorry sir, but it does not have the correct signature. You will have to talk to our supervisor in the office—I'm sure this can all be corrected; please follow the officer."

"Wait a minute—where are my bags? I want my bags at the carrousel!"

"Again, I am sorry sir, but you cannot proceed to the carrousel to claim your bags until you are properly and legally admitted into the country; please accompany the officer, your bags will be safe." End of discussion.

It must have been one hundred and twenty degrees in the small, non air conditioned office. I was sweating, I was alone, and I was angry. The Sikh sergeant left me alone with the sweet smile and phrase, "Somebody will soon be here to attend to you, sir." Thirty minutes later, a young kid came in and asked if anyone was taking care of me. I said no and explained my plight; he nodded his head knowingly, and, I hoped, sympathetically. He asked for my passport, looked at it, and said he would be right back, then disappeared with my passport—my lifeline to identity and freedom.

Another half hour elapsed, and another man appeared. He looked at me quizzically and asked what I was doing in his private office. I repeated my story.

"Where is the young man who was here half an hour ago and took my passport?"

"What young man?" he responded. I described him; he said he knew no one who worked in his office by that description. Now I knew I was in deep trouble, but I did not yet know how I was going to extricate myself from this can of worms and get on to New Delhi.

Another thirty minutes, and I heard loud voices arguing, the loudest being spoken in American English, approaching outside the door in the hallway. In strides the Indian official who claimed I was in his office, followed by two American Flying Tiger pilots in uniforms who were madder than bees in a hive that has just been turned over. The senior captain, with four stripes, yells, "That gross weight is in pounds, and you know it; there is no way I or my company will accept that as kilograms! You're just harassing us Americans and trying to charge us 2.2 times what is legal! I want this in writing and I want a clearance to fly my freight out of here to Istanbul; you've already illegally held us up all day with this nonsense!"

The captain and the official went into another room where the official said he would call his chief. The second pilot stayed with me, and I asked him what was going on, after first explaining my waiting and frustration. He explained, "It's a simple matter, but disgusting. The United States sides with West Pakistan, India with East Pakistan, and apparently the word has gone out to hassle all American citizens."

I said (showing my ignorance), "But I am traveling on an official U.S. government passport, and they should let me go on with my official business."

He replied, "You'd have been out of here if you only had a tourist passport. They're playing games with you and laughing up their sleeves. Why don't you exercise your rights when that jerk 'official' comes back with my captain, and tell him you're calling your embassy in New Delhi collect right now—the one telephone call you are allowed all over the world." I thanked him for his advice. They got their problem solved, got permission to take off, and left in a hurry.

The official now asked me again what my problem was. Another Indian gentleman appeared, but this one was in a business suit. He heard me explain my situation and threatened to call my embassy. The official got a telephone call, and while he was talking, the gentleman politely quizzed me. He told me he was a professor at Hyderabad University. When I told him who I was and that I used to be an associate professor at Ohio State University, it was like old college reunion time. Ohio State had helped build Hyderabad University to prominence with USAID/India funding, and he had done graduate work at OSU under our program many years before. He said, "Let me handle this nasty situation for you; they have no right to treat you this way."

My new professor friend knew how to deal with the junior official by making him an offer he couldn't refuse (he later told me he threatened to have the man fired by the professor's friend, a brigadier general who just happened to run the airport) if the man did not find my passport immediately. It was amazing how quickly the kid who had taken my passport an hour earlier showed up with it. The professor arranged for them to come running with my bags, hired a boy to carry them, and then accompanied me all over the airport, helping to run interference for me until I got a reserved seat on the next Indian Air Line plane to New Delhi, which was no simple task. I thanked him profusely; we exchanged cards (and later letters), and I was on my way. What a godsend that he showed up at that place at that time, otherwise I might still be waiting to recover my passport.

When I finally arrived in New Delhi and called USAID, they sent a driver for me, and in the car were Ron Pollock and his Indian assistant. When I explained the situation, he wrote down a telephone number for me and said to keep it in my billfold. "You may need it when you come back. These minor Indian officials are being told to harass every American citizen, especially American government people. This number scares them; it's an emergency U.S. consular number that has been widely advertised. This is a serious telephone number, Howard; don't be afraid to threaten to use it!"

When I returned to New Delhi from Nepal two months later, the immigration officials tried to harass me again at New Delhi airport. This time my visa supposedly had expired. I threatened to use the consular telephone number and it worked. They apologized; they had been "reading it incorrectly." One more reason international frequent flyers get gray.

Oh, Those German Tourists!

On the way from New Delhi to Kathmandu, the capital of Nepal, I was flying up front in the flight deck with the Royal Nepal Air Lines captain and first officer. We were in a two-engine propjet aircraft called an AVRO. It probably seated about forty people. I noticed as we loaded, before I was invited up to the flight deck, that most of the passengers were speaking German, and each had at least one camera over their necks, many two. Ah yes, the German tourist trip to the Himalayas.

From New Delhi, the first half hour or so we were in heavy clouds, the visibility was zero, and of course the Royal Nepal captain had the AVRO on automatic pilot tracking a known safe route at a safe altitude. He and I (I was sitting on a jump seat just behind the captain and the first officer in the middle) were discussing our respective training programs while the first officer was monitoring the instruments and occasionally communicating with India air traffic control, then Nepal air traffic control as we crossed the border east of the Ganges River Basin in the Tarai Plains.

The clouds parted, and there on our left were the magnificent snow-capped Himalayas towering above us at some fifty miles safe distance. But just as we saw the sun, the blue sky, and the mountains, the AVRO took a dangerous tilt to the left, almost at a 45 degree angle. The captain let out an expletive, grabbed the yoke and literally twisted it clear stop right to straighten out the plane's wings to level, or we would have gone into a spin toward earth. All the tourists on the right side of the plane had run to the left windows to try to take pictures of the snow-capped Himalayas.

Once more I was reminded how little the average person knows about aircraft sensitivity to changes in forces, such as a change in the center of gravity, or weight, or snow (even frost) on the wings. I recalled a statement made by a friend of mine, an aeronautical engineer, while I was training for the pilot instrument rating at Ohio State University: "You know Howard, an aircraft and its airfoil are engineering miracles that almost do not work!" I suspect that details like this are not something we who love aircraft, piloting, and flying wish to share freely with our passengers and friends. But as the Nepal captain said after our AVRO was stable again in the air stream and the German tourists were back in their seats, "Well, they have no idea how dangerous their desire to snap photos was to this flight, but thanks be to the Almighty One, we escaped death again!"

"So you have a pilot's license, Steele! May I see your credentials?"

Those were the words of Arizona Helicopters Inc. head pilot Aaron Aupperle when I arrived at the Kathmandu Airport early one morning with my USAID colleague to fly down to the Tarai area near the Indian border to look at some experiment stations that had planted new miracle varieties of rice, the hot item in agriculture in 1971.

In those days, I carried my logbook, medical certificate, pilot's license (with its ratings), radio operator's license, and my pilot's flight kit everywhere I went—just in case there might be a chance to fly. Aaron had a very serious look on his face. After he read my documents and was convinced that I was indeed a current instrument-rated pilot, he broke into a smile.

He said, "Thank God! We've been looking for somebody like you to show up here for two weeks. You see, two weeks ago we began flying rice from the Tarai up to the hill and valley Sherpa people, who are starving." Monsoon rains had wiped out their barley crops in the Himalayan river valleys, which were flooding.

"We lost one of our pilots," he continued. "It was in one of our Robinson helicopters. They dropped into a small, remote village, dumped out half the bags of rice on board, and were starting to take off for another village over the mountain. The Sherpa men saw that there was more rice in the helicopter, and as the pilot lifted clear of the ground they jumped up and grabbed the rungs of the helicopter. It struck, tilted, and the rotor struck the ground. It cart wheeled and killed our pilot and six Sherpas.

"So I and our other three pilots have been flying constantly with our two remaining helicopters and this Pilatus Porter STOL [short take off and landing plane]. Would you be willing to fly for us?"

Would I? "You bet! I'd love to."

Aaron Aupperle enthusiastically showed me all the important control features of the outstanding Swiss-manufactured plane, one designed to fly at very high altitudes. We opened the cowl and looked at the 695 shaft horsepower engine, surprisingly small for such a long fuselage. Then we climbed aboard, and he briefly showed me the main critical speeds, operational temperatures of the jet engine, and critical safety features unique to that aircraft. We fired up, were rolling after clearance from ground control and tower, and were airborne in seconds.

"It's all yours, Howard," Aaron said. "Climb up to the left there, through Pokhara Pass," he said as he unfolded a National Geographic map of Nepal with pencil lines drawn on it and pointed. "Take up a heading of 210 degrees after clearing the pass, climb to and maintain 9,500 feet until you cross this river at the bend, and wake me up when we get to the river!" That was the extent of my instruction. The sweat came out on my forehead and my hands. My hands were so wet I could hardly hold the control stick.

But that plane was so stable and balanced that it was much easier to fly than I had imagined when I first looked at it. I had no problem whatsoever. I soon settled down and even enjoyed the scenery. Now at that time there were only navigational radios around the mountains to guide planes into Kathmandu and none in the rest of Nepal; there were no communication radios at any of the airports, except at the airports in Kathmandu and Pokhara, and no radar anywhere. Thus, you used a National Geographic map and flew by the seat of your pants. Later in our flights together, Aaron taught me how to read the winds from the snow blowing off the Himalayan peaks and smoke from the Sherpa huts in the villages—very crude navigation and piloting.

On a later flight with Aaron, we were taking bags of rice way up into the Himalayas, close to the Chinese border. It was the middle of the Cold War, and relations with communist China were poor. I had second thoughts about that trip when the U.S. embassy took my official passport away and gave me a "trekking pass" with my picture on it. The pass was written in Chinese and Nepali, neither of which I could read. For all I knew it said something like: "If you capture this man, throw him in jail. We do not want anything to do with him."

We landed about an hour later at a grass landing strip deep in the Tarai, a flat, hot plain in the Ganges River Basin, where an agricultural experiment station doing miracle rice varietal research trials was located. I also wanted to visit the local market to interview middlemen to see where the food crops were being shipped to, their prices, and the costs of transportation. When we stopped at the end of the grass strip and taxied the plane off the landing strip, a young Western man with a large beard approached us as we stepped out of the plane. He could hardly walk and was obviously in great pain. He told us his name and explained that he was an American Peace Corps volunteer. He was very sick with dysentery and perhaps other parasites, and had been waiting at the strip for an airplane to arrive and take him to the hospital in Kathmandu for nearly two weeks.

We told him that he was welcome to ride back to Kathmandu with us, but that we would be working for several hours before going back, and we were going to fly up into the Himalayas with a load of rice bags and drop them off at two different villages. He could, however, lie on top of the rice bags. He did this as we supervised the loading of the hold of the plane. I have never seen any young person look so ill. It was obvious that he had been dehydrated for a long time, had lost a tremendous amount of weight, and could not keep food down. He was happy to get on the flight to safety.

"We're flying to the Tibet border; bring your trekking pass, Howard." Those were Aaron Aupperle's words a few days later. Now I knew what that meant. We would be flying on oxygen as we climbed up past Anapurna Peak (nearly 27,000 feet above sea level), then dropped down into several deep valleys to snow-covered landing strips where we would drop off our bags of rice for the hill and valley people. Winds, landing, taking off, and avoiding down-drafts and updrafts all are very tricky in the Himalayas. If we did not watch our plane and its movements closely, we could be casualties in those frigid mountains.

About one week before this trip, we went one evening to a local restaurant run by expatriate Americans, which was on the embassy-accepted list. As we approached the entrance, we heard loud singing and upon entering saw a large group of Japanese dancing and singing to Asian music. It was a climbing team that would set out in the morning for the top of Anapurna, which had failed the year before, due to an avalanche. The team leader's brother, who led the climbers the year before, had been killed in the avalanche, along with six other Sherpas and Japanese. This time, the team proposed to finish the climb, then on the way back down, recover the bodies of those killed and give them proper burials. We danced and sang with them and toasted the team's good luck before leaving.

"Aaron, can you imagine the risks those Japanese climbers take?" I asked as our plane climbed up close to 27,000 feet to get past Anapurna before dropping sharply into the valley beyond to a strip called Jumbla, almost on the Tibet-Nepal border.

"Yeah, Howard—look at the snow blowing off that mountain top; why would anybody be so foolish as to take that kind of risk climbing that thing?" Aaron replied.

Ironically, the climbing team might have said the same of us. Looking up from the face of that mountain in the wind, snow, and ice, they might have exclaimed, "Look at those idiots up there in that single-engine airplane; what will they do if their engine quits?" It is all a matter of perspective.

All during my flying training, instructors warned of the dangers of flying at high altitudes without supplemental oxygen or pressurized cabins. When brain cells become starved for oxygen, the result is hypoxia—a feeling first of euphoria and invincibility, followed by headaches, difficulty breathing, and finally loss of consciousness and/or temporarily paralysis.

On that trip to Jumbla, as we ran through our pre-flight check list, Aaron asked me to check the oxygen bottle behind my seat and to put on the masks, hook each one up, and ensure that oxygen flowed through them. I did this, and I also looked at the gauge on the bottle and reported that it was three-fourths full. Aaron said that was sufficient—about a three-hour supply. We should be above 11,000 feet (oxygen is required of all pilots at that altitude or above) for only about two hours. But he forgot one important fact; two of us would be drawing on that supply, not just one! I failed to recognize it too.

About the time we passed Anapurna Mountain, we discovered our mistake. Aaron said, "Let's take turns with one mask; when you feel a bit woozy, I'll pass the mask to you, you can breathe oxygen for a minute or two, and then you can pass it back. That way we'll have plenty left over."

I suggested another plan. I had seen copies of the handwriting of pilots suffering from hypoxia who thought they were quite lucid and capable, even as they scribbled gibberish. I would try an experiment; every five minutes, without any supplemental oxygen, I would copy down on paper our altitude, indicated airspeed, and the elapsed time. I would keep this up until I either got a headache or dizziness. The results were predictable and shocking. I thought I was doing fine, although half way through the experiment, I started making corrections in my writing. When the dizziness hit, after about fifteen to twenty minutes, I asked for the oxygen mask. After drawing on it for a couple of minutes, everything came into focus. The last couple of entries were absolutely unreadable. As one instructor once told a group of us green instrument-rating hopefuls, "You don't have to pay attention to these lectures if you don't want to—just remember that what's at stake here is your life."

"USDA? Sure Steele, we know who you work for." Wink.

Those were the words of a U.S. Army sergeant in communications at the U.S. embassy in Kathmandu. I was housed in a nice little guesthouse on the grounds of a former queen's palace. The palace itself housed many U.S. Government offices associated with both the embassy and USAID. There was a nice restaurant and recreation building with ping-pong tables, pool tables, a reading room, a small commissary, and a bar.

Before I started flying with the Arizona Helicopter people in their Pilatus Porter STOL, I used to play ping-pong and pool with some of the other single men from the embassy and USAID. One of my buddies was an army sergeant who did cable encryption for the ambassador and other officials. His office was near mine in the former queen's palace. We would tip a few at the bar on occasion, after a rigorous ping-pong or pool round-robin competition after work.

Obviously, he knew that I had a top-secret security clearance, which I had since first going to USDA in 1971, because he had produced the incoming cables for the embassy and USAID before my arrival. When they took away my official U.S. government passport and issued me a Trekking Pass in Chinese and Nepali, and then I started flying with the CIA-contract airline company (Arizona Helicopters Inc.), he made an assumption. He thought that I worked for the CIA, and "development economist" with the USDA was my cover.

The first day I flew up into the Himalayas to deliver rice to the hill and valley tribes people, I came back at about 6 p.m. tired and in need of a drink. The sergeant was at the bar, "three sheets to the wind." He called for, "Drinks on the house: in honor of our good friend Howard Steele, who has just returned from another dangerous mission at the Chinese border."

No matter what I said to him or to any of his colleagues about being a USDA development economist, who just happened to be a pilot currently helping Arizona Helicopters because of the recent crash, they just laughed and winked knowingly. "Oh yeah, we understand," they said, and kept believing that I worked for the CIA. After several days, I quit trying to convince them and let it go.

Tara Manandhar was my secretary at the offices of the Nepalese Ministry of Agriculture in one of the old queen's palaces. Tara, who spoke excellent English, was about twenty-three years old, a Buddhist in a Hindu country, and one of the fastest, most accurate typists I have ever seen. She also had a great sense of humor and loved America, which she hoped to visit some day. Her brother, Rawan, was about nineteen and was an accomplished artist who had won a scholarship to the Sorbonne in Paris.

Tara always wore Western-style skirts and blouses at the ministry while all the other women employees wore traditional Hindu saris. I asked her one day if she did not wear saris because she was a Buddhist, and not Hindu. She held her hand to her mouth, as she always did so as not to be disrespectful (she told me), and let out a hearty laugh. "No, Dr. Steele, it has nothing to do with religion; I trip in saris when I try to walk in them!"

About a month after my arrival in Kathmandu, working daily with Tara, she said to me one evening, "Dr. Steele—I would like for you to meet my mother and father, and my brother, Rawan. Would that be alright?" I said I would consider it an honor. Immediately she said, "Oh, I am sorry; that would not be possible." I asked why. She said, "Because we are so poor and ashamed—we do not have nice furniture for you to sit on; we sit on the floor." I replied, "That's O.K.—I sit on the floor a lot at my home. "Oh wonderful; we have a heavy Nepali rug on the floor which is quite comfortable. I will ask my father and mother tonight!" She seemed quite excited.

She said nothing about it the next morning, and late in the afternoon my curiosity got the better of me, so I asked if she had talked to her parents. "Oh yes; they would be so pleased to meet an American (which they have never done before), but I'm sorry, you cannot come because we all agree our home is not good enough to entertain somebody like you."

"That doesn't sound right to me—I would love to visit your parents with you," I said.

"But we have no stairs to our living quarters; we use a ladder made out of a tree," she replied.

I said that was O.K. by me. "Remember Tara, I told you I used to work on a dairy farm and milked cows. I can use a ladder."

"Oh wonderful—I will be so happy to tell my parents!"

Well, this kind of back-and-forth went on for a few more days until I was finally invited to dinner. It was a great evening, eating her mother's special goat and rice dish with Nepali spices by candlelight and one kerosene lamp. Rawan showed me some of his sketches and paintings, and before I left, he gave me one of his oil paintings of Anapurna Mountain, which hangs in my family room today. I liked it so much that after flying rice to the Sherpa hill and valley tribesmen, I commissioned him to draw a picture of a Sherpa couple, which also hangs in my family room. The lad had such talent. I surely would like to know what he is doing and where he is now.

"That is Buffalo Steak, Sir, very tasty, don't you think?"

Those words were spoken by my waiter at a five-star hotel where we ate some Sundays—a special treat after the USAID cafeteria all week (which was pretty good, and inexpensive). The meals at the hotel were extra expensive for Nepal.

My dinner partner one Sunday said, "Yeah—buffalo meat my foot." (We were speaking of the Asian water buffalo, not the North American Bison, which we often call buffalo.)

I said, "What are you talking about? The waiter said we are eating buffalo steaks!"

He answered me, "But obviously you have never eaten Asian water buffalo meat before; this is beef!!"

I was thoroughly confused. This was a Hindu country; cows, bulls, and steers—considered sacred—roamed the streets. Only small children with small sticks were allowed to touch the animals, to shoo them away from their parents' vegetable stands.

My companion explained to me that he had done a small research project on his own after his first year in Kathmandu. The number of water buffalo sold and slaughtered weekly (being a beast of burden, the water buffalo was not sacred to the Hindus in Nepal—please do not ask me to explain this one) accounted for probably only ten percent of the total disappearance and consumption of "buffalo steaks and meat" per week in Kathmandu, he said.

"So where does all this bovine beef you say we're eating come from?" I asked him.

"What do you think happens to all those sad looking cows, steers, and bulls after dark?" he asked, with a smirk on his face. "Kathmandu would be overrun with cattle if they didn't have some way to control the cattle population. The only thing native slaughterers have to watch out for is that they don't try to capture the animals when a Hindu religious official is near," he said.

"Come for Dinner, Howard. We have some Fresh Fish from India."

My American friends were so kind to invite me and three other bachelor, short-time consultants to their home for dinner. I guess it was a rare occasion to have fresh fish come in from India—like when I was a boy growing up in Pennsylvania, and fresh seafood came from Chesapeake Bay. This was a treat for Sunday guests. Only in my case, it was a roasting hen that was the delicacy. It was a marvelous, full Sunday meal prepared by the Nepali cook under the supervision of the hostess. It was delicious.

However, when I got back to my USAID guesthouse at about midnight, something was amiss. By 2:00 a.m. I wanted to die! I have never been so nauseated and sick to my stomach in my life. I did not sleep a wink all night. The next morning, as soon as I knew that the embassy nurse would be at her office, I went. Later it became evident that the fish had been tainted, and all of us had pretty bad food poisoning. The host told me later that they decided they would never again buy "fresh fish" on the local market; these were "fresh fish from Calcutta, India". He figured they had sat in a railroad car for days in 120 degree heat, and then somebody threw ice on them before they were unloaded in Kathmandu to make them look fresh.

"We will meet you at the Yak and Yetti Restaurant, Dr. Steele," one of my former short-term students at Ohio State University said to me during a visit to my office. He worked in the Ministry of Agriculture in Kathmandu in a nearby building, and he and another former student at OSU invited me to be their guest at the famous restaurant. It was run by a former Russian (White Russian, I assumed) named Boris. Even before arriving in Nepal, I had heard of the place, which served great borscht soups and other goodies. Succulent goat meat and lamb dishes were also specialties, plus many more (including "buffalo steaks," no doubt!).

The night of the dinner, I arrived a bit early and went to sit at the open fire pit with the ancient brass hood and chimney. The restaurant was housed in one of Nepal's early queen's palaces and had been quite elegant in its time, many centuries before. The fireplace was huge and had large logs burning, with perhaps twenty people sitting around its square perimeter.

Soon I heard a throng of voices approaching from the rear and many voices calling out my name. Just as my students in Taiwan had done, the ten Nepali students I had taught in short courses at Ohio State University had come from all over the country to honor me. That was also a night I will never forget. We had a great time telling stories about our times together in the United States, what they were doing, and how they were applying what they learned in America to improve their own agricultural situation. I loved Nepal and Nepalis, and returned there in 1983 on a trip with my family.

My home in the Mt. Lebanon suburb of Pittsburgh, 1931–1946

With Beverly Farms, Inc., 1946–1956.

Washington & Lee University senior, 1950

Washington & Lee University, Lexington, Virginia, 1946–1950, B.S. degree (that is daughter Jennifer Steele on a visit I made in 1995).

We had this house constructed in Clemson, South Carolina, in 1960, total cost $25,000. David, 9 years old, Pat 7, John 11.

Escola Superior de Agricultura "Luiz de Quieroz" (the Luiz de Quieroz Superior College of Agriculture) of São Paulo State.

Market Square in downtown Piracicaba, Brazil.

"Modern" agricultural transportation near Piracicaba, Brazil, 1965.

Rich red soils surrounding Piracicaba produced superior sugar cane.

The coffee cooperative at San Jose do Rio Preto, where I helped establish a farm service center for co-op members, 1965–1967.

Brazil's Congress Buildings in background, from Itamarati, the Ministry of Foreign Relations building.

Back from Brazil at our farm, Kingwood Acres, Somerset County, Pennsylvania, 1967.

I earned the coveted Pilot's Instrumental Rating from the FAA at OSU in 1970. Here I am at the Royal Singapore Flying Club with instructor O'Brien

Crowded streets in Saigon, South Vietnam, 1972–1974.

Much "higgling and haggling" before a sale is completed in Saigon.

9

Dodging Bullets in Vietnam

Nasty air travel has provided more than enough background music in my life. The most discordant notes came on a thirty-six hour return from Saigon near the end of the Vietnam War in the fall of 1974. Everything was collapsing; the U.S. military had basically left the country and the fighting to the South Vietnam Armed Forces. Uncle Sam was chartering special Boeing 747 jets to fetch American families back home.

Pan Am had reconfigured one of its Boeing 747s to hold the most passengers possible, all in expanded coach-type seating—a warehouse in the air. That flight surely had more than five hundred crying babies, screaming kids, exasperated mothers, and the occasional civilian government worker (including me). We stopped at every major airport in eastern Asia and in the Pacific to let people off, take people on, refuel, re-supply food and beverages, and sometimes even clean toilets. I had planned to fly all the way back to Washington, D.C. and take my twenty-four hour rest stop at home, but as the sun was coming up inbound to Chicago O'Hare Airport, I realized I could not go another hour. I left the airplane while it was again being refueled, spotted a row of motel telephones, picked one up, and asked the attendant on the other end, "Do you have a bed that doesn't move? A bath with scalding hot water and soap I can rent for about twelve hours?"

Both answers were positive, so I stayed. I did not even bother to get my bags off the plane, but went out the next day and bought a clean shirt, underwear, socks, and pants.

On the flight, there were Vietnamese war brides and fiancés, most of who had never been away from their villages or on an airplane. They were so scared and nervous—they were on their way to a new world, with a poor command of English, knowing little about our country or culture. Many of them were afraid they would not be met by their American husbands, fiancés, or relatives. They had very little money, and most were clutching their plastic sacks with their chest x-rays, legal documents, pictures of their loved ones, and a letter or two all dog-eared from re-reading.

The small woman sitting next to me, twenty or twenty-one years old, said in her halting English that she was going to "Taxus" to meet her husband. She shook visibly on every landing and take off. I told her I was a pilot and could explain every noise the plane made so they need not scare the daylights out of her. She relaxed a bit, especially when the couple with their kids behind us—he a U.S. Navy sailor, she his Vietnamese wife—helped interpret for me. Somewhere near Taipei, Taiwan, en route to Washington D.C.'s Dulles Airport (that charter plane landed in Manila, Taiwan, Yokohama, Tokyo, Okinawa, Guam, Honolulu, Los Angeles, San Francisco, and then Chicago), she confessed that she was not yet married to her American GI, but only engaged. When I asked her where he was going to meet her, after seeing his picture with her and reading the letter she carried from him, which she shyly let me read, she said at Sam Houston. Well, then we had to establish that there is no city called "Sam Houston," but rather he was stationed at Fort Sam Houston in San Antonio, Texas.

She would connect in San Francisco to a flight to Dallas. The Navy couple and I promised to help her get on the right plane in San Francisco. What would happen to her at Dallas was anyone's guess. Somewhere around Guam, she had gained enough confidence in me that she confessed she only had ten dollars with her. What a risk taker! Her biggest fear was that she would not be allowed to enter the United States at immigration when we landed in Hawaii. She showed us all her documents, which seemed to be ample in quantity and coverage, including all her medical x-rays and an American GI M.D.'s report, but what did I know about our immigration laws? The sailor and I promised to help her in Hawaii at immigration, and then he and I each came up with twenty dollars to give her for taxi fares, telephone calls, food, and so on, in case there was a mix-up in "Taxus." The sailor also gave her information about Traveler's Aide and how it could help her in the airport in Dallas.

She got so nervous inbound to Honolulu Airport that she could not eat her food. Sure enough, at immigration, the U.S. Officer was very firm in his questioning. He kept looking at her papers and pointing out that she had only ninety days to get married, or she would be sent back to Vietnam. Then he told her she had to have a medical exam and directed her to a room off on the side; she started crying. The sailor, his wife, and I promised to wait for her. In about fifteen minutes, she emerged with a U.S. Public Health Service nurse, smiling from ear to ear. The report was excellent;

the immigration officer even smiled and wished her a pleasant wedding and a happy marriage. The trip to Los Angeles and San Francisco was quite relaxed and lighthearted. We got her on the right plane to Dallas in San Francisco amid many "thank yous" and smiles, plus a tear or two. The sailor's Vietnamese wife took down names and addresses at Fort Sam Houston and vowed to follow up with her, so I continued eastward feeling the arrangements were in good hands.

What was a Pennsylvania agricultural economist doing in Vietnam? That is a very logical question. When President Richard Nixon's National Security Advisor (and later Secretary of State), Henry Kissinger, was negotiating behind the scenes in France to end the Vietnam war, we in the Department of Agriculture (USDA) got the word confidentially that as the U.S. military pulled out, somebody had to study what could get the Vietnamese economy back on track again. What could the Vietnamese export to earn badly needed foreign exchange with which to rebuild society?

In the winter of 1972, we analyzed all the trade information we could find for the largest free port in the world at that time, Singapore, and the Japanese market, then tried to match food and agricultural commodity availability in Vietnam with imports into these two gigantic markets. We evaluated about twenty-six agricultural commodities. The ones that held the most promise were fishery products from the South China Sea and the Gulf of Thailand and tropical hardwoods from Vietnam's highlands. Of course we faced a major obstacle; the war was still being fought everywhere in the country, and our experts needed to look at supply availability and stocks, interview producers and fishermen, and then mount a marketing research effort in Singapore and Japan. Not an easy task. But the U.S. Agency for International Development (USAID) had ample funds to mount the effort, and I became the Chief of Party to kick off these phases of the research.

I was most fortunate that the Chief of USDA's Forest Service named S. Blair Hutchison, one of their best forestry economists, to accompany me on our first (and subsequent) forays to Saigon, Singapore, Tokyo, and other points in the east. Talk about an enthusiastic traveler! Our June 1972 mission was Blair's first overseas work trip, and I was his mentor. We spent a good deal of time developing our research methodology and analyzing the trade and production data made available to us by our Washington, D.C. statistical teams. Then it was off to Saigon. We presented our methodology to the officials of USAID, got their approval, and then interviewed a number of Vietnamese Ministry of Fisheries and Ministry of Forestry officials, private sector fish processing and exporting entrepreneurs, lumber dealers, and sawyers—all the time avoiding the war zones when we could or postponing trips until areas were cleared to travel in. Inevitably, we had some close calls.

Singapore was our favorite city. We wasted no time setting up our office there and hiring employees to begin testing our development methodology for the benefit of the South Vietnamese government and economy—which, of course, all of us believed would soon be at peace with North Vietnam. (Believe me, we had less than perfect information about what was happening then.) We had reservations at the lovely Singapore Hyatt Hotel. I wanted to negotiate for an office room, plus rooms for Blair and me for about six weeks. We were also expecting other U.S. team members later, so we had that as an additional bargaining chip. Blair could not believe that I could "dicker down" the room rate by going higher and higher in the management chain over the next several days at the Hyatt, but I did. We also interviewed candidates to run our office and serve as head secretary.

We hired Doris Lim [Lim Boc Nho], about 23 years old, who spoke three Chinese dialects perfectly, plus British English, Malaysian, and French. She was also studying German. How talented those young people we came in contact with were. Next I rented office equipment, and then we interviewed a research organization called Far East Research Probe, Ltd., a subsidiary of the McCann-Erickson advertising conglomerate. The Singapore firm was managed by an Australian. During our first interview in his lovely office one hot afternoon, he pushed a button under his desk, and a whole wall rotated to reveal a liquid refreshment center. Those British and Australian subjects from the old Empire surely knew how to cool off on a hot tropical afternoon.

"Gin and tonics, gentlemen?"

I called for bourbon and ginger ale; no problem.

"We try to satisfy the most discerning tastes," said the manager.

Of course his firm got our contract, for this and many more important reasons.

We hired the firm to help us interview Singaporean importers and exporters, fish and timber processors, and so on. It was not long until Blair and our other U.S. forestry and fisheries people were interviewing Chinese businessmen, with the help of the Far East Research Probe interpreters. One afternoon at the giant fish port and wholesale market, Changi Port, I was interviewing a Chinese fisherman who had several boats operating in the waters around Indonesia and Malaysia. My young Singaporean interpreter, Rosie, sat on my left with a yellow legal pad between us. I asked the interview question from my questionnaire, she translated into the Chinese dialect of the interviewee, and then, as the person answered, she wrote the response in English on the yellow pad. Such versatility!

About halfway through the set of questions, the fisherman/wholesaler began to talk about the South Vietnamese fishermen he had observed. He got quite excited. He jumped up, went to a roll-top desk, and brought out a large dried sea horse with the eyes and tail. Rosie and he started an animated conversation back and forth. She quit writing on the yellow pad, she was so excited. Finally, I got them to stop and explain what was so fascinating.

Rosie said the fisherman was absolutely furious that the Vietnamese fishermen, when they pulled in their nets from trawling on the bottom, would save the shrimp, red snappers, sharks, and other pelagic and dimersal fish, but were throwing back into the ocean as trash all the sea horses. He said of course he would buy snapper, shrimp, sharks, and other edible fish from the Vietnamese, but for goodness sake, he would pay twelve dollars per pound for dried sea horses with the eyes still in!

Well this had both Rosie and me excited; why twelve dollars per pound for dried sea horses when really good eating fish like snapper or shrimp were commanding only one or two dollars per pound at the time?

Ah yes; cultural differences. The ground up, dried sea horse was in great demand among certain Chinese men who believed it was a strong aphrodisiac which would give them all sorts of great powers. You can be sure that the first opportunity I had back in Vietnam, I told the Ministry of Fisheries to spread the word: save those sea horses—there's a heck of a market for them in Singapore!

"Yes, I'm with Gandy's Raiders"

How often have you wished for the opportunity to engage in the perfect put-down when dealing with an arrogant snob? I had that pleasure on one of my trips back to Saigon from Singapore on Air Vietnam. Blair Hutchison, I, and the members of our teams had flown a lot on the CIA-operated airline, Air America. In fact, on several occasions when we flew Pilatus Porter STOLs of Air America on the trip from Can Tho in the Mekong Valley to Rach Gia on the Gulf of Thailand, I would actually fly for the pilot in the copilot's seat, since I had logged about ten hours flying that plane in Nepal in 1972. The word got around the civilian flying community at Tan Son Nhut Airfield, and I was called captain.

There is a comradeship among pilots of all types; we all started out the same way, and we all face the same risks. I flew on Air Vietnam's two Boeing 727s and its one Boeing 707 so often that the crews knew me, and every trip they would invite me to fly in the jump seat behind the captain. Waiting at the Singapore airport one day to fly back to Saigon, I was sitting in the duty-free lounge when the head stewardess for Air Vietnam recognized me and asked if I was flying back to Saigon with them. I said yes, and she said she felt sure that Colonel Pham, the captain in command of the Boeing 727, would want me to fly up front with the crew. I thanked her, and she said she would have a seat in the small first class compartment for me when we boarded.

True to her word, she greeted me as soon as I passed through the door saying, "Good afternoon, Captain. Welcome aboard; your seat is right here!" There was one other man, a Caucasian, across the aisle from me in a three-piece business suit, with all his papers spread out— obviously a VIP from somewhere who had been pre-boarded so he could do his important paper work. I said a cheery, "Good afternoon sir!" No response but a guttural grunt.

After all passengers were accounted for and we were taxiing out, the stewardess asked me to come forward to the flight deck. I got up to go into the flight deck and switched my glasses, putting on my prescription sunglasses as I walked past "Mr. Important." I was up there for about a full hour. Captain Pham actually put me in his seat while the first officer was flying, and then he went back to talk to some passengers. Soon the first officer had me taking amended clearances from Singapore Air Traffic Control and reading them back. Then he had me dialing in the new headings and altitudes assigned on the computer, which was actually flying the plane. Then the first officer got up to get a soft drink, and the flight engineer and I were in charge—except I was the one sitting in the captain's seat. Technically, I was flying the Boeing 727 until the first officer came back. This, of course, was illegal, since I had no Air Transport Pilot's rating, but such was the informality of these Vietnam Air Force pilots forced to fly the civilian airline, which they hated. (They were paid the grand sum of sixty dollars per month equivalent, plus all the things they could load on the plane duty free and bring into Vietnam.)

Soon the stewardess came and said that dinner was about to be served. Would I prefer to eat in the jump seat, or in the first class seat? I chose the latter since it would be better for her and me. Captain Pham said, "Come back up here after dinner—we're going to have some nasty weather the last half hour or so, and I want you to see how we Vietnam pros handle it!" As I left the flight deck and emerged into the first class section, I took off my pilot's sunglasses and put my regular glasses back on. Now "Mr. Important" had become all friendly.

"Excuse me, sir", he said, "but are you a pilot by chance?"

"Yes I am," I replied.

"Oh, were you flying this plane? You were up there quite a while, and I saw two of the pilots come back through the cabin while you were up there!"

"Yes," I said matter of factly.

"Well," he asked, "May I know who you are flying for?"

Here was my chance: I looked around the plane conspiratorially, opened my attaché case, and pulled out my shirt patch, which has a Vietnam dragon breathing fire in the middle and GANDY'S RAIDERS and VIETNAM around the outside, cupped it in my hand, and showed it to him in confidence. He nodded his head knowingly, and I started to eat my dinner. I'll bet that guy is still trying to find out who Gandy's Raiders were during the Vietnam War! In truth, it was the brainchild of John Gandy, one of our U.S. foresters, who spoke excellent Vietnamese. He had found a young woman with a naked baby cringing and crying outside the wall by the presidential palace in Saigon one day during a tropical rainstorm while passing in a USAID car, and he ordered the driver to stop. On questioning the girl, he found that she was from a village in the Mekong Delta, had the baby out of wedlock, and was banned from her family and village. She had come to Saigon on a truck hoping to find work as a domestic. He gave her one thousand piasters, the equivalent of perhaps six dollars at that time. Back at the USAID guesthouse, he told us the story, and we organized GANDY'S RAIDERS. All of us who passed by would stop and give her a few piasters.

Eventually, she was able to build a lean-to at the wall, had clothes for the baby, and was selling fruits and vegetables. A year later, she had another woman living with her who also had a small child, and the two were cooking curbside meals for laborers. We had the Gandy's Raiders patches designed and sold them to each new USAID worker who came in for about one thousand piasters. Believe me, I was a proud member of Gandy's Raiders and was happy as a dues paying member of the group to be able to put down "Mr. Important."

Cultural shock—Women in the Men's Toilets!

When Blair Hutchison and I first arrived in Vietnam aboard the Air France Boeing 747 nonstop from Hong Kong, we had a bit of cultural shock. That was the first time I was ever asked to deplane—

after fully loading and hassling about seats, storage bins, and so on, we had to walk a half-mile across the tarmac so each passenger could identify his suitcases because of a terrorist bomb threat. Blair and I wondered if we were doing the right thing by taking this assignment in a war zone.

Back in Saigon and our complicated clearance through Vietnam immigration and customs, customs officers were collecting the bribe, "black taxes," with gusto. The customs officer, when he saw I had a carton of American cigarettes in one of my bags, tore the carton apart (without asking permission from me, and smiling all the time) and took out four packs for himself. Not one word was spoken by either of us. He knew he had a new "pigeon" he was dealing with. The next time it happened, I took two packs back, all the while shaking my finger at the man in the "no, no, not today" syndrome, which you were never sure would work. You either won the game or faced some nasty time in a private room cooling your heels.

Well, I had to go to the bathroom very badly, so I headed for what I recognized as the men's room from my sketchy knowledge of French. As I approached the urinal, I saw out of the corner of my eye that a person was cleaning several urinals to my right. But I was in such need of relief, that I did not pay much attention. I was about to gain that relief when a very feminine voice said, "Bonjour, Monsieur!" Excuse my French, but I wet my pants. I had no idea that women worked in men's restrooms in France and former French colonies, like Vietnam. It took me a long time to get used to this; in time, after I found out that it was a low, menial job for very poor women, I finally began to casually say, "Bonjour, Madame!" and went right ahead with my business. Of course, they always had a fresh towel waiting for me after I washed my hands, and their hands would be out for a tip. Cross-cultural training is what all Americans, especially this American, need before traveling to new countries.

"Goodbye GIs! Come back to see us again!"

That's what the "ladies of the night" yelled at us from the roof of the "hotel" in Rach Gia (pronounced "RockYah" in Vietnamese) one morning as the USAID drivers arrived in jeeps to take us to the local airport. We were low level VIPs and had been bumped out of the U.S. government compound guest quarters in the city. Because the only five star hotel was packed with South Vietnamese military leaders and their U.S. Army advisors, the fishery experts were given rooms at the only other hotel in town—the "Pleasure

House!" The local South Vietnamese army commander simply told the mayor to "clear those women out of the first floor of Hotel X, and I'll post army guards at the entrances to that floor to protect the U.S. GIs."

Apparently, the prostitutes took serious exception to this interference with their livelihoods. We were hassled nearly all night as the women played all kinds of games with our "guards," and the noise and traffic was incredible. I think the "guards" got drunk, with some obvious help from the ladies, and I finally barricaded my door with chairs. I got maybe two hours of sleep.

It was the first and only time I can remember brushing my teeth with Jack Daniel's Tennessee Sipping Whiskey! I did not trust even the bottled water they gave us. The next morning, as we stood bleary-eyed on the sidewalk waiting for our USAID vehicles and drivers to arrive, about a dozen of the ladies were on the roof, about five stories up, lining the railing, with American whiskey bottles held high, and shouting for all to hear in both Vietnamese and English, "THANKS A LOT GIs—HURRY BACK—WE GIVE YOU GOOD TIME AGAIN. BRING LOTS OF GOOD AMERICAN WHISKEY GIs!" We innocents just waved and yelled goodbye.

"Hey GIs! Over Here!"

One evening, Blair Hutchison and I were tired of eating at the USAID Guesthouse and local restaurants. We had heard that the noncommissioned officers' mess had good, cheap food and large Manhattans for twenty-five cents each, plus first-run U.S. movies. The mess was about five blocks away, and one had to pass along the wall of the presidential palace to get there. We went at about 7:30 p.m. At this time (in 1974) there was a strict curfew from 11 p.m. until dawn.

A corporal was showing "Watermelon Man" (one of the funniest movies either of us had ever seen) on a 16-millimeter sound projector in the courtyard after dinner, but the film kept breaking. We wanted to stay to see the end, but curfew was fast approaching. At about 10:45 p.m., the movie did end, and Blair and I left the mess running to make it to the USAID Guesthouse before 11 p.m. There was so much Viet Cong terrorist activity at night during this period that the South Vietnamese soldiers shot curfew violators first and asked questions later.

As we rounded a corner to dash the two blocks past the presidential palace wall, we ran right up to barbed wire that had been placed there while we were watching the movie. Somewhere in the dark a soldier yelled "HALT!" in both Vietnamese and

English. Blair and I froze with our hands in the air, and he appeared out of the dark with a Girand M-1 pointed at our heads. Then he said, after giving us a long, hard look, "Hey GIs—opening in fence over here, follow me!" We breathed a sigh of relief and followed him to the opening. Then we started running again, down the two blocks past the palace. Sure enough, at the next intersection we were challenged again to the same effect. This time the South Vietnamese soldier dropped his rifle and asked, "Hey GIs, what time you got?" Then he pointed to a wristwatch he was wearing and said, "Japenses watch, no good! Come with me—opening in fence over here, and hurry up or you get shot by next guard!" Man, did Blair and I hightail it out of there. The next time we went out for dinner, we started at 5 p.m.

On one of my trips to Rach Gia on the Gulf of Thailand, we flew from Saigon to Can Tho in an Air America Caribou airplane. Then we transferred to a Pilatus-Porter STOL, also run by Air America, for the hour flight to Rach Gia. The pilots normally climbed up to 7,000 feet immediately and stayed at that altitude until just over the Rach Gia airport, then spiraled down to avoid Viet Cong small arms fire from their jungle strongholds. Our pilot that day was a thirty year veteran who had just learned he would be laid off soon. As I sat in the copilot's seat, he unloaded his concerns about his future work. He did not follow usual flight procedures and gradually descended to the Rach Gia airstrip. At about ten miles out and perhaps a thousand feet above the ground, a "WHOMPF" shook the plane's right wing. We had been hit by Viet Cong automatic weapons fire from the ground! There was no fuel explosion, and no control surfaces were severely damaged, but it got our attention. The pilot shouted a few choice Vietnamese words as he shook his fists at "Charlie" in the jungle below.

On Halloween night in October 1974, we were comfortably sitting in the USAID regional director's home in the USAID compound in Can Tho enjoying refreshments. Neighborhood kiddies from the compound were trick-or-treating at the door in their costumes as the Vietnamese maid passed out popcorn balls and candy to them. All of a sudden, three tremendous explosions rocked the building and smashed windows upstairs. Professor Harlan Lampe, from the University of Rhode Island, and I simultaneously dove for the floor. The USAID regional director never moved from his chair and was laughing at us prone on the floor.

A little breathlessly, we asked, "What the heck was that?"

He said, "Oh, the Viet Cong try to blow up the government rice warehouses with 105-millimeter rockets fired from bamboo rocket launchers at the edge of town just at dusk, but they usually miss, then melt back into the jungle."

Some consolation—to nearly be a war casualty "by mistake." But, such were the risks taken by every American in Vietnam during this period.

Japan Was a Pleasant Cultural Surprise

Blair and I spent a lot of time in Japan, traveling there from Vietnam often during the 1973 and 1974 trips. We had perfected our research methodology for developing Vietnamese fisheries and forestry exports in Singapore. USAID officials in Saigon trained South Vietnamese government officials and private sector exporters in our methodology and then turned them loose together in Singapore. There the ethnic Chinese traders had cultural and economic empathy with their Indochinese cousins, so things were progressing quite well.

Japan was another case. The big market for Vietnamese commodities that we had been optimistically aiming at—Japan— was a tough nut to crack. We discovered earlier than many other Americans that Japanese played the international trade game strictly by their own rules.

Blair Hutchison and I opened an office in the Tokyo-Kanku Hotel in Akasaka, Tokyo, in February 1973. This was a small, conveniently located eight-story hotel in the center of Tokyo, with four floors of Asian rooms (i.e., mats on the floor and pillows like wooden blocks) and four floors of Western rooms. We had several rooms of office space, and eventually I had ten Americans and fifteen Japanese interpreters, translators, and secretaries working for me out of that office. We selected this small Japanese hotel because our Vietnamese counterparts were operating with very modest per diem amounts and could afford this hotel.

Our USAID colleagues in Saigon had told us to go to the U.S. Defense Department Hotel Sano near the U.S. embassy in Akasaka, Tokyo, and in the basement where the U.S. Army had an information center, to ask for Michi Nakamura. She was a long-time bilingual secretary who could help us locate other bilingual secretaries, interpreters, and translators to interview.

Michi not only agreed to help us locate, interview, and hire the types of Japanese employees we needed, she had some premium leave and asked if she could come to work for us the first month to serve as an overseer of the people she recommended and we hired. We were pleased and relieved. Getting good help is rarely easy, and getting it across language and cultural barriers can be excruciating.

Michi worked out so well, in fact, that after she went back to her regular job at the U.S. Army Information Center, she insisted on coming back to our offices after her 4:30 p.m. quitting time to: "Make sure my people are doing good quality work, and are keeping their American bosses happy." We were most impressed.

Blair, I, the other eight American foresters and fisheries experts, plus the Vietnamese officials who came and went, were not slave drivers. We insisted on paying Michi a good Japanese hourly wage, even though she offered to do the work for free. One evening around 7:30, Blair and I came back from a meeting with officials from the Japanese External Trade Organization (JETRO), and there was Michi at her typewriter, looking quite upset and tired.

"What are you still doing here Michi?" I asked.

"Oh, your Japanese workers did bad work today, and I am correcting mistakes—not good if we give American forester poor work when he comes back from Niko tomorrow!"

"That's O.K., Michi," I said. "You're tired; you worked all day at the Army—go on home and leave a note for whoever made the mistakes. I'll follow up on it in the morning."

Of course Michi said, "Don't worry about Michi. I will stay and do the work right!" She said it with emphasis and also said they would not charge us for the time.

Blair and I were going out to dinner and would be back in a couple of hours. We told her to just turn out the office lights and lock the door.

"See you tomorrow. Don't stay late."

"O.K. Bossman," she said with her usual big smile. "See you tomorrow afternoon!"

Blair and I lingered over dinner and the restaurant's entertainment and got back to the hotel around 11 p.m. Walking down the hall of our floor, where we also had sleeping rooms, I saw the door to the offices open and the lights still on. We walked down, looked in, and found Michi with her head on her arms, resting on the top of her typewriter. She was sound asleep.

"Michi, did you fall asleep?" I gently asked. She awoke with a start. "Ah, oh, Sandman musta got me," she said in her best American slang. We took her downstairs to the hotel restaurant, which served until 1 a.m., and insisted on getting her some dinner since she had not eaten, then hired a cab for her long trip home to the Shibuyaku-area of Tokyo. She went, but said we spent too much money on her.

That was how we found all of our Japanese employees—hard-working, loyal, kind, and always wanting to please. Of course this was a cultural awakening for Blair, me, and most of the other professional Americans who worked in Japan with us from 1973–1974. Most of us had lived through World War II and the horrible experiences of fighting the Imperial Japanese Army and Navy as civilians like me, or in the military like some of the others. We did not know the Japanese people, only the generated image of "cruel killers." But the people we met knew the benefits of hard work, loyalty to their organizations, and quality work. (I had no trouble understanding how the Japanese were able to penetrate our new car markets in the 1970s and 1980s—superior workmanship and pride in the finished product, their company, and its brands were built into their psyches.)

However, it has been pointed out to me that these traits were the very same ones that made the average Japanese citizen such a strong force in the Imperial Military government during World War II. I just happened to witness them still being practiced, but in an economic context during the postwar era following the reorganization of Japan's political economy by General Douglas MacArthur and his staff.

We had one secretary that Michi located for us, a woman who worked at a U.S. Air Force base near Tokyo for twenty-seven years, since 1946, who had been told that she would be furloughed as the United States was phasing down its work and eventually closing the base. This woman, according to Michi, was contemplating suicide. She came from a cultural background in another part of Japan where they believed that you worked for the same employer and company for life. You were never fired or told you had to quit, or, as we American government types euphemistically call it, "furloughed". With Michi's help, we convinced the woman that the U.S. Air Force was a U.S. government employer, and we were a U.S. government employer, so she would still be working for the U.S. government, and we would help her continue to work for "Uncle Sam" after that job was done. She turned out to be the best worker with the highest quality of output that we had. Michi found her another job when our work was finished four months later.

Near the end of our work in Tokyo, Blair and I invited Michi to have dinner with us as a thank you for all she had done. We picked out an elegant restaurant with a show to take her to. She told us about how her father, a Japanese civil servant in Japanese-occupied Manchuria, where Michi and her brothers and sisters were all born, refused to accept the fact that Japan had lost World War II and refused to return to Japan. He gave Michi's mother enough money for the ship steerage passage for her and the kids and did not return to Japan until he was an elderly man.

Michi said that they had gone to live with poor farmer relatives in the north of Hanchu Island but hardly had enough to eat. She said that her hands turned green from picking vegetables and grasses in the spring and early summer and orange from picking squashes in the fall and early winter. She said the last was embarrassing because at that time, squashes were usually only fed to hogs, "but we were starving, and they kept some of our hunger away." They had a small amount of rice in the winter but no meat, just some fish once in a while. It had been a grim existence and a common story, though one seldom told here in the United States.

Michi related some funny, yet tragic, stories. Finally, at dinner, Blair asked, "Michi, how is it that such a woman as you—so pretty, fun, hard-working, and loyal—has avoided getting married?" (We figured from Michi's personnel papers that she was about forty-two years old at the time.)

Her response was quick and given with a hearty laugh, "Oh, Mr. Blair, never mind about Michi and her future; I'm too Japanese for American man, and too American for Japanese man. Not to worry, Michi will take care of herself!"

We knew that Michi was the youngest daughter in the family and that she felt an obligation to take care of her mother, a charming, elderly Japanese woman whom it was my pleasure to have met. But those first few years after World War II had been very difficult for her and her family. She said that her older sister and she, as teenagers, used to read books on the roof of a small barn by moonlight (when the moon was bright enough) to conserve candles, and occasionally by candlelight before everyone went to bed. Quite often during the day they could not read at all, unless it was storming, because they all had to work hard in the relative's farm fields.

Michi's older sister was teaching herself English. Soon her mother had saved enough money for her to take the train to Tokyo to look for a job with the American occupying forces of the new "shogun," General MacArthur, who had replaced the emperor as the major deity in the country. Michi said it was difficult for her mother waiting for a letter to arrive. Soon one did, with the good news that the sister was working as a maid for an American army colonel. She would soon have enough money to come home. When she did, they all danced around their small living area. The sister said, "Michi, Michi, you must come back to Tokyo with me—they give you three big, hot meals every day, clean uniforms which you can wash in their automatic washing machine as often as you want, and there is heat in your room and the whole house all the time! What's even better, the pay is fabulous!"

Michi told her mother and sister, "But I cannot speak English." The sister said not to worry—she would teach her all the immediate phrases she would need to know on the train back to Tokyo. Michi was afraid to go, but when her mother heard of all the benefits and the money her second daughter was earning, she told Michi she must go. Soon her sister arranged for a job for Michi through the American army colonel's wife. But first Michi had to overcome a cultural/religious stigma. She and her mother were devout Shintoists, and one of the sect's beliefs about self-gratification was that when someone offered them something, they must properly decline politely three times. Then, and only then, might they accept the gift.

The first night in her new home with the U.S. Army major and his family, the wife offered Michi some of the dinner they were eating out in the kitchen where Michi was washing dishes, pots, and pans. Being the devout Shinto she had been taught to be, she politely said, "No, thank you," in English. The Major's wife said, "O.K. Michi—maybe tomorrow morning you will be hungry," and put the food away in the freezer. Michi said she went to bed so hungry she cried herself to sleep. Next morning, she figured out what to do to satisfy her hunger, her religion, and both cultures. When the major's wife offered her breakfast, Michi said, as fast as she could pronounce the words in English, "No thank you, no thank you, no thank you, THANK YOU VERY MUCH!" and grabbed the plate from her employer before she had a chance to put it in the refrigerator.

As much as we liked our Japanese employees and all the common people that we came in contact with on a daily basis, we disliked working with Japanese government officials. That was and still is, I am told by some of my Foreign Service colleagues, the pits! At all of our official visits at the Japanese External Trade Organization (JETRO) or at the Ministry of International Trade and Industry (MITI), all appointment visits were quite proper and courteous, and one could never figure out what the Japanese position was. Everything was, "Ah so, oh yes, very interesting; we will have to take this carefully under consideration and study. This sounds like a very interesting possibility." Could they tell us yes or no? Always it was maybe, or come back in two weeks and we will discuss it further. "You Americans must realize that this is a very serious proposal requiring very serious study by our top officials at the highest levels," etc. ad infinitum.

We finally appealed to the diplomats. First I talked to our head attaché in Japan, a wonderful man by the name of David Hume, who later became administrator of the full Foreign Agricultural Service of the USDA and all the agricultural attaches around the world. He said, "Howard, why don't you and your specialists try to work through the South Vietnamese ambassador here in Japan? Perhaps he can help open up doors for you! I'll do all I can to help you, but since the benefits will accrue to his country, he should have an extra incentive to help you." I had already met His Excellency, and he seemed like a very cooperative man, but my first visit was strictly protocol and a broad-brush explanation about what we would be trying to do in Japan with some of his government officials and private sector fisheries and forestry leaders. Of course he agreed with the general objectives of our work at that time.

So I made another appointment by telephone to see him. His chancellery was in his residence (later he told me how little money his government gave him to run his whole embassy, thus the doubling up of residence and offices), and it was so far out of the central area of Tokyo that I thought my cab would never get there, nor that I would have enough Japanese yen to pay for the ride (we had met downtown at the Sano Hotel for lunch, at my expense, for our first encounter). He and his wife entertained me with a lovely Vietnamese luncheon that included just the three of us. Here I learned to love the famous Vietnamese fish sauce called nuoc mam (pronounced "nook mom"). I had tried nuoc mom before (it is made of the oil of rotting fish, but if properly prepared, filtered, and purified, it is absolutely great with all kinds of foods), and I obviously had obtained the cheap, low quality version of the product. Forget it. Then I tried the ambassador's wife's high quality product and learned the proper way to use and savor it with my meal.

After dinner, local cigars, and the customary diplomatic brandy, we began to discuss the project, my concerns, and alternative approaches to the Japanese government officials in earnest. The ambassador picked up his office phone and started making calls on our behalf. In about a half hour, he lined up meetings for himself and me for the rest of the afternoon. We lingered at the chancellery; I was beginning to worry about the time and looked at my watch, as the first meeting was in about half an hour, and it had taken me one and a half hours to get to his place from Akasaka by cab with all the stoplights and traffic congestion. He noted my concern, and said, "Do not worry Dr. Steele—we have good friends here in Japan." I had no idea what he meant, but I trusted his word and relaxed.

Soon the ambassador said it was time to go. We went to his garage, and there was a driver and a large black Cadillac with the flag of South Vietnam on one fender and that of Japan on the other. Much to my amazement, as we pulled out onto the main street, the driver accelerated to about 50 miles per hour! I was as nervous as the cat on a hot tin roof.

I should not have worried. The driver used a radio phone; all traffic lights were green for us, with Tokyo police holding up opposing traffic, and we were at the Japanese MITI offices for our first meeting in about fifteen minutes. I had never before had that kind of experience and have never experienced that kind of deference since. (Where did I go wrong?)

With the South Vietnamese ambassador's help, things began to happen. After a whole series of meetings with him present, he suggested that Blair Hutchison and I accompany him to some dinner meetings in the Ginsa with some of the very same officials we had been meeting with formally during daytime work hours at MITI and JETRO. Decisions were made on a one-on-one or two-on-two basis over private dinners, with service by the famous geisha girls (very professional waitresses and hostesses; nothing untoward when I was present. Of course, I did not know what, if anything, occurred after I staggered home to my room at the Hotel Tokyo-Kanku in the wee hours of the morning. Boy, those Japanese could put a lot of sake away!)

In any case, we began to get agreements of cooperation. The projects got on line. I was told years later that the South Vietnamese businessmen who wanted to sell their fisheries, forestry, or other agricultural products to Japan had to pay finder's fees, purchase special import licenses, and so on. These forms of "black taxes" were never discussed in my presence. Perhaps the Vietnamese ambassador or his people took care of those details.

South Vietnam was corrupt from top to bottom, and I have always believed that was a major reason for its demise. The average person was hard working, with the same kinds of aspirations all of us have: peace, a decent wage for labor, education for the kids, some leisure time, savings for old age, and good medical treatment when needed. But it was obvious to the average Vietnamese in the South that there was too much corruption at all levels. A two-ton truckload of freshly caught, good looking red snapper, tuna, shrimp, or shark fins, leaving the far southeastern fishing ports on the Gulf of Thailand or the South China Sea for the nine hour trip to Saigon's central fish market would be stopped an average of fifteen times to pay "black taxes." This was in the autumn of 1974, but the practice was, and had been, endemic. Only three of the fifteen stops were, on the average, by the Viet Cong. This was what demoralized the U.S. government professionals working with me. The trucker—representing the hard-working fishermen—would be stopped and forced to hand over part of the load by the South

Vietnamese sergeant on the river bridge, by the village chief, or by the policeman at a highway check point, so that by the time he got to Saigon, half the truckload had been stolen—excuse me, taxed.

And it did not stop there. I mentioned above that the highly qualified pilots of the Air Vietnam jet transport planes, Vietnamese Air Force officers forced to fly the civilian planes, were paid the equivalent of only U.S. $60 per month, but were encouraged to smuggle in all the plane could hold in untaxed (so-called duty-free) liquor, cigarettes, other tobacco products, girlie magazines, and who knew what else. Of course the pilots would sell these items on the black market in and around Saigon and pocket what they could.

The fishermen were hit doubly hard; not only was their catch and product stolen, but on the high seas they were not allowed to have ocean navigation charts, marine compasses, or two-way radios. Why? How can a fisherman navigate dangerous waters without such equipment? The South Vietnamese Navy's theory was that if a poor fisherman in his homemade boat had this equipment, he automatically was involved in smuggling supplies to the Viet Cong!

Here was the incongruous part: the fishermen from the same fishing village banded together and sailed and fished together. One would have a compass and the navigation charts, and another boat would have a two-way radio, used sparingly and mostly for emergencies so as not to be interdicted by the South Vietnamese Navy. But interdicted they would be; their charts, compasses, and radios would be confiscated, and all the fishermen would be fined for "obviously helping the Viet Cong." Miraculously, several weeks after the confiscations, the same exact items would be presented for sale to them in the local bar by some mafia-type Vietnamese criminal. We were told this happened repeatedly in the later years of the war.

My eyes were opened while visiting a very successful shrimp company with a fleet of trawlers, a shrimp processing and freezing plant, and a modern hog farrowing and carp fishery complex that used the hog wastes. The owner had connections in high places in the South Vietnamese government, and most of the equipment I saw had, at one time or another, belonged to the U.S. Army or Navy. There was not even a pretense to hide the serial numbers or manufacturers. I do not know how the Vietnamese acquired this expensive equipment (boilers, compressors, blast-freezing and packaging equipment, quick-chill freezing and long-term, low-temperature holding rooms), which was worth hundreds of thousands of dollars, even when it had been used. I inquired about the situation back in Saigon with the USAID officials there. They just shrugged their shoulders.

One day Professor Harlan Lampe, a great marine economist from the University of Rhode Island, and I were traveling to the little fishing village of Fuc Tui to interview fishermen about their catches and where they were fishing. We had a South Vietnamese military escort and a representative of the directorate of fisheries with us, both of who spoke English. The army lieutenant had a powerful radio with him since we were traveling through the Mekong Delta jungle country. Many places in the delta were, from time to time, overrun by the Viet Cong. The VC would swoop down from the hills where they had been hiding since the night before to make a "tax collection" raid for their cause from the peasants.

The lieutenant would radio ahead to the next bridge at which there should have been a sergeant or corporal and a squad of privates with heavy weapons guarding the bridge. If he did not receive a radio response to his coded calls, we would stop while he called zone headquarters to see what was going on and to determine if it was safe for us to proceed. Sometimes the word was that the bridge had been blown up early in the morning and the troops killed, and we would have to detour and try another route. Other times, zone headquarters would raise the soldiers who had either been snoozing or for one reason or another away from their radio.

This particular day we were rolling along between bridges for a stretch of about fifteen miles, enjoying watching the Vietnamese peasant farmers and their families threshing and winnowing rice in their small fields. Men and women were cutting the ripe rice with large knives, somebody was running a small threshing machine with a small, stationary gasoline powered motor, and others, usually the teenagers and children, were winnowing the harvested grain—that is, getting rid of the chaff. They used large woven baskets for the winnowing, and it was picturesque to see the baskets being deftly thrown up and down in the air in a rhythmic syncopation. We watched group after group as we drove and radioed the morning away heading toward our objective.

Suddenly as we watched one group of peasants near the end of one field, perhaps a half mile away near a jungle hill and woods, they threw up their equipment and began to run toward the highway we were traveling on. Coming out of the jungle at the edge of the field, also on the run, were Viet Cong soldiers firing their weapons into the air. Our driver floored the accelerator on our carry-all. We asked what was happening and what the danger was.

The lieutenant replied, "Oh, the VC are collecting their taxes— they will just take all the rice the farmers have threshed and bagged since early this morning. They don't want us, and they won't kill any of the farmers, unless the farmers try to avoid paying their 'taxes;' we really aren't in any danger as long as we keep going!" I was not as blasé as he was. Harlan Lampe said that he hoped the VC were not going to "tax the fishermen we are about to visit while we are interviewing them."

On one of our visits to Can Tho, which is on the Mekong River Delta, one of the USAID workers suggested that we try the famous Mekong River Pepper Crab, as prepared in one of his favorite open-air restaurants overlooking the water. We all went—a party of about eight. The pepper crabs were selected from a batch of live ones and dropped unceremoniously into a fifty gallon drum on top of a roaring wood fire. You could tell from the marvelous odor wafting out of that drum of boiling water, spices, and other secret ingredients that this was going to be a meal to remember.

Naturally, the crab was served with steaming rice, different kinds of local vegetables, and the usual nuoc mam sauce for the various delectables to be dipped into. Sitting at tables covered with plastic tablecloths, we were given metal nutcrackers, with which to crack the cooked crab, and the ever-present chopsticks, which I must say I was quite accomplished at using by this time. (Learn to use them in Asia, or go hungry.) The meal was so delightful, and the price was ridiculously low by American standards.

As we entered the place, we noticed that hanging around just beyond the railing that separated the raised restaurant floor from the surrounding streets was a bunch of teenagers who looked to be perhaps eleven to fourteen years old. There were also several old men, perhaps in their seventies. None of them was dressed well; they were pretty much in rags. As we ate, they started moving closer and closer to the railing just beyond our tables. We became satiated with our more than ample meal, and all of us had leftovers, either on our plates or in serving bowls on the table. Then a strange thing began to happen. With much jostling and yelling in Vietnamese, it appeared that the teenagers were fighting for pecking order. The old men joined the haranguing, and the teenage boys started to beat them and the small boys. It was appalling. They were all fighting for the right to eat our leftovers, according to the local USAID workers. They were starving, emaciated, and had no sources of income.

Finally, as several of the bigger, stronger ones started to brazenly enter the restaurant over the fence, the owner shooed them away, then asked us if we were finished with our meals. When we said we were, he took our plates with the leftover scraps and threw the food into the street. Such a scramble for food scraps I had never seen before, even as a kid growing up in Depression-stricken Pittsburgh. Watching that sad scene took the pleasure out of what had, before the fight, been a most enjoyable culinary experience.

"South Vietnam Will Be a Recreation and Vacation Paradise"

That was the conclusion of the mayor of one of South Vietnam's coastal cities, revealed to us when Harlan Lampe and I were there looking at shrimp trawling and processing facilities one day in late 1974. The mayor was a sharp businesswoman who was involved in the shrimp business and a number of other activities. She entertained us royally at a marvelous dinner party at one of the city's five-star hotels, which she also owned.

We promised to visit the mayor's office the next day for a presentation of the master plan, developed by the city's planning group at the mayor's prodding (at great cost to the city) and using foreign architects and their services. The presentation included all kinds of scale models, detailed schematic diagrams, blueprints for the main buildings, a redesign of the city's streets, new beaches, a redesigned harbor, commercial district, vacation housing, and more. It was a very professional master plan.

There was one problem though, as far as Harlan and I were concerned. The planners seemed oblivious of the inroads being made by the North Vietnamese Army and the Viet Cong in the Northern provinces. Both of us felt that the South Vietnamese Army could not stem the tide without massive assistance from some other source, especially since the U S. military had almost completely departed. As I have indicated, corruption was so rampant at the higher levels, both in the private sector and the government, that it seemed the country was doomed to fall to the communists—and soon.

When we presented our concerns to the mayor privately the next day, we heard loud denials that the South would ever fall to the North and the communists. The mayor also indicated that the master plan for the city would be useful no matter who controlled the country. It seemed to Harlan and me that this was evidence of the mayor's real feelings. A sort of blanket resignation, shared by other South Vietnamese officials we knew, that the South would either be victorious or make an accord with the North Vietnamese and that in addition, the South's economic prowess was so great and badly needed by the communists that accommodation was practically guaranteed.

While neither of us could deny that the plans would be useful and valuable to whoever held power, we doubted that many high-ranking officials appointed by the South Vietnamese government, such as the mayor, would retain their positions. In fact, rumors were heavy that many South Vietnamese officials were already bailing their families out of the country for the United States, France, and other European countries. Several years after the fall of the South, we heard that the mayor had also left South Vietnam for France, having sent money to that country and to Swiss banks during the war. I have no proof of this, but many former officials were accused of similar actions.

On all of our trips to the fishing villages on and around the South China Sea and the Gulf of Siam, Professor Lampe and I were curiosity items—a previously unseen form of homo sapiens. Most of these Vietnamese, especially the children and teenagers, had never seen a civilian American or Western Caucasian up close in their lives. In the war zones where they lived and worked, this was due partly to their survival instinct.

Typically, Harlan and I would arrive in a fishing village with our Ministry of Fisheries interpreter/guide, our Vietnam Army protector, and driver, and within what seemed like only seconds, a crowd of twenty to one hundred people would gather. The teenagers would crowd closest to us to hear what was being asked of the village chief and elders, the smaller children were behind them, and the women and elderly stood in the rear.

While we asked economic and technical questions of the elders and fishermen, which were laboriously translated by our Ministry of Fisheries counterpart from English into Vietnamese, the circle grew smaller. We heard whisperings behind us. Soon the teenagers literally would be surrounding Harlan and me. The first time this happened, I felt a bit claustrophobic—we were quite closed in. Then I felt a sensation on my right arm. I looked down, and the most brazen of the teenage boys was feeling the hair on my arms with his fingers!

Those Vietnamese teenagers had heard that American G.I.s had hair all over their bodies, something that Vietnamese men had very little of. The biggest risk-taker of the teenagers was being encouraged, hence all the whispers behind us during the questioning of the elders, to go and feel their arms and tell the Vietnamese kids what it felt like.

The first time this happened, I swiftly turned around having sensed what the boy was doing. As if I had a machine gun cocked and aimed, all the teenagers and younger children surrounding us fell back in a mad dash. Then as we all realized the humor of the situation and Harlan and I laughed, they all guffawed too, and our friendship was restored.

Cultural differences around the world are absolutely mind-boggling, and this was just another new one for both Professor Lampe and me. Obviously, it also was one heck of a learning experience for those Vietnamese kids, to be retold over and over again in the next years by the bold teenage boy who felt the hair on the arm of the North American!

"The Country is Running Out of Rice, Howard. What Can We Do?"

Those were the words of Shelby Roberts, director of agricultural marketing for USAID/Vietnam and an old friend from my teaching days at the universities, when I returned to Saigon from Tokyo in September 1974. "Will you help us evaluate the problem, and then help develop a strategy to provide sufficient stocks if needed?"

"Of course," I replied.

We recruited some trustworthy researchers from the South Vietnam Ministry of Agriculture and developed a research methodology to try and determine the facts. Earlier forecasts of the South Vietnamese rice harvest had been quite favorable—it had been a good year. Although we knew that the Viet Cong were collecting their usual "black taxes" by raiding farmer's fields at harvest and threshing time, reports of this activity were not alarmingly high. Plans to import U.S. surplus rice for the South Vietnamese Army and to purchase rice from Thailand and Taiwan were modest compared with previous years. Thus, the South Vietnam Ministry of Agriculture had reduced the guaranteed price slightly, based on the optimistic yield and harvest forecasts.

The mystery to be unraveled was: What happened to the rice? Was it illegally exported? If so, how much and to where? If not, were the forecasts and projections of a bumper crop erroneous? If so, why? Had there been a Viet Cong sympathizer, a 'mole' in the ministry, creating disinformation? The array of possibilities to be researched grew!

Several of us concentrated on researching the ending stocks, harvest, and pricing variables. Things just did not add up. We began to wonder if the South Vietnamese government's reduced guaranteed price for the harvest might be a significant causative variable. We sent a team of young ministry of agriculture technicians to interview warehouse managers and review their records (and also to estimate stocks in the warehouses) and another group to interview peasant rice farmers on what they did with their harvests

Our teams found thousands of tons of rice hidden, basically by the farmers but also by some of the warehouse managers, in the ground or in unauthorized locations like school yards, truck garages, and houses. They were hiding the rice as a form of speculation, hoping that either the South Vietnamese Ministry of Agriculture would panic and raise the guaranteed purchase price, or in some instances (we suspected this, but had little, if any, proof) they were waiting to see if private traders would offer higher prices.

What economists call a "down and dirty armchair calculation" based on intensive interviewing in two provinces, when expanded, accounted for about seventy percent of the missing harvest. The crisis was not a crisis for long, and heavy advertising and arm twisting by the South Vietnamese government, plus a modest increase in the guaranteed price, started the rice flowing back to the government warehouses again.

Blair Hutchison and I worked for two different groups in USAID/Vietnam during our nearly three years of activity there. The fisheries work was under the associate mission director for capital and commercial assistance, while the associate mission director for food and agriculture oversaw our forestry work. Our administrative assistant and secretary for the fisheries work was a Vietnamese woman named Jeanne Pham. We all deeply admired Jeanne, whose skills and kindness were unsurpassed. She worked for us on lunch hours and after hours to help us make our deadlines for reports and papers. When we left for our frequent trips back to Singapore, Tokyo, Hong Kong, or Manila and had unfinished work to be done, she would always say, "Dr. Steele, Mr. Hutchison, do not worry, your work will be finished and waiting for you when you return." She never failed us.

One day, we had a formal report and presentation to make to a group of U.S. government officials late in the afternoon. We gave our short texts to Jeanne midmorning. She took her lunch period to finish typing for us. An officious State Department supervisor came into the office and saw Jeanne typing for us at about eighty words per minute. She stopped and, in our presence, berated Jeanne for working during her lunch hour, which was supposedly not permitted. Jeanne just looked at her and politely said, "Yes madam; I know madam; but Dr. Steele and Mr. Hutchison must have these copies finished for their 4 p.m. meeting with the associate mission director and his staff, and you have not given me any extra help with my duties as I have requested."

The State Department representative exited, uttering a string of salty words as she stormed past us. Jeanne looked at us and said,

"Don't worry about her—she has a whole bundle of problems!" Then she started typing at about ninety-five words per minute.

Jeanne Pham had a marvelous family, some of whom (I believe her mother and one or two sisters) had left for France long before the terrible end of the war. Jeanne's one sister, Hue Pham (or Pham Hue in Vietnamese), was a great artist and gave me a painting of a young Vietnamese lady in the traditional long, split-skirt dress (called an Ao Dai). The painting hangs in my hall at home as I type these experiences. Several of Jeanne's other sisters, including Hue, left Vietnam before it fell to the communists and ended up in California. Jeanne's father and one sister stayed and suffered for many years. Finally, Jeanne was able to get them out about eighteen years after the fall. Jeanne came to the Washington, D.C., area where her former associate mission director, Bud Hougy, sponsored her and helped her get a job.

Jeanne became a successful administrator for one of the best consulting firms for the U.S. government and still lives in the northern Virginia suburbs. Blair and I agreed that Jeanne Pham was outstanding, yet typical of the wonderful Vietnamese people we were so fortunate to know, admire, and work with. I just wish that more of our Vietnamese friends and coworkers could have escaped the communist "reeducation," i.e., concentration camps. Some of our former associates never lived to see the better times coming to their homeland.

Porters at Customs Are Also Very Helpful

On our trip back to the United States from Vietnam over Labor Day in 1973, Blair Hutchison and I were unable to get a confirmed flight all the way from Saigon to San Francisco on Pan American Airways. Their flight from Honolulu to San Francisco was already full because of the holiday, but the USAID travel agent was able to get us a connection from Honolulu to San Francisco on a Northwest flight. The only thing that concerned us was the very short time between flights, during which we had to clear U.S. customs in Honolulu, sometimes a time consuming chore.

As luck would have it, our Pan Am flight was late in leaving Saigon and lost time at stops all across the Pacific Ocean. By the time we arrived in Honolulu, our Northwest flight was long gone. Now we were in a bind. Blair Hutchison had been in Singapore and bought a number of watches, had four suits tailored, and also bought some cameras to give as presents next Christmas. All of his purchases required customs declarations and the payment of import duties. In the meantime, I was guarding our suitcases, figuring that when Blair got finished with customs, we would start the process of trying to find a flight to the U.S. mainland.

A baggage porter was watching me. Now this gentleman had some age on him and looked like a real "professional". He approached me and asked what flight we were taking and if he could check our bags through for us. I explained our plight, pointed out that Blair was negotiating with the customs people about his import duties, and that I did not know what we were going to do, it being a holiday weekend. He said that the Pan Am flight we had just arrived on would be in the servicing modality for at least another forty-five minutes and wondered if he could try and get us back on the flight to San Francisco.

I said, "Fine, but sir that flight has been full for the past three weeks; our U.S. government travel agents in Saigon tried to get us on it way back then." He said, "Please permit me to try something." I replied, "Go for it, what do we have to lose?" He picked up a phone at his station, dialed a number, and said to the person who answered, "Tea for two." After a brief conversation with whomever he had called, he hung up and said to me, "How soon can you and your friend cut loose and follow me? I think I have two seats for you. You may not like them, but they're on the flight you just came in on and will get you to San Francisco in good time. The seats are in the lounge on the upper deck of the Boeing 747, usually reserved for cabin crew breaks. But they have seat belts and are legal for passengers like you!"

Man, I ran and got Blair just as he paid his import duties and quickly explained while running with him what had just happened. The porter took our bags and told us to hop on the back of the trailer taking passengers from terminal to terminal and to jump off at the second stop it made, run up the stairs with our tickets, and ask for Maria at the Pan Am desk. Maria, he said, would get our tickets changed for us so we could reenter the Pan Am flight to San Francisco.

Taking the man at his word, Blair and I gave him a huge tip and did as he said. Maria had all the wheels greased, and in no time we were entering our Pan Am Boeing 747 once again. This time a new cabin crew of attendants welcomed us, looked at our boarding passes and must have figured we were some important company officials. One was assigned to take us up to the lounge immediately and wanted to get drinks for us without our even having asked for beverages.

I have never been treated so royally before, nor since, on any airline flight. The lovely crewmembers kept coming up to the lounge for their break and to engage in conversations with Blair and me. Talk about being plied with food and drink! I barely remember landing at San Francisco and deplaning that flight. In fact, it seems to me they had to push Blair[9] and me to get off that plane—we were having such a marvelous time we did not want to leave!

So, you never know who will come to your rescue when in a tough situation. I wish I had the name of that baggage porter now so that I could write and tell him how much we appreciated his helpfulness back then.

Dr. Pollock to the Rescue!

When Blair Hutchison and I first landed in Saigon, who should turn out to be the administrative assistant for USAID/Vietnam and the Food and Agriculture group but Dr. Ronald Pollock.

And what a great administrative assistant he was. You could not imagine the complicated requests that my team members and I made of Ron Pollock. Some of the logistics problems were almost insurmountable. Our forestry team members would want to go up into the highlands to look at tropical hardwoods, and this was a war zone! My fisheries team members would want to traverse the Mekong Delta region to interview native fishermen at their ports. Ron was the man who arranged: transportation; accommodations; competent bilingual Vietnamese/English interpreters (in some locations we needed to have trilingual interpreters who knew French as well); authorizations from the U.S. Military Command, still in charge of U.S. personnel and activities in the country; South Vietnamese army or navy guards to accompany us; South Vietnamese military approval for our trips; and finally, USAID/Vietnam approvals for all of the above and their official authorization for all the expenditures.

Our requests usually exceeded normal logistical parameters, and Ron's calm demeanor and his smiling, positive approach to solving our needs amazed us. Over and over again I heard him say, "Well that's an interesting request; wow, that may take quite a few radio and telephone calls, but let me see what I can do. Will answers by three o'clock this afternoon be soon enough for your group?" Ron was a U.S. government bureaucrat's dream come true!

Ron also had other positive attributes; he loved to entertain "visiting firemen—and firewomen," and he had a marvelous Vietnamese cook who was as sweet as could be. Ron had so many Vietnamese friends from all walks of life; it was both entertaining and culturally enlightening to visit his large apartment, and we were invited quite frequently. We also met some of the most beautiful Vietnamese women you can imagine. Ron was a very eligible bachelor at the time, and the word had spread, especially among the eligible female employees of USAID. We met his future wife, an educator named Quynh, but neither we, nor she I think, knew at the time that matrimony lay ahead. Ron and Quynh have been married for more than twenty years now and live in Sun City, Arizona.[10]

Late in the autumn of 1974, it was obvious to many of us who had spent significant periods of time with Vietnamese government workers that things were going downhill fast. We feared the worst. Ron Pollock was busy helping his legions of South Vietnamese friends, most of who had worked for the U.S. government in one form or another and would probably be marked for prison, torture, or death if the North Vietnamese and Viet Cong won. He helped them get their medical records together, documenting things like shots, x-rays showing they were free of tuberculosis, and blood tests showing they had no communicable diseases. Then he helped them think about their finances and what they would need at a minimum if they wished to join relatives in France, the United States or elsewhere. Finally (and only Ron knew the facts and numbers about this), I am convinced that he helped many South Vietnamese families apply for U.S. visas to emigrate.

The final disillusionment for me, just before the fall of South Vietnam to the North Vietnam Army and their Viet Cong allies in April 1975, was a small item sent to me from an English-language weekly paper in Tokyo. It said that the wife of the South Vietnamese ambassador to Japan—the beautiful and charming woman who had served me lunch and dinner on more than one occasion at the ambassador's residence and chancellery—had been arrested by the Japanese immigration service. She was caught allegedly trying to smuggle into Japan a large quantity of heroin in a suitcase while traveling on a diplomatic passport from Saigon to Tokyo.

During my last trip to Vietnam in October 1974, just five months before the fall of the country to the communists, we became aware that the end was near. The Vietnamese people who had worked for the U.S. government or our armed forces were frantically trying to get their families and themselves out of the country. After the war, one retired South Vietnamese general—a friend of Blair Hutchison's and Ellen Lew's who escaped to the United States—told me that many of his flag officer colleagues could not be trusted by President Nuygen Thieu. A number of them ended up surrendering to the North Vietnamese Army in February and March 1975 without firing a shot, and they turned all their U.S.-supplied equipment over to the North Vietnamese as well.

Those corrupt generals were not typical, however. The vast majority of the Vietnamese people I had worked and associated with were fine, kind, hardworking people with a great sense of humor and lovely families. They were caught in a no-win situation by their own politicians and by world powers, such as the United States, France, China, and the Soviet Union. These forces made the Vietnamese people pawns in the Cold War, which, unfortunately for all of us, was a very hot war.

The Last Days and the Fall of Saigon, April 29, 1975

Ron Pollock was one of the last USAID officials to leave Saigon by helicopter from the U.S. embassy that April day in 1975 as the North Vietnam Army and their Viet Cong allies were battling to break through the outer defenses of Saigon from the north. U.S. Ambassador Graham Martin finally declared an evacuation of all American citizens. The sad part, Ron told me several months later when he finally made it to Washington, D.C. for a visit, was that the U.S. Navy had small aircraft carriers, lots of helicopters, and Marines to aid in the evacuation off the coast near Saigon for days, perhaps even weeks. But Ambassador Martin had held back, not making a firm decision to declare an all out evacuation effort until the last minute, so their usefulness was reduced.

Ron was particularly upset because the best he could do was get fourteen of his friends and their families out at the eleventh hour. He said that when he had to abandon his apartment to go to the U.S. embassy, he left behind approximately forty people he had promised to help. There just was not enough time, and this caused Ron much trauma in the years to come. Unfortunately, nearly everything in Vietnam was rife with errors, false assumptions, poor planning and execution, and a horrible loss of civilian and military lives—including those of fifty-eight thousand Americans. One of the few honest politicians during this unfortunate period was castigated as a "war monger" and went down to ignominious defeat as a presidential candidate during the early days of U.S. involvement in Vietnam in 1964. Senator Barry Goldwater (R-Arizona), who ran against President Lyndon Johnson and lost, had quoted Union General William T. Sherman's assertion that: "War is hell; you either enter it with all you have to win, or you stay out!"

With 20/20 hindsight, we tried to fight a guerrilla war using massive firepower tactics from the "set battles" approach of the past, as directed by civilian politicians who would not let trained military professionals make the military decisions. Further, there was no strategic plan to proceed to a military victory and since there was no news media blackout, bloody scenes were on televisions in millions of U.S. living rooms every night. Finally, our military and civilian leaders were lied to about body counts as a measure of accomplishment, and the civilian leaders in turn lied to the American people about supposed successes. The cliché that we fought the wrong war, at the wrong place, in the wrong time was true about Vietnam.

I am proud of the work that my teams did to help the Vietnamese people. (South or North, it doesn't matter to me now. Although I was always a staunch anticommunist in principle, now I empathize with the common people in these developing countries.) We developed a sound economic strategy to earn badly needed foreign exchange and to create employment opportunities and agribusiness investments in forestry and fisheries products. I hope that the work we left behind has been used to positive ends. If so, our part was worth the effort and risks.

10

Under the Desert Moonlight

In 1973, the Organization of Petroleum Exporting Countries (OPEC) reduced oil production, causing a shortage of oil products and skyrocketing prices worldwide: the price of a barrel increased quickly from ten dollars to more than thirty dollars, and each OPEC country soon had huge surpluses of U.S. dollars. Shortly after OPEC cut back on pumping oil to raise prices, Secretary of State Henry Kissinger started secret negotiations with specific OPEC countries. The intent of these negotiations was to raise the cartel's daily production of crude back closer to pre-1973 levels, easing shortages and prices in the United States, and to use a lot of the banked dollars in the cartel countries for internal economic development and defense purposes, using American hardware and technicians. This was at the height of the Cold War with the Soviet Union and its allies, and the United States did not want to be vulnerable for lack of petroleum products, nor did we want to let communist influences grow in the Middle East.

These negotiations resulted in the establishment of what came to be called the "Joint Economic Commissions." The work of these commissions in OPEC countries was soon referred to as "recycling petrodollars" by U.S. government types as they planned ways to spend the oil profits being realized in those countries using American technicians and buying American products of all types.

Even before the announcement of the agreements Kissinger and his staff had reached with Saudi Arabia, Iran, Venezuela, and Egypt (all of who were our friends at that time), we in the government were gearing up to propose a variety of development programs that would use these funds being stashed away by the OPEC countries.

When Kissinger announced, with great fanfare, in early 1974 that the United States had just signed a technical cooperation agreement with Iran for $15 billion over a ten-year period, a $10 billion agreement with Saudi Arabia, and a $3 billion agreement with Egypt, things got very exciting within the executive branch of the U.S. government. Every salesman in the United States wanted to promote his business overseas and get some of that development money, and much of the development activity was in agricultural and rural development, to be managed by USDA. Since the United States was by far the largest market for petroleum products for these countries, we had an edge over other countries in proposing the agreements and negotiating favorable terms that gave priority to the purchase of American products, such as military hardware, road construction, irrigation equipment, and in hiring American technicians.

Based on my many years of experience living and working in underdeveloped countries and on my success working with government officials in those countries, USDA named me leader of Middle East Programs. I had not worked directly in that region in the past, although I had helped train a number of their agriculturalists at Ohio State and the USDA. Truthfully, I had some fears for my future success.

However, I had assurances of strong support from my administrators, so we started recruiting teams of specialists to conceptualize a number of developmental projects based on what the ministries in each country considered their priority needs. My job was based in Washington D.C. and did not involve moving my family to the Middle East, but I spent a lot of time there researching, supervising, and monitoring projects. These projects included mapping the soil types in each country; recommending, researching, and implementing the use of diversified crops that would grow under irrigation; establishing agricultural research stations and programs; and developing the agricultural marketing infrastructure. Equally important was the development of training programs in the United States for the locals who would eventually have to return home and run all the organizations and programs the expatriates had helped launch.

In Saudi Arabia, we had to build special compounds for the American families to live in because of their Islamic codes that had the force of law and were designed to keep Western influences under control and out of sight. We built walled-in groups of houses with private swimming pools, tennis courts, and social centers. In the early days, the compounds varied in size from four to twelve houses. Later the program built bigger compounds, including high-rise apartment buildings and small shopping centers stocked with American and European goods.

Construction costs were high by the standards for U.S. government housing at the time: we were budgeting $150,000 (in

1974 dollars) per family to build these compounds. That would be close to $800,000 in today's dollars, and some Washington bureaucrats thought we had gone too far. However, there were legitimate reasons for the high cost of building. Since Saudi Arabia is a desert, all of the materials had to be imported into the country at high prices. Labor was imported; Turks, Filipinos, or Yemenis were brought in to provide all the labor. Nomadic Bedouins did not have the training or skills, nor were there enough of them to perform the needed labor. The imported laborers were paid high daily rates and were transported home by air on rotations. Finally, the contractors and subcontractors were Europeans and Americans, and their services were also very expensive.

My first problem was in selecting specialists to go to these countries for two to four year assignments. It was the wives and children, rather than the technicians, who I was concerned about — especially in Saudi Arabia, where women were not allowed to drive cars or to be out on the streets alone or unveiled. In the early days, American children had to either attend boarding schools in other countries or be schooled at home by their families, as no international schools that taught in English existed. Nor were American children allowed to enroll in local Saudi schools that only taught in Arabic and emphasized Islamic religious studies.

We looked for a special type of family who understood the cultural differences and the challenges of living in such a place, and we only chose those families we felt would be able to cope with them. We interviewed wives and daughters to try and discern if they could accept the "no women may drive" law of the country, who were willing to move outside the compounds only in groups and honor the local dress code for women (no shorts, miniskirts, and so on). They also needed to understand the educational limitations and accept some sacrifices for their children in that regard.

Officials from the Arabian-American Oil Company, which had been operating in the oil fields for many years in the Jedda region of the country, had warned us that the pressures on families in that desert region often led to substance abuse, divorce, depression, and even suicide. We were admonished to choose the technicians and their families very carefully. The Company also told us that they were often confronted with the expense of having to send technicians and/or their families home before the end of their contracted tours because of the difficulties Americans faced living there.

Conducting business with the royal family in Saudi Arabia was both a crucial and delicate matter. The U.S. government recognized this and trained employees before sending them over on business. One of the best cross-cultural training programs I ever experienced was a program jointly run by the George Washington and Georgetown Universities for U.S. government employees heading to assignments in Arab countries. It was an outstanding four-week program tailored for technicians and their families who were going to Saudi Arabia, one of the most conservative Arab countries at the time.

After studying authoritative texts about Saudi history, religion, and culture, we watched two instructional videotapes. The first tape showed an arrogant Western businessman trying to persuade a Saudi government official—a member of the royal family, which has thousands of members—to quickly sign a contract committing royal funds for a project. We had to evaluate the Westerner's performance and identify the mistakes he made. He was nervous, showed impatience when his conversation with the official was interrupted, kept trying to touch the official with both hands, and so on.

There are certain specific protocols required when dealing with members of the royal family and government officials in Saudi Arabia, and the purpose of the video was to show these protocols being ignored or dismissed. For example, before discussing any business, you must first inquire about the official's family members and their health. You listen intently, and then respond to his questions about your family. Much discussion relates to sons in each family, more evidence of the macho nature of the society. Also, there are certain faux pas you must know about and never make: for example, you never cross your legs in such a way as to show the sole of your shoe to another person, as this is considered very crude and offensive. Similarly, the left hand must never be extended to touch an individual, as the left hand is used only to "clean oneself after toilet" in Arab cultures.

In Saudi Arabia in 1974, all official meetings were held in a public office, and there were twenty or thirty Bedouin tribesmen sitting in chairs lining the office walls while you were trying to interview the Saudi official. At any moment, one of the visitors may get up from his seat, walk up to the official—often a member of the royal family—and bend down to whisper in his ear. The official will apologize to you for the interruption and will then turn his attention fully to hearing the tribesman's petition or complaint, in whispered conversation. During all this, the Westerner is expected to wait patiently.

Once, Ed Watkins, an agricultural marketing specialist I had sent for from Ohio State University to come and help me evaluate the Saudi marketing problems, and I were reporting to a deputy minister of agriculture and water about our trip to the newly irrigated lands near Unezah and Buraydah and presenting our recommendations about market cold storage and other infrastructure needs. We were interrupted about ten times in a single hour; the deputy minister apologized profusely for each interruption. Finally, since he was keenly interested in hearing our report, he suggested that we go to another office where we would not be interrupted, and he locked the door to the new office behind us. But that was not good enough! We started our report again, but his assistant soon came banging on the door and insisted that the minister sign yet another petition. We finally had to come back a second day to deliver all the facts to him.

Our GWU/Georgetown training included eating a typical Saudi dinner of mutton and rice served out of a huge, round cooking pot as we sat in the middle of the floor with our legs crossed, using only our right hands—no cutlery—to eat. In traditional Saudi style, the host serves the choicest piece of mutton to the honored guest first. If there is round bread, such as nahn, you may use it to scoop the meat, rice, vegetables, and broth, remembering never to use your left hand! Also, if the sheep's eye, considered a delicacy by the Bedouins, is offered to you, you must eat it, since the host has given you the highest honor he could think of. It is very chewy. Those who were willing were given small samples to taste and chew during the meal and then described the experience in detail to their more timid classmates.

During the training, it was assumed that in all official activities we would be dealing with Saudi leaders who had been trained abroad, and this was most often the case, though not always. These leaders and their wives—mostly from Saudi Arabia, but some from other Arab countries—had attended some of the most prestigious universities in Europe and North America. Many times while I was inbound to the airport in Riyadh, perhaps fifteen minutes before landing there would be a big rush for the toilets by all the young Arab women aboard. They had been unveiled for most of the flight and usually were wearing blue jeans. They would emerge from the toilets one by one, wearing their veiled chadors, the only acceptable dress for Arab women in Saudi Arabia at that time, as dictated by the religious police, or mullahs.

Our training taught us that when westernized Arabs entertained privately in their homes, women and men would sit and converse together, as they do in Western countries. However, if at some point during the gathering somebody came to the door, there would be a flurry of excited movement while a servant went to answer it. Meanwhile, someone (usually the woman of the house) would rush to hide any evidence of alcohol, and the women would all dash to a separate room, where they were supposed to have been in the first place, segregated from the men, and put their veils back on. (American women who might have been visiting were expected to be with the Saudi women, separated from men in the house. While they were expected to honor the conservative standards of dress for women in that country, they did not have to wear veils.) If the visitor turned out to be a trustworthy westernized friend, everybody laughed, the veils came back off, drinks reappeared, and the sense of relaxed camaraderie would return. It was an odd thing to experience, this secret life that went on behind closed doors.

As part of our training, we role-played and practiced all of these correct behaviors until the instructors were convinced that we had the necessary cultural orientation to function successfully in the Royal Kingdom. However, remembering to carry them out in all real-life situations was more difficult, as I learned through experience.

While I was preparing the ground for our work in Saudi Arabia, I stayed in a large four-story guesthouse owned by JECOR (the Joint Economic Commission, Riyadh) in an official compound. Across the street from the guesthouse, behind a high wall, were four beautiful houses in a Saudi compound. We learned that a Saudi merchant from the gold market lived there with his four wives and many children.

Every evening when I returned from the ministry of agriculture and water and parked my car, the kids from next door, who wanted to practice their English, would greet me. They liked to play soccer in the street between their fenced in compound and the walled U.S./JECOR guesthouse.

"Hallow Meester," they would say. I would greet them back; one would throw me the soccer ball they were playing with, and I would either kick or throw it back amid much laughter and smiling.

One evening, as we kicked the ball back and forth, the gate to the gold merchant's compound opened, and a beautiful seventeen- or eighteen-year-old girl came out, unveiled, to call her brothers in for supper. And—horror of horrors—OUR EYES MET! She immediately jumped back behind the gate as if she had had an electric shock—this was something that was not supposed to happen! All the kids laughed uproariously. Two nights later, the same thing happened again, but at a different gate a little further up the street where I had just happened to park. This time, she shrugged and smiled, as if to say, "Oh, what the heck. Our eyes have already met, so now we know each other. Anyway, who really cares besides the mullahs? I certainly don't." I got the feeling she knew I was a friend, not an enemy, and was not going to be bothered about it.

The USDA had a letter of understanding with the U.S. Department of the Interior to jointly conduct soil surveys, build a national park and forest by the Red Sea in the southwestern corner of the kingdom, and develop irrigation and soil conservation districts. This was one way the USDA could fulfill the U.S. government's commitments in a timely way. The agreement with the Department of the Interior effectively doubled the pool of highly specialized American technicians available for recruitment for this important work. The Saudi Ministry of Agriculture and Water endorsed this cooperative agreement enthusiastically. They concluded that together the USDA and the Department of the Interior could bring about a timely implementation of the highly specialized projects the Saudis wanted.

The assistant secretary of the interior and the coordinator of international programs there was a fine woman named Barbara Burns, who had been the administrative assistant to former Senator Kenneth Keating from New York. Barbara was dearly loved by all of us at JECOR and was a very good manager.

As a hands-on manager, Barbara insisted that she needed to go to Saudi Arabia to check on all the projects her people from the Interior Department were working on. This concerned both Saudi and U.S. officials. We knew from conversations with our Saudi Arabian counterparts that as far as they knew, no woman had ever been in the ministry of agriculture and water. But, because they liked Ms. Burns after meeting her and discussing the projects with her in the United States, they said they would try to get permission from the royal family for the event. It took a while to arrange, but finally the great day arrived. When Barbara arrived in Riyadh, many Saudi ministry officials accompanied her on her trip from the airport, which gave her visit legitimacy. Well aware of Saudi customs, she was immaculately attired in a long dress with long sleeves (even though it was hot as blazes there in the desert).

As we walked down the corridor to the minister's office for a welcoming and briefing meeting, we met a waiter coming the other way carrying a full tray loaded with at least 20 small cups of cardamom coffee and saucers. Obviously he had never seen a woman in the ministry building before and probably had never even seen a woman unveiled in public, certainly not a Western woman with beautiful, striking red hair. And there she was, right before his eyes, marching down the hall alongside all the Saudi officials in their flowing robes and headdresses. The waiter turned his head to follow her with his eyes (I was about four people behind him, so I saw his every movement), and then the predictable happened: he got his feet all tangled up, lost his balance, and fell down. The tray and cups went flying and crashing to the floor. The sound of breaking china cups and saucers rang through the hall, and cardamom coffee flew in every direction.

Wondering what all the noise was about, men came charging out of their offices to see what had happened. Barbara, the deputy minister, and our whole entourage never missed a step but proceeded, with all decorum, right into the minister's reception area. Only then, when the doors were closed behind us, did we all break up laughing. Ms. Burns was concerned that the coffee man may have been hurt, but one of the deputy minister's English speaking assistants said, "Do not worry Ms. Burns, I will take care of everything. Please stay here in the office until the minister summons you and the deputy." (I think he feared that more mayhem might occur if the lovely Ms. Burns were to reappear in the hall!)

Ed Watkins and Howard in the New Lands

As part of the analysis of Saudi needs for improved agricultural marketing infrastructure that Ed Watkins and I were doing, we planned a trip to the "new lands" (formerly barren desert that the government was now irrigating with water from an aquifer deep in the earth), about 280 miles northwest of Riyadh. The government was also teaching former nomadic Bedouin tribesmen how to raise fruits, vegetables, and alfalfa under irrigation.

Ed and I spent time in the new lands analyzing the losses of perishables, such as tomatoes and melons, establishing the costs of those losses, and then recommending improvements in handling and storage methods to protect the commodities until they could be sold to final consumers. We discovered that about 60 percent of the tomato crop and 40 percent of the melons were rotting in the heat in the period between harvest and final retail sale. The cost of those wasted resources was high; refrigerated storage facilities and insulated hauling trucks would quickly pay for themselves and would also add profit to both farmers' and middlemen's accounts.

Before we left Riyadh for the desert, my intuition told me that we should do some shopping at the JECOR commissary. As I loaded up on supplies, Ed wondered aloud why I insisted on buying a huge supply of nonperishable foods—potato and corn chips, canned sardines, Spam, corned beef, smoked oysters, canned fruit, crackers, soft drinks, and pretzels—in short, just about anything that would not spoil quickly. He thought I had lost my mind. I gave him a knowing look and asked him if he had ever been to the "new lands" before, and he got the message.

After loading up our provisions, Ed, a Saudi ministry counterpart, an interpreter, a driver, and I headed across the desert to the new lands. Our driver was dressed in typical Bedouin headdress and flowing gown and had a mouth full of teeth glittering with gold inlays and fillings. When he smiled, which he did frequently, he looked like Fort Knox!

He spoke few words of English, but when he did, he spoke in a loud, authoritative voice, smiling the whole time, clearly very proud of his limited vocabulary. I am quite sure his name was Mohammed. I am also quite sure that he knew only one speed to drive our Chevrolet Sierra carryall van—full throttle!

I was in the back seat where I could see the speedometer. I knew that the ambient desert temperature was probably 120 degrees Fahrenheit, and from my days driving dairy trucks in western Pennsylvania, I knew that the inside of tires heat up to extraordinary temperatures at high speeds and can easily blow out. So as Mohammed sped over those desert roads, my eyes were fixed anxiously on the speedometer; he was driving between eighty and ninety miles an hour. I feared for our safety, but did not say anything. (I was too busy praying!)

All of a sudden, Mohammed was braking the car frantically, and we were screaming along the stone-strewn side of the road, raised perhaps forty feet above the desert floor. I was sure we were going to blow a tire and crash; the noise was deafening. But by the grace of God, Mohammed brought that missile of a three-ton Sierra van to a screeching halt. Then he turned around, flashed his gold-toothed smile at us and said, in his best English, "Time to pray!"

It turned out he had spotted a water hole on the desert floor, a good spot for him and the other Arab passengers to wash themselves and do the prayers they were required to do at that specific hour. As I prayed my own prayer of thanksgiving (for our deliverance from an untimely death) and supplication ("In the name of God, Mohammed, don't do that to me again!"), the driver, our counterpart, and the interpreter said their prayers and practiced their late afternoon ritual.

After their prayers had been offered and we set out again, Mohammed and the representative from the ministry of agriculture and water who was traveling with us got into a terrible argument, which I demanded to have translated. Mohammed wanted us to stay in the only hotel in Buraydah, but the ministry official wanted to drive another hour to Unezah, where he said there was a better hotel. Initially Mohammed won the argument; we stopped and inspected the hotel at Buraydah, but it was filthy. We then drove the extra hour to Unezah, where we found the "better hotel," which was even worse—a filthy flophouse. We insisted on driving back to Buraydah. That drive was made in silence; there were a lot of unhappy people in that car.

By now it was about 10 p.m. Not only had we not eaten dinner, but our stomachs were raw from the tension and nervousness of the two-hour hunt for a decent hotel room. We had a filthy, noisy room, and the restaurant was no better. What a mess! The spinach soup was full of sand, the mutton was stringy, tough, and tasted like the wild ram it must have been, once upon a time (a long time ago). The only decent thing we were offered there was warm Coca Cola, which at the time tasted like wine from heaven to Ed and me!

After "dinner," Ed and I quickly said our goodnights and headed for our room, where we tore into the canned food and snacks we had bought in Riyadh. At that moment, Ed decided that I was a genius, but I explained to him that I had been in this predicament before, and this practice was purely a basic survival tactic for any Westerner, especially the "spoiled American beast."

The next morning, after a fitful night of sleep, we started our research. We interviewed middlemen in the central market places of two cities that had been small oasis towns before the development of irrigation and new lands schemes by the government two years earlier. We learned that produce was spoiling everywhere in the desert sun, and by talking to the middlemen, we got our first estimates of the total daily losses. Later that day, we visited the camel auction, where some little Bedouin boys watching after their baby camels asked us to take pictures of them. Although I remembered from our training that Bedouins do not want people to take photos of them (which they believe will bring bad luck), it was hard to resist the request, especially coming from innocent children. Ed started to take shots of the boys with their camels when a loud ruckus started, and men began running toward Ed, shaking their heads frantically and shouting, "NO, NO, NO!" One of them tried to take the camera away from Ed.

Then another man came running and screamed at us in English, "Those are mullahs—you cannot take a picture of a Bedouin—any Bedouin! That is a graven image, and it will bring many years of bad luck to the person's family." Ed hastily tucked the camera back into his attaché case before the mullah who had started all the fuss could confiscate it. Finally, with the help of the English-speaking man, peace was restored, and Ed and I went on with our work.

While Ed finished interviewing some wholesale fruit and vegetable buyers in the market place, I wandered up the hill to where I could see a line of people engaged in animated conversation, standing in front of a store. Looking in, I saw that it was a butcher shop where people were lined up to get their meat. On further inspection, I saw that the butcher was wielding a large double-edged axe, rhythmically yelling something in Arabic. POW BANG! went the axe, over and over as it smashed through the carcass and hit the giant chopping block. As I looked more carefully, I realized that the carcass being butchered was that of a camel.

Now, camel meat may taste fine—I had never had any, to my knowledge (and frankly, anything would have been better than the stringy, wild-tasting mutton we had the night before) —but those people sure were excited about the event going on before our eyes! I seem to remember someone telling me that camel meat is very stringy and had quite a wild flavor. Ed and I were glad to leave it at that and depart from the scene.

Our Ministry of Agriculture and Water counterpart wanted us to visit a prominent Bedouin farmer in the area before heading back to Riyadh several days later, but it was already late in the afternoon. Ed and I were hot and tired, but diplomacy won out and we agreed to make the visit, if it could be a short one. So Mohammed, upon the word of our counterpart, floored the Sierra, and out through the desert we went, this time at close to one hundred miles per hour.

After what seemed forever, especially at that frightening speed, Mohammed drove down off the asphalt highway onto a gentle slope, following some tire tracks. Off in the distance, we could see the green vegetation of an irrigated farm. As we got closer, we could see buildings. Suddenly, we saw what looked like half a dozen penguins running out of a field of onions where they had been hoeing. Black chadors were flying as they ran. The Arabs in the car laughed uproariously, and our interpreter explained that we had surprised the women and girls as they worked in the field. Since they were unveiled, they had to dash for the cover of the compound when they saw us coming. Mohammed was happy he had almost caught them with their veils off; apparently he had played this game before.

We found the farmer working in another field—this one a field of beautiful, pear shaped Italian Roma tomatoes—where he was weeding with four of his teenage sons. Introductions were made all around through our interpreter. As we had been taught in our orientation course, Ed and I congratulated the farmer on having such big, strong sons to labor for him and help bring much wealth to this family. He smiled and said he had six younger sons too in the compound with his four wives.

The farmer inquired about our families and how many sons Ed and I had, their ages, and the type of work they did. Then he announced that, as the sun was going down, it was time for him to pray, but said that his eldest son would accompany us to the meeting area outside the main wall to his compound and serve us coffee, tea, and sweets until he and his other sons returned for conversation. When he asked if we could stay for supper, we thanked him and said that we would not offend his family by coming for a meal unannounced and uninvited—another bit of protocol we had learned—but hoped to come another day.

Back in the meeting area, the eldest son seated us on an expensive carpet where we could rest our backs against a wall and placed carpeted arm rests at our sides. We were in the gathering place where men conversed, drank cardamom coffee, smoked tobacco in water pipes, and ate, all under the desert moonlight, which was now shining brightly. Soon the eldest son reappeared with a big metal teapot, cups, saucers, and some kind of coconut sweet. We started to drink the cardamom coffee, and it soon became evident that this was the traditional bottomless cup! Another son arrived from prayers to make sure our cups were never empty. Then a third son arrived with his father, carrying a tankard of hot, steaming tea. More cups, more sweets, more cardamom coffee, and the conversation began.

As Ed Watkins and I fielded their questions about the United States and then asked a few questions of our own, I became aware that gradually, quietly, more Bedouin farmers were joining our group. Where they came from, how they got there, how they knew that American strangers were at their neighbor's farm, I have no idea. This went on for at least another two or three hours. Such questions and open conversation I have never had before. Those former nomadic Bedouin tribesmen and farmers wanted to know all about our agriculture, marketing, family life, and how we protected our daughters on the streets without them being veiled.

They asked very frank and open questions about males' sex lives in America, for example, how often the average American male engages in intercourse, and how many American men have more than one wife. Ed and I concluded that not only were these Bedouin farmers chauvinistic, showing fierce loyalty to their tribe and its leadership, but they were absolutely macho and paranoid about the role of women in their society. We did not see that this kind of attitude would change in the near future. The Arab male has such a strong mindset about his manhood and his role in making the family decisions.

These men's answers to our questions about the role of women showed a consistent pattern: women are to bear children, especially sons, and pretty much live in servitude in the households of these rural Arab communities. Wives and daughters cook, clean, sew, carry water, gather fuel (such as camel dung) for cooking fires, and so on. Their roles in these households showed them relegated to hard physical labor, as we had seen as they hoed onions in the field when we arrived.

Daughters serve the family in this manner and are protected until puberty. At that time, most Bedouin fathers make an arranged marriage for their daughter with another member of their tribe. The daughter is then expected to create more boys for the society. While the mores of these Bedouin farmers seemed quite antiquated and autocratic, Ed and I thought that as some of the sons (and perhaps the daughters too, in time) received education in other countries, these mores might change. We reminded each other of the changes in the roles and freedoms of women that had taken place in Egypt, Jordan, Tunisia, and even in Iran under the Shah. Later we talked about how even in the United States, women did not have the right to vote in elections until 1920. Social change can be slow and tedious. How rapidly will it come to the Bedouin Arabs? It will take many decades.

I have not been back to Saudi Arabia since 1976. I have heard from those who have been there recently that the society has not changed much regarding its mores and religious rules, nor significantly relaxed its rules concerning the role of women. There has been some advancement in the number of young women admitted into the local universities. They are studying technical courses such as computer science, business and accounting skills, and word processing. All hospital nurses are still imported from countries such as the Philippines and Thailand. Saudi women do not touch males in public. I am also told that the weave of the veils worn by these young college women is getting wider; so far, however, they still stay covered and no cosmetics are allowed to be seen in public.

It was an amazing evening as these new Bedouin friends were quite open in sharing their personal lives and feelings with us. They also gave Ed and me very candid information about the government's new program in these newly irrigated farmlands. They complained about how slowly the ministry of agriculture and water responded to their requests. They were concerned because they had trouble getting timely credit with which to buy their seeds and fertilizers. They thought that the price they had to pay for irrigation water provided by the government was too high. Ed and I had often heard complaints like these from American farmers in the past. I had also heard the same types of complaints in Brazil, other countries in Latin America, and Africa. In that regard, most farmers' values and complaints about their agricultural problems are pretty much the same all over the world.

The farmers showed greatest interest in what Ed and I said we might suggest to the ministry regarding facilities to significantly reduce spoilage of their crops. We said that we did not have all the details thought out yet, but we would recommend that the government build and operate protected storage and refrigerated facilities in the towns where farmers could store their beautiful produce, protecting it from the high quality and quantity losses they were currently experiencing. We also said that we felt the government should subsidize the purchase and operation of insulated trucks for transporting the farmers' products to Riyadh and other distant markets in the unfavorable weather conditions that exist in the kingdom. Their enthusiastic acceptance of our ideas was encouraging.

Finally at about 10 p.m., we headed for our flophouse hotel completely exhausted but educated anew about the Arab male's world and some of his thought processes. They were outstanding hosts and conversationalists, and we benefited a great deal from our evening with them.

11

Iran, Tunisia, and
Yemen Happenings

The $15 billion development program with Iran was another exciting experience for me as leader of Middle East programs for USDA in 1974 –1976. I remember my first trip there in the winter of 1975. It's a long way from Kennedy International Airport in New York City to Tehran. We arrived around one in the morning in Tehran. It had been snowing hard, and the airport was blanketed.

The Treasury Department ran the Joint Economic Commission program in Iran, and an assistant secretary flew in on Air Force Two with his entourage. We "grunts" from USDA, Commerce, Interior, and Defense came on a commercial flight together in tourist class, as arranged by the Joint Economic Commission office in Treasury.

The protocol officer from the U.S. embassy in Tehran was a nervous wreck. In the first place, our flight landed three hours late. Secondly, there were literally hundreds of people ten deep in the lobby of the Inter-Continental Hotel waving their reservation confirmation slips and yelling at the room clerks, who were paying absolutely no attention to them. Talk about overbooking practices. That was what upset the embassy protocol officer: the U.S. delegation had arrived so late she feared that our reserved rooms were gone, rented to the highest bidder. Her fears were well founded. We learned later that the assistant secretary of the Treasury had changed his reservation while in flight from two three-room suites to four three-room suites.

I was the lowest-ranking U.S. government official in our group. The others from the Departments of Commerce, Defense, and Interior had their rooms assigned ahead of me. The protocol officer assured me I would have a room. By this time in the morning, after some eighteen or nineteen hours traveling, I was beat, sweaty, stinky, and out-of-sorts. Finally, the protocol officer came to me and said, "They've found a room for you—the Pan Am Crew Room."

Well, I had no idea what that was, so I stupidly asked, "Does it have a bed and bathroom with a toilet and a bathtub or shower?"

"Of course," she replied, "The bellhop will take you right up."

After thanking her for her help, I followed my Iranian bellhop. As soon as he opened the door to "my room," I knew I was in trouble. Cigarettes were still smoldering in ashtrays and there were half-empty drink glasses on the desk and coffee table. I kept trying to communicate to the bellhop that somebody else was occupying this room. The bellhop kept saying, "OK, no sweat!" (Apparently this was the full extent of his command of the English language). Getting nowhere with him, I gave him a couple of American dollars, he bowed and said something nice (I assumed) in Farsi, and out the door he went.

I called the front desk, and staffers assured me that this was my room for the night. They also said that they would move me to a nicer room in the morning. I started to undress to take a steaming hot bath so I could perhaps get relaxed enough to sleep.

While I was half undressed, a knock came at the door. I opened it a crack. A surprised American gentleman asked, "Isn't this the Pan Am crew room?" I said I had been told that it was, but that the crewmembers had been moved to another room.

"Where?" he asked.

"Don't know—why don't you ask downstairs at the reception desk?" I said.

He grumbled something and exited. Blessed relief—the hot bath relaxed me, and even though it was in the wee hours of the morning, I believed I could finally get some badly needed rest. Not necessarily. Just after putting on my warmest flannel p.j.s and crawling under the covers, I reached up to turn off the light, and another knock came at the door. A second American male had a very surprised look on his face. I was definitely not one of the Pan Am stewardesses he was expecting to answer his late-night amorous visit.

"Where are the Pan Am crew members?" he asked.

"Beats me—all I know is that they have been moved," I replied. He wished me a good night and apologized for disturbing me. Finally my mind was clear enough to evaluate my situation. Am I going to be answering furtive knocks on my door all night, or am I going to get smart and get some sleep? "A-ha!" I thought, "I will put the 'Do Not Disturb' sign on the outside of the door and get some sleep." I slept for at least five hours undisturbed, thanks to the precious "Do Not Disturb" sign turning away who knows how many others!

"Howard: What did you do with those classified materials you had last night?"

Those were the words of my administrator, Dr. Quentin West, who had not only hired me in 1971 but was also responsible for naming me USDA's leader of Middle East programs in 1974. Quentin had been in Rome at the Food and Agriculture Office of the United Nations and sent me ahead to start the negotiation process with the Iranian Ministry of Agriculture, based on our approved strategy formed prior to leaving Washington, D.C. Soil surveys, agricultural agronomic research, livestock improvement, and agricultural marketing changes were high on the list of activities desired by the Iranians.

I managed to move the negotiations along, with a few disagreements to be negotiated after Dr. West arrived. Fortunately, I had the help of a fine assistant secretary of commerce, James Tabor from Pennsylvania, in Dr. West's absence. Tabor and I agreed that Dr. West should make the final commitments for the Department of Agriculture.

Quentin West arrived, and we spent an afternoon of tough negotiations with the Iranian Ministry of Agriculture officials. The Persian people were, and obviously still are, tough traders. Quentin and I had separate dinners scheduled, but we agreed to meet in his hotel room after dinner to add the finishing changes agreed to in the U.S. draft document. Hopefully, the document would be approved the next morning in plenary session, signed, and become part of the Iranian Joint Economic Commission master plan.

At about 1 a.m., Quentin said that he was very tired from his travels and the protracted negotiations with the Iranians. Would I mind taking the draft document up to my room to finish it while he took his bath and said his prayers? (Quentin was a devout Mormon, and I knew the importance of prayer to him.) He was very apologetic and went on to say that he had ordered a U.S. embassy car and driver to pick me up at the hotel at 8 a.m. and take me and the revised draft document to the embassy to be typed. He also had a crew of American typists waiting to correct and complete the finished document, then make twenty copies for the 10 a.m. plenary session back at the Ministry of Foreign Affairs, where he would meet me.

I went to my hotel room and slaved away until I finally finished with all the changes in the text, probably around 2:30 a.m. Then I made a very frightening discovery. I had a whole bundle of highly classified cables and materials that, when in a foreign country, were supposed to be locked in a secure embassy safe. Surely Dr. West did not expect me to hire a cab in the middle of the night in dangerous Tehran, cross to the other side of the city to the embassy, and deliver the classified material to the Marine guard on duty, did he? He had not said anything about having an embassy car and driver for me at that time of night. I really shouldn't disturb his sleep! What should I do?

Common sense finally struck this Pennsylvania boy far away from his Keystone State roots and Old Dominion home. "I'll put them under my mattress, sleep on them, and hope I do not get robbed during the night," I said to myself—and so I did. Up at the crack of dawn, shaved, showered, and shined, I met the driver at the lobby entrance; he whisked me across some of the most congested streets I have ever seen, and the staff was waiting for me at the American embassy. All was completed on time, and another car and driver took me to the plenary session at the Foreign Ministry.

There was Dr. West, all rested and decked out in his finest "memorandum of understanding signing clothes." He saw me carrying the twenty copies of the document, came over to me, gave them a quick glance, and thanked me profusely for all my late night and early morning efforts. Then he asked,

"Howard, didn't you have a number of classified cables and other documents with you in your room after you left me last night?"

I casually answered, "Yes."

"What did you do with them?"

"Dr. West, I slept on them—put them under my mattress—I figured you wouldn't want me out on the streets at 3 a.m. with them in a cab."

Quentin let out a hearty laugh and, turning away from me with the twenty copies of the memorandum of understanding, said over his shoulder, "I didn't hear that!"

During preliminary meetings in Washington, D.C., before we left for Iran, some strategy sessions took place where people from the participating government agencies got to know each other and the official members of the U.S. delegation. When the newly appointed assistant secretary of commerce, James Tabor, was introduced, I took special note. His name was familiar, and on inquiry I was reminded that he was formerly Pennsylvania's secretary of commerce under Governor William Scranton.

The day before Dr. West arrived in Tehran, I had been negotiating with ministry of agriculture people about USDA's proposed projects, program of work, and corresponding budget, as per our "official briefing book and script" worked out in Washington. I was told that Secretary Tabor wanted to go with me to meet the Iranian minister of agriculture early the next morning, and I was to brief him on the way in the embassy car, which would pick me up at the Inter-Continental hotel (the secretary was staying at the ambassador's residence).

The long limousine arrived at my hotel at the appointed time. Tabor was very friendly. He asked how long I had worked for USDA, my background, and my original home. I pointed out that both of us were from the Pittsburgh area—he from Squirrel Hill, I from Mt. Lebanon.

After my briefing in the car, he handled himself with the minister as if he had written the document, having grasped and then repeated every nuance and detail. Tabor did not stay in Washington, D.C. very long and was replaced by the famous Texan James A. Baker III at Commerce late in President Ford's administration.

I wish I could say that our projects in Iran were as successful as those we had in both Saudi Arabia, which was really the Joint Economic Commissions' showplace, and Egypt. Sadly, that was not the case. Behind the scenes in Iran, there was a lot of political unrest. We from the technical departments of the U.S. government were not fully aware of how close the country was to anarchy and how much the Shah and his cronies were disliked by the common people.

When we tried to talk about this subject with our Iranian counterparts at many of the dinners and lunches, they either avoided direct answers to our questions or often changed the subject. I do know that our technicians in Iran had difficulties with honesty among their Iranian colleagues and struggled to keep the project plans operational. My colleague Dr. Ken Laurent, who headed the USDA livestock project in Iran for several years, had a counterpart who tried to divert project funds. Ken was leery of his every action.

When Ken and his family went on a vacation out of the country, his counterpart tried to talk Ken into leaving some signed, blank project checks with him. (All checks required Ken's and the Iranian counterpart's two signatures.) Ken refused, and the counterpart tried to have Ken removed from the project by the U.S. government. Later, after Islamic radicals overthrew the Shah and Ken's counterpart escaped to the United States, he tried to get Ken to loan him money and find him a job. Ken was furious over the man's arrogance and complete dishonesty about events he caused in Iran.

Tunisia Is a Great Relief after Saudi Arabia's "New Lands"

After leaving Saudi Arabia following one of my trips there, Dr. West asked me to go to Tunisia and negotiate a Participating

Agency Service Agreement (PASA)—a contract between two U.S. government agencies, in this case the Agency for International Development (USAID) of the Department of State and the Department of Agriculture. The objective was to provide technical assistance and training to improve the efficiency of agricultural production and marketing in the rural sector of Tunisia and to train Tunisians in the United States in various agricultural disciplines, who would then become the human capital that carried on the work after the Americans' departure.

I was met at the Tunis airport by the director of the USAID Mission in Tunisia, Kenneth Johnson, who welcomed me warmly. I had flown into Tunis on a Saudi Arabia Airlines Boeing 707 jet, having sat up front in the jump seat behind the Saudi Airlines pilot in command. The other two pilots were Trans World Airline (TWA) pilots who were training the Saudis. There was also a TWA master mechanic on board in the cabin with us. The plane was being leased to Saudi Airlines by TWA.

After waiting at least a half hour after the plane had departed for London for the baggage to be unloaded, it became evident that my luggage with all my suits had not arrived. We filled out the necessary forms amid excuses from the Saudi Airlines ground personnel and assurances that they would deliver my clothes to my hotel as soon as they arrived.

Ah yes, to my hotel, which again was supposed to be the Inter-Continental in downtown Tunis—not exactly. The USAID mission director explained that the Tunisian presidential inauguration was to take place later in the week and that the U.S. Vice President, Nelson Rockefeller, and his group had preempted my room and those of a USDA national agricultural statistics service team also in town. Not to worry, said the mission director,

"We have a couple of villas for you at a resort on the Mediterranean Sea—a bit far out of town, but we will provide you with cars." Oh darn!

I had visions of the trip to Saudi Arabia's "new lands." But believe me when I say that the villas on the Mediterranean Sea and Tunis looked like heaven. There was a swimming pool, casino, marvelous restaurants, a nightclub, a beach on the seaside, and gorgeous Europeans for company. We USDA officials were in "hog heaven" and said a few silent thanks to the vice president for preempting our rooms in the Inter-Continental.

"We are so sorry we have been unable to locate your suitcases, Dr. Steele."

That was the message I received by telephone every time I called Saudi Airlines over the next couple of days. Finally I got frustrated — wearing the same suit I had worn and slept in on the way over from Saudi Arabia — and asked to talk with an official. He was understanding and suggested that I buy a couple pairs of slacks and sport coats, keep the receipts, and in due time Saudi Airlines would reimburse me. I did this and began to feel like a properly dressed USDA negotiating official once more.

I had a feeling that I would never see that wardrobe again. There was a shooting war going on in Lebanon, and Beirut had been the normal stop for that Saudi Airlines plane, but we overflew Beirut airport, with its rocket holes in the runway, and went on to Tripoli, Libya — not at all a friendly country to Saudi Arabia at the time. Dictator Muammar Gaddafi hated both the United States and Saudi Arabia, and I figured my wardrobe had been either stolen or off-loaded and dumped.

Those up front in the flight deck of that jet (I was monitoring the communications with a radio headset from the jump seat behind the captain) knew that the Libyan air traffic controllers were ordered to harass our flight. While they cleared about fifteen flights that arrived near the airport after we did (including five Soviet Aeroflot flights), they kept us out over the Mediterranean Sea in a "lazy eight" holding pattern.

The Saudi Airlines captain became furious. He finally told Tripoli air traffic controllers that he was very low on fuel, had one hundred and fifty persons on board, and demanded immediate clearance to land. After a lot of arguing back and forth, he finally declared an emergency, and they reluctantly cleared him for the approach to the active runway. Our problems were not over.

Once we landed, cleared the active runway, and switched to ground control, they cleared us to taxi far away from the terminal. Then they let us sit in frustration, refusing to clear us to the ramp and gate, or even assigning a gate to us. But they did clear other commercial flights to gates. Finally, a big Soviet Aeroflot intercontinental jet landed and was immediately cleared to a gate. Then they cleared us to follow the Aeroflot jet and kept telling us to follow the jet as closely as possible. We never saw a ground director until I spotted a man to the side of the Aeroflot jet, which had stopped and been secured, holding his "follow me" paddles behind his back. I pointed him out to the crew, and they asked the tower and ground control to please order him to assist us.

Sure enough, he waved us to a spot right behind, and under, the huge tail of the Aeroflot intercontinental jet. He kept telling our captain to continue, by waving his paddles on and on, until the captain and the rest of us in the flight deck thought we would hit the Soviet jet. As soon as the captain cut our jet engines, the TWA mechanic sitting in the jump seat next to me went down through the escape hatch under the flight deck and started waving off all the Libyan ground personnel who were about to open the baggage compartment and the other access doors under the plane. He told me later that he absolutely would not let anybody touch any of the plane's equipment unless he was there watching. He claimed they had broken several door handles and other delicate instruments on the outer skin of the plane. That was why he was on the plane whenever it was scheduled to land in Libya.

He also told me that one time they refueled there, the Libyans put the wrong grade of jet fuel in the plane. He thought it was to purposely tie us up for hours while they pumped the fuel out. That also cost the airline more money for being on the ground longer, probably another reason for the "error."

We finally off-loaded all the passengers destined for Libya, the air freight and baggage (later I just "knew" my wardrobe disappeared in the Tripoli airport—which turned out to be false), and tried to get permission to start our engines and taxi out for take off for Tunis, Tunisia.

This time, the air traffic controllers in the tower would speak to us only in French, which of course none of us in the flight deck spoke. Not to be daunted, the Saudi captain, nearly scarlet with rage, called one of the stewards forward who spoke French to communicate with the ground controller and air traffic controller in the tower.

More confusion and arguing ensued until we finally got a logical clearance to taxi. Now the reason the ground director had parked us so close under the tail of the Aeroflot jet became clear. We had a very difficult time turning the front end of that Boeing 707 jet without hitting the Soviet plane with our wings or fuselage. That great intercontinental jet of the Boeing Aircraft Company just could not turn on a dime under its own power, and the Libyans suddenly could not find a tractor to push us back! There was more hassling, more swearing, and more frustration, until finally we were at the end of the runway and rolling. All of us in the flight deck celebrated with shouts when we finally cleared Libyan airspace and were handed off to the Tunisian air traffic controllers. Another Cold War interlude!

Continuing with the saga of my missing wardrobe, I spent the next six months back in Washington, D.C., in conversations with a very kind American representative of Saudi Arabia Airlines in a New York City office. He finally gave up trying to locate the wardrobe, and we began a running drama with the airline's insurance carrier. I had to convince the insurance representative, with what little proof I had, of exactly what was in the wardrobe, when I had bought each item, and what each item cost.

After many more months of haggling with the insurance agent, we agreed on a cost that they would reimburse. "Don't forget the Warsaw Convention of 1939," the agent warned me many times. In accordance with that international agreement, missing luggage or personal items could be reimbursed at U.S. $6 per pound—terms that used to be printed in the tiniest print on the back of every airline ticket.

"Pretty ridiculous," I said. The story was not over yet.

One day, in the middle of the night, my wardrobe case was mysteriously dropped on the front stoop of my home in Fairfax, Virginia. How do I know it was in the middle of the night? My oldest daughter, Pat, was late leaving to catch the school bus that morning and tripped and fell over it as she rushed out the front door. This was almost one year after my trip to Tunis from Riyadh. Would you also believe that the check for the settlement from the insurance company arrived the next day?

I immediately called my friendly Saudi Airlines representative in New York City and asked him what I should do. He said, "Forget it," and asked that I please not call him again. "I've already closed this account, and I want it to stay closed." The bottom line was that the wardrobe had been off-loaded at our quick stop in Jedda and sat there in a corner of a hangar—dank, humid, salty, and hot—for nearly a year. I opened the wardrobe to find the clothes rotted. Case closed!

All of us in USDA were so happy that Vice President Rockefeller had made it necessary for us to stay in the villas at the Tunisia resort on the Mediterranean Sea. The food in the restaurants was fabulous, as were the casino, nightclubs, the swimming pool, the beach on the Mediterranean Sea, and the European beauties in their bikinis. I said in all seriousness when I returned home, that to me, Tunisia had the best mix of European and Middle Eastern cultures and people that I had seen up to that time. I think it is still true, although some of my peers who have lived in Morocco feel likewise about it.

I saw my first authentic belly dancer at one of the clubs attached to the resort. Now that is something to behold: so much lovely human anatomy in constant motion at the same time. We didn't know where to focus our attention next. I considered it a very interesting art form. The food and music were enjoyable also. After all the time Ed Watkins and I spent in the grim new lands of Saudi Arabia, Tunisia seemed like heaven on earth.

"Which of you two gentlemen is Mr. Steele?"

That question at the Tunis airport rather startled me. The USAID mission director and I were waiting at the airport for my early flight to London. As we discussed details of the Participating Agency Service Agreement between USDA and the USAID Mission that he and I had just signed at his office, the query came from behind us.

We both turned around to confront about a half-dozen people in uniforms—pilots, stewardesses, stewards, and people in business suits and lovely dresses.

"I am," I replied.

A gentleman in front of the group said: "Welcome, Mr. Steele, as the first customer on British Caledonia's newly reestablished nonstop service from Tunis to Gatwick Airport, London."

Then a flight attendant stepped forward and presented me with a large bouquet of beautiful orange blossoms. Another flight attendant handed me a pretty gift-wrapped package. I thanked them sincerely. I was really surprised, since nothing like that had ever happened to me before. I handed the orange blossom bouquet to the USAID mission director and asked the assembled crowd if they would mind my giving the orange blossoms to him for his wife, who had been so kind to me during my stay in Tunis. They agreed that I would have trouble getting them to London in a fresh condition.

I tore open the lovely package they had given me and found the most beautiful pair of silver cuff links. Etched into the middle and outlined in black and gold was the British lion, the logo and symbol of British Caledonia Air Lines. It was a lovely gift, and I thanked them profusely. A young gentleman in a spiffy business suit then identified himself as the airline's vice president for sales for all of the Middle East and Africa and said he would talk to me when we boarded, as they had more surprises for me!

After saying goodbye to the USAID mission director, I and the other thirty or so passengers boarded the Boeing 737 airliner and found our seats. The young vice president took a seat immediately across the aisle from me. A cameraman arrived to take our picture together, and he quizzed me about who I worked for, why I was in Tunis, where I was going after London, and so on. All of this for their company house organ and/or a news release, I thought.

Then the V.P. presented the other surprise. He was authorized to present me with chits for any entertainment free of charge (courtesy of British Caledonia Air Lines) while in London. Would I be staying long in London, he wanted to know. I responded that, no, I had been away from the United States in Saudi Arabia, was quite tired of traveling, and really just wanted a good hot bath at my hotel—the Sheraton at Heathrow Airport—which had been reserved by my travel office at USDA before I left some weeks before. I was to leave Heathrow Airport for New York City on Pan Am's flight at noon the next day.

He said they would honor any request that I might make and not to be shy or worry about the cost. It was a pleasure to welcome me properly as their first customer and to treat me quite royally! I said I was a licensed pilot and would love to fly up front with the crew over the Alps, as that was our route for the early part of the flight.

"No sooner said than done!" So, as had often been my custom, I sat up front with the two-man crew, and we had a lovely chat for about an hour. This was a brand new Boeing 737 with some state-of-the-art navigation equipment for that era, so the visit was doubly enjoyable as the crew demonstrated its capabilities to me

I must admit that the head stewardess kept plying me with cocktails while the crew drank soft drinks and coffee. It was soon time for a late lunch, or afternoon tea as they called it. I suggested that I would eat back in the cabin where it would be easier for them to serve me. Immediately, the vice president came to me with a copy of the *Times* of London newspaper, and started reading all the concerts, plays, and other evening activities.

"Wouldn't you let us get tickets for you to a concert, a play, a cinema, a jazz club, or something?" he asked. I demurred with thanks. Then he "hit me between the eyes" with, "Perhaps you would like the company of a 'lovely birdie' for the evening?"

Now I knew this was a serious young vice president trying to please a customer and, frankly, going way out of the bounds of rationality as far as my values were concerned, to do so. So, I decided to help him out: I asked for a tour of the countryside between Gatwick and Heathrow airports and a call to my fiancée in America from the Sheraton Hotel at the Heathrow Airport. These he arranged, and after arriving at the Sheraton, having a hot bath, and a great meal—courtesy of the airline—I called Jane and we talked for the first time in over a month. I finally relaxed and had a marvelous sleep. Thank you, British Caledonia!

Work in North Yemen

A decade later, I found myself once again in the Middle East, this time in North Yemen. My colleague and friend Dr. Larry Boone was associate director of the Consortium for International Development (CID) in the early 1980s, working out of CID's headquarters in Tucson, Arizona. CID consisted of a number of cooperating universities in the western states, from Alaska through Washington and Oregon to California, New Mexico, Arizona, Utah, Idaho, Colorado, Oklahoma, and Texas. At one time all eleven western and northwestern states were cooperating members of CID.

In April 1989 Larry called to say that the CID program leader stationed in Sanaa, North Yemen needed an agricultural marketing specialist to take a quick look at marketing problems in that country and to make some recommendations for improvements. Larry wanted to know if I was interested and asked if I could be temporarily released from my USDA duties to work on the problem in Yemen for about six weeks. CID was to reimburse USDA for my salary during the time I would be gone and pay all the other costs of my work there—for transportation, housing, and food allowance, in-country travel, and so on.

This was about a year before the unruly, tribal-based North Yemen and highly unstable Marxist South Yemen merged on May 22, 1990. In 1989 when I was there, many tricky crosscurrents were at work, including fighting among several tribal warlords. North Yemen was "a friend of the United States," while South Yemen was under the influence of the former Soviet Union. The geopolitical situation dictated that America give technical assistance and humanitarian help to this small but strategically located country, with coastline on both the Red Sea and the Gulf of Aden. The Red Sea includes shipping lanes from Egypt and western Saudi Arabia, while the Gulf of Aden blends with the Persian Gulf encompassing strategic shipping lanes for oil and other petroleum products essential to Western industrial nations.

When I got to Yemen, I was reminded of the low mountains of southwestern Pennsylvania where I had grown up. But unlike Pennsylvania, Yemen is mostly desert land, just south of Saudi Arabia's vast, desolate, uninhabited, sandy desert quarter, the Ar Rub-Al Khali. Yemen's soils are primarily sandy; the low mountainous areas are rocky and sandy, with little organic material. Along the west coast on the Red Sea the climate is hot and humid. The mountains offer more temperate weather and seasonal monsoons. To the east stretch Yemen's extraordinarily hot, dry, harsh desert lands.

The northern city of Sanaa is the political capital of today's united Yemen. The southern city of Aden, with its refinery and port facilities, is the economic and commercial capital. A low level of domestic industry and agricultural production has made northern Yemen dependent on imports for virtually all of its essential needs. Large trade deficits have been compensated for by remittances from Yemenis working abroad and by foreign aid. This remains true today.

Once self-sufficient in food production, northern Yemen had become a major importer. Land previously used for export crops— cotton, fruit, and vegetables— was now planted in khat, a mildly narcotic shrub chewed daily by Yemeni men, with no significant export market.

One look at the quality of domestic produce displayed in the central market in Sanaa convinced me that the domestic agricultural marketing system was in serious disarray. It would be my responsibility to look at the few assembly markets for domestic produce—closer to the cooler mountainous area of the country— and determine what, if anything, could be done to improve the quality and quantity of the perishable produce being shipped to Sanaa.

CID had leased a large house for the use of bachelor members of the group and as a place to house short-term specialists like me. The house had about eight bedrooms on two floors, several bathrooms, a large kitchen, dining room, and lounging room. We were quite comfortable there. CID also had an office in a small commercial building near the Yemen Ministry of Agriculture. I, like most of the CID specialists, had a small, plain office in an outbuilding of the ministry of agriculture, a "secretary"—a young boy who could type—and a counterpart from the ministry, a young officer who had recently graduated from college. Both my counterpart and my secretary spoke English.

I dutifully reported to my ministry office every morning, and then returned after lunch every afternoon. But I soon learned that my counterpart and the other Yemini professional staff never came back to work in the afternoons following lunch. Then I learned why—every afternoon and late into every evening they whiled away the ministry's time, and their own, chewing the khat leaf.

Once I had started traveling around the country looking at the produce and fish marketing activity, I saw how truly devastating the khat was to the local economy. In fact, it had a deleterious influence on the whole society. Demand for the narcotic leaf was so strong, and the prices paid were so high, that farmers were tearing out other agricultural crops and planting thousands of acres of khat bushes. Consequently, food products were now being imported from other countries at high prices to feed the population.

In effect, this narcotic habit was imposing a double tax on Yemeni society. Male workers chewed the stuff every afternoon and night, suppressing their labor productivity. They were also not eating properly, with the eventual result that disease and generally declining health would become widespread. The medical profession has been researching this possibility and has at least convinced the Yemeni president, 'Ali' Abdullah Salih. (I recently read in the *Washington Post* that he has publicly announced, with much fanfare, that he personally has abandoned the chewing of Khat and is encouraging all Yemenis to do the same.)

My counterpart at the ministry wanted me to concentrate my study at a large assembly market northwest of Sanaa, about sixty miles away. He kept mentioning a name for this assembly market, but I could not find a city or location by that name on the maps we had at the CID office. Finally, a CID specialist who had been in North Yemen some time told me that the "assembly market" was nothing more than a bunch of sellers, buyers, and truckers that would line up along the main highway at an intersection with another highway that led into the mountains.

So we arranged for a vehicle and a translator, and my counterpart and I drove to the "assembly market." It was the dirtiest, most congested and disorganized place by that name I had ever seen. There was absolutely no protection from the elements, which included heat, dust, rain, mud, and cold. There was no refrigeration, no covered storage of any kind, no potable water, or any sanitary facilities. Farmers' trucks, independent haulers' trucks, and buyers' trucks jammed the two main highways for a mile or so in each direction, and open produce was spread out everywhere. At the time of year I visited, the dust was horrible. What the "assembly market" would be like in a monsoon I could hardly guess.

After an hour or so of discussion as we walked around the place, my counterpart discovered a colleague. He told me that his friend lived in Sanaa and that he would ride back with him later; then they disappeared to chew khat together. "No need to wait for me" he had said. "Just proceed with your study."

With my Arabic-speaking interpreter to help me, I started interviewing farmers, truckers, buyers, and other sellers. Two large buyers who supplied Sanaa with all kinds of locally grown produce from up in the mountain valleys, which they bought at the assembly market, gave me estimates of their losses between their location and Sanaa at different seasons of the year.

They were most cooperative when they found out that I was there to develop a tentative design for permanent facilities that would make the area a real assembly agricultural market. I told them that I planned to recommend building a covered loading and unloading facility some distance back from the main highway. Adjoining it would be a refrigerated warehouse with rental units for the most perishable produce. That facility would be "all-weather" and would include a deep-drilled potable water system, an appropriate sanitary septic system, sanitary facilities inside for the users, a system of chlorinated water for washing produce and for employees' use, and sanitary facilities outside for the use of the general public. I determined this was a priority after observing dozens of people using a drainage ditch running away from the main highway as "the only place to toilet in the area."

Then I suggested that the government should encourage the establishment of a gasoline and diesel filling station with truck repair facilities near the junction and convenient to the new marketing facilities. I also suggested an adjacent food service facility, especially for those who had to wait for trucks to be loaded or unloaded, citizens waiting on negotiations between buyers and sellers, and so on. We were not talking rocket science here, just basic, necessary improvements. Now, we had to find the economic data to help us estimate total costs and benefits, calculate an internal rate of return, and so on.

I was fortunate that one of the CID agricultural engineers back in Sanaa had excellent estimates of construction costs in Yemen, well-drilling factors, and costs in that part of the country, and was willing to help me estimate the other construction and operational costs. I had some pretty good input cost information of my own, which I had tucked into my suitcase before leaving Washington—information about the cost of "packaged" or prefabricated refrigeration units, their compressors and condensers, by sizes and capacities, which we had imported for use in Saudi Arabia during the Joint Economic Commission/Riyadh days. These updated data, when added to freight costs for hauling by sea to Aden from Saudi Arabia or Qatar, then by truck to the proposed new market site, were helpful in making gross cost estimates.

But estimating losses and prices of produce to calculate the value of benefits were a bit trickier.

I made several return trips to the site with my interpreter, who now knew how to frame my questions, and who had become quite interested in what I was trying to do. Together we interviewed farmers about their produce sales and estimates of losses from the farm to the assembly market. We interviewed independent truckers about their costs and their problems and talked to other buyers in the market.

Through all this, my counterpart and his assistants in the ministry were of little help. They did, however, put me in touch with a dedicated elder Yemeni in the ministry who had some good marketing and price data. (Perhaps there was a connection between the usefulness of his information and the fact that he did not chew khat every afternoon.)

One more field trip was required to gather raw data—from Yemeni fishermen and middlemen at a port on the Red Sea. The fishermen would sell to middlemen if their trucks appeared at port when boats returned from sea. When this did not happen, which was often, the fishermen had to hire small trucks to carry their catch to the "assembly market" I was working with. Again, high losses and bad sanitation were endemic due to lack of refrigeration. I needed hard data to estimate the fishermen's costs, prices, losses, and returns, as well as marketing costs and losses. Fish consumption was important in Sanaa and was a fairly reliable domestic product—no khat bushes grew in the Red Sea—but without proper refrigeration from port to market losses were extremely high.

My young counterpart at the ministry and his friends persuaded me to join them at the ministry official's home for tea to discuss my proposed project. I felt a diplomatic need to go, even though I knew that they would spend the afternoon and evening chewing khat and smoking tobacco in the traditional hookah water pipe. They tried to get me to try khat; I thanked them graciously, said that I was not interested, and suggested I had a tender stomach. They took that to mean that I had the "Sanaa Two Step," or common diarrhea, which got me off the hook socially. Then, after all the business had been discussed and they were ready to resume their consumption of khat, I asked for a driver to take me to the CID residence "for dinner with the other CID specialists."

Later my counterpart wanted to accompany me to the fishing port on the Red Sea. That was fine with me—he could see how well the interpreter and I were getting along with the Yemenis we were visiting and questioning. And, he could have had a more complete knowledge of the basics of my proposed facilities had he not instead spent the time visiting a former neighborhood in a small village, looking up school chums, and chewing khat with them.

Exhausted from the trip and a day of interviewing, I went into a social hall for men, drank some hot tea, ate coconut sweets, and watched the men chew khat and gossip until I nearly fell asleep. As I needed to go out to the van to get some sleep, I thanked everyone, and took my leave. I spent some fitful hours in the van until, around midnight, they finally left the hall for the drive back to Sanaa. I told myself I would not again get into a situation like that, where I was dependent on unreliable people like my ministry associate. And I did not. But I did something even worse.

One Sunday a CID specialist who spoke excellent local Arabic suggested that we ride out in his personal vehicle to a lovely, small oasis in the desert about twenty miles from Sanaa. The oasis had an impressive artesian spring, date palms, and a well used to irrigate some crops grown nearby. He had visited the place several times before. I was intrigued, so I said yes, and we headed east on the highway out of town, then left the road and started across the desert on sand tracks toward the tall date palms in the distance.

We had seen what we thought was a farm worker near the oasis as we approached, but when we reached there, no one was in sight. We were about to get out of the carryall and explore a bit, when the CID specialist let out a long whistle, followed by a curse. "Look at our welcoming party," he said, pointing back to the way we had come. My heart sank as I saw five large pickup trucks filled with Yemenis bearing down on us. Small machine guns were mounted in the beds of two of the trucks. Putting on a brave face, our CID specialist smiled broadly and greeted the new arrivals formally, in the local dialect.

The leader in the first truck did not return the specialist's smile. It was obvious that the leader was asking him what we were doing there—on his landlord's personal property—who we were, and so forth. Our CID friend asked if he could interpret for us into English. He told us later that he had said that we were invited guests from the United States whom the president of North Yemen had asked to help the country with technical assistance and money. Then he pointed to "our" diplomatic license plates, which were actually his.

As he spoke to them, all the men in the trucks began to relax, lit up cigarettes, or shoved khat leaves into their mouths. Then the specialist remembered that we had stopped at a small supermarket on the way out and bought some sardines, smoked oysters, crackers, and canned tomatoes. We had intended to leave them with any caretaker we found at the oasis or, failing that, use them ourselves back at the house in Sanaa. Instead, the CID man offered the groceries as gifts to our welcoming committee. That did the trick.

The chief of the group took all ten cans of our produce and the giant box of crackers. He headed back for the first vehicle after telling us we had better go back to Sanaa. The CID specialist then asked who the landlord of the property was. The answer sounded like "Mohammed something or other," but as soon as we got to the highway our CID friend said we had been trespassing on the private property of one of the most powerful warlords in Yemen. He also said that the chief told him his landlord had taken the oasis back from a competitor after a brief war two weeks before. Another lucky escape!

Back in Sanaa it took two more weeks of crunching the numbers until I was satisfied that the rough assembly market plan and layout were correct. Then it was necessary to compute the estimated benefits and costs of the proposed facility. Finally, before submitting the proposal to USAID for possible funding and to the North Yemen government for approval, I needed to compute an internal rate of return, which would prove whether or not the project was viable. In fact, the projected benefits loomed so large compared with the facility's total cost that they made the internal rate of return exceptional.

I submitted one more request to the CID leadership, asking for the use of an engineer/artist to sketch a drawing of the proposed facility. This would give the officials a visual idea of what the new assembly market and its separate facilities would look like. Then we made a number of presentations of the proposal and its economic numbers, and I headed back to northern Virginia. I have heard since from a former CID specialist that the new government of the combined North and South Yemen has constructed the facility we recommended, and it has been very successful, so much so that they are designing and planning to construct several more at other assembly points in the country.

Recently, I have been doing a lot of thinking in an effort to understand why so many people in the Middle East dislike Americans and the United States. Many acts of kidnapping, terror, and murder have occurred in that region for a number of years culminating in the terrorist attacks on New York City's twin towers and the Pentagon and the aborted attempt to use United Flight 93 for the same purpose on September 11, 2001. Perhaps these acts by Middle Eastern terrorists were the "wake-up call" the United States should have had many years earlier. But, those attacks killed more Americans and others—three thousand—in one hour than the Japanese sneak attack on Pearl Harbor, Hawaii, on December 7, 1941, that brought us into World War II.

The signs of hatred for the United States and other Western countries run much deeper. Recall the overthrow of the Shah of Iran in 1979 and the holding of a large group of Americans hostage in the U.S. Embassy for more than a year; the bombings and killings of American soldiers stationed in Somalia and Saudi Arabia; the bombings of our embassies in Kenya and Tanzania; the bombing of an American pharmaceutical company in Khartoum, Sudan; the first bombing in the basement of the New York Trade Center; the attack on the USS Cole in the harbor of Aden, Yemen, and many more.

I have concluded that the Middle Eastern countries and many of their people, especially their Islamist radicals, still consider themselves beholden to a new colonialism, whether rightly or wrongly. They look on Western industrialism and liberalism as a threat to their beliefs and way of living. They are so used to being governed by despotic leaders and taught by extremist clerics that participating peacefully in a democratic evolution remains unacceptable.

It seems to me that the number of these young radicals who would blow themselves up and simultaneously kill many of their fellow citizens is relatively small. But, the damage they do, and the number of lives they take, receives immediate, worldwide media coverage. Unlike good news, bad news travels fast in today's cyberspace. The international media rarely cover the new schools, hospitals, roads, power grids, health posts, and other advances, often funded by Western generosity. Think of the millions of Afghans and Iraqis who have voted in recent democratic elections and held dyed fingers high in the air with smiles of pride about their new voting freedom. Yes, many problems still exist and require solutions and hard work in these countries. But Israel, Egypt, Palestine, Lebanon, Afghanistan, Yemen, Jordan, and others are enjoying more freedoms and peace than they have perhaps known in hundreds of years, if ever.

I am convinced that the work our specialists successfully completed in the rural and agricultural sectors of these countries, working closely with native counterparts, has been well appreciated. The participants that we sent for training have, for the most part, returned home to take up positions of authority and responsibility and plan more improvements. We wish them well. We also wish that we had accomplished more in our thirty or more years working with them and their fellow countrymen. On balance, I think we have made lifelong friends of these people, and must be patient yet consistent in helping them achieve more lasting freedoms.

12

Guatemalan Adventures

I spent so much time traveling for USDA and USAID from January 1971 through my last trip to Vietnam in October 1974 that I was nearly exhausted. By this time all international hotels looked pretty much alike, the planes were all the same inside and even the airports began to look alike.

I kept asking my administrator and deputy administrator for a resident assignment overseas, preferably in Latin America, which I loved best (and also understood the languages and culture). Nothing happened. In the meantime, my marriage to Sally was falling apart, especially with all my traveling.

With eldest son John away at Miami University in Coral Gables, Florida (one of the more expensive private universities), and son David poised to graduate from W.T. Woodson High School in Fairfax, Virginia, and raring to go to Clemson University in South Carolina, we would need the money Sally could earn. In addition, daughter Patricia was just two years behind David at W.T. Woodson and also was planning to go to college. Sally began employment teaching piano and in a flower shop.

At the time, a chance to go overseas in residence looked very good to me. The first opportunity came from another agency—the foreign agricultural service (FAS). I had met the new administrator of FAS, David Hume, in Tokyo on my numerous trips in and out of Japan on the Vietnam project. David was our attaché there for a number of years and was very helpful to my team members and me. He had outstanding credentials in FAS and was soon named its new administrator.

David and I met accidentally in the hall of the main building of the Department of Agriculture one day in the spring of 1976, and he asked me what I was doing now that the Vietnam work was over. I told him about my work as leader of Middle East programs at the economic research service and all my travels to Iran, Saudi Arabia,

Tunisia, and so on. He asked me if I would like to apply to become an agricultural attaché.

In a later discussion I called his attention to the fact that I spoke Portuguese and felt I could quickly learn Spanish. He took me immediately to meet his assistant administrator for the agricultural attaché service, Dr. Bill Horbally.

After some interviews, my name and resume were introduced to a selection panel that met regularly to recommend candidates for consideration as agricultural attaches and counselors. Dr. Horbally called me to his office to say that the panel had considered me favorably and asked if I wished to have my name actively entered into the final round of considerations for an attaché position. Of course I replied in the affirmative.

As is common practice at USDA, Mr. Hume and Dr. Horbally contacted my administrator and deputy administrator to let them know of my application. My administrators in turn contacted me to ask if I was unhappy with my supervisor, my work or something else. I repeated my often-mentioned desire to have a resident assignment overseas and to get some rest from the constant travel.

Administrator Quentin West, one fine gentleman, said: "Well, I have never believed in standing in the way of an employee who wants a change and/or a chance to be promoted. Besides, we need good people like you from the Economic Research Service in FAS, and they will benefit too!" It was hard to leave a superior like Dr. West.

Other candidates had better political connections, and I ended up number two for the open slot as attaché in Brazil, and also number two in Venezuela. Then one Monday in August 1976 my director, Dr. Bill Hoofnagle, came to my office and asked if I would like to go to Guatemala with him the next week to try to get a contract signed with the USAID Mission there. I quickly agreed.

Off to Guatemala

Two weeks later Bill and I were flying to Guatemala City. We met the USAID officials, signed a PASA contract, and I got ready to move. But there was a bit of a problem. Since the agreement was for less than two full years, USAID could not pay a housing allowance or my moving costs. So, we worked out a substitute arrangement—which later drove the USAID executive officer in Guatemala nearly crazy.

I had to maintain my apartment and pay rent in the U.S. while away in Guatemala. Sally and I had separated in June 1976, and I had moved into a two-bedroom apartment in Falls Church, Virginia, while she remained at our five-bedroom home in Fairfax County. I also had to rent an efficiency apartment in Guatemala City for the year or so I would be working there.

The USAID mission director approved my being paid the stated per diem rate in Guatemala City, Guatemala (as if I were staying in a hotel and purchasing all my meals), up to the maximum allowed. I believe it was something like eighty-nine days. Then, I would be called back to Washington, D.C., to headquarters for consultations to report on progress of the work under the PASA contract. After a few days in Washington and some strategy meetings, perhaps interviewing consultants to come down and help me with the work, I would return to Guatemala City again at the full daily per diem rate.

This arrangement worked fine for me. I could pay rent in both places (and the rent for my little efficiency apartment on Avenida Reforma in Guatemala was very expensive). The small apartment— there were four in a complex, which included a boutique, all owned and rented by the Dupree family—was in a convenient location, had a neat little kitchen, a sitting room with a television, and maid service. I could walk to the U.S. embassy where my offices were located, and there were lots of nice restaurants in the area, known as Zona 10. I made my own breakfasts, and many days my lunches too if I was not traveling. Most evenings I would either join friends from USAID or the embassy and eat out or test new locations on my own

Two important things should be noted about my time in Guatemala: (1) A devastating earthquake had hit Guatemala in the spring of 1976, with its epicenter close to Guatemala City, which killed an estimated 30,000 people and, (2) in 1968 a U.S. ambassador was assassinated in Guatemala City by communist terrorists, and Americans on official or diplomatic missions were heavily protected by the Guatemalan police and military.

As a consequence of these two events, the U.S. government was providing massive quantities of money and technical assistance to help the Guatemalan people recover from, and rebuild infrastructure destroyed by, the earthquake. The United States was also trying to promote democracy in the country, whose native peoples of Indian origin had been subjugated and did not enjoy many basic rights or suffrage under a number of Guatemalan dictators and military men.

Enter the U.S. Department of Agriculture, with USAID funds, to develop an agricultural marketing system for temperate fruits and vegetables from the highlands produced by indigenous Mayan farmers and marketers. The goal was to help increase productivity, decrease marketing losses (thus costs), provide better incomes for indigenous producers and marketers, and supply higher quality produce to the general public at lower prices. A noble concept, but not easily accomplished.

My first responsibility was to take a rough project outline, flesh it out, get USAID mission people to agree (and/or modify), and then review it with the appropriate officials in the Guatemalan Ministry of Agriculture, where U.S. government loan funds to support the project were managed. This required a number of trips around sprawling Guatemala City for meetings. Dutifully, I would put in a request for an embassy vehicle with driver to take me to the various Ministry of Agriculture offices.

Imagine my surprise the first trip when a driver pulled up to the loading location at the embassy with a four-ton Chevrolet sedan, complete with lead protection from possible grenade explosions, bulletproof glass all around, and a plain-clothes goon riding in the right side of the front seat with a sawed-off shotgun on his lap wrapped in burlap!

At every stop the goon jumped out, moving his burlap-wrapped shotgun around in all directions as he looked for terrorists. I thought: "Please do not do this—I am a lowly USDA economist, and not worthy of your precious lead bullets."

I quickly decided that I no longer wanted this type of "protection" from the U.S. embassy. Some poor terrorist might have been hiding out with instructions to blow away whoever is in that armored sedan they send around the city with a plain-clothes guard, and it could have been Howard Steele. What a waste of effort that would have been—and very injurious to my health!

For weeks and weeks, I asked the embassy to assign me a vehicle to drive myself. I had no fear, because of the devastation from the earthquake and the basic kindness of the indigenous people I was working with in the highlands.

Finally the big day arrived. I went to the USAID motor pool to pick up my vehicle. Many of the drivers were waiting for their next trips and were playing ping-pong in the garage. As soon as I arrived, all eyes were on me as the supervisor of the motor pool led me to an ancient Chevrolet. He gave me the official check-out papers to sign and the key to this worn, old "bomb" and said: "Please be careful. The brakes are not too good."

I inserted the key, started the engine, and a huge cloud of smoke, accompanied by much belching and backfiring, filled the garage. The other drivers could hardly contain their laughter. But, I floored the accelerator, and up the ramp I went, pistons clamoring for more gas and air. Once on the street, I discovered that the steering wheel had enough play in it to be rejected by any state inspection service in the United States. Oh yes, the driver's seat had a large piece of cardboard on it because the fabric was ripped.

I fought that car for three days up in the highlands of Guatemala. But, undaunted, when I returned it to the USAID garage in another cloud of blue, oil-fueled smoke (obviously the thing had needed a piston ring repair), I jumped out—again to a full audience of drivers—and in my best Spanish declared: "Boy I LOVE this car—I want this car every time I take a trip!"

What the executive officer of the USAID mission didn't know was that I used to be a truck driver in the dairy business and had practice driving all kinds of weird vehicles. Many of those duds we affectionately labeled "bombs on wheels." Recall that this individual did not like me anyway because he had to pay me per diem rates for my stay, when he wanted to cut the cost of my services to his mission.

You can imagine what happened. The motor pool supervisor probably told the executive officer of USAID what he heard. "That crazy USDA official Steele loves the old Chevy and wants it every time he takes a trip. That Chevy's not safe to drive up into the western highlands where he's working, and I'll have to send a vehicle and mechanic up to rescue him when it breaks down. Please give him one of our new jeeps."

Sure enough, the next time I ordered a vehicle, a week or so later, John O'Donnell, my supervisor in the agriculture and rural development division of the USAID mission, said: "Howard, we won the battle with the executive officer—they are assigning you one of the new CJ-5 Jeeps, bought to provide transportation for technicians following the earthquake. The only problem is the executive officer is insisting that you turn it into the embassy motor pool every evening you are in Guatemala City." I said: "If that's the only price I have to pay for flexible transportation, lead me to it."

After a few quick trips up into the highlands I concluded that Guatemala could produce beautiful temperate fruits and vegetables, although the country's marketing system was a disaster. I gained a lot of insight into what was happening by interviewing other growers and Americans who had lived and worked in Guatemala for years. I am referring to those like Dave Warren, a kind of "Johnny Appleseed" of the 1970s, who started providing improved seed and technology packages to the Mayan growers and encouraged them to produce snow peas (Chinese peapods) and garlic.

David Fledderjohn was another source of help and information. He was from an active Indiana Farm Bureau Federation family. His father was a top official, had worked overseas when David was young, and loved Guatemala. He bought a farm above beautiful Lake Atitlan and experimented with raising all kinds of temperate fruits and vegetables, then shared his successes and failures with growers all over Guatemala's highlands.

The fascinating experiences of Henry "Dutch" Schultz, resident manager in Guatemala of Hanover Foods, a Pennsylvania firm, require special mention. Schultz was trying to establish a fresh vegetable-freezing plant near Guatemala City in a highland valley called "San Jose Pennula."

"Dutch" Schultz told me the first time I met him that "Guatemala farmers suspect contract farming and forward pricing." He said that Hanover Foods had made some detailed research about the richness of the alluvial soils all over Guatemala's highlands and knew that great yields, long growing seasons, and quality produce could be profitably produced there. Hanover Foods intended to open a freezing plant for products such as cauliflower, broccoli, snow peas, okra, English peas, snap beans and other vegetables. But it could not get a sufficient number of farmers to agree to raise the vegetables under contract to the company.

I had observed that most farmers sent their beautiful produce to the congested central market in Guatemala City from distant growing areas in places like Quezaltenango, Solola and Huehuetenango. Much of the Mayan growers' produce came in on the top of buses in large cloth bags called bolsas, rotting in the sun or damaged terribly by rough handling. The food then commanded very low prices; the process was extremely wasteful.

Hanover Foods resorted to the expedient of renting land from local Mestizo farmers to demonstrate the quality, yield, and value that producing the kinds of vegetables they wanted for supplying its freezer line could bring. Reluctantly, a few innovative farmers in the San Jose Pennula valley contracted a few acres to Hanover and Schultz the next year. Yields and prices were exceptional.

What Schultz had to do was demonstrate that, contrary to common belief, only good quality produce, raised under very controlled conditions and utilizing cultural practices developed by the processing company, made a good frozen vegetable product that commanded a higher price. The common belief in Guatemala was that you sent the poor quality products that the consumers in the market place had rejected to the freezer plant. Just the opposite was true.

The USAID project I was helping to develop suggested building storage facilities near production areas to help maintain quality and avoid spoilage in transporting and handling. Our reasoning went like this: "Why pay the very expensive cost of transporting produce to a central market under primitive conditions, with all the losses of quantity and quality in route? Why not keep the produce close to the point of production, grade it and store it there, then ship full truckloads, well protected from the elements, to distant markets such as El Salvador, Honduras, Nicaragua, or to a freezing plant such as Hanover Food's?"

That seemed like a logical idea, certainly tested and proven in the United States and in other developed countries. But this was a very radical idea among the Mayan farmers of Guatemala's highlands, I soon learned. So, to put together a marketing project of this type to be loan-funded to the government of Guatemala by USAID, required a lot of research, and the development of reliable data. That is where USDA development economist Howard Steele and his team had to "bite the bullet."

The USDA Team Contained Diverse Specialists.

I hired a local consulting firm, owned by Lionel Gonzalez, a Guatemalan who had studied agricultural economics at Michigan State University, to gather reliable data for me on a whole list of temperate fruits and vegetables: How much was being produced in each region, where was the produce being marketed, by whom, and for what destinations, prices, stocks, losses, seasonality, and so on. One of the group's most important accomplishments was verifying that national statistics on agricultural production of these minor crops, as the government at that time considered them, were unreliable and imprecise. We were "plowing new ground" in Guatemala; the ministry of agriculture and natural resources was still thinking of import substitution, i.e., making Guatemala "self-sufficient" in basic foodstuffs, and opposed to importing grains at world prices.

Here are some of the crazy things this policy led to: "Look at the golden sunset on that mountainside!" That was my comment on the first trip with USAID technicians high into Guatemala's western highlands during my first week there. "Howard, don't you know what that is?" They explained that the Guatemalan government had set a very high guaranteed price per bushel of wheat to encourage farmers to increase their plantings and supplies. The guaranteed price was something like the equivalent of U.S. $4 more per bushel than the world price at that time.

Farmers are "economic beings," and at that price they were planting all the seed they could get, even by hand around the rocks on that mountain side, which would eventually have to be harvested with sickles or knives. Thus the "golden color" on the mountainside—ripening wheat clear up to the top. What a foolish policy of Guatemala's government! Economically, it would make much more sense to promote the production of temperate fruits and vegetables, and some of the luscious tropical ones in the lowlands, market them efficiently, earn high prices for quality exports, and then buy the basic grains at world prices. But in 1976, this was a bit too logical—the U.S. Government's Caribbean Basin Initiative was still seven years away.

Ivon Garcia Morenco headed my statistical team, Dr. Marshall Godwin my cooperative development team. Two more different people you could never meet; Ivon was a former Jesuit priest, who had left the order and married a librarian at Ohio State University, where he had just finished his master's degree in agricultural economics, and was extremely liberal. Dr. Godwin, a retired Marine Corps colonel who had fought at Iwo Jima in World War II, was a gruff, no nonsense, right-wing conservative who believed in the business principle of cooperative marketing development. I had fun with both of them, but had to keep them on the research subjects, and not politics!

Ivon was one of the best statistical technicians I ever had the pleasure to work with. This was before the days of personal computers, but I bought Ivon a programmable calculator that would do things like simple correlations and multiple regressions. He did a fabulous job analyzing our growing database for me. Unfortunately, as the Sandanista rebels in his native Nicaragua gained support and power, I saw a rotating group of Jesuit Order people "camping at the Garcia residence" from time to time. Ivon completed every chore I assigned him, but sometimes his mind was in his homeland. I was told later that he had become a uniform-wearing Sandanista in Managua, working in the ministry of agriculture.

Marshall Godwin was a deep-thinking economist and cooperative organizer, who had taught agricultural marketing from a business and profit-making perspective for many years at the University of Florida, then at Texas A&M. He was so sure of his principles of business management that he had little patience with anybody who disagreed with him. The problem I had was that the Mayan culture was quite different from that in the United States, and Marshall and I had a lot to learn.

Enter social anthropologist Bill Kaschek. We were blessed that Bill, a former Peace Corps volunteer who had lived with Quetchua Indians in Central America for a couple of years, and who spoke their language, was available to test some of Marshall Godwin's concepts with them. Marshall thought we should pay the producers a percentage of the value of their beautiful produce upon delivery to the local cooperative storage facility we planned to organize and have built, then settle up at the end of every month after all sales prices were known for the co-op's activities that month. This was accepted practice in the U.S. and developed countries.

After about two weeks living with the village Mayans in the producing areas, drinking chicha (a corn-liquor) with them, playing his guitar and singing with them, Bill returned to Guatemala City and told us: "No way, guys, your idea will not work!" It seemed that the producers did not even trust their neighbors who took their produce by bus or truck to market in Guatemala City. They insisted on cash payments upon delivery. Even then, they had other contacts who had access to radio or telephone reports on prices in the capital city's market place. They would "check up" on the testimony about prices from their neighbors who had taken the produce to Guatemala City upon their return, and always would make final payment that same day.

So much for the American scheme to pay a percent of average market value upon delivery to the producers' association, then settle at the end of the month. You notice I switched from using the word "cooperative" to the term "producers' association." The history of cooperatives in Latin America was checkered at best. In the worst case, many cooperative managers historically stole money from their producer members by manipulating the books. There was little, if any, oversight of accounting procedures or practices. Most producer members were not educated about finances, bookkeeping and so on, and many could not read or write. They were often fleeced by dishonest "managers."

A second reason we began using the term "producers' associations" is that term was usually understood to mean an association of agricultural producers having a common marketing problem, and consequently, a common reason for banding together. Latin American cooperatives, on the other hand, were usually broad in character and quite often were based on some social justice concept as their unifying reason for being.

Their common interest might be around a political party petitioning the national government for a school, teachers, and books in a village or region. Thus the cooperative consisted of many dissimilar members such as corn growers, bean growers, vegetable growers, cattlemen, and often common rural laborers who were landless. The issue of landlessness was frequently used as a political rallying cry. These types of cooperative organizations would petition the government to confiscate land, on which the landless were squatters, from an absentee landlord. This would also be used to form a cooperative, which became a splinter political party. Without formal education, these landless peasants were often at the mercy of unscrupulous organizers. Economic and business programs, which specific producers groups always needed, were frequently ignored by those organizers.

So we changed our ideas about financing quickly after Bill Kaschek's report. The next problem was figuring out how best to finance repayment of the government loan we were planning that would be made to the producers' association to build cold storage and the grading and handling facility, buy the office equipment, standardized packing and shipping containers, and delivery trucks needed for protected transportation, and so on.

Latin American farmers, especially small peasant farmers, are very reluctant to give up their hard-earned money to anybody outside their extended families. To get them to check off a part of their returns from sales of produce to build a reserve account in a bank somewhere for bad times was a very difficult sales job ("*Carumba*—a stock of money just sitting there to be stolen by some dishonest manager—how do I know I'll ever get it back? I'll keep it myself, thank you!").

So we had to come up with some kind of scheme. We finally settled on a modest check-off coupled with a significant underreporting of total sales price in the United States by having our broker send a very liberal "first payment reporting," which would be immediately paid to each farmer based on his or her recorded delivery to the packing facility. Though a "under reporting" of actual market prices, the price reported was so good by Guatemala standards that we knew it would be accepted immediately as cash payment, with the "sweetener" that final settlements in the U.S. market would probably yield even more payments. The final settlement—put in a trust account in the capital city and drawing liberal interest income—could be used as collateral for capital loan purposes, and the check off would pay the capital borrowing interest costs.

We sold the basic concepts to leaders of the producers' associations and to the ministry of agriculture officials, and incorporated them into the USAID project and loan proposal for the Guatemala government. Next came a competitive fight between directors of the two large associations of campesinos whom we needed to make the project work. Typically, it was a turf battle to see who would get the most political credit if the program was successful. While we were trying to resolve that battle, real shooting battles started between the Guatemalan army and the communist-inspired guerrillas deep in the highlands, and in the lowland jungles. The conflict soon ended the possibility of USAID launching our project, even though the Guatemalan Ministry of Agriculture had approved it.

The Malas de Mayo

While in Guatemala, I learned all about the *malas de Mayo*"! My fiancée, Jane Cornelius, stopped in Guatemala on her way to Brazil to pick up a planeload of Youth for Understanding Brazilian high school kids planning on spending time with American families and attending American schools. We went down to the Pacific Ocean to swim and sun and had a lovely time. After I put her back on a Pan Am 747 to fly nonstop to Rio de Janeiro, I sensed that old "Guatemala two-step to the toilet" feeling in my stomach. So I popped a Lomotil, which usually worked within a couple of hours. Not so, Americano! Despite liberal doses of Lomotil, my diarrhea got worse and worse. I panicked, fearing the dreaded dysentery amoeba or chagella protozoa.

So I got an appointment with a Guatemalan parasitologist recommended by the U.S. Embassy medical office. He quizzed my symptoms in Spanish, looked in my eyes, had me stick out my tongue, looked in my mouth and announced in Spanish: "I know what you have—you have the '*malas de mayo*', literally the "bads of May." I said: "What? I'm going to pay you the equivalent of US $25 for you to tell me I have the 'Bads of May'! That's a rip off!"

He broke up laughing. Then he gave a scientific name to the malady in Latin, prescribed some huge German-manufactured pills, and said I would be O.K. in a couple of days. But, he wanted to see me the next week. I got the pills, took them as prescribed, and felt much better in a matter of hours.

So I came back the next week, all cured although weak, and he was quite pleased with himself. I was curious about his training and medical experience. He said he graduated from New York University Medical College, and had done his intern and residency work at Bellevue General Hospital in Manhattan. I had heard some strange things about Bellevue from my college roommate Bill Walther's brother, who also graduated from there. The Guatemalan M.D. said he spent eleven years there.

When I asked him why he returned to Guatemala when he probably could earn much more money in the U.S., he said he felt he should help the medical field modernize in Guatemala. Then he got animated and said: "Look, I'm a parasitologist—I want to practice on the cutting edge of my discipline. You don't have any significant parasites in the United States of interest to my field. Here I get to examine your Peace Corps volunteers—plus my people—and your Peace Corps volunteers come up with every parasite known to medicine, and some we haven't even identified yet!"

Now we both broke up laughing. I loved my work in Guatemala and the Guatemalan people. We had some really fine parties at the U.S. Marine Security Guard barracks, or "House." It was a large home, somewhat like fraternity houses on large university campuses, at which they had the latest first-run movies delivered and showings every weekend; all American personnel were warmly welcomed. They also let all Americans use their swimming pool, and their well-stocked cash bar and lounge were open every evening. Dancing was the stock-in-social-trade every weekend night. At that time Guatemalans were also invited to participate.

Ed Watkins from Ohio State University "Bails Me Out Again."

I contracted once again for Ed's services on fruit and vegetable handling economics, his specialty at Ohio's Cooperative Extension Service back in Columbus. The reader will recall that Ed and I had some strange, amusing experiences traveling in the desert of Saudi Arabia looking at, and planning, marketing facilities to protect perishable fruits and vegetables from spoilage, described in a previous chapter

I arranged for Ed to rent the small efficiency apartment from Madame Dupree across the hall from mine. Ed and I could share cooking and dishwashing chores when we were in Guatemala City, and it made it convenient to check our experiences every evening, talk about the problems we saw during the day's travels, and so on. After about two weeks traveling and working together in Guatemala's beautiful highlands (including seeing the volcanoes, beautiful Lake Atitlan, Antigua Guatemala—the first Spanish capital of Central America, nearly leveled by an earthquake in the 1700s) Ed said to me one night: "Howard, I'm sure glad you had me go to Saudi Arabia's desert lands first, and here to Guatemala second! Had it been the other way around, I don't think I could have 'toughed it out' the full time with you in Saudi Arabia. Guatemala is 'heaven' by comparison!"

Ed and I "banged around Guatemala" together (literally, with the CJ-5 Jeep's metal roof and Guatemala's rough gravel and potholed roads) for a number of weeks. We interviewed Mayan and Mestizo farmers, Mennonite land settlement farmers from Canada, and American expatriate farmers and marketers. We learned a heck of a lot about Guatemala's agricultural sector and its problems. We worked, and argued, and compromised, and drew up plans, and rejected plans, and got opinions from USAID officials and other members of our teams, and finally wrote up our recommendations for the loan paper. Ed could cut to the core of any marketing problem faster than a speeding bullet, and his technical recommendations were absolutely on the mark—very impressive —I was fortunate that he was there to give our teams and USAID the experienced guidance we needed.[11]

Guatemala Has Much Beauty and Charm

Now for the glorious tourist part—traveling over the extinct volcanoes to beautiful Lake Atitlan. That sparkling jewel lies in a valley that you have to approach over a volcano and then drop several thousand feet. When you first spot the lake from high up on the mountain-volcano, it resembles a large diamond sparkling in the sunlight, truly impressive. You just have to stop and take in your breath at the spectacle. It is—in the vernacular of today—awesome!

The same expression may be used to describe a Sunday afternoon luncheon at Hotel Antigua Guatemala, in the heart of the colonial town of Antigua Guatemala. As mentioned above, it was the original Spanish capital of all of Central America. This was the seat of government of the Spanish conquistadors. Selected Catholic bishops were given special rights by the kings or queens of Spain, and they became "the intelligencia" of the 1600s in Central America. All of this followed the defeat and virtual enslavement of the Mayan people and suppression of their culture. It was the region's major city until a series of devastating earthquakes leveled most of the buildings and the ornate churches. There were a series of earthquakes in the 1600s and 1700s and after the most serious quake in 1773 the Spanish government finally gave up and moved away from the city. The many cathedrals, now ruins, are tourist attractions.

Ah, but luncheon at the modern—yet quaint in its colonial Spanish architecture—Hotel Antigua Guatemala was a rare experience! As one exits into the interior tropical garden (the hotel is built in a square, with a large and luxuriant tropical garden with pools, waterfalls, and lush tropical plants, orchids, parrots and macaws in the middle), one hears the lovely music of marimba bands as one can hear them only in Guatemala. This is a haunting music played by 10 or 12 musicians on wooden marimbas of various sizes (marimbas are like large xylophones, but made from tropical hardwoods rather than metal, which gives them their unique sound).

In one awning-covered area young Mayan women were making tortillas out of ground, native white corn (called *maize* in Spanish), dipping the ground flour and other ingredients in light moisture, then hand-patting and pressing the tortillas in the correct, round shape for baking in the charcoal-fired beehive oven in front of them. If you have never tasted one of these thick tortillas of Central America, made in the fashion described above, filled with refried beans, you have missed something special.

My Boss from Washington Wants to See Where We Work

Dr. William Hoofnagle, my director from USDA in Washington, D.C., had been an acquaintance and friend since 1963. He became the director of the technical assistance division of the office of international cooperation and development, and my boss, in 1974. I mentioned above that when I was sent to Guatemala in the summer of 1976, Bill had helped set up the PASA contract with the USAID Mission in Guatemala for my services.

After about six months into my labors in Guatemala, Bill let me know in no uncertain terms by telephone that he wanted to come down to see the project area. I can hear his strident voice over the phone from Washington, D.C. now: "Howard—I want to see the interior of Guatemala—where the troops work and sweat it out every day—hell Howard, I know what Guatemala City looks like— take me to where the development action is, o.k.?"

"Sure, Bill, I'll work it out for you," was my quick reply.

So I scheduled a trip up into the highlands to visit a small Indian-dominated cooperative that was selling temperate fruits and vegetables to the main terminal market in Guatemala City. Those campesinos were transporting their produce in sacks by mule to a paved road 15 miles from their village where it would wait for a bus headed for Guatemala City. They wanted to participate in our project to locate storage facilities and handling facilities closer to their fields of beautiful produce. It was a Mayan village called Tahutla.

First we had to make the drive over asphalt highways from Guatemala City to Quetzaltenango, perhaps a four-hour drive up over many mountains and volcanoes into the western highlands. Before Bill and I left Guatemala City I suggested that we take a short shopping trip to the U.S. embassy commissary. Bill could not understand why I was buying toilet paper, Ritz crackers, canned smoked oysters, cheese, sardines, canned fruits, Spam, canned beef brisket, and so on. (Remember my similar shopping excursion in Riyadh, Saudi Arabia, with Ed Watkins before traveling to the "new lands"?)

In response to his questions, I said only: "Bill, we might break down in our Sierra vehicle up in the mountains and need something to snack on until we get help and get back to a town." He seemed to accept that.

The next day when he saw our U.S. government Chevrolet Sierra carryall with a winch on the front, an assigned driver and ministry of agriculture counterpart, he asked: "Why does that vehicle have a winch on the front?"

"In case we get stuck in a mud puddle and have to hook onto a tree to get out," I answered.

Bill was beginning to get the picture.

"Where is this place Tahutla that we're going to?" he asked. The U.S. embassy driver, who spoke English, said: "Oh, doctor—it's a hard place to get to in any weather, but we'll make it; it's up a stream bed in the shadow of a volcano."

Bill immediately asked if there was any danger that the volcano would erupt while we were near; the driver just shrugged his shoulders and said in Spanish: "No, if God is willing." (*No, si Dios quiere.*)

It was a bone-jarring trip some three hours away from Quetzaltenango, Guatemala's second largest city. We did indeed travel up a dry streambed, which was the mule trail and the last bit of "interstate highway"—10 more miles to Tahutla. Near the top of the mountain from which this stream ran, we hit a thunderstorm, with hail and high winds, and torrents of water. We barely made it over the top (they call it *la cumbre*, or the pass, in Spanish) without getting flooded out. Bill was becoming nervous.

Well, the local cooperative president and his directors could not have been more hospitable. After meeting at the cooperative's office and discussing our proposed project, answering questions, and getting the "spin" on the project from the ministry of agriculture representative for the region who was traveling with us, the president said:

"Now we must go to the cathedral and meet the Monsignor, who has a great interest in your project—he wants to know how it will benefit his parishioners."

This was an important lesson I first learned in Brazil many years before. Here in the United States we would go first to the county agricultural extension agent from the land-grant university in the region in order to convince him of, and then get legitimization and support for, a specific project. Not so in Latin America—you go to the Catholic parish priest, monsignor or bishop for approval first. Without that approval, nothing will work!

Then we had to tour the cathedral and admire each and every icon. There was much gold in those statutes, and some precious gems too, all given probably at great sacrifice by the indigenous

Indians of the region who had accepted Roman Catholicism. This is not to be critical. My Presbyterian and Methodist forefathers made a lot of sacrifices for the right to be able to practice their particular religious beliefs too. But it pays to pay attention to this part of the colonial culture of Latin America's past.

Bill Hoofnagle nudged me and whispered to me about 2 p.m.: "Howard, I'm starving—when can we go to a restaurant and get something to eat?"

I made the suggestion in Spanish after hearing about the history of the 17th statue inside the cathedral. Our host replied: "I am treating you distinguished Americans to lunch at our town restaurant, in honor of your visit to our humble cooperative and village."

If Bill expected there to be a choice of restaurants, or a McDonalds in the vicinity, he was way out in "left field." I knew pretty much what we would find. Around the corner from the cathedral on the main square we came to Tahutla's only restaurant. Bill Hoofnagle was floored. He whispered to me: "Can we find another restaurant—this place is filthy!"

I explained no, this was it!

The "restaurant" was open to the street. It had a mud floor. Gobbling turkeys were tied to the tables by cords attached to their legs. In back behind the open, wood-burning stove the owner cooked on was a mud puddle in the "floor" full of little pigs. In the middle of the wallowing piglets was a girl, perhaps five years of age, drying dishes that she was washing in a metal tub at her feet while some of the piglets drank water from the tub. (It was probably 100°F in that place, and all of us were sweaty and thirsty.)

Bill said to me; "I can't eat in this place; I'll throw up. What are you going to do?"

I said "It looks to me like that pot of turkey soup the owner has made has been boiling for some time. I'm going to order a bowl of it and eat with the Guatemalans. She's boiled all the bacteria out of it by this time. Why don't you order one too? At least drink a warm Coca-Cola with the natives, even if you do not want a bowl of her specialty, turkey soup." He said; "Okay, I'll have a warm Coke, but can't we go to the car and eat some of those canned meats and crackers you bought in Guatemala City? God, I'm glad you had presence of mind to buy that stuff. I had no idea this place would be so primitive!"

Then Bill asked if I could suggest that the owner get the piglets out of the restaurant. I diplomatically asked if they could possibly shoo the pigs out of the restaurant, which the little girl did after instructions from her mother, the restaurant's owner.

Bill responded, "That makes me feel better, but they missed one piglet over there playing in the mud."

I took a hard look. "Bill, that's a baby," I said. The little girl told us that it was her baby sister. Life in the developing world. No wonder life expectancy is so short in many such countries.

Later Bill gave me the opening I was looking for as we walked to the embassy car from the restaurant a half hour or so later. I reminded him: "Bill, you said you wanted to go to where the development action is—to the boonies. So I have brought you. This is the way our people live in these developing countries. They are dedicated public servants, trying to help the people of these countries find a way to have a better level of living. It's hard, dirty work, but the rewards are so great—to see people accept new, improved ways to do things in agricultural production and marketing, to accept innovation, and to enjoy better incomes and be able to afford better living conditions."

Bill said; "Howard, you cannot understand this in the written reports that we get about these development projects back in Washington, D.C. One must see it in person to completely understand. By the way Howard, I'm going to recommend that you be assigned to stay and work here in Tahutla for a four-year assignment. You and your team are doing such a fabulous job I wouldn't want to see the work interrupted. Don't call us. We'll send a helicopter to supply you and get your messages out, o.k.?"

We have laughed about his statement many times since early 1977 in Tahutla, Guatemala. And, I believe, we made a "development economics believer" out of Bill Hoofnagle with the trip to Tahutla back then. I can not tell you how civilized, modern, and great Quetzaltenango looked when we came down out of the mountains and stopped for a day of rest and recuperation there in Guatemala's second largest city.

We finished the USAID loan document within the year—actually it took me only 11 months, and I attribute that to the fine team members working with me. The USAID mission in Guatemala was pleased with our USDA work, and that was my biggest reward. Mission Director Fred Scheick even helped rewrite a few sections that last week in Guatemala; he was that interested. We held a seminar about the project at Lake Atitlan for the USAID and Guatemala government people plus the cooperative leaders. John O'Donnell ran the seminar in Spanish.

Civil warfare broke out in the highlands between the military and the communist-inspired revolutionaries. There was still unrest there on my last trip (2001), even though the highlands are now full of temperate fruit and vegetable fields, and lots of freezer plants processing exports.

Of course, the reason for my being in Guatemala with the USDA team related to the humanitarian effort the United States and other countries had launched following the devastating earthquake there in March 1976, as related above. It was the powerful earthquake aftershocks, of which there were thousands, that leveled the adobe homes of the peasants, cracked or destroyed larger buildings, and led to most of the 30,000 or more deaths.

I used to feel minor tremors nearly every day in my apartment even up to one year later. I would feel and hear a "ratta-tat-tat-tat" vibration and sound, especially when eating at my kitchen table, which was set against an outside, supporting brick wall. That fault under Guatemala just kept on moving and shaking the earth, and my brick kitchen wall kept telling me the "news." I was a bit apprehensive, although the one full earthquake I experienced in El Salvador probably only registered a 5.0+ on the Richter scale. Trust me when I say that being in an earthquake is a frightening experience no matter how mild or strong on that scale!

Jen and I Return to Central America in 2001

My youngest daughter Jennifer and I left Honduras for Sri Lanka in 1982 when Jen was three years of age. She remembered some things about our home, our maid Norma and life in Tegucigalpa, Honduras, but not much, as one would expect. So when it was confirmed that she would finish her bachelors degree program at Boston University in December 2000, with a double major in international relations and economics, I said I would honor her accomplishment with a trip to the place of her choice. "Let's go to Honduras, Dad, and see where I used to live." she said.

Fine, I said, but with Honduras you get Guatemala and Costa Rica. Jen had never been to either Guatemala or Costa Rica and I knew she would enjoy visiting both countries.

In January 2001 we made airline reservations via the Internet and reserved a room at the pension called "La Casa Grande" near the U.S. Embassy in Zone 10 of Guatemala City.

On the airplane trip from Miami to Guatemala City I sat next to a pleasant, middle-aged Guatemalan woman who spoke excellent English. We bantered, about half in Spanish—I always try to practice my Spanish so I do not lose it completely—and half in English. When I told her what Jen and I were going to do in her country, and what I had done there in the highlands in the period of 1976–1977 following the devastating earthquake, she became very confidential. She whispered to me how bad security was in her country, and cautioned about a recent rise in violent crimes.

She said that she and her daughter had been followed to their home from the airport after their last trip to the United States, accosted in their garage by armed gunmen and robbed of an automobile, jewelry, TV sets, and other appliances. The woman said things were terrible and getting worse. At the end of this flight she and her daughter would be met at the Guatemala airport by her own hired security people.

The woman said that she and I had much in common—both of us were interested in agriculture. I asked her about her farms. It turned out that she owned farming operations throughout Guatemala that her deceased husband, an entrepreneur, had started and operated for many years despite continuous civil war in Guatemala. When I asked her what crops she produced on those farms in the highlands she said, "Irish potatoes"—she provided all the potatoes to all the McDonalds restaurants in the country, more than 50. I let out a low whistle in appreciation; I had been in Guatemala City in 1976 when the first McDonalds opened near the Hotel Eldorado-Americana around the corner from my apartment.

She also said that she raised different varieties of potatoes according to Guatemala's ecological zones so that she could supply a constant quantity of potatoes to McDonalds throughout the year. Her operation, of necessity, included potato processing and freezing facilities under carefully controlled sanitary and quality control conditions. The woman's story was just one indication of the sort of economic changes taking place in the developing world.

Jen and I attended a security briefing at the U.S. Embassy before we started our touring of the country. They recommended we not rent a car and travel on our own, but suggested letting the management of the pension where we were staying, which had a super reputation at the embassy, make arrangements for our travel with licensed tour guides.

So that was the way we toured Guatemala City, Lake Atitlan and the towns of San Francisco, Solola, Antigua Guatemala and the Mayan ruins at Tikal. I was delighted to see temperate fruits and vegetables growing on many of the Guatemalan hillsides and in the valleys. These were big, important changes from the time I was there after the devastating earthquake in 1976–1977. Jen and I had a fine time together there, and had no security problems or scares.

A Short Assignment in El Salvador

It was in El Salvador that I received my "wake-up" call about the frustrations and potential violence that would boil up in Central America among the landless peasants and lowly paid rural workers, including those in Guatemala. The comparison with events in Guatemala, and also in Nicaragua, is worth explaining here.

I was nominated to be part of a tripartite team brought to analyze El Salvador's agricultural sector in the fall of 1974. The team consisted of twelve specialists divided equally between the World Bank, the Inter-American Development Bank and the United States Agency for International Development. I was the agricultural marketing specialist on the USAID third of the team.

We stayed at the lovely Camino Real Hotel in San Salvador, the crowded capital city of the country. El Salvador is about the size of Massachusetts, with a population then of some 5.5 million people, and a rapid growth rate of more than 2 percent per year. The country had the most concentrated population of any of the Central American countries, and land and resources were mostly owned by the wealthy extended family members of the twenty-five richest families in the country, a true oligarchy. We noted landless squatters everywhere in the rural countryside, poor living conditions, primitive subsistence agriculture, and a lack of rural infrastructure, such as schools, health posts, and so on.

My responsibility was to look at the agricultural marketing facilities and recommend improvements. In the second and third largest cities in the country, Santa Anna and San Miguel, no modern central markets existed. In these cities, at what were called central markets, produce lay in the open sun or rain, there was no cold storage, no sanitation facilities, no chlorinated water, and so on. I soon started developing the economic justification for proposing that the central government build and operate new facilities in each city.

All of us on the team fanned out each morning, covered most of the country by vehicle, conducted interviews and research in our respective areas of responsibility and then returned to the Camino Real Hotel each evening to meet and discuss our findings. At these meetings over beverages and food we also discussed problems, research, and travel plans for the following days.

Several of the team members spoke no English. My Portuguese was still quite good, but my Spanish was weak, although I could understand the spoken Spanish. When I tried to speak Spanish it came out some mixture of mostly Portuguese and some Spanish (some called it "Portunole," for Portuguese-Espanole). Nevertheless, I tried to speak Spanish. This turned out to be very dangerous.

For example, in the Camino Real lounge one evening while waiting for other team members to return from their daily trips so that we could eat and discuss experiences, several of us had ordered beverages. The Ecuadorian cooperative specialist sitting next to me spoke no English, but was deeply interested in quizzing me about Brazil and my experiences there. He asked me in Spanish what the favorite Brazilian alcoholic beverage was in São Paulo state where I had lived. Just as the waitress approached our table with our beverages, I answered him loud and clear, and truthfully, I said: "*Pinga.*" This was, indeed, the Brazilian name for the sugarcane alcohol beverage in São Paulo. (In other areas of Brazil it had names such as *Cashasa* or *Auguadenta*, but in our area it was *Pinga.*)

The waitress backed away from the table with our drinks; the men, all of whom spoke native Spanish, frowned or covered their faces. I asked "*Que pasa?*" (What happened?)

They told me that I had just used the local slang expression for the man's sexual appendage! I was so embarrassed.

So I said: "*Desculpe, estoy embaraçado*" ("Excuse me, I am embarrassed," I thought I said in Spanish). They started to howl with laughter. This time I asked: "*Que foi?*" (What was it that made you laugh?)

They said: "You just said that you are pregnant, as they use that word here in Central America!"

Now I was red-faced for sure. The poor waitress did not know what to do—to approach our table with the drinks, or to go back to the bar. So this time I remembered a Portuguese phrase to tell them how truly embarrassed I was with my two terrible errors in public. So I "laid it on them": "*Um mil desculpes; tengo verguenza!*" The Ecuadorian next to me laughed so hard he fell off the end of the bench we were sitting on.

Now I switched to English, and asked those who spoke it to please tell me what I had said. They explained that this time I said that "I was pregnant and not married" in the slang of El Salvador. I said that from then on I would speak only in English and they would have to translate. Obviously my Spanish was not up to speed, and my Portuguese knowledge could only get me into a lot of trouble, as it already had!

One night after a full day of travel throughout the country, following a good dinner and planning session, I went to bed after taking a good, hot bath, and fell into a sound sleep. Some readers may remember the old motels along U.S. two-lane highways. Many of them had beds equipped with vibrators to massage the weary traveler. You put a quarter in a slot on the head frame of the bed, and it vibrated for ten minutes or so, very pleasant. At perhaps 2 a.m. I awoke in my bed vibrating!

In my semiconscious state, I thought: "Hey, I didn't put a quarter in that bed slot!" Then I heard the pictures on the wall start to shake, and things began to fall on the floor, then a loud warning bell outside my door began to clang and I realized that I was living through an earthquake. The whole hotel started to shake, as did my legs.

Somehow my subconscious self took over. In a flash I was up out of that bed, had pulled on my pants, grabbed my money, my passport, and my airplane tickets and was out the door and down to the ground. It was all over in a matter of a couple of minutes, but I am here to tell you it is one frightening experience. I do not ever want to witness a really big one!

The upshot of all our work in El Salvador was that the final report, in addition to recommending many physical and operational improvements for the country's agricultural sector, strongly recommended that the government begin to find a way to distribute land to the peasants who were working it. Most were paid slave wages (if paid at all) to absentee owners, or were tenant farmers charged exorbitant rents and "shares" of the crops.

Revolution was in the air. Of all the agricultural sector studies those three groups did in Central American countries in this period, the El Salvador report was the only one that the host government refused to grant permission to publish. We had gone from "preaching to meddling." So I was not at all surprised when the revolution broke out in El Salvador in the 1980s. Thank goodness some progress is now being made in finding ways to help the rural peasants and to develop land markets and land distribution for their benefit.

Thankfully, too, a peace process has been negotiated recently in Guatemala after the longest civil war in Central America, going back to 1960. The indigenous Mayan Indians and many mestizos still do not have universal suffrage. I guess that it is very difficult to reverse values and procedures ingrained into a society for nearly 500 years. But other countries in Central America have made significant progress, and I am convinced that Guatemala will too. The human and natural resources there are incredible and deserve to be developed in freedom and peace.

13

On to Bolivia

I have mentioned the unraveling of my first marriage and my attraction to Jane Cornelius, who had arrived at USDA from the Iowa State University in August 1974. Jane had worked for Iowa State's Office of International Student Affairs and came to the International Training Division of our agency to work with foreign student participants.

She and I soon found we shared many interests regarding developing countries and their students, a number of whom would become future leaders in their countries. Jane was intrigued by my desire to work in residence in developing countries under USAID technical assistance development programs. I convinced her that we should get married and live overseas.

First, however, I had to legally separate from Sally, explain my intentions to our three children, and wait out Virginia's separation time requirement. Fortunately, USDA sent me to Guatemala soon after I moved to an apartment in Falls Church, Virginia in June 1976.

In May 1975 Jane, having become disenchanted with her job at USDA, accepted one as regional director for Youth for Understanding (YFU), the high school international youth exchange program. YFU's international headquarters was in Ann Arbor, Michigan, so Jane packed up, bought a new AMC Gremlin, and moved. She traveled to about twenty-two states and often went to Brazil, YFU's biggest country program at that time.

We carried on our romance by telephone, letters, and visits at every opportunity. Fortunately for me, Jane often flew to Brazil with participants, and Pan Am stopped in Guatemala City on its way to Rio de Janeiro, so we would see each other on her trip down or on the way back. I was also called to Washington, D.C., frequently for consultations, and found a way to route myself via

Detroit Metropolitan Airport coming up or going back at a small additional cost, which I paid myself.

We married at the Methodist chapel just off the campus of the University of Michigan on July 30, 1977, after a courtship of more than two-and-a-half years. My three older children all participated in the ceremony, which pleased me very much.

Prior to our marriage in Ann Arbor, Michigan, I was asked by the rural development officer of USAID in Bolivia, Daniel Chaij, if I would come to Bolivia and manage USAID's development program with peasant farmers entitled "The Coca Crop Substitution Project." After consulting with my superiors and with Jane, I accepted. I had mentioned to Dan that I would be marrying and taking a month-long wedding trip to Europe and would need training to convert my Portuguese to Spanish. He agreed and set October 1977 as the target date for me to arrive in La Paz, Bolivia. But how does one convert Howard, no linguist, from Portuguese to Spanish? First came the Department of State Foreign Service Institute's (FSI's) Spanish exam to see what training needs would be required.

"Your Portuguese is quite good," said the Spanish examiner. Nobody has ever been able to explain to me why native Portuguese speakers can understand Spanish, but the average Spanish-speaker has a devil of a time understanding Portuguese. I have noticed this frequently in my thirty-four years traveling and working all over Latin America and around the Iberian Peninsula. It is a mystery, and my experience with the Foreign Service Spanish exam was typical.

The USDA obtained an examination date for me at FSI. I arrived at the appointed day about 9 a.m. and was ushered into a small cubicle where a man and woman greeted me courteously in Spanish. Of course I responded in Spanish. They began by asking me a series of questions in Spanish about my background, my work with USDA, my family, where I proposed to live in Latin America, my work assignment there with USAID, and so on. This seemed a way to relax me before the exam was to begin, I remember thinking.

Then the woman opened a loose-leaf notebook she had in front of her to a letter and asked me to translate it verbally into English for them. I struggled quite a bit in the next five minutes, and she said, "Oh that is quite a difficult, formal letter," and leafed back toward the beginning of the notebook to another printed page in Spanish, and asked me to translate it. I made quite good progress on that one, in my opinion. She then closed the notebook, and the gentleman asked me some additional questions. You get the point: I understood everything that they asked me, and answered them in my best Spanish.

The gentleman thanked me for coming and told me to call the FSI after 2 p.m. for their evaluation. I said: "You mean I have already had the exam? I thought this was just a warm-up to the formal exam." (The whole experience lasted about 15 minutes.) They smiled and both said: "Yes, we've just examined your Spanish."

"Well, how did I do?" I asked.

The gentleman, who had told me he was from Ecuador, replied; "Your Portuguese is quite good." "Thank you," I said, "but this was an examination in Spanish!"

They both nodded their heads, and the gentleman said; "Yes, we know. Call back after 2 p.m. for our formal evaluation and recommendation."

The bottom line was that they recommended I take formal Spanish lessons at FSI for four months and/or until I tested at the FSI grade of 3+ (5 being their rating of native speaker). When USAID rural development officer Dan Chaij heard this bit of news, he "blew his top," telling me by telephone from La Paz, Bolivia, that he would approve only a thirty-day intensive Berlitz course, nine hours per day for six days per week. That would be sufficient, in his opinion, for me to do quite well in Bolivia. "After all, you got along quite well in Guatemala the past year with your mixture of Spanish and Portuguese," he said.

"*Usted*, Dr. Steele: *Usted-Usted-Usted!*" said my Berlitz teacher. Talk about frustration. I do not know who was more frustrated — me, or the two and three instructors who confronted me each day at Berlitz. I was not even allowed to speak English during the lunch hour when one of the instructors would take me to one of the fast food establishments near the Seven Corners area in Falls Church where the Berlitz School was located then. After nine hours of straight Spanish, I virtually crawled home on my knees every evening.

One instructor from Cuba nearly gave up on me. She talked so rapidly, I fell into the same habit in answering her questions in Spanish. I would make a linguistic slip and use the Portuguese familiar you ("*voce*") in addressing her instead of the correct Spanish *usted*. She flipped every time I did it and with a slow burn in her voice said with utter frustration:

"*Usted*, Dr. Steele, *usted-usted-usted*. Never, never, NEVER, use *voce*! Will you finally understand?"

But, I really made progress in Spanish the last couple of weeks, so they issued me my certificate, and Jane and I took off for a month "riding the rails" in Europe before attending orientation for our resident assignment in Bolivia.

To the Andes and the Altiplano of Bolivia

The trip to Bolivia, courtesy of Braniff International Airlines from Miami, Florida., arrived at Kennedy International Airport (also known as *El Alto*, The High One) in La Paz three hours late, at about 2 a.m. Later we would name Braniff "the world's largest unscheduled airline," as it struggled unsuccessfully to avoid bankruptcy. Seldom did flights arrive or depart on time, and often they just over flew La Paz and did not stop if there was snow on the runway or heavy fog. El Alto is the highest commercial airport in the world. It sits on the *alto plano* (high plain) near Lake Titicaca, far above the city of La Paz, at nearly 14,000 feet above sea level. The runway is about three miles long, otherwise airplanes can not get up enough speed and lift to become airborne in that thin air.

The airport personnel keep bottles of oxygen and face masks in plain view of all arriving passengers. Many must have supplemental oxygen at that altitude if not accustomed to the thin air, or if they have respiratory problems. Otherwise they would pass out. We were warned in our orientation about the shortness of breath, dizziness, headache, and so on, the first week after arrival. The admonition was: "Don't smoke, don't drink alcoholic beverages, and don't try any vigorous exercise the first week or so in La Paz." For the most part, we heeded the warnings and did not suffer much altitude sickness, though I tried a German beer at lunch that first Friday with my colleagues and got really woozy!

The deputy rural development officer for USAID, and a friend of his there as a consultant, met Jane and I at the airport. They had been waiting in the airport bar since around 10 p.m. and were in a mellow mood. My wife and I were exhausted from the long trip from Washington, D.C., compounded by uncertainty about our new home, work, living conditions and so on.

Our host called his wife, and with a local driver and van, down the mountain with all our luggage we went, to be met at the house they had picked out for us by his wife. She had hot coffee and snacks for us and quickly showed us how to turn on our kerosene space heater, boil and filter drinking water, and other basics before we crashed and fell asleep. She promised to come back in the morning to help get us oriented to where we were and to other basic safety and sanitary rituals and requirements.

Even though our little house was only at 10,500 feet above sea level, coming from close to sea level in Northern Virginia to that altitude really had an effect on us. The majority of expatriates, including most of the American community, lived "down the mountain" from the city of La Paz in suburban communities like ours, which was called Calacoto. The houses were quaint. They had no central heat though they had fireplaces and the U.S. embassy furnished kerosene space heaters. We shipped our own electric space heaters and electric blankets in our sea freight as supplemental heat.

I must say that even at that high altitude with cold nights hovering around the freezing mark, (because La Paz is close to the equator) and one is in thin air closer to the sun, the routine was to dress warmly with wool and sweaters in the early morning, and then start peeling clothes as the sun warmed the city. Again in the afternoon, we put the warm clothes back on. None of our offices in the Ministry of Agriculture, nor my other office at the development institution called PRODES, had central heat. We had electric space heaters that served to warm our feet and legs under the desks. For the three years that we lived in La Paz, I believe we had a beautiful wood fire in our fireplace at home every evening, except six or seven.

"You don't have to take this house if you don't like it."

Those were the words of the deputy's wife before leaving about 4 a.m. the "night" of our arrival. The next day, after sleeping six or seven hours, then waking up with a headache from the high altitude, we looked the house and neighborhood over and decided to take up her offer to look at a couple of other houses that the embassy had available.

We found a little house that suited us just fine on Calle Solodad (Solodad Street), with a great big yard, lots of room for a garden, and a maid's patio area in the back that I could make into a greenhouse for raising tomatoes and other warm weather vegetables. We had agreed that we would not have a live-in maid, with all the problems we heard they created, but just a day maid.

Anyone who knows my former wife Jane also knows that when this Bolivian woman who "came with the house" told Jane that she would handle all the food purchases and cooking and did not want anybody (meaning the "lady of the house") bothering her in the kitchen, her days were numbered! She came well recommended too, but we figured out her scam very quickly. She was taking "garbage" home to her chickens, with our permission, but her chickens were eating "high on the hog"! That was the method she had perfected to rip off Americans and the food money they allocated for her use. When Jane showed up regularly in the kitchen and then took over the purchasing function, the maid quit immediately. End of free food for her family!

The Amazing Construction Workers All over the Developing World

We noticed an interesting phenomenon everywhere we served in Latin America and elsewhere too. It was as true in Brazil as it was in Bolivia, Honduras, Guatemala or Sri Lanka. The workers never work from blueprints or drawings. Everything that they do comes out of their heads. I should not have been surprised at this since those Pennsylvania German relatives of mine on my mother's side, especially the Amish, are renown for "raising a barn in one day" without a single blueprint. For some reason it surprised me to see these skilled carpenters running around talking to themselves as they measured our windows and doors for frames to hold screens in Piracicaba, Brazil, and never wrote any numbers down on paper. The frames fit perfectly, believe me; we had four different sized doors in that house in Piracicaba and probably six different sizes of windows.

"Step and Fetch It", was what wife Jane called the two construction workers building our new bathroom in La Paz, Bolivia. She called them that because they were so slow and they also operated "free style" i.e. no plans. They were as slow as the proverbial "molasses in January". But again, as with those who worked for us in Sri Lanka, one never saw a drawing or a blueprint. It was a source of wonderment to me. I can not even saw one piece of wood without measuring, writing down the measure, re-measuring, consulting my drawing at least ½ dozen times, and even then I sometimes cut the sucker the wrong length or width! Oh well, that is why I am an economist and author and not a contractor I guess.

Other Craftsmen Build Our New Bathroom off the Master Bedroom

One of the requirements that the USG demanded before leasing the house we were assigned on Calle Solidad in La Paz was that a bathroom be built adjoining the master bedroom. Typical of Bolivian work timing, the laborers did not start the construction until after Jane and I moved in on about October 15, 1977. One morning at about 6:30 a.m., before Juan or Christina had arrived, we heard loud voices outside our bedroom window, then heard the crashing of timbers being thrown to the ground, then other construction materials. Finally a foreman knocked loudly on the front door. When I answered he told me in Spanish that they were there to start the new *cuarto de bano* (the new bathroom). However, he wanted me to open the gate to the driveway since he had a truckload of rocks he needed to drive into the back yard and dump. These turned out to be what the Bolivian workers would use for the foundation, once they hand-dug a rectangular hole large enough to hold them. Later, after these large rocks had been placed in the dug foundation some concrete was smeared around them to hold the "foundation in place". Let us face it: cement and concrete were expensive items in La Paz, but rocks were in every dry streambed.

Before they had a floor laid, a framework for the room in place or a roof on top of the former, guess what they did? They took out one of our bedroom windows, cut the wall to the floor and hung a dirty quilt and blanket up in their place. This was to be the door from our master bedroom into the new bathroom. The blanket and quilt were to keep out the cold Andean air at night! But why cut that out first before the other construction? No logical explanation was given in Spanish except that was the way they always added rooms to houses; the contractor could be sure that by doing it this way the door and other framing would be in the place he wanted it! Oh well.

It took those workers months to erect the walls of cement block and the framing of the roof. Once these were all completed, the electricians and plumbers came to laboriously cut channels in the cement blocks for electrical wiring and the same in the flooring and foundation for plumbing. Now I am not a professional craftsman. I have done some good carpentry, remodeled some rooms, put in false ceilings, installed drywall, and so on. But dear reader, I think that everything those Bolivian workers did was done backwards. They also broke the blue bathtub while installing it, and had to replace all the ceramic since there was not another bathtub in La Paz the same color as that broken.

But their final act convinced me that this might have been the contractor's, certainly the workers', first western style bathroom. Yes, they put the sink, bathtub and commode in the right places. They even hung a medicine cabinet with mirrors and lights in the correct location, although we had to have them raise the medicine cabinet so I could see above my neck to shave. But the toilet paper dispenser threw them for a real loop. They cut an opening in the cement block for the toilet paper holder, where? Clear across on the other side of the bathroom from the commode, about six steps away! Of course we insisted that it be moved closer to the toilet. We gave no explanation.

"What are you doing, Juan? It's raining!"

That was our question to Juan, our gardener, one afternoon when we came home in a rainstorm and found him watering our lawn and flowers. "You told me to water the lawn and flowers every afternoon at 4 o'clock and that's what I'm doing madam," he said in Spanish.

"Yes, but Juan, it's raining," we said. "I know it is: I seem to be getting wet all over."

At that point it was hard to get mad at Juan: He wanted to please us so badly. Juan was an Aymara Indian from the Alto Plano and needed the money badly. Where he came from it was stony, muddy or dusty, and without much vegetation. So he would not cut any of the flowers and shrubs in our yard. If it was green or colorful, Juan wired it on up the wall or fence. We had hollyhocks and daisies six to eight feet tall, all neatly wired to the wall or high fences.

My project when I arrived in Bolivia to work as project manager for the U.S. Agency for International Development (USAID) was called: "The Coca Crop Substitution Project." I immediately concluded that the project was incorrectly named. I could not see any technical or economic "substitute" for coca to be made into cocaine that would satisfy users' drug cravings, or the drug mafia's craving for huge profits, unless it was something like opium poppies for heroin and its various derivatives. This approach did not win me many friends in the U.S. Drug Enforcement Administration (DEA), but I prevailed. We renamed the project "Diversification in Coca Zones."

The two main areas of coca production in Bolivia were the Yungus high valley about 60 miles (as the crow flies) from La Paz, and the major coca zone for manufacturing cocaine hydrochloride out of coca leaves, the Chapare. The Chapare was actually a part of the Amazon Basin, only about 600 feet above sea level, yet 2,000 miles from the Atlantic Ocean. It was tropic rain forest with nearly 6,000 millimeters of rainfall per year. (That is about 15 feet of rain: It rained every day, and the few days it did not rain, you wished it would; the heat and humidity were so stifling!). By contrast, the U.S. Great Lakes region receives about five feet of rain per year. The Chapare had rivers and water running everywhere, and flooding is a constant threat.

"Cocaine is a harmless recreational drug of the rich"

That was what we were told in a weeklong seminar in Miami, Florida, about "Controlled Substances, Their Abuse and Control Methods," by no less an "authority" than President Carter's scientific advisor at the time. Nothing could have been farther from the truth, we soon learned. The American public learned later the hard way. Other than that pronouncement, the seminar was excellent. We attended halfway houses where former addicts poured out their experiences, their shame, and their hearts to us.

We watched behind the scenes at a methadone clinic and saw the addicts and their pain, yet unable to withdraw from their habits. We also saw demonstrations by the DEA's drug-sniffing dogs and their handlers, Customs Officers, and went on board a U.S. Coast Guard cutter active in interdicting drug shipments on the high seas and were given good briefings.

Coca Leaf Use Is Legal in Bolivia, Not in the U.S.A.

One reason that the United States underestimated cocaine's danger in 1977 was that most of what was being distributed by the mafia and smugglers then was only about 5–10 percent pure, being cut with milk sugar and other neutral additives. Not so in Bolivia where local authorities were trying to hush up what had become an epidemic of huge proportions among the youth, who were smoking crack cocaine or injecting nearly pure cocaine various ways. Remember, too, that chewing coca leaves and/or using coca leaves in tea were both legal and popular in Bolivia.

Researchers at the University of California Medical College conducted a controlled experiment with nearly pure cocaine using Rhesus monkeys. The monkeys were free to push one of several levers, each of which would dispense a product. I believe they used things like banana flakes, sugar water, and apples, and one lever delivered the cocaine. Once the monkeys tried the cocaine they kept pushing the lever and consuming until they died in about two weeks. Not addictive indeed! Cocaine hydrochloride in its purer forms is highly addictive. Of course our experience with the substance in the United States since the early 1980s has been frightening, and points to serious social problems.

It was a fact that tin and silver miners in Bolivia would strike if they did not have their daily ration of coca leaves and lime given to them for chewing while they labored deep inside the earth. That habit left them with a mild numbing sensation in their mouths and stomachs. Coca tea (i.e., pouring boiling water over one or two coca leaves) was a pleasant tasting drink — much like drinking unsweetened black tea. The stimulation could also be compared to that of a cup of strong coffee or strong tea, and much similar in taste to the Mate leaf tea very popular in Brazil and Argentina.

So most Bolivians saw nothing wrong with peasant farmers producing coca leaves, as they and their ancestors had done for centuries. Only in the Santa Cruz Department, and to a lesser extent in the slums of Cochabamba and La Paz, did the Bolivian medical profession and social workers begin to question what was happening to their society. Teens and young adults were becoming addicted to strong cocaine hydrochloride pastes and powders, injecting as well as snorting and smoking, and the substances were beginning to ruin many Bolivians' lives.

Again the "experts" were wrong about the benefits derived from chewing coca leaves by natives to relieve high altitude sickness. Medical research workers from UCLA and the University of Manitoba discovered that the second highest per capita users of coca leaf chew, after the tin and silver miners, were colonists who had had emigrated from the alto plano to the Amazon Basin at less than 1,000 feet above sea level.

Why? Further research showed that these colonists, who were born and raised in the alto plano (most above 14,000 feet mean sea level), but who migrated to the tropical lowlands, maintained their very high carbohydrate diets—based on many varieties and large quantities of potatoes, the staple food of the Andes Mountains' natives. There was some endemic digestion problem with this high carbohydrate intake among the Aymara Indian population. Coca leaf chewing aided their digestion; it did not relieve the lack of oxygen in their systems.

In reality, Bolivia is at least five different countries. There is no railroad that connects the alto plano with the central, southern, eastern, or northeastern provinces. There is no direct access to the sea. The Andes Mountains run the full length of the western side of the country, and roads to the east—few in the 1970s—were treacherous at all times of the year and subject to rock and mud slides in rainy weather. The Andes are snowcapped all year long. The eastern two-thirds of the country are actually in the Amazon rain forest in the north, and the River La Plata lowlands in the south. The central part of Bolivia contains the high valleys and lower mountains, which are still much higher than our Rockies.

Consequently, the most efficient way to travel—though expensive for the natives—is by airplane. We also used a lot of large, four-wheel-drive "Suburbans," jeeps, and vans. The USAID Suburbans were equipped with winches on the front end. Frequently we had to hook those winches up to trees to pull us out of a mud hole or swampy situation. Most of Bolivia's interior roads were dirt then. In the rainy season they were nothing but quagmires; in the dry and arid upper reaches, they were suffocatingly dusty.

Having mentioned the worst of the topographic conditions, I quickly tell you that I have never seen such fantastic scenery or beauty in my life. One must call it stark beauty in the Andes. It is snowcapped from about 18,000 feet and higher. We here in the

United States expect snow year-round from about 10,000 feet and above, but Bolivia lies near the Equator, and the nearness of the sun, plus the thin air, keeps the snow line higher. We only saw snow in our yard one time in the three years we were living at 10,500 feet above sea level in our La Paz suburb of Calacoto. I have seen lots of snow at the La Paz airport during the "rainy season," however, and it is at about 14,000 feet.

The barren landscape of the alto plano where the Aymara Indians live is striking. The air is so thin that one can see clearly for anywhere from 50 to 60 miles in all directions. The sunsets on those Andes mountainsides every evening can only be called awe-inspiring. The only things that the Aymara Indians seem to be able to grow in that rocky, barren alto plano soil are various kinds of potatoes (150 plus varieties, all native to the area), some barley, a grain called quinoa (known here as "pigweed of the Andes") whose tiny seeds are high in protein and quite nutritious, and a root crop called oka. We learned to eat and enjoy these native foods. Our Peruvian maid Gertrudes showed us how to prepare them.

This is to be contrasted to the various ecological zones and crops one encounters as soon as you "start down." Almost every other zone in Bolivia is "down," but the mountains and valleys you have to climb and descend to get "down" are formidable.

Most "roads" (dirt or gravel, for the most part) are one lane as you climb or descend the mountains. There are infrequent "pull offs" where the vehicle going down must pull off and give the right-of-way to the vehicle coming up. Most often this means quickly stopping, then backing up until reaching one of the pull offs. How many vehicles failed to stop before striking the upcoming truck or vehicle on the narrow curve, or who backed off the highway and dropped several hundred feet off the mountain, I fear to imagine. But there is ample evidence that the number is great as measured by the number of stone, metal, and wooden crosses one frequently saw along the sides of the roads.

"Let us show you how and where we changed government in 1947"

Those were the words of Bolivian colleagues from the research arm of the Ministry of Agriculture (IBTA—The Bolivian Institute of Agricultural Technology) and my University of Florida research professors as we traversed the very narrow, winding road to the experiment station in the Yungus. We came to a very sharp curve, and on the edge of the curve facing a drop-off of about 1,000 feet was a stone monument.

It seems that during a coup d'etat in 1947, the military rounded up the President, Vice President, Speaker of the House and Chief Justice of the Supreme Court and drove them to this spot. The military asked the civilian officers for their resignations. When they refused, the military declared a new federal government for Bolivia, lined the civilian officers up with their backs to the valley below, machine-gunned them and "buried them" at the same time as they blew backwards from the blast of the machine guns and fell the 1,000 feet to the valley and their rocky burials. So said my Bolivian companions. The memorial's explanation was less dramatic, only mentioning a disaster on the road, the deaths of the individuals involved and a change of government as a result.

We Had Seven Presidents in Three Years

You read that correctly. We lived through five coups d'etat, three of which were shooting ones, in the three years we lived in Bolivia. One day three different people claimed to be president. A Bolivian Air Force general, broadcasting via radio from Santa Cruz; the former lady speaker of the House, broadcasting from Cochabamba; and, the previously appointed president, speaking to the public from the Presidential Palace in La Paz.

Talk about confusion. The Air Force general, who had been minister of agriculture during my first two years in Bolivia, wanted to bomb the central labor union and the military college buildings in La Paz, but his officers talked him out of it. Why? They said their pilots had such little practice bombing, and they had so few bombs, that strafing with machine guns would be more accurate and more effective. "Please don't kill civilians, sir," said the general's younger officers.

Bolivian Army generals arrested the air force general in a couple of days and took over the government. They sent the air force general to Argentina as the military attaché in the Bolivian embassy in Buenos Aires. So was politics practiced in Bolivia in those days.

"Da-nos chocolati, doctor," said the campesinos

The main thrust of my work in the Chapare and Yungus regions was to find alternative crops that the peasant farmers (*campesinos*) could produce and would yield sufficient income for them to maintain a reasonable level of living. We called in a number of specialists to help us identify alternatives to producing coca leaves for processing into cocaine by the international drug traffickers. Many of the syndicates of campesinos (sort of labor unions of native farmers in a particular region) hated being forced to produce and sell coca to the drug traffickers but had no alternatives.

One syndicate in the middle of the jungle some distance from Villa Tunari, where the "improved" gravel road ended in the Chapare, met us on the other side of one of the many rivers. We had crossed the river in a dugout tree canoe, and I was mighty glad to get to the other side—dreading having to come back the same way later. The campesinos pleaded with us to give them cacao (cocoa) seedlings so they could produce chocolate beans. They wanted the government entity called PRODES that we had helped organize to buy and transport their cocoa beans. They told us that the drug traffickers controlled all the trucks that came to the other side of the river's edge, and how that mafia demanded the farmers' bananas, citrus, and other products along with the bags of coca leaves and would pay practically nothing for the other products.

This was a frustrating part of the job. We knew there was so much corruption at every level of government, including the army and local police, that without an honest program of military/police interdiction of the international drug mafia by the Bolivian government, run from the highest level, none of our diversification programs would work. There was just too much illegal money that could be made in cocaine.

In fact, the U.S. Drug Enforcement Administration calculated that the farmers were receiving about $260 for a 100-kilogram bag of dried coca leaves which, when processed, would yield one kilogram of pure cocaine hydrochloride. This, when cut to 5–10 percent purity and sold in the industrialized countries of Europe, the United States or Japan, would yield anywhere from $250,000 to $500,000 at that time. So as we made progress with some of the Chapare syndicates of campesinos by helping build all-weather gravel roads, bridges, schools, health posts, and helping them to grow and market alternative crops, the price paid by the mafia for a 100-kilogram bag of dried coca leaves doubled, then doubled again and yet made little dent in the mafia's profits.

The International Drug Mafia Plays Hardball

Cocaine's profitability was so great that the mafia could corrupt police, politicians and the military suggesting they "look the other way" as the mafia engaged in the cocaine business. Remember that coca leaf production and marketing for chewing and teas was legal by Bolivian law. However, the processing and distribution of cocaine, its derivative, was illegal. Strong-arm tactics were used by the cocaine mafia to run their operations, and any interference often resulted in injuries or death.

We had ordered and received about forty-two vehicles of different kinds for PRODES people to use in working with the campesinos. These were pick-up trucks, Jeeps, Suburbans, some larger trucks, and trail motorcycles. The four-wheel vehicles all carried the PRODES logo on their doors. PRODES stood for the Spanish equivalent of "Project for the Development of the Yungas and Chapare," and the drug traffickers all knew it.

As we began to make some progress with the campesinos, these PRODES vehicles would have problems—flat tires, distributors stolen during the night, and so on, and then later, just before the "Cocaine Coup d'Etat" of General Garcia Mesa in July 1980, they were shot at as they drove along rural roads. The same thing happened to the University of Florida team's vehicles, and they asked me for permission to remove the logos from them, to which I agreed.

We had a high-level project evaluation team of three specialists in Bolivia in early 1980 when another coup d'etat occurred. The military junta that took over in a few days announced that they were going to "close down the cocaine laboratories and start arresting the cocaine traffickers in the country." This caused a lot of unrest, particularly in the Yungus area where coca leaves had been grown for centuries. The military junta foolishly talked about destroying farmers' coca fields, which I had always opposed. I felt that it was wrong to put the monkey on the backs of poor farmers, who were only trying to survive. I believed the correct approach was long-run education of U.S. and European youth and other consumers to reduce the demand for the stuff, interdiction of traffickers to disrupt the market, and the development of alternative income sources for small peasant farmers.

The mafia organized guerrilla teams in the Yungus to try to neutralize the military. They rolled boulders onto the narrow roads, felled trees and dug ditches, all designed to paralyze traffic into and out of the zone. This it did. My three "specialists," who had never been in a coca- leaf producing area, all insisted on visiting one in Bolivia on their way out.

Finally the embassy approved our trip. Its information indicated that Bolivian elite paratroopers had defeated the Che Guevara Maoists in the Yungus (who were trying to incite peasant farmers to revolt against the government), had restored order, and reopened the roads. We were advised to stop at the ministry of agriculture experiment station near Oripata, which the specialists wanted to do anyway, spend the night, and get the station director's approval to transit the Yungus coca zone. The specialists had finished their basic report and were on their way back to the United States, so they could catch a plane in Santa Cruz for the trip to Miami.

The station director said that things looked pretty much back to normal. Our driver was from the coca growing area, and I said that I would ask him to take the vehicle and visit relatives/friends near Coroico, where we had heard the paratroopers had a firefight and took control back from the guerrillas. The director said that was a great idea. We relaxed, toured the experimental plots with the IBTA director, his staff, and the University of Florida team members working with the staff. We had a swim in the guesthouse pool and a great dinner.

The next morning our driver returned at breakfast and said the roads were all open and that his relatives said the natives were moving about again. The director said he thought we could traverse the coca zone but cautioned us not to stop or take back roads—just do a "windshield" survey. I asked if we could stop in Coroico for lunch—I knew of a good restaurant there, the La Florida—and he said it would be all right to do that and then proceed to Chulumani and Santa Cruz. He threw a bag of fresh oranges of different approved varieties into the Suburban for us to sample on the way. This turned out to be most helpful, but not as intended.

The trip started uneventfully. But I got a bit nervous as we passed through the little *pueblos* (towns) I had visited many times before and nobody was out on the street. No dogs, no cats, no goats, no chickens, no people. This was highly unusual. I could sense our driver was nervous too.

Now my specialist colleagues included a naturalized American horticulturalist from Ecuador (a native Spanish speaker), chairman of a department of rural sociology at one of our land-grant colleges who had grown up the son of missionaries in South America (nearly a native Spanish speaker), and an agricultural economist who had spent many years in Central and South America speaking Spanish. My Spanish was the poorest of the four of us.

Around the last bend on the narrow gravel road, in sight of the town of Coroico up on the hill in front of us, our driver suddenly slammed on the brakes and we ground to a halt just as six armed guerrillas came up from the embankment below the road and surrounded our vehicle. They ordered us in Spanish to get out and to hold our hands high in the air. Quickly the three specialists said I should do all the talking with my Spanish still tainted with a Portuguese accent, and that we were tourists on our way from La Paz to Santa Cruz.

The gunmen were armed with Soviet-made AK-47 automatic rifles and a couple of old U.S. World War II M-1 Garand rifles. These guys were dirty and wore peasant clothes. Talk about shaky knees and scared—we all were. I felt that this was not only the end of my interesting overseas career, but maybe my life.

In my worst Spanish I asked, "*Que pasa?*"

They told us "*Revolución*"—"We're having a revolution against the corrupt military government, and you cannot pass beyond here. Where are you coming from and where are you going?"

I told them we were tourists from La Paz, and one of my companions was a citrus lover, and we heard there were great new types of oranges here and at that town Chuluuummoony (I purposely mispronounced the name, and they relaxed a bit as they corrected my pronunciation), so that's where we're going. Then I pointed to the bag of oranges in the Suburban and said we found some good ones at that big nursery farm back at the last town. Would they like to eat some?

The guy holding the AK-47 at my chest never relaxed or smiled. He said: "You cannot go beyond here, and even if we let you go they will shoot you up ahead. We killed 12 Bolivian paratroopers here last week. And don't make any move toward your car, or I'll shoot you!"

We concluded later that they probably thought we had weapons hidden on the floor of the car. I said in my worst Spanish to open the door of the van, and bring out the oranges so we could all have one. The answer was: "You're Americans, aren't you?" And when we answered in the affirmative, they asked if we had any American cigarettes. Boy, our two smokers quickly found a couple packs of American cigarettes as soon as I faked a translation to them. We opened the packs and helped the guerrillas light up.

Then the scariest thing of all happened, although they lowered the automatic rifles as they enjoyed the American tobacco taste. The leader asked if we had any money. The truth was that my three specialists were loaded with American and Bolivian money, travelers' checks, and airline tickets and had expensive cameras and all kinds of jewelry and artifacts that they had bought in their suitcases. I said in Spanish: "*Muy poco*" (very little) because we were being met by our leader in Chulumani. "Why did you ask if we had money?" "Because we're thirsty—we've been here four days in the hot sun without anything good to drink, and would like to send Juan there up to town to get some soft drinks and beer!"

We found some peso coins after my slow translation to the "non-Spanish-speaking colleagues." I think this did the trick, because they soon put their rifles down, smoked some more cigarettes, and, after telling us we would have to turn around and go back to La Paz, began to ask us questions about America.

Had they been real, committed revolutionaries, I would not have left there alive. After they helped us turn the Suburban around in that very narrow road, and we started back for La Paz, my knees did turn to jelly. Two weeks later we found out through U.S. intelligence people and Ambassador Paul Boeker that they were left-wing university students trying to foment the peasant uprisings. Real Maoist gunmen would have killed us on the spot, stolen the money, cameras, the car and other valuables and then buried us in hard-to-find shallow graves. That was literally too close for comfort.

Tent Camping and Trout Fishing in the Zongo River

After climbing up over *la cumbre* ("the pass") at about 18,500 feet, just a few miles past the La Paz airport, the gravel road starts a rapid descent in a series of switchbacks. In about 20 miles one has descended through a number of ecological zones and is at 8,000 feet. Here are lush temperate forests, much like those of the northeastern U.S. mountains. It was a protected area owned by the Bolivia Power Company in 1977–1980. Bolivia Power had Canadian management people maintaining the small hydroelectric generating dams and power network on the Zongo River, and the river was full of rainbow trout. We Americans had permission to camp and fish there, which we did on a number of occasions.

The native boys using string and tree limb fishing rods with safety pins as hooks would come by our tents grinning from ear to ear and carrying 20-to24-inch trout they had caught. We, with our several hundred dollar Orvis rods, Shakespeare reels and exotic collections of expensive, hand tied artificial flies, could only show off our 6-to-10 inch "baby rainbows." But the climate and camaraderie on that beautiful mountain river were a great elixir from the rigors of La Paz.

Jennifer Lynn Steele Is Born June 21, 1979

Sometime before our marriage plans were firm, Jane told me that her physicians in Iowa said that she probably could not bear any children; did this bother me? I said no, after all I already had two grown sons and one daughter. She asked, "Could we, perhaps, adopt a waif who needs a good home? There are so many starving kids in the developing countries!" I agreed and said that this was no impediment to our marriage.

Soon after arriving in Bolivia we were introduced to an American priest, Father Jaime, who did show us the well-run orphanage he had some responsibility for. However, he said that the present government of Bolivia was making adoption of the orphans a very difficult and expensive proposition. Perhaps we should wait until the next coup d'etat. So, we waited and waited. In the meantime, our American friends the Bitners had adopted a baby girl and a very young boy, went through all the paper work and costly negotiations, and were ready to leave for Peter's next USAID post. They could not get the two children out of the country. It was nearly devastating to them, although they did succeed about a year later.

So, on rest and recuperation leave in 1978, Jane had a thorough examination by our physician Dr. Bob Poole, who declared her very fit. She said to me, "I'd like to have a 'chip off the old block'—what do you say?"

I said, "Yes!"

Jennifer Lynn Steele was born about 11 p.m. at the St. Francis Hospital in Waterloo, Iowa, on June 21, 1979. I do not know how I lived without her all those years; she has most certainly brought very much joy into Jane's life, as she definitely has into mine!

Jenny Needs Special Permission from State to Go to Bolivia

Soon after Jenny's birth, I had to go back to my job in Bolivia. The Department of State would not let Jenny go to that high altitude post until she passed a cardiopulmonary examination at six weeks of age. Then, and only then, would they issue her an official U.S. passport and apply for her Bolivian entry visa. Well, she and her mom had quite a trip back. They were both crying at El Alto Airport when I met them. Jane from relief to be back after a very difficult journey from the United States—and five months absence from her home, having left in April for Iowa as a precautionary measure dictated by her physicians—and Jenny probably from fatigue and the thin air at that altitude.

I Fly the Ambassador's C-12 Air Force Plane

I had maintained my currency as a pilot with an instrument rating since 1970, and always enjoyed talking about "and actually flying with all the pilots I met." One evening Major John Heide called me at home in Calacoto and asked if I could fly copilot with him on the ambassador's Air Force Beech King Air prop jet (designated the C-12 by the U.S. Air Force, to whom it belonged). He explained that the lt. colonel, who was the commander, had to go to Panama for surgery unexpectedly, and the ambassador had a number of trips planned.

I was excited, and gave a quick "yes." Major Heide said he would get a waiver from Southern Air Force Command in Panama to let me—a civilian—fly as copilot. He said not only would I relieve his fatigue on the trips, but this would give him a chance to see if the emergency landing fields in Bolivia, shown on our World Aviation Charts (WACs), were actually there. The weather was forecast to be CAVU ("ceiling absolute–visibility unlimited"), a most infrequent event there in the Andes Mountains.

The first trip was to be from La Paz to Sucre, the "official" and historic capital of Bolivia, where Ambassador and Mrs. Boeker, and the Minister of Cultural Affairs and his wife, were going to inaugurate an art exhibition of U.S. masters. Major Heide said he would pick me up at 7 a.m., we would go to the hanger, meet the Beech Aircraft maintenance engineer for his briefing, preflight the plane, and tow it over to the main terminal. There we would await the ambassador and his entourage for a 9 a.m. departure.

Major Heide had me compute the weight and balance data, pressure altitude, liftoff speed and other technical data, then file our flight plan to Sucre with Bolivian Air Traffic Control. I was wearing a sky blue jump suit, and my "Fudpucker World Air Lines" captain's cap, with the golden scrambled eggs on the visor. Heide said, "You look magnificent: let's stand below the entry stairs to the plane, you in front, and when the ambassador and Mrs. Boeker start to enter, we'll both give them a smart salute, and you say 'Welcome aboard, your excellency,' o.k?"

Now the ambassador and I, and Major Heide, had played softball together on the Embassy and USAID teams, so I knew he was a good sport. How good a sport, during an official function such as this, I did not know. But we did it. As soon as he and Mrs. Boeker approached the plane, we performed our greeting. He took one look at me and said to his wife, "Margaret—look who our crew is going to be. I think we had better go back to the residence and postpone this trip!"

Then he burst out laughing, shook my hand and Major Heide's, and introduced us to the other ministers and their wives, then climbed aboard. As copilot, I served them coffee before we started the engines. (Memories of being listed as "stewardess" with Rio Airlines in Texas came rushing back!)

I handled all the communications on the trip to Sucre, sitting in the right, or copilot's seat, and flew some to relieve the Major as he went back to chat with the passengers. On the way back—we left the ambassador and his party in Sucre—I sat in the left seat and did all the flying while Major Heide did the communications and kept trying to locate the fields on the ground for future reference. I must say I was saluted a lot in the Sucre airport by the officials there. I do not think they knew that "Fudpucker World Air Lines" was in jest, but they sure recognized the word "Captain" on my pilot's cap, and all honored "scrambled eggs" on anybody's visor. I also think that Ambassador Boeker had been "tipped off" to my presence at the bottom of the plane's stairway ahead of time. It was fun flying with Major Heide, and the Super King Air 300, the Air Force C-12 in this case, was a jewel to fly, very responsive and docile.

Max, the Wonder Dog, Bags a Chola's Chicken

We inherited Max, a sixty-pound, German shorthaired pointer with yellow eyes, red nose and paw pads, and a loving family dog, from Dick Arche, a USAID colleague, who was suddenly transferred to Africa. Max was very intelligent but stubborn and headstrong. Every evening when I came home, Max would be waiting for me at the front gate and then would take off running all around the house at high speed, making at least two complete circuits. On the last circuit he would bring me some kind of toy to play with him — usually a stick, but sometimes a rubber bone, or a tennis ball.

And Max loved little Jennifer, who at this stage was just beginning to sit up and crawl. She loved him too but did not know how to show it. Often she would pull his ears, or his tail, but he would never hurt her — maybe just give a tiny yelp and pull away. Sometimes something would please Max, and that big, thick tail would start to wag, and if Jenny were sitting up but in the way, WHACK, and down she would go, and start to cry as she hit the floor. Max, of course, knew that something was wrong with the little human, but not what, and in sympathy would go and lick her face.

They even played together with Jenny's toys and dolls. I would take Max out for runs and try to train him to work for birds in the fields. It was useless. He had a nose, all right, but he would race far a field, and I had a hard time keeping him close.

He loved to go to the Zongo camping with us. Surprisingly, he listened much better there than around La Paz. Perhaps it was all the strange scents. Or, bad memory of his first visit when he leaped out of the car as I opened the door and told him to "GO" and ran right to the river where some of our friends' children were splashing in the water, could not stop in time at the bank, and fell on the rocks. I heard this very loud yelp and found him splayed on top of a boulder. That could have changed his social outlook the way he landed. He was very docile for the next few hours!

Well, on the way back to La Paz on that trip, as we climbed from 8,000 to 18,500 feet, switching back and forth, we came to a small pueblo. I had the window open halfway, and just as Jane said, "Don't you think you had better close your window more so Max doesn't try to jump out?" and I answered, "It's too narrow; he can't get out!" Max spotted a bunch of chickens in the road in front of the car and was out that side window—someway—in a flash before I could do anything to try and stop him.

The next thing I saw, Max had a hen in his mouth and was shaking the life out of it as feathers flew everywhere!

By the time I got to Max, the hen was dead at his feet. He had a mouth full of feathers and the triumphant look in his eyes as if saying to me, "See master, I am a bird dog—have been all along—and just needed to prove it to you!"

By this time a crowd of Indians had gathered, and a Chola woman (native Aymara women were called "Cholas") came up crying. She was wailing in Spanish: "Your *perro* (dog) killed my best laying hen—there goes my income from selling her eggs. Now what am I going to do?" The other natives were all in sympathy.

I knew that Max and I were in deep trouble. Would you believe that escapade of Max ended up—after much negotiation with the Chola's husband and the village chief—costing me about $6 U.S. in Bolivian pesos, one heck of a lot of money there at that time.

But what could I say? There were a lot of witnesses to the Gringo dog's actions, and the white chicken feathers in his mouth (and the doggy-smile on his face) as I led him back to Jane and Jenny in the car were irrefutable evidence. I felt compelled to pay up to avoid another international incident!

Again, My boss from Washington, Dr. William Hoofnagle, Goes to Where the Troops Work

This involved a trip to the Amazon rain forest in the Chapare. The only decent motel in Villa Tunari (capital of the Chapare) was run by a German-Bolivian woman who had some screened cabanas overlooking the river, had her own electric generator, and a good Bolivian cook who followed her recipes. The cabanas all had good screening to keep the mosquitoes out and ceiling fans to stir up the humid, hot night air. During every day it rained sheets of water.

We arrived from Cochabamba, after a grueling four-hour ride in a terrible tropical downpour, at the motel in Villa Tunari. Water was running across the property, as it did every afternoon, about four inches deep. The German-Bolivian lady had cut-off ends of tree trunks installed in the ground every couple of feet as a sort of walkway above the water. The boss asked, "Where are the bellboys to carry our bags to those cabanas?"

I answered, "Here in Villa Tunari, Bill, there are no bellboys, except us."

He moaned: "How the heck are we going to get through all that water to our rooms?"

"Roll up your pant legs, take off your socks and shoes, and lets make a run for it—we can come back to the Suburban later for the shoes and socks," was my response.

Later that night the landlady's generator broke down. This was bad for two reasons: 1) no refrigeration in the kitchen to keep the beer, eggs, milk, and other perishables the proper temperature, and 2) no power to run the ceiling fans in our cabana rooms so we could sleep in that 100 degree heat at 100 percent humidity. About 2 a.m. Bill yelled over to me in his sleep in the adjoining room in the cabana:

"Howard, lower the air conditioning unit, I'm burning up"!

The next day the cook did not show up—some local holiday— and all the landlady had for us to eat was bread, eggs and warm beer. The boss said on the way back to La Paz a couple days later (we ate fish and fried potatoes two or three times a day at the little local restaurants the rest of that trip), "Boy, the living conditions our people suffer here are unbelievable, and you can't truly understand them from just reading their monthly progress reports. You really have to experience this primitiveness to understand what they go through. They earn every cent they are paid, and then some. Don't anyone in the U.S. government tell me these aren't hardship posts, 'cause I'll clobber them if they do!"

A Return to Bolivia —Memories and More

The rural development officer of USAID/Bolivia, T. David Johnston, contacted me at my State Department office in April 1985. He said that the mission was putting together an agricultural marketing workshop in early May to be held in the city of Cochabamba and he wanted me to be part of the team. It included some acquaintances of mine who I respected, such as Dr. Kelly Harrison from Michigan State University, and Cheri Rassas and Alvero Silva from Development Alternatives, one of the larger consulting firms in Washington, D. C. My boss "Scaff" Brown at USAID/Latin America and Caribbean Bureau approved, so off I went to La Paz for the first time since 1980.

There in the Rural Development Office of USAID/Bolivia—in new quarters on the Avenida Principal was our ever efficient and kind administrative assistant Elffy Vasquez and my former secretary Sonia Mendizabel. Seeing them again was "old home week" revisited! Elffy and Sonia were putting the paperwork together to take to Cochabamba in support of us participants. T. David Johnston said the workshop organizers were expecting about one hundred agribusiness leaders, cooperative representatives and government workers. Two days later we climbed aboard a Lloyd Aeria Boliviana jet plane for the half-hour flight from La Paz to Cochabamba. The workshop was held in the city's largest hotel, and that is where we all stayed.

The workshop, with its combination of formal presentations in Spanish —including mine (my Spanish was very passable at that time, since I had spent nearly two years in Guatemala, three years in Bolivia and two years in Honduras honing the language daily) —plus the breakout sessions in smaller work groups was enjoyable and, I think, beneficial to all the participants. We were proposing agricultural marketing improvements for Bolivia's rural and private sectors that were innovated and greeted with enthusiasm by the Bolivians. We concluded with a banquet and comedy show at a nightclub near the hotel.

Back in La Paz, I invited Elffy and Sonia to lunch one day before I had to leave to return to the United States. Late in the luncheon conversation I asked Elffy how she liked working with T. David Johnston. He and I had been a part of the USAID/Honduras rural development office from 1980–1982, and I had a great deal of respect for him. Elffy, always the diplomat, said, "Oh, Dr. Steele I get along with all my rural development chiefs and I like them all. You know Mr. Johnston is the 25th USAID Rural Development Chief I've trained here in La Paz since I came to work for the USAID Mission!" This was typical Elffy, and her statement provoked much laughter. Sonia had married a Bolivian since my departure in 1980 and seemed to be very happy after an unpleasant first marriage.

Did I Mention Mud Slides in Bolivia?

A group of three families rented a "summer cottage" —translation: large mansion—for several days over New Years in 1980. Ambassador Paul Boeker's wife Margaret had discovered the house and grounds and felt the location would be a good place for American families to use for relaxation and recreation. The fine house and grounds were fairly high in the Andes Mountains and set amidst beautiful scenery. The house was located by a main river about 40 miles northeast of La Paz just off the main gravel road leading to the town of Chulumani. The U.S.-based Grooms Construction Co.

was building a new road higher up the mountainside that would be paved when finished, but in 1980 only rough grading work was in progress.

Fortunately for my family the group included the defense attaché at the U.S. embassy, Colonel George Fisher and his family, and the deputy defense attaché, a Navy lieutenant commander and his family. With all the children, including Jenny who was six months old, our party was eight kids and six adults. The mansion provided plenty of space. We were quite comfortable with the kerosene lamps for light, the propane gas stove and oven, fresh water from a mountain spring and so on. But it had been raining for several days high up on the Andes and the river was a torrent of water. There would be no trout fishing on this trip, one of the attractions for the men and teenage boys. The rain got stronger and stronger, but we still celebrated New Year's Eve with a fine meal cooked by the women, then songs, games and beverages. We were oblivious to our coming fate.

That night the sound of large boulders and huge rocks smashing into each other in the nearby river woke me. The sound reminded me of the crash of glaciers on Jungfrau Mountain in the Swiss Alps as they melted and cracked, pieces breaking off and plunging into the river below.

We were still innocent about what was happening. Fortunately, the Navy Lt. Commander, his wife, and kids had a social commitment the night of New Year's Day back in La Paz. The four of them jumped into their Jeep soon after lunch, and with fond adieus left to return up the winding mountain gravel road to La Paz. At dinner time that evening we heard voices coming up the driveway to the house. It was the Lt. Commander's wife and two teen-age kids. They had walked four hours, perhaps 12 miles, from where a series of three gigantic landslides completely blocked the road to La Paz. The husband had stayed with the Jeep to guard it and in case bulldozers might arrive to open the road.

Colonel Fisher and I decided to drive toward Chulumani and check out that route. We had brought enough food for only two days, so if the road to Chulumani was open, we would bundle up the three families and head there where food was available and hotels open for shelter. But about four miles from the mansion we found four huge landslides had blocked the road.

Now, stuck on the mountainside, we worried about our survival. At a bridge over a stream we found a truckload of dressed chickens. The owners had been driving the poultry to La Paz when they heard about the landslides ahead of them, and were trying to keep the chickens cool in the frigid mountain stream as the landslides thundered down behind them. They, like we, were trapped between three landslides to the west and four to the east.

Colonel Fisher and I bought two of the birds. Then we located a small *tienda* (retail store) lighted by kerosene lamps and operated by an Aymara Indian woman. We bought the last small tank of propane gas that she had, a gallon jug of kerosene for our lamps, ten eggs, and all the canned meats, vegetables, crackers and soup that she would sell us. We returned to our families as heroes, of a sort.

We fed the group sparingly from our new cache of food, hypothesizing that we might be stuck for days. The next morning the rains slacked off some and occasionally one could see breaks in the clouds. The lieutenant commander had returned with his Jeep late the night before after learning from road workers that it would be days before bulldozers could break through to where his jeep and other vehicles were stuck. He and Colonel Fisher were optimistic that Ambassador Boeker would find some way to rescue us.

At about noon we heard the sound of a helicopter. We ran up the hill and around a curve to a wider, straight stretch of the road. There the helicopter, owned by Groves Construction, landed. The helicopter and pilot had been hired by Ambassador Boecker and the embassy to find us and bring us out. The craft was jammed with all the commissary canned and boxed food, beverages and bottled water that it could carry.

Quickly we decided to fly the women and small children out first. It was a fairly small helicopter, and at 10,000 feet above sea level, the thin mountain air limited lift capability. The pilot took about three individuals out per trip and, on return flights, brought more food and supplies. Finally, by the third day all of the teenage boys and us men were lifted out. We left our three cars there; it would be several weeks before the road was reopened and the autos could be picked up.

To us, Ambassador Boeker, the pilot and helicopter mechanics were heroes. They were, it seemed to us, the answers to our prayers.

About a year later, we heard that the helicopter crashed high in the Andes, and the Groves Company pilot was killed—how very sad for all in the American community.

Cocaine "Mules" Claim to Be Working on My Florida Team

My project was called "Diversification in Coca Zones" and included a number of studies and agronomic trials of alternative crops in the two coca leaf producing areas of Bolivia at that time, the Yungas and the Chapare. The Yungas was the traditional growing area for coca leaf, which was legal to chew and use in teas. It was not legal in Bolivia to convert the leaves into cocaine hydrochloride, the very addictive narcotic. The big growth in coca leaf production, and also in the number of clandestine laboratories for converting the leaves into cocaine paste and powder, occurred in the tropical Chapare rain forest.

The Chapare was actually a part of the vast Amazon River Basin, extremely hot and humid, and less than 1,000 feet above sea level even though 2,000 miles inland from the Atlantic Ocean. It rained every day in the Chapare and when it did not the humidity made you wish it had. The area received between 5,000 and 6,000 millimeters of rain per year: that is nearly 15 feet of water annually, about five times the precipitation in the well-watered U.S. Great Lakes region. Rivers and water ran everywhere and flooding was a constant threat.

The main road —it was gravel —from Cochabamba terminated in the little town of Villa Tunari. After Villa Tunari any roads, if they existed, were mud. Many times we took dugout canoes on rivers to get to a particular peasant (*campesino*) community. We would fly from La Paz to Cochabamba, about 150 miles over the Andes, then drive in big Chevrolet Suburbans or large Jeeps with winches on their front bumpers the remaining 150 miles to Villa Tunari. Many days we got mired in mud holes and had to rely on the winches, their cables attached to trees, to pull the vehicles out.

We had a team of twelve agricultural specialists from the University of Florida, there with their families, working on the project with counterpart specialists from the Bolivian Ministry of Agriculture (called El Ministerio de Agricultura y Asuntos Agropecuarios, the Ministry of Agriculture and Rural Affairs). They reported to me as the project manager since their funding came through the U.S. Embassy and USAID. We also had a large group of Bolivian specialists working with the farmers in the Yungas and Chapare in an effort to get them to diversify and produce crops other than coca. This group was called PRODES (Projecto Para Desenvolvimiento Las Yungas y El Chapare—Project for the Development of the Yungas and the Chapare) and was also funded primarily by the U.S. government. I had two offices, one in the ministry of agriculture and one in PRODES. The chief of party and administrative offices of the Florida group were also in the building housing PRODES. Most of the Florida specialists worked in the field during weekdays, either in the Yungas, in Cochabamba or the Chapare: their families were in homes in La Paz or Cochabamba.

PRODES and the Florida/Bolivian teams were making progress gaining some support and loyalty from several of the campesino organizations (called *sindicatos de campesinos* or campesino's syndicates) in both the Yungas and the Chapare. We were showing our interest in the campesinos' welfare by building bridges over flooding streams, building and supplying health clinics, schools and graveling roads. Some of the *sindicatos* started raising cacao for harvesting chocolate beans; others were raising black tea, spices, bananas, citrus, pigs and so on.

But none of the alternative crops or enterprises would yield as much income as did coca leaves. This was especially true as the cocaine mafia kept raising the price of a *bolta* of dried coca leaves (a bolta or sack contained 100 kilograms, 220 pounds, of packed coca leaves) in those areas where campesinos were trying new crops. The diversification projects could not succeed without a serious interdiction program by the police or military to stop the buying and selling of cocaine paste and the running of laboratories to produce cocaine powder by the mafia. Corruption, including bribery by the cocaine mafia of local politicians, police, and even some army commanders was rampant.

This bribery and corrupting of police, military and public officials was very similar to what I had witnessed in South Viet Nam in 1972–73 which I reported in *Food Soldier*. It will be impossible, in the case of the growth and marketing of coca leaves to be made into the very addictive cocaine powder, to reduce the supply in a region where bribes free truckers and the international narcotic mafia to control the activities of the small *campesino* growers of the leaves. The only long-run solution to this very serious addiction problem in the developed countries is education which reduces the demand of cocaine. Not easy to accomplish.

One afternoon at my PRODES office I received a call from the head of the U.S. Drug Enforcement Administration (DEA) at the U.S. embassy. He and I, with a number of other embassy officers, were members of the U.S. Embassy Committee on Narcotics and Controlled Substances, which met weekly in a secure conference room to discuss problems, events, and strategies. The committee was chaired by Ambassador Paul Boeker the three years I was in Bolivia.

This afternoon the DEA head read off a list of four names, two women and two men, who claimed to be working for the University of Florida on my project. I did not recognize any of the names and asked what was up. He said they were being held in the Holiday Inn in the city of Santa Cruz by Bolivian authorities under suspicion of being "cocaine mules", i.e. hiding a kilogram or two in their luggage and flying on one of several airlines serving Santa Cruz and major cities in the United States. The authorities—the Bolivians and the U.S. DEA agents—needed evidence that they were lying before they could legally search their belongings.

I said to hold on for a few minutes while I talked to the Florida chief of party and two of his specialists I knew were in the building. The DEA head said that all four of the suspects showed University of Florida student identification cards with their pictures affixed. He also said that they told the Bolivian and DEA agents that they were working on the "Coca Crop Substitution Project" in Bolivia.

I told the DEA head this made me very suspicious because we had changed the name of the project from that to "Diversification in Coca Zones" two years ago. Even short-time consultants from the University of Florida would know this fact before they came to the country. The Florida chief and the two specialists had new student, faculty, and staff directories in their hands and quickly confirmed that nobody by the names given were employed by the university. I relayed this information to the DEA head, and he said the quartet probably was using stolen student I.D. cards. That could be verified quickly once the individuals were thoroughly searched. He thanked me and said he would call back soon so the Florida chief of party could alert the office of international programs at Florida in Gainesville with the facts.

About an hour later the DEA head called back and told me that the authorities had found two or three bogus passports on each of the four individuals. A simple examination by magnifying glass showed the student I.D. cards also to be fakes. When the four suspects were told they were going to be booked for being in Bolivia illegally, for lying to Bolivian authorities, and for presenting multiple and false passport documents, things got serious. Then, informed they would be sent to Bolivian jails to await sentencing, they started "squealing like stuck pigs" in the words of my DEA friend.

At that point, one of the young men asked that he please be turned over to the U.S. authorities as there was an outstanding warrant for his arrest in Florida and he was really an American citizen, although he was using a bogus Canadian passport and also had another fake British passport from England. If he was going to jail, he preferred a comfortable American one. No European or North American wants to be incarcerated in a Bolivian jail. All you get is bread and water —someone has to bring additional food from outside, not to mention bedding, clean clothes, and so on.

Separating the suspects and interrogating them individually, the DEA agents and Bolivian authorities were able to put the facts

together. Three of the four were habitual coke users; the fourth—
the older man and leader of the group—was British and apparently
did not have a cocaine habit. One of the women was an American,
the other Swiss. The cocaine mafia in Colombia had provided them
with the false documents.

The Americans were turned over to our Consul and jail in La Paz
until American authorities and prosecutors decided their fate. The
other two were turned over to the embassies of their countries in
Bolivia. The DEA explained at our next embassy committee meeting
on narcotics that "professional mules" such as those four would be
paid $10,000 per kilogram brick of pure cocaine hydrochloride (2.2
pounds) they successfully smuggled into the United States, Canada
or a European country. Further, that the 2.2 pounds of cocaine, when
cut to 10 percent purity as was being done then, would retail in the
States or Europe for between $250,000 and $500,000. Markups this
big were sufficient to corrupt many officials and still leave huge
profits for the cocaine mafia.

And how much did poor Bolivian, Peruvian or Ecuadoran
campesinos, who provided the leaves, earn?—between $200 and
$300 for his 220 pounds of leaves necessary for the production of
one kilogram of cocaine. The only long-run solution to this "supply
side" problem as I mentioned above is "demand side" reduction.
Education ought to be able to help reduce demand in developed
countries for this extraordinarily harmful substance, along with
social intolerance of its use and ostracism of those who persist.
In Washington, D.C., for example, we saw in the 1980s and 1990s
that what heroin addiction could not destroy, cocaine use—with its
attendant violence—often did, especially in the inner city.

We Have to Fire the Head of the University of Florida Team

The Chief of Party of the University of Florida research team
working under my "Diversification in Coca Zones" project, turned
out to be a fool. There is no better word for it.

He was charged with completing research and extension activities
with campesinos to help them diversify out of the production of
coca leaves for making cocaine. He also was determined to show
the U.S. Embassy and USAID/Bolivia how important he was and
how important the University of Florida was to the program in
Bolivia. Finally, he had a serious drinking problem.

Matters came to a head when he announced that he would
not permit the University of Florida to recruit for the remaining
members of the twelve member professorial team to come to Bolivia
until all twelve vehicles promised for their personal as well as work-

related use had been received in country. But there were only three members of the Florida team in Bolivia at the time.

Asked how his agricultural economics analyses were coming, he insisted that he had so much administrative work to do that he had not been able to find time to complete his analyses. "Too much administrative work to do —managing yourself and two others?" he was asked—ridiculous.

The USAID Mission/Bolivia contacted the Office of International Programs at the University in Gainesville, Florida describing the "Chief's" statements and taking strong exception to them. The next thing we knew, the Director of International Programs at Florida was on his way to La Paz to "negotiate conditions of the University of Florida contract."

Our Ambassador, Paul Boeker, met with the Director, with my USAID Rural Development Office Chief and me, and told him in very strong terms to return to the campus and tell the various department chairmen that the embassy in Bolivia wanted them to continue the recruitment process for the project immediately and to supply the names of three viable candidates for each of the nine unfilled positions as soon as possible for USAID/Bolivia and the embassy to choose from. Ambassador Boeker had put this in writing and handed his letter to the Director during the meeting. The ambassador also said that the embassy and USAID/Bolivia wanted Florida to recall the then chief of party in Bolivia for incompetence. The director was shaken by the seriousness of the situation.

In the next few weeks two interesting things happened. First, we received a telegram from the Office of International Programs at Florida stating that the department chairman and the dean of agriculture at the university insisted that the chief of party in Bolivia stay until the end of his two-year contract. Second, the chief of party of the Florida team in Bolivia started drinking heavily during work hours, and engaged in lewd conversations with Bolivian employees. The Bolivian government sent USAID/Bolivia and the embassy an urgent request that the American chief of party for the Florida team be removed and asked to leave the country immediately.

The Mission Director of USAID/Bolivia had been on home leave during most of this scenario, but had returned to post at the time the Florida University telegram was received. Steve Wingert and I were not sure how the Mission Director might react. His reactions were often unpredictable. He read our letter of dismissal and explanatory memos: "Fire the SOB right now —this letter isn't strong enough. Call him and his wife and tell them to report to me immediately. And start the process of getting him airline tickets to leave La Paz tomorrow. Give his wife a month to clean up their affairs here before she leaves the country." Case closed.

We asked Florida to name Dr. Larry Janicki acting chief of the team. We respected Larry, and he agreed to take the additional responsibility until a new, permanent chief was appointed. That soon happened. Dr. Joe Goodwin was named and did a fine job recruiting and supporting the remaining nine members of the Florida team, filling the twelve positions specified in the contract with USAID/Bolivia and the embassy.

An Encounter with a DEA Agent Under Cover

Living in La Paz and a participating member of our "American family", there was a very debonair Brazilian-American DEA agent married to an American woman. They had several adorable kids. The agent was always impeccably dressed and cut quite a handsome swath in the community. Both were very active members of the small theater group we called "Waaay Off Broadway", bowled in our little American bowling league, were active in our softball tournaments, and so on. In informal conversations with the agent I found that he was often assigned to fly arrested American citizens charged with violating Bolivian (and/or American) narcotics laws to the States to stand trial. He also was involved in sting operations to catch stewards, stewardesses, or other airline crewmembers smuggling cocaine hidden in the jets connecting La Paz and Santa Cruz with American cities.

As mentioned above, crewmembers would be paid $10,000 or more if they succeeded in delivering a kilogram of cocaine hydrochloride (called a "brick") to contacts at airports in Miami, New Orleans, New York City, and elsewhere. DEA watched American or other employees of Braniff International Airlines, Lloyd Aereo Boliviana, Lufthansa, Aero Argentina, and so on. The agent related some exciting stories about these sting operations. Once he had dinner with a stewardess in Miami, a known coke addict who had been bragging about her big bank account and real estate investments. The DEA doubted her financial success rested solely on her stewardess' salary and suspected her of working as a cocaine "mule".

The agent told us the Drug Enforcement Agency inspectors found that the stewardess would hide the brick of cocaine in the rest room ceiling at the rear of the jet by lifting up the acoustical tile and securing the brick to aluminum braces inside a small handbag she had adapted for the purpose, then replacing the tile until offloading in Miami. The DEA found this activity of hers by assigning one of their trained agents as an "airplane cleaner" at the Miami Airport, with the cooperation of the airline.

The agent was vigorously cleaning the toilets in the rear of the aircraft while carefully watching the "enterprising stewardess" who kept delaying her departure from the aircraft until she slipped up trying to recover her valuable "brick" of cocaine and the agent caught her in the act. She was arrested and later convicted of trafficking in cocaine. According to our La Paz DEA friend, she is now serving time in a federal penitentiary for her brazen behavior.

While I was in Santa Cruz for some USAID meetings, colleague Dick Peters suggested we lunch at a Chinese restaurant (called a *chifa* in Bolivia) that he knew. Dick and his wife, Ching, had lived in Santa Cruz for a number of years before he joined USAID/Bolivia and moved to La Paz. Dick said that the *chifa* was located in a run-down section of Santa Cruz behind the new Holiday Inn motel, but that the husband-and-wife team who owned and ran it had been there for many years and their out-of-the-way place was well known. Dick assured us that when the owners saw him we would indeed be in for a gastronomical treat, and at a very low price. So a half-dozen of us joined Dick and walked through the back streets of Santa Cruz toward the *chifa* with anticipation.

Around one corner hanging onto a light pole stood a man who looked drunk. His clothes were disheveled and a bottle of liquor hung out of a back pocket. His beard was long and straggly, his hair matted and uncombed. As I passed nearby, I smelled the stench he gave off. Then I looked at him and thought, "That derelict looks like my DEA friend from La Paz. But no, that can't be—must be just a vague facial resemblance." I walked on to the restaurant and did not mention the coincidence to my colleagues. We enjoyed a marvelous meal, good beverages, and lovely hospitality prior to returning to our meetings.

But as we walked back toward the center of Santa Cruz, we caught up with the derelict. He was staggering up the street, weaving from side to side. I passed him at close range. Our eyes met, and he winked at me. It *was* our DEA friend from La Paz.

Some weeks later I saw him again, at the embassy. He was dressed impeccably. I said, "Boy you really surprised me in Santa Cruz in your 'Waaay Off Broadway' costume." He laughed and replied, "Howard, I was afraid that you would blow my cover when you stared at me the second time and I thought you recognized me. That's why I winked at you —it was a signal, I hoped, to keep quiet!" Once more, I was reminded that flexibility, and discretion, contribute to successful overseas assignments —whether one is a narcotics agent or an agricultural economist.

Entertainment from "Waaay Off Broadway!"

What do international specialists do for off-duty entertainment in developing countries like Bolivia? I have mentioned trout fishing, camping, bowling, interdenominational church activities, and sightseeing. Another welcomed activity was producing plays and musicals and presenting them at the International School auditorium. We were fortunate in La Paz that many families from other embassies had talented actors, actresses and experienced directors on their staffs. Such talent sought expression, and found it in an amateur thespian group we called "Waaay Off Broadway". I myself always had been involved in acting ... and long ago decided to consider the nickname "Pure Pennsylvania Ham" a compliment. So I was interested in joining the group and finding some way to contribute.

Finishing Touches was the first play I participated in. It told the amusing story of a college professor, his wife, a rather dysfunctional group of teenagers, and me —a bachelor colleague of the husband living in a small apartment above their garage. My character was "always there"—always in their living room, their kitchen, their dining room, witnessing all their problems, especially those brought to the wife by the family's kids. With her husband slaving away at college trying to get a promotion, the wife turned to me for counsel. I was not overly interested in academic achievements, and, in fact, was growing quite fond of my colleague's wife.

After some false starts at romance between the wife and me, almost always interrupted by the unannounced arrival of one of the teenagers, a surprise visit from a neighbor friend or an insistent telephone call, and so on, virtue and morality won out. Our characters agreed the romance just would not work, and we had to resign ourselves to friendship alone.

Finishing Touches' three-night run drew large audiences. As for my own notices, no less than Ambassador Paul Boeker was quoted as saying: "Howard Steele was right at home playing the role of lecher!" Thanks, Mr. Ambassador. With friends like you a Pure Pennsylvania Ham could get canned.

Finishing Touches featured a fairly small cast. The biggest production presented by the group during my three years in La Paz was the Broadway musical comedy *A Funny Thing Happened on the Way to the Forum*. The show was in English, but the lead actor was from Turkey, and others in the cast hailed from France and Germany, as well as England, Scotland, Ireland, and the States. The director of the extravaganza was an American who worked for the Groves

Construction Company, which was building an all-weather road high in the Andes Mountains. The director had much experience in amateur theater groups in various parts of the United States and helped us put on a first class show. This time I played the farcical role of Sennex, played on Broadway by Zero Mostel. It was a fast-moving comedy with lots of singing, dancing, people chasing other people around the stage, down the aisle of the theater, outside the high school auditorium windows on the walk, and so on. It was a great hit with the international community and with the Bolivians who understood English.

My biggest challenge was trying to remember all the words to the song "Everybody Ought to Have a Maid," as three other principal actors and I sang and danced on the stage. I kept mixing up the lyrics, but with aplomb the other three followed whatever crazy arrangement I sang and the audience never knew the difference. But the musical director, wife of the USAID mission director, could have killed me.

As Sennex, I had been chasing the principal maid in the play all evening. Once more, Ambassador Boeker said he thought that I had done a great job of playing myself. In fact, I had been playing against type—really.

The "Waaay Off Broadway Players" were a fun group, and the ambassador and his wife helped make it that with their constant support and encouragement. It should be noted that I was a much better actor than a player on the ambassador's softball team. But in the theater or on the diamond, Ambassador Boeker was a quite tolerant fellow.

Jennifer Sleeps through the Night, at a Former Convent

One of our best Florida specialists, Dr. Larry Janicki, an agronomist trained at the University of Florida, who just happened to be born near Pittsburgh at Aliquippa —so in my opinion he could not be all bad—was working with a coffee cooperative and Catholic boys' high school run by Hermano Jaime (Brother James), a Roman Catholic educator from Baltimore. Hermano Jaime allowed Larry to conduct some controlled coffee experiments in his coffee orchards. This was basic research Larry was doing for his PhD dissertation in agronomy. His inquiry followed these lines:

Arabica coffee, the most flavorful type, is grown in high mountain valleys around the world under native shade trees. Expert opinion at the time held that the shade of these tropical trees gave the coffee its marvelous flavor and high yields. But Larry and his committee at the University of Florida had another hypothesis, which would need proof.

Larry's hunch was that the shade trees were nitrogen-generating species that somehow transferred this nutrition to the coffee bushes growing under them, and this transfer facilitated increased yields and flavor in the coffee beans. How to prove it scientifically?—by a controlled experiment, of course.

For the experiment, Larry planted coffee bushes out in the open in a series of plots. Some plots received heavy inputs of chemical nitrogen fertilizer, some plots received no fertilizer, some plots had nitrogen-fixing legume crops planted between the rows of trees, and of course there was the control plot with the native shade trees above the coffee bushes. The results after a number of years of observations on Hermano Jaime's plots were conclusive.

The coffee bushes with no fertilizer applied had the lowest yields, those with the heavy nitrogen chemical fertilizer applied had the highest yields, and those with the nitrogen-fixing legume crops between the coffee bushes yielded similar results as those planted under the native shade trees. These results were recognized in agronomic circles as an important contribution to knowledge about coffee culture and Larry Janicki was awarded a doctorate for his pioneering research at the coffee cooperative near Coroico, Bolivia, on Hermano Jaime's lands.

Quite often my wife, Jane, and daughter Jenny would accompany me to visit the experiments being conducted in the Yungas at Hermano Jaime's farm, and at the ministry of agriculture experiment stations where diversification experimental crops were being tried under University of Florida specialists' watchful eyes. At Hermano Jaime's school, which also included a dormitory that had held a convent in earlier years, but was now Jaime's visitors' quarters, we enjoyed some marvelous food and hospitality. On one trip there when Jenny was about eight weeks old in the summer of 1979, she, Jane, and I were assigned a room in the former convent. For the first time in Jenny's life, she slept clear through the night without awaking for a feeding. Jane and I felt that there was an aura in that former convent that told Jenny's subconscious: "Be quiet little girl, you are in God's special place —please sleep through the night and give your mother some peace!"

Bolivia Talks about Regaining Access to the Pacific

Bolivia has not been successful in any of the wars it participated in. One war it lost dramatically was against Chile and Peru in 1879. All during 1979, commemorating the 100th anniversary of Bolivia-Peru-Chile War in which Bolivia lost its corridor to the Pacific Ocean, all government stationary carried the motto "Bolivia Will Regain Its Access to the Sea, 1879–1979". This was during the first presidency of General Hugo Banzer; he was a tough old warrior who pushed his diplomats to try to restore Bolivia's old boundaries.

Diplomatically, Bolivia sought to gain a strip of territory extending from the port of Arica on the Pacific Ocean (just at the border between Chile and Peru) northeast to the Bolivian border. This encompassed the province Bolivia lost in 1879. Commentators in the Bolivian press did not give the initiative much chance.

My counterpart at PRODES was the delightful Dr. Winston Estremadora. Winston was the director of PRODES and a strong supporter of the United States. I visited my PRODES' office, next to Winston's, every afternoon. He had earned a PhD in anthropology and sociology from UCLA and he and I got along famously. Bolivian to the core, Winston was very patriotic. But Winston also had a rare sense of humor. He had been in the Bolivian army and still hobnobbed with many of his former army buddies at their officers' club or retired military club.

One afternoon as soon as I arrived at my office in PRODES, Winston's confidential secretary, who sat immediately outside our office doors and "guarded against unauthorized entrances," came to me and said, "Dr. Estremadora wants to see you as soon as possible in his office."

"Good," I replied, "please show me in. I have some urgent things to discuss with him today too."

Now I could tell immediately that Winston was in a humorous mood. He opened up by telling me, once the door to his office was shut by the secretary as she left, that he had been with a number of his old military college buddies, now mostly colonels and brigadiers, at the officers' club the night before. They had been discussing the government's goal of regaining the country's access to the sea on the Pacific. Winston said they figured out the most expeditious way to do it with a minimum of casualties and deaths. They would invade Brazil, the most powerful country in Latin America, by crossing its border to the northeast with their fastest motorized units, then quickly turn around and retreat to the Pacific, as the very professional Brazilian army pursued them, then on arrival at the Pacific Ocean, lay down their arms and stay! Now how can you get mad at a country's military with ideas like that?

But during my three years plus there, the Bolivian military's actions were not always humorous and were shooting affairs. One particular day three different people claimed to be president of Bolivia. Nevertheless, we were told that when a group of generals decided to plan a coup d'etat, it was usually resolved peacefully. There would be a lot of discussion among the senior officers about whose turn it was to enjoy the spoils of government. That is to say, the fraternity of colonels and generals practiced a form of usually collegial round-robin leadership. Still, if negotiations bogged down among the officers, a shooting war could start. The first to be shot at usually would be the denizens of the "free university," a hot bed of leftist radicals and other "professional students," and the COB, the national federation of laborers' headquarters.

So as long as one kept his or her distance from these targets, one felt relatively safe. We Americans were told by telephone, radio or visit from our area captain what precautions to take. One Saturday during peaceful times my wife Jane and I took a long walk for exercise and passed in front of the military college several blocks from the house we were renting. A small crowd had gathered, so we walked up to see what the excitement was about. Several military cadets were trying to maneuver a light tank back through the gate of the college. They could not get the mission accomplished. They kept using the wrong steering levers and braking mechanisms and succeeded in wedging the small tank between two telegraph poles.

"Let this be a lesson," I said to Jane. "The young military types here could aim at someone else and hit us, so if there is a coup attempt, let's get far out of their way. Their lack of skill could be dangerous to our health!"

The lesson did not prevent me from experiencing three frightening episodes during the shooting coups. One, when three colleagues and I were held up by guerrillas in the rural Yungas, as described above. The second time the general staging the coup had transported troops into the city from his home region in the jungles around Santa Cruz. Our American block captain contacted us and told us not to venture outside our walled property into the streets until further notice. Most of the rebels had never been in a city before and were extremely nervous. Worse, their leader had issued them rifles and live ammunition.

"So," I asked, "what's special about this?"

The block captain responded that American intelligence had discerned that the soldiers were raw recruits who had never fired rifles before. Under these circumstances, a lot of random firings, wounding, and deaths were anticipated in La Paz. We did not leave the house until the shooting stopped four days later.

The third such scare occurred near the end of our tour in Bolivia in June and July 1980. A general by the name of Garcia Mesa had staged a coup d'etat with the aid of cocaine mafia financing and some Argentine urban guerrillas. The latter rode around Bolivian cities in paneled vehicles with green crosses painted on their sides. They seized, tortured, and murdered people who were opposed to General Mesa's attempted takeover.

Mesa's insurrection became known as the "Cocaine Coup d'Etat". Our new ambassador, who spoke out vigorously against what was happening, was quickly recalled to Washington, D.C. Jane, Jenny, and I also left the country, taking a timely vacation. We flew home to the States and went directly to our farm in Somerset County, Pennsylvania, following my father's second serious stroke and hospitalization.

We were scheduled to move to Honduras in late August 1980. With my vacation nearing its end, we needed to return to Bolivia to pack. I asked my office in USDA to draft a cable to the embassy in La Paz indicating our itinerary for return to Bolivia. But the program manager in the State Department Bureau of International Narcotic Affairs refused to sign off and send the cable my USDA office had prepared.

I called to ask why. He said that neither Jane nor Jenny could return with me. Further, I had to pack up, sell my vehicle, write my final report and leave the country within two weeks.

I wanted to know why Jane and Jenny could not accompany me, and pointed out that I could not do all the things he mentioned by myself in only two weeks.

The program manager claimed that the embassy was evacuating American personnel. I did not believe him, especially when I said that if he refused to let Jane and Jenny return with me I wanted it in writing, and also his approval to pay them separate maintenance funds. He refused.

I called the Charge d'Affairs at the embassy in La Paz, Alexander Watson III. Alex said that the shooting had died down, that Jane and Jenny should return with me, and asked if one month was sufficient time to accomplish all the tasks. I thanked him profusely and said it would be done. Alex explained that the embassy was having a "phase down" of its programs and personnel to show Gen. Mesa that Washington opposed his government and its actions. Alex Watson also cleared his instructions to us and our travel plans with his superiors at the State Department. Under the circumstances, we were glad to be leaving Bolivia.

Braniff International Airlines Is on Its Way Out

Braniff was the only American carrier serving La Paz when we were stationed there. As a U.S. government employee I was obliged to fly it on return trips to America. Quite often, especially in the rainy season when there might be snow on the runway at El Alto Airport, nearly 14,000 feet above sea level, Braniff would simply overfly La Paz and go on to Lima leaving a number of passengers stranded. That happened to me the night my father died in August 1980, even though I was able to get a seat for the flight on very quick notice (and under the emergency provision one may use when there is a death in the immediate family). As the USAID driver was taking me and my bag up the four-lane highway toward the airport to catch the 10 p.m. flight, it started to rain. The rain turned to snow as we climbed higher and higher. In Spanish, the driver said to me, "Doctor, I have a feeling that Braniff will fly on to Lima tonight and not land at La Paz." He was right.

So I got up early the next morning and drove immediately to the Lufthansa office on the main Avenida and stood in the doorway until it opened at 8 a.m. Soon there were about twenty-five people waiting with me, all of whom Braniff had stranded the night before. The Lufthansa manager was kind to me when he heard why I desperately needed to fly to New York City. He checked with the airline's main reservation and operations office in South America and found that the flight from Santiago, Chile had about ten vacant seats. I was given one of them, and Lufthansa even accepted my Braniff ticket once I got Braniff to endorse it, following my trip to the Braniff office.

It was sad to have to make the arrangements for my father's funeral, and deal with related family matters. But while I was gone, Jane and Jenny moved to Honduras, and that helped ease my mind.

Missing the direct flight back to the States was not my worst experience with Braniff. This occurred previously, when I had been called to Washington, D.C. by USAID to help defend the mission's request for additional funding for the Diversification in Coca Zones' project that I was managing. The cable from Washington authorizing me to come up for the several days of meetings at the State Department was late in arriving in La Paz.

I'm pretty sure I got the last seat available for La Paz passengers on that Braniff flight for the next night's departure, usually about 10 p.m. Braniff was using old DC-8 jets on those flights through La Paz. These "tired old birds" made the trip from La Paz nonstop to

Lima, Peru. At a layover there ground crew filled the planes with jet fuel for the all night, nonstop flight to Miami, Florida, where we would arrive about sunrise.

I had been working hard in the jungles of the Chapare with my Florida and PRODES team members. As a result, I was quite tired and knew that I would have trouble sleeping sitting up in those cramped seats of the DC-8. That would turn out to be the least of it.

First came a ridiculous exercise the cabin crews of Braniff always went through. Two flight attendants would go up and down the aisle with mechanical counters counting the number of passengers on board. They did this even though all the DC-8's Braniff flew on that route were configured identically and all held the same number of seats. Nevertheless, the flight attendants always had trouble reconciling their numbers. In part, this was because they could not get people to sit down, to quit juggling with their baggage in the overhead bins, stop running back and forth to the toilets, and so on.

I made the mistake of thinking that the easiest way to take that count was to take the known number of seats the aircraft had, say 125, and simply deduct the number of empty seats any given evening. Apparently this was too simple. The crew argued about the correct count that night, and recounted repeatedly. Meanwhile, Braniff's operations in La Paz would not let the captain of the plane start his engines until the numbers were identical for their manifest.

Sitting across the aisle from me was the new USAID Mission director, his wife and one of their teenagers in the bank of three seats on my right. I was in an aisle seat on the left side, and the two seats to the left of me were occupied. I knew that the new director was a talker: he certainly did not disappoint me that evening. He wanted to talk, talk, talk about my project, his hopes for the mission under his leadership, and on and on.

Wondering how I would ever get some rest on that flight, tired as I was, I had an idea. I will turn on the light and start to read the project paper I was going to defend in Washington. I hoped that would shut up the new director.

I reached up to turn my seat light on, but nothing happened. I called the nearest stewardess. She apologized and said they would try and get it fixed during our layover in Lima. "May I move to one of the unoccupied seats further front?" I asked. "Sorry sir, but those seats are assigned to the passengers we will pick up in Lima."

Next, I decided to feign great fatigue —not hard, since I was exhausted —and push my seat into the reclining position and close my eyes. But the seatback would not recline. It too was broken.

All right, I thought, I will pull up the tray table, spread out the documents I was carrying, and pretend to be working on them. Of course, the tray table was jammed into its nest at the side of the seat and would not budge—all this before takeoff.

After what seemed an eternity the two flight attendants with the mechanical counters agreed on the number of passengers in the cabin. The captain turned on the "Fasten Seat Belt and No Smoking" signs and started to cycle the fanjet engines.

I reached down to grab the two ends of my seat belt so as to fasten them together. One side of the belt came completely up into my right hand. It was not fastened to anything. Again I called a flight attendant. By now we had taxied out and were nearly to the end of the runway for takeoff when she arrived.

"What do I do now?" I asked. "Can you move me to another seat?"

"No, I cannot."

"But madam, I am a pilot and it is illegal to take off unless all passengers are tightly secured in their seat belts", I continued. "Sorry sir, the signal has been sounded and I must return to my chair and get buckled in. Just snap the belt buckle, hold it in your lap and pretend that it is secured snug and tight; thank you sir."

Now my mission director, who had observed and heard everything wanted to discuss the whole Braniff Airlines situation. I got no rest that night. As for Braniff, it hung on for another decade, obviously scratching for every penny. We in Bolivia referred to it as "the world's largest unscheduled airline."

Aerolina Ecuatoriana Flies a Bit Differently

With the number of coups d'etat in Bolivia, the frequent presidential inaugurations meant that sometime I was going to get caught in the States on consultations and have difficulty getting back to La Paz. During one inauguration period my travel unit at USDA had a very difficult time finding a way to fly me back. All the direct airline flights were booked solid, they told me. Finally, the head of our travel unit called me and said, "Well, I have reservations for you. You will get back to La Paz, but I'm sure you will not be too happy with it. It's the best I could do under the circumstances."

Let me have it, I said. She did.

"You take the last flight from National Airport on Eastern Airlines to Miami leaving about 10 p.m. Sunday and arriving in Miami about 12:30 a.m. Monday. Then you take Aerolina Ecuatoriana from Miami about 2 a.m. to Guayaquil and Quito, arriving in Quito midmorning on Monday. Midafternoon Monday I have you on an

Aero Peru flight to Lima. Finally, late Monday night you take a Lloyd Aereo Boliviana flight the last leg to La Paz. You'll arrive in La Paz about midnight. Sorry about that Howard, but all the good flights are booked solid for the inauguration of the new president in Bolivia."

I thanked her for her perseverance.

So off to Miami I went on Eastern Airlines. Believe it or not, that flight left National Airport on time and arrived in Miami on time. What would happen to my checked luggage with all the changes in airlines and delays in flights I had no idea. However, as usual I packed an extra shirt, underwear, handkerchiefs and socks in my carry-on bag along with my toilet articles in the likely event my luggage and I parted company.

I had never seen the Miami Airport so empty. Usually during the daytime there, one could hardly move through the thick crowds. Being a stranger to Aerolina Ecuatoriana, I asked a janitor where its check-in counter was. He directed me to the farthest concourse in the airport, Concourse E. When I finally located the check-in counter there was no one in sight. However, there was a sign instructing passengers to report to Gate 46 on Concourse E for check-in at 2:00 a.m. That seemed a bit strange, but oblivious to what I might find, I walked all the way out to the end of Concourse E to the last gate there, Gate 46.

It was now about 1 a.m. Nobody was behind the counter at the gate. There were, however, about forty young people in an alcove by the gate sleeping on the floor or playing cards or reading. Their overstuffed backpacks were everywhere. The young people looked like Peace Corps volunteers to me. I took a seat near the far end of the long gate check-in counter and started to read a book I had brought. I dozed off.

The next thing I knew, conversation and other noise awakened me. Close to one hundred people crowded around the check-in counter waving their reservation forms, tickets, passports and so on at the one middle-aged airline employee behind the counter. The people besieging the counter looked and sounded angry, and I wondered if the flight had been "overbooked," a not-atypical practice then for airlines from developing countries — or today, by almost all lines. Discretion being the better part of valor, I decided not to try to penetrate that crowd to get to the clerk. Instead, I adopted another tactic.

I put my official passport and my tickets up on the top of one end of the counter, leaned on my elbow, and just smiled at the harassed gentleman. He would reach up and grab a set of documents out of the hands of a member of the mob, look at me, shake his head and disappear into an office behind the counter. Soon he would reappear and hand the person some official-looking pieces of paper. Then he would look at me over his half-glasses and repeat the process with another member of the mob.

About the fifth time this procedure was completed—and I had not budged from the end of the counter there all by myself, nor had the smile left my face—he walked down to me and asked in Spanish if I was flying to Ecuador with them that night. I handed him my official U.S. government passport and tickets. He grabbed the passport, opened it to my picture, gave it a huge, loud sniff up close to his nose, and declared: "*Es legal, señor, es absolutamente legal!*" and we both began to laugh. Then he said: "*Un momento, Señor Steele,*" having looked carefully at my passport and ticket-holder name.

He disappeared into his office but was back in a flash. He handed me my documents and a boarding pass with a seat assignment. I thanked him profusely in Spanish. Then, as he walked away from me he said in Spanish that he wished all the passengers were as calm as I was.

That flight was on a well-kept Convair 227, clean as a whistle, everything worked marvelously, and the cabin crew was a delight. The next morning inbound to Guayaquil the cabin crew served a marvelous breakfast. Then the crew served another fabulous meal for lunch between Guayaquil and Quito. I was impressed with Aerolina Ecuatoriana. It was a pleasant departure from most of the flights I took in and out of Bolivia those days.

There was not much help though for the boring layovers in Quito and Lima. I read so much that I finished the book I had brought and bought another one in Lima. I finally got home to Calacoto early the next morning, bone tired, but so glad to be back with my family.

Negotiating an Aerial Mapping Contract with General Saldias

DEA and the Bolivian government were alarmed at the rapid growth of coca leaf, cocaine production, and coke smuggling. The major portion of this criminal activity took place in the Chapare rain forest and basin. Spontaneous colonization was growing quickly, but how quickly was a matter of conjecture, since no census had been taken in that region.

Our problem was how best to estimate this growth in population and also in coca leaf production. We decided that aerial photography done by professionals, and the mosaics that could be produced from that photography, could provide two things:

1) Since the Chapare had never been fully mapped, this would establish a benchmark which would be useful for census and other future comparisons; and

2) Skilled photo interpreters could estimate how much new coca was being produced.

That information would be valuable for the American DEA, Bolivian customs, military leaders, and the Bolivian president.

I was soon introduced to a General Saldias of the Bolivian Air Force by my counterpart at PRODES, Dr. Winston Estremadora. Winston had told me that it was common knowledge General Saldias had studied aerial photography procedures, equipment, and the use of airplanes for that purpose in the States. Further, he had been able to purchase a Lear Jet 45 configured and equipped to take high altitude aerial photos at high speed. In addition, he had several Cessna pressurized propeller driven aircraft that could photograph much closer to the surface either high in the Andes Mountains or at lower altitudes. This was important because we knew that cloud cover prevailed in the Chapare and all over Bolivia. One final bit of information Winston passed to me was that General Saldias hated the cocaine activity and was said to be an uncorrupted member of the Bolivian military establishment. So we negotiated a contract with him to map the Chapare with his equipment and airplanes.

In the process of negotiating the contract, someone at the State Department in Washington began to raise questions. He was concerned about the total cost of the work, including the necessity of re-flying patterns when cloud cover would make production of mosaics for detailed study unfeasible. The Washington expert was operating from a "private sector contracting" bias, regardless of the advisability of using General Saldias's planes.

The acting mission director in Bolivia, Dan Chaij, took our proposed contract for the work, including examples of mosaics the general and his staff had made in other areas, and Saldias's proposed budget to Washington on one of his periodic trips.

The person who had questioned USAID/Bolivia entering into this arrangement with the Bolivian Air Force because of its high cost and sophisticated technology, now questioned the total cost proposal. This notwithstanding that the price was only about 20 percent of what his private sector alternatives would have charged.

We did have an advantage: General Saldias did not have to include charges for depreciation on his aircraft and equipment in the accounting procedures used by his government at the time. The Bolivian Air Force, at no prorated cost charged to the operations, supplied the expensive aircraft, photography equipment, and other capital goods for his work.

Meanwhile, the State Department official had to admit, as did some of our specialists in the USDA's National Agricultural Statistical Service (NASS), that the general's mosaics were marvelous. In fact, the work of General Saldias, his pilots, cameramen, and lab technicians was outstanding. I asked a specialized team of USDA's NASS people, who happened to be working in Ecuador mapping agricultural areas by airplane, and developing mosaics of those regions, to come to Bolivia to evaluate the air force's mosaics. The USDA specialists were most complimentary —they said that 90 percent of the work by the Bolivian Air Force team was above average compared to what they were used to in the States.

This pleased me because I was the person who insisted on the contract even though I was not at all knowledgeable about substance of the mosaics or their level of technical precision. I had committed myself, and the USAID Mission in Bolivia, to stand behind a multimillion dollar contract.

Believe me, I did not want my "posterior in a sling", and the assurances that my NASS colleagues gave about the quality of the work General Saldias' professionals were doing was well worth the price of round-trip tickets and per diem we paid the NASS specialists for coming from Ecuador.

When we finally were able to bring both Bolivian government and U.S. DEA and embassy officials in for a briefing, we were all shocked —and impressed. Spontaneous colonization was growing in the Chapare at a much faster rate than anybody, Bolivian or American, had forecast. This had serious ramifications for interdiction and control of cocaine production as well as implications for my project to try and develop alternative crops for coca leaf production and profitability. But as project manager, I found working with the general and his staff advantageous, and pleasant.

The General and I Disagree

I had a great deal of respect for what General Saldias was trying to do for his country. He told me once at a private lunch the two of us had together that he had been asked by one of the new presidents to head the military district of La Paz, the most responsible position in the Bolivian army. He turned it down.

General Saldias explained that he had "fought the succession and corruption activities in the Bolivian army for many, many years." And, he was sick of it. Therefore, he asked for, and received, an assignment to go to the States to study photographic mapping techniques and equipment. He said that before he retired from active service for his country he wanted to do something positive and lasting that he could be proud of. Mapping the country with the first reliable base maps, including the program he was doing now with U.S. development funds, was the honest work he sought.

Then he looked into the future. He said: "Howard, with the funding help of the United States and its DEA, we can wipe out farmers' fields in the Chapare that are full of coca bushes. We can aerial spray them and kill those bushes immediately. All we need is another thirty or forty helicopters, and we can do it. The end of the cocaine madness will quickly be at hand."

I responded quickly. I said the same thing to General Saldias that I had been telling U.S. government officials since the beginning of my work on the "Diversification in Coca Zones" project: "General Saldias, I believe it is immoral to put the burden of stopping this curse on humanity on the backs of the poor campesinos of Bolivia, Peru, Ecuador, Brazil or wherever. They and their families are on the edge of starvation, and are just trying to survive.

The problem to me is twofold: (1) We must reduce the demand for this mind-altering drug in the developed countries; and (2) We must interdict and arrest the mafia traffickers in this marketing system. I do not want one campesino or his family members to be hurt by our spraying his fields and the land where he and his family live with our lethal chemicals. We must, however, work with honest Bolivian government officials and find alternative crops for him and his family that will yield a reasonable standard of living for the campesinos."

To prove his point about the feasibility of control of the skies and the potential ability of his pilots and helicopters to overfly and spray fields and crops of coca, the general invited me on a trip to the Chapare with him and three of his helicopter pilots. First we loaded up in his Lear Jet at El Alto Airport in La Paz for the nineteen-minute flight to Cochabamba. The general, always the astute politician, had me sit in the right seat of the Lear Jet, as copilot, knowing that I was a licensed, instrument-rated pilot in the States. I was thrilled. I had never flown a Lear Jet, one of the fastest airplanes in the civilian inventory of aircraft, and this would be exciting.

I had a total of about five minutes in control of the Lear, somewhere between La Paz and our approach to the airport at Cochabamba. I looked at the altimeter and airspeed indicators as I was piloting the plane. We were flying at 41,000 feet above sea level and at a speed of .9 Mach, that is 90 percent of the speed of sound! I felt like a professional pilot and a plutocrat at the same time. Piloting a Lear Jet over the Andes Mountains of Bolivia? I was sure a long way from my Pennsylvania roots.

In Cochabamba at the Bolivian Air Force Base, we entered three helicopters for the flight to the Chapare. This time, General Saldias had me sit in the copilot's seat of the lead helicopter with himself just behind me as a passenger. The pilot, a Bolivian Air Force major, soon gave me instructions on how to handle the jet-powered helicopter. I had the earphones on and could hear his commands to the other two pilots in the helicopters behind us. Then we lifted off and headed toward the Chapare in the fastest trip I had ever made there. We landed on the grounds of the best motel in Villa Tunari then, one that I had stayed at many times before, owned and operated by a friendly German-Bolivian woman who welcomed us with open arms.

Some of the other guests were a bit scared when they saw three Bolivian Air Force helicopters roaring out of the sky to land close to the swimming pool. But our hostess soon calmed them. It was not an invasion or coup d'etat, she explained, but a visit from her favorite air force general and his team.

I had serious reservations about flying safely the next day because of our dinner that evening in one of Villa Tunari's best restaurants. The general knew all about the proclivities of his troops, so on the dinner table in front of us were large bottles of imported Scotch whiskey. Where General Saldias obtained those imperial quarts of that potent Scotch whiskey, I do not know. I do know that his pilots, a major and two captains, knew how to drink copious quantities of Scotch and tell risqué stories while doing so.

Around midnight I looked at my pilot, the major. He was head down on the dinner table, sound asleep. The Scotch bottle in front of him was empty. "In the United States," I thought, "it's eight hours between bottle and throttle, but we're supposed to leave for some overflights of the Chapare at 8 a.m. How will this guy be up for the task?"

I need not have worried. I awoke at 7 a.m., and saw the major in coveralls examining every working part of his ship. I felt reassured.

We flew into the Chapare coca fields with those three helicopters. On several occasions we landed where workers were harvesting coca leaves. We would get out and quiz the campesinos about where they were drying their leaves, who was buying them, when, where, and at what price.

The approach of the DEA is to wipe out the fields of coca bushes with killing chemicals. They used that technique in Peru and now apply it in Colombia. But not only does it penalize poor campesinos, as I mentioned, it also "displaces" the problem: As soon as the U.S. DEA and local military forces wipe out coca in one region, it moves to another, even jumping from country to country. By the early 2000s, Brazil and Mexico had become prime producing countries. In my opinion, the "supply side" problem will not be eradicable until the "demand side" stimulus is lowered.

I failed to convert General Saldias to my philosophy. With no influence over foreign demand, he, of course, focused on domestic production. So, he wanted more helicopters. Regardless, General Saldias made a permanent contribution to his country by mapping and photographing the vast Chapare region of Bolivia using U.S. taxpayers grant funds.

Jumping through Hoops, U.S. Government–Style

When I arrived in Bolivia to take over management of the "Coca Crop Substitution Project" for the USAID Mission there, the USAID Mission Director, Frank Kimball, objected to the justification for the project. His position, reflecting that of USAID/Washington, was that the coca farmers were not the "poorest of the poor" and were not, therefore, in the U.S. government's interest. He said that the embassy could not justify these kinds of expenditures out of USAID/Mission funds since the farmers were not a part of the USAID/Washington's target group at the time.

I sat through many "Controlled Substance Committee" sessions chaired by Ambassador Boeker at the embassy, in which Kimball continued to make those points. At one session I remember noticing the ambassador beginning to tap his pencil against his cheek. Thanks to my own numerous meetings with him, I recognized this as a signal he was losing patience with Kimball and his arguments.

Finally, but with a smile on his face, the ambassador said, "Frank, that was a fine defense of the USAID/Washington position about this project, but I must ask you the following: 'What is the U.S. government's interest here in Bolivia at this time, and who determines it?'"

Eventually, Kimball replied, "O. K., Mr. Ambassador—I recognize that you and the Department of State are in charge of American policy here in Bolivia." With that, the prolonged argument ended.

But that was not the end of my management problems with the project. The project was approved for expenditures of about $12 million annually. The expenditure of funds I approved went for jeeps and carryalls for the University of Florida team of specialists and also for PRODES (the "Project for the Development of the Yungas and Chapare", the Bolivian counterpart development team). These tax dollars paid salaries, living expenses, a contract with the

Bolivian Air Force, seeds, fertilizers, trucks and road improvement equipment, school and health clinic construction, and so on.

I was informed that the Department of State's Office of International Narcotics Affairs was about to become a full State Department Bureau, with an Assistant Secretary of State in charge, and that the Diversification in Coca Zones Project in Bolivia would now be in the new bureau and no longer managed by USAID/Washington. My management position under the USDA PASA arrangement would continue, but daily discussions and approvals would be directly with the embassy executive officer, the deputy chief of the embassy, and the ambassador, not with the USAID/Mission Director.

I knew all three personally and expected to be quite content working with them. But a serious problem of the time arose. At the time, an embassy finance officer could only expend a maximum of $2,500 without prior cable approval from State/Washington. As project manager, I was authorizing thousands or tens of thousands of dollars of expenditures for specific project support, which, under USAID rules, could be approved by the local USAID controller. In fact, I could dispense up to $250,000 of funds for an approved project without prior approval from Washington if it met the criteria of the approved country plan at USAID headquarters.

These State Department regulations were going to hold up important disbursements under my project if we could not find a solution. The impasse worried the embassy State Department finance officer into a dither. She had no idea how we could solve the problem. But my colleagues and I from USAID/Bolivia did. We suggested that she obtain approval from State Department/Washington, Bureau of International Narcotics Affairs, to draft a series of U.S. government checks for $10,000 each, undated and without her required co-signature, and deposit them in the embassy safe until I submitted vouchers for her approval and the deposit of the funds into a special Bolivian bank account for disbursement. It worked, finally —but I still believe the finance officer lost uncounted nights of sleep to fear that we were doing something illegal.

Not illegal, but the arrangement certainly was innovative. It did permit us to advance the project —until the cocaine coup d'etat in July 1980. Then, many of us had to close our projects and leave Bolivia.

We left Bolivia a bit prematurely ourselves, in the middle of our second two-year term. We hated to go, but the cocaine coup d'etat of General Garcia Mesa made it necessary. Given the circumstances, I was more than happy to accept the employment offer of Steve Wingert and the USAID/Mission in Honduras.

My father passed away on August 25, 1980, so I headed for Pennsylvania, made arrangements for Dad's funeral, and took care of mother's needs while Jane and Jenny finished the move to Honduras. That was a difficult time for me because Mom had always relied on Dad to do most all the heavy work and take care of all the financial matters. Again, wonderful relatives came to my rescue, and she began to take an interest in her "investments." We also hired some good people to help her with the heavy work in her retirement cottage, and to take care of the garden, mowing, and maintenance at the farm. I was very happy to rejoin Jane and Jenny, however. Now I was on my way to the lovely Honduras.

Street market in crowded Kathmandu

I am in the pilot's seat of this Pilatus Porter 695 shaft horsepower STOL (short takeoff and landing), getting ready to fly from Kathmandu to the Tarai, Nepal, 1972.

272

My bilingual secretary, Tara Mhirandar in Kathmandu—efficient and so pleasant.

Chinese traders dominate the rice market in Nepal's Tarai.

The temperate climate and productive alluvial soils of Central America make for outstanding harvests of temperate fruits and vegetables in the highlands.

Central American marketplaces are crowded, yet product moves in and out daily.

Painful physical labor is still the norm in the Americas.

Handmade white-corn tortillas with refried beans are a gastronomic delight in Central America

Beginning in 1981, these men succeeded in helping *campesinos* export 110 trailer loads of outstanding cucumbers per year from the Comayagua Valley of Honduras to the United States and Canada.

Many festivals, with costumes and dancing, partially relieve the grim life of the Aymara and Quechua natives in the Andes Mountains.

La Paz, Bolivia—one of the world's highest capitals at 12,000–14,000 feet. [Paramount]

Improving Agricultural Marketing Seminar, Cochabamba, Bolivia, May 1985.

USDA and USAID staffs honor the retiring director general of the Inter-American Institute for Cooperation on Agriculture (IICA) Dr. Martin Pineiro [at right], for eight good years of service.

14

Honduras: Turning Winter into Spring

In August 1980, Steve Wingert, who had been my boss in Bolivia, called me from Honduras, where he was the deputy rural development officer for the USAID mission, and asked me to come and manage several large projects for him.

Jane and I were both excited about this possibility: Jane had enjoyed riding horseback with Steve's wife Marilee in Bolivia and Marilee had already told her about the excellent equestrian activities in Honduras. Further, the country has beautiful mountains and seacoasts on both the Pacific and Atlantic oceans.

Steve wanted me to manage a project developing temperate winter vegetables for exportation to the East Coast of the States during the time of the year when fresh vegetables were not available from Florida. He also wanted me to look into converting the Honduran Food Marketing Institute (IHMA) from a monopoly that bought, stored, and sold all basic food grains in the country to a research and information arm of the Ministry of Agriculture. IHMA had been losing much of the taxpayers' money over the years, and was believed by many Honduran government officials and USAID advisors that its functions could be more efficiently and better handled by the private sector.

In October I flew directly from Pennsylvania to Tegucigalpa. Jenny, who was fifteen months old at the time, had a wonderful surprise for me when I met them there. She waited until we got to our new temporary home, an apartment we were staying in until our house was ready for us. Then she took off from her mother's knee and zoomed across the wide floor on her own two feet at top speed, laughing with joyful pride at the top of her lungs. What a wonderful homecoming that was!

Within a few weeks we were able to move into a lovely home Jane had rented for us in a suburb of Tegucigalpa called Colonia Los Angeles, high above Toncontin International Airport. This area had been developed by an interesting, and very successful entrepreneur named Wladimir Kestenbaum, who became a good friend. Wladimir had arrived in Honduras as a small boy, a Jewish refugee who, along with his mother and sister, escaped from Danzig, the international city between Germany and Poland that the Nazis had annexed to Germany in the late 1930s. Wladimir's father had stayed behind to try to protect his business, and his family never saw him again.

When Wladimir came by the house one day, to welcome us and to fix a minor water supply problem, we developed a rapid friendship: Like me, he was a graduate of Penn State, so there was an instant connection there. We also learned that we were both licensed pilots, and he told me about his factory-fresh, four seat Cessna Skylane II, which was sitting in a hanger at the airport just two miles away.

At Wladimir's suggestion we flew his plane the next day. He put me in the left seat, the pilot- in-command's place, and with him doing the radio work, I did three takeoffs and landings, whereupon he declared that I was a smoother pilot than he was.

It seemed Wladimir had bought the plane for his son, who was at the University of Florida in Gainesville, and when he realized that the son was spending more time flying than studying, he took it away from him, and brought it back to Honduras, where it sat unused for long periods of time while Wladimir was busy with his work. Sitting idle is very bad for an airplane, and when he asked me if I would be interested in flying the Cessna now and then, of course the answer was yes. I answered that I would love to fly his plane, but wondered what he would charge me.

"I won't charge you anything, Howard," he said. "Just keep it full of fuel in case those damn Sandinistas invade Honduras, and I have to escape in it!" Always willing to help a fellow Penn State alum, I graciously agreed to the deal.

The Cold War was still on, and Honduras was positioned between two active revolutions in Central America. Fidel Castro had encouraged both the civil war in El Salvador to the northwest, and the Sandinista revolution in Nicaragua to the south. The United States supported the Nicaraguan "Contras," who were fighting the Nicaraguan Sandinistas. The United States also supported the government of El Salvador against the left-wing insurgents in that country. Honduras supported both U.S. positions.

While there was no fighting on Honduran soil, there were many refugees in Honduras who had fled the wars in their countries. The U.S. government, with help from the Honduras government and other countries in the Organization of American States (OAS), was endeavoring to house and feed these needy refugees, and also make arrangements for their emigration out of Honduras.

At that time there was no radar surveillance in Honduras. And, although English is the official language for air traffic controllers worldwide, my concern—after listening to a lot of Honduran air traffic communication—was that there was plenty of room for dangerous miscommunication with the quality of English spoken by some Honduran air traffic controllers. Besides, my pride made me want to get a Honduran license to go with my American pilot's credentials. So, I took the Honduran medical exam for pilots, took Honduran instruction until I was cleared to solo, and applied for a license. It was granted, and I started communicating only in Spanish as I flew around Honduras. Since I was flying all over the country and wanted to continue flying to my project in the Comayagua Valley —about a two-hour, 80-mile drive over the mountains by narrow, congested roads, but only twenty-eight minutes by Cessna HR-AAC—I wanted to fly safely, and I trusted my Spanish more than I trusted their English.

Another challenge was presented in the fact that meteorology is somewhat less than a pure science, which of course is true in the United States as in other countries. Pilots are always advised to "not trust forecasts—plan on the worst—go take a careful look at what you see out the window, and plan accordingly." And, especially in small planes, it is important to always assume the worst. If conditions look marginal, it is best to stay on the ground, or, if you are already in the air, to do a 180 degree turn and go back to where you came from and land until things improve.

As a licensed pilot in Honduras, it was always my habit to go to the operations section of the airport and obtain a weather briefing before starting any flight. The weather briefers all knew me and would usually ask if I was flying to Comayagua today. When I answered yes, they would ask when I planned to return. Usually I said in the late afternoon. Many and many a time they would tell me: "Oh, the weather over there is wonderful; you are going to like it, clear skies, not much wind. Wish I were going with you," and so on. Then, nine times out of ten, the minute I crossed the first mountains northwest of Toncontin airport, I would run into a heavy rainstorm! So much for the reliability of Honduran weather forecasts at that time. I understand that their predictions have improved drastically since the installation of radar, which took place with American help during the wars in Nicaragua and El Salvador.

The Winter Vegetable Export Project

My manager-in-residence at Comayagua for the winter vegetable export project was Dr. Donald Braden, another fellow Pennsylvanian. Don held the terminal degree in Weed Science and Agronomy from Rutgers University in New Jersey. He had been working for Standard Fruit Co at its vegetable experiment station near La Ceiba on Honduras' north coast on the Caribbean Sea: Don was an experienced specialist in producing crops of vegetables, and in packing, storing, shipping, and selling them. He took a great deal of pride in producing superior quality produce and really knew how to work with the local campesinos.

Fortunately for me, USAID/Honduras, and the ministry of agriculture there, had hired Dr. Braden the year before my arrival in the country. Standard Fruit Co. had decided to close down its vegetable breeding work and to concentrate only on banana, citrus, and pineapple cultures, processing and exporting from its Honduras operations. This made Dr. Braden available for other work, and the USAID winter vegetables export project in the Comayagua Valley needed an on-site manager with his knowledge and experience. Two years before I arrived from Bolivia, Don had started working with the Ministry of Natural Resources, using USAID funds to encourage cooperatives of peasant farmers, who had recently obtained land grants from the Honduran government, to diversify into nontraditional crops in the dry season.

The Honduran government was in the process of condemning the lands of absentee owners who had not been utilizing those lands for productive enterprises for many years. After paying the absentee owners fair market prices for their lands, the government gave title of them to *sindicatos de asentiamentos* (a form of land reform cooperatives) of peasant farmers featuring long-term purchasing rights. These were the groups that Don Braden had been working with to teach them how to grow high-value vegetables under irrigation in the dry season. This was a bit tricky since most of these campesinos were former tenant farmers or day laborers on big haciendas owned by absentee landlords. The campesinos really only knew how to raise corn and beans or to provide labor under trained overseer's directions. They were anything but entrepreneurs, and they were used to farming only in the rainy season and seeing land lie fallow during dry seasons, Don Braden had a lot of attitudes to change! But they did respond well to training when urged on by their cooperative's leaders. And I soon saw how effective Don Braden was in training these peasant farmers; together, he and I made for a very good team.

In the beginning, there was some skepticism about our project: the capital development officer of USAID/Honduras referred to it as "the golden cucumber project" when I took over its managership in the fall of 1980. He felt that the grant funds used to train Hondurans in the United States, and the total cost of the project, were too high, and he would rather have used that money for other projects.

It is true that USAID had provided a large amount of grant funds to get it started. Some of the money went to send Hondurans to the University of Florida in Gainesville to study horticulture, agronomy, and economics and management so that they could take over and run the project successfully when we left. This type of participant training, paid for in development programs by American taxpayers was, in my opinion, one of the best long-run benefits resulting from the U.S. government's efforts in developing countries. Yes, it was costly, but the social benefits had long-run payoff potential for the developing country.

But true, and effective, development work is always both tedious and expensive. For example, in 1988, five years into the U.S. Government's Caribbean Basin Initiative, we at USAID's Latin America and Caribbean Bureau commissioned an evaluation of the initiative's successes and problems. As a control, the private sector investigators traveled to Chile and Mexico to analyze their export development history—their successes, problems, and schedules. The researchers also gathered factual information about the changes occurring in Central America and the Caribbean countries, which were to benefit from the U.S. initiative that would remove all import taxes on agricultural commodities from the region (except on sugar, cotton, and their by-products). Of course those import taxes on goods, called tariffs, raise the prices consumers must pay for them and make them noncompetitive in the local markets. In other words import tariffs are barriers to trade which discriminate economically against the exporting countries.

The bottom line of our later research was that Mexico's export efforts had a thirty-year history, and Chile had more than twenty years' export experience. I knew this from having studied the U.S. and Taiwan experience with the Joint Commission for Rural Reconstruction, another agricultural development success that required many years of development work with peasant farmers until it was economically viable on its own. My knowledge of the long-term nature of Taiwan's experience in sustainable development, borne out subsequently in the study of the Mexican and Chilean experiences, was that this type of development project requires many years of financial support before it becomes sustainable on its own. That does not mean it is not worth doing: unfortunately, many a valuable development project has been cancelled prematurely, before it had a fair chance to prove its worth.

I pointed all this out to the USAID officers in Honduras, some of whom agreed with the capital development officer and shared his skepticism. I built a strong case that the project was good for not just the 600 cooperative families in the valley who were benefiting directly from the project, but some 8,000 Hondurans, through its employment and income generation and multiplier effect in other areas of the country. The capital development officer had been analyzing the cost of the project for the year by dividing monies received by only the 600 cooperative families who benefited directly, and was then declaring that it was too expensive. However, the USAID mission director agreed with my arguments, and we continued with all due speed in developing the project.

Dr. Braden soon proved that we had the right concept with the cucumber production and export marketing project. In this successful project, campesino farmers, who had up until then only grown corn and beans in the rainy season, were now learning how to produce high-value, high-risk, very perishable, fresh winter vegetables under drip irrigation, on trellises to be exported to the United States and Canada. The leadership of the *asentamiento* cooperatives had to learn how to recruit and manage labor gangs, tractor drivers, irrigation foremen, harvest foremen, packing house employees and bookkeeping, none of which they had done before. Next they had to understand the value of employing a reliable brokerage firm or representatives in the United States and Canada to market their perishable products and look out for their interests — at a cost of course — at the far end of the marketing chain.

Finally, the campesino's leaders had to understand the importance of shipping only high-quality produce that would be able to survive the seven-to-fourteen-day transportation under carefully controlled, refrigerated conditions. And — most difficult of all for the campesinos to understand — they had to accept the necessity of holding onto a portion of the money they received from each shipment for placement in a reserve account, to be drawn on in those periods when things would — as they inevitably do in agriculture — go wrong.

Disease, weather, fluctuation of market prices, refrigeration breakdowns, damages incurred in transportation and so on, all add to the economic risk involved in shipping fresh vegetables long distances. This was the most difficult lesson for us to get across to the Honduran campesinos. They wanted all the money from their crop sales, they wanted it in cash — and they wanted it now! The concept of reserve accounts — even if the accounts were in their own names—to be held for a "rainy day" just did not make sense to them.

In truth, they were making more money than they had ever dreamed possible. But they could not seem to understand that they would need a reserve stock of money to carry their enterprise through a difficult time, whether related to weather, disease or market conditions, at some unknown future time. They were impatient, and lacked knowledge of the high risks involved in the shipping and long-distance marketing of perishable vegetables.

Following a test shipment of a couple of trailer loads of super-select cucumbers to the States during the winter months before my arrival on the project in 1980, and the success of the brokers that Dr. Braden had selected to market the product, we started construction of a small packing and storage plant in the town of Comayagua in the summer of 1981. We also made big plans to plant, harvest, pack, and export a large number of refrigerated trailer loads of cucumbers to Florida beginning around the Christmas holidays in 1981. Our marketing strategy was to follow the market prices in Miami very closely. We calculated that when the crops of cucumbers from Florida and the Bahamas were finished, and when Mexico only had enough production to supply markets from Colorado to California, the price of a bushel and a ninth would reach the point at which it would pay for Comayagua farmers to pick and pack super-select cucumbers and export them to Miami.

During this time period, under Dr. Braden's supervision, the packing plant would continue to receive cucumbers from the five cooperative members' fields while the price climbed, until about mid-February, when it would peak and start to drop again to the "breakeven" price, sometime in late March. It also signaled us that farmers in Florida, the Bahamas, and Mexico were again producing and shipping to eastern U.S. and Canadian markets.

At this point in the year, some of the Honduran cucumbers could be sold in local markets (although at that time Hondurans did not eat many cucumbers), but the amount of product still in the fields was greatly above the local market need, so the crop was only being harvested for animal feed, or plowed under as "green manure."

That first year was a huge success. As I recall, we shipped about 110 trailer loads of outstanding Honduran cucumbers, and marketed them through our distributors' sales to supermarkets from Denver, Colorado, throughout the Midwest, the East Coast and even up to Ontario. The money made by the campesinos and their families, plus the purchase of new tractors, trucks and other capital equipment by their cooperatives, exceeded everyone's expectation. In fact it was almost too successful. Let me explain.

The fresh produce business is an economically volatile one. There are so many risks: weather can wipe out a year's effort in a matter of seconds when a hailstorm or tornado rips through a region. There can be an unexpected wet weather season or lack of sun. Or, there can be drought, or scorching heat at the wrong time when fruit flowers or when juvenile fruit is susceptible. And disease can strike without warning and ruin a crop before it can be brought under control.

Those are some of the natural risks. But the market risks are equally great. New competition can appear unexpectedly, suddenly forcing prices below your breakeven point. Or, there can be storage problems in transit or at ports, and large quantities of good produce can be spoiled or ruined before they get to market, and losses are high as agents must repack and re-grade the produce, discarding ruined fruit and probably taking a lower price for the marginal fruit remaining.

For all these, and for other reasons as well, prudent fresh produce marketers can do one of two things. They can take a portion of profits and build a financial reserve account to protect their interests against that time—impossible to forecast but also inevitable—when things go wrong. Or they can take out crop insurance. The Honduran peasant farmers we were dealing with, although hard working and quick to learn production, could not accept the idea of withholding hard cash from sales of their produce for "a rainy day." Buying crop insurance, by paying a cash premium out of their receipts, did not interest them in the least either.

Dr. Braden had, with great effort, and building on his rapport with the campesinos, managed to persuade the cooperative presidents that a reserve account should be established at the local bank for each cooperative to protect the membership in case one of the disasters described above should occur. He had many years of experience with the fresh produce business and told me that usually there would be one bad year in every four or five years of production and sales, making a reserve account crucial to survive to plant a crop the next year.

Being familiar with the mindset of Honduran peasant farmers, Braden insisted that any withdrawal from a cooperative's reserve account would require both his and the cooperative president's signature. One day when I was there, the board of directors of one of the cooperatives came to the packing plant to request that its members be able to withdraw money from their reserve account to buy a second, new truck for the cooperative. Braden told them in front of me that they did not need a second truck—though they may have wanted one for prestige, or to do other work on their farms—and in his opinion they should not be allowed to tap their reserve account for that purpose. With their hats in their hands, respectfully they thanked Braden for his concern and time and said they would take the matter back to their cooperative's membership meeting that night.

The next day the whole membership of the cooperative, and their families, were outside the packing plant, in all kinds of vehicles. Some trucks were rented, the new cooperative truck they had bought with proceeds from the outstanding earlier cash payments for their exported cucumbers was there jammed with people, and so were cooperative tractors pulling wagonloads of members and their families. They respectfully requested to see Dr. Braden. Don was very courteous with them. He carefully and patiently explained, this time to the entire membership, his position and his concerns for their welfare, probably for the twentieth time. At a certain point, a spokesman for the group jumped up on the top of a truck and shouted out in Spanish: "But, Doctor, that is our money, and we want it now. You shouldn't be able to keep it away from us!" Shouts of support came from the crowd.

Dr. Braden held firm. He said: "I know it is your money and not mine. But if you insist on depleting your reserve account for such an unnecessary purpose, I can no longer be responsible for your economic well-being. At this packing plant I have helped you and the other four cooperatives make more money than you ever imagined possible these past two years. But we will have a bad year—maybe next year—and having that reserve account in your name is the only way for you each to survive. If you take the money out, you cannot ship to this packing plant next year. I cannot take responsibility for your financial health if you do not listen to me."

Dr. Braden was right. The cooperative withdrew its money that year, and he refused to let them ship to the packing plant the next year. Two years later that particular cooperative had a massive disease problem, and all the members suffered horrible monetary losses along with their crops of cucumbers and tomatoes.

But the cooperative leadership and its members who remained in the project seemed to understand and accept the financial facts. When my daughter Jennifer and I returned to Honduras in 2001 and returned to the Comayagua Valley for the first time since we had moved away in 1982, I was very pleased to see our grading and packing shed in full operation, and a number of other temperate vegetable processing and freezing plants operating there. And I was told that most of them were owned and operated by Hondurans. That is one project I am very proud to have managed for USAID and my government.

15

"Civil Disturbances" in Sri Lanka

Jane, Jenny and I stayed on in Honduras through October 1982 to help the USAID Mission assist a special presidential mission appointed by President Ronald Reagan to travel and interview throughout the country. We then reported to Washington for a day of debriefing on our Honduras projects and two days of briefings on our new assignment in Sri Lanka, the former Ceylon, off the southeastern coast of India.

I can still hear the USAID executive officer in Honduras saying "we are packing all your sea freight and air freight for direct shipment to the U.S. embassy in Sri Lanka—it's going direct from here. Just pack enough baggage for your three days in Washington, D.C., the rest into your unaccompanied air freight to Colombo, Sri Lanka."

Not necessarily. My unit in USDA did not even have a contract signed with USAID/Sri Lanka for my services—another one of those PASA agreements—and we ended up at a Quality Inn efficiency apartment in Arlington, Va., for a month. Every day I would contact my office at USDA and suggest that we wanted to take a small trip and get out of that apartment because we were getting "cabin fever." "Permission denied—you will probably be leaving in a couple of days." Hardly—this turned out to be wishful thinking by the Asia program leader.

Jane finally said she and Jenny were going to fly to Iowa to see her family. "If our tickets and passports come through for a departure for Sri Lanka, please call me, and I'll catch the next plane for Washington from Waterloo, Iowa," she said. "I can't stand this infernal waiting and twiddling my thumbs here in this dinky apartment any longer!"

Jenny Sees Her First Snow in Pennsylvania

Just before Thanksgiving 1982 I made another check with my office and with USAID/Asia Bureau/Washington: still no agreement and no immediate departure. So I announced that we would be going to our little farm in Somerset County, Pennsylvania, called Kingwood Acres, for Thanksgiving. My office had its address and telephone number.

My parents and I had bought the 22 acres, barn, outbuildings, and house in 1966 as a place for Dad and Mom to enjoy in their retirement. It was great therapy there in the forest land for them and for my family. We raised only Christmas trees, blueberries, and summer fruits and vegetables, so we could "lock it up" in the winter. We younger Steeles also enjoyed winter fun in the snow, trout fishing and hunting in their respective seasons.

After my mother died in May 1982, I made arrangements for a local neighbor to check on the farmhouse daily and hired a young man to mow and take care of the garden in my absence. Jane and Jenny returned from Iowa, and we drove up to Pennsylvania in a rented car for Thanksgiving. We had a great dinner at a Mennonite restaurant called "Penn Alps" in Grantsville, Maryland. Jane and Jenny were introduced to such Pennsylvania "Dutch" delights as shoopeg corn, shoofly pie, schnitz and knep at Penn Alps—not all of which made a hit with them, but I was in heaven!

As we started to climb up Negro Mountain, in the Allegheny Range (the highest range in Pennsylvania), we hit a heavy snowstorm. Jenny was excited. She was three years and five months old and had never seen snow firsthand before. We got to the farm, surrounded on two sides by heavy forest with a small stream running through, and the large hemlock trees and other conifers that my dad and I had planted in the mid-to-late 1960s were all covered with beautiful white snow. There was about eight inches of snow on the ground, and the temperature was down into the teens.

We quickly found heavy clothing for Jenny (she had lived only in the tropics and been home to the United States only in the summer up to this time) and I started a big fire of piled brush in the upper field. Jane went out to buy some hot dogs and rolls, and we had a great time playing in the snow and eating around the warm bonfire. Naturally we had to make a snowman with Jenny in front of the old farmhouse next to the road for everyone to see. Jenny was so excited with all these new experiences she could hardly sleep that night.

Your Tickets Are Ready: You Fly across the Pacific Tuesday

Finally all was in readiness for our departure. The normal routing would have been across Europe, but a coast-to-coast price war in the United States prompted Uncle Sam to send us to San Francisco and across the Pacific instead. That was fine by me. I wanted to show Jane and Jenny my favorite city, Singapore, anyway. So we planned to take our twenty-four-hour rest stop in Singapore and to add a couple days of annual leave there so we could tour the island. We left on November 30, and after a six-hour flight to San Francisco, entered a Pan Am Boeing 747-SP (Special Performance) for the nonstop, thirteen-hour flight to Hong Kong.

Passengers: I Have Good News and Bad News

Those were the words of the salty old Pan Am captain after some eleven hours into the flight—all in darkness, as we raced across the Pacific ahead of the sun. Jenny had settled down to sleep after a great meal.

"Folks, I've been flying the Pacific since 1942, nearly forty years, and in all those years I've never seen head winds like we're having this year," said the captain. "You don't know it, but I even changed flight plans and took us up over Alaska to try and beat these head winds, but we've lost. The bad news is we won't make Hong Kong nonstop; we must stop and refuel at Okinawa. And, you Singapore passengers: we won't make it there tonight. The crew and I must stop, by law, for six hours of sleep. The good news is we have hotel reservations and dinner chits for you at the Hong Kong airport. And, it will be my pleasure to fly you on to Singapore tomorrow morning at about 8 a.m."

Jenny slept through the refueling at Okinawa, and we awakened her as we started our descent into Hong Kong. "We have good news Jenny. We're going to stay at a hotel in Hong Kong for about six hours, then go back to the airplane and fly to Singapore!"

Her response? "You mean stay in a hotel and sleep? I don't want to sleep any more; I just finished sleeping!" It was pretty hard to argue with that logic. But she did stay quiet playing with her dolls and with Jane while I caught up on my rest.

Singapore Has Changed: Wall-to-Wall Buildings

I had made reservations at my favorite hotel in Singapore, the Hyatt, where Blair Hutchison and I had our offices, our rooms, and so many wonderful experiences off and on from 1972 to 1974 during our work for USAID and South Vietnam. But at that time there still was a lot of green space in the city and elsewhere on the island. Imagine my surprise to see the Singapore Hyatt Hotel walled-in with high-rise office buildings where eight short years before it was surrounded by green parks.

But the city was still as exciting, as clean, and busy as before. Even though Jane was suffering from serious jet lag, we planned a sightseeing trip around the city the next day. We saw a crocodile breeding and rearing farm, the original Raffles Hotel, made famous by Rudyard Kipling in his tales of the British Empire, a small rubber plantation to show tourists (although actual operating plantations on the island, which still existed when I was there in the early 1970s, were a thing of the past), and the Chinese fish market where I had spent so much time interviewing fishermen and middlemen, with the help of translators in 1972–1974.

Jenny Makes a Hit Wherever She Goes

Right outside our room a gigantic office building was going up, and the operator's cupola of the very large crane swung close to our window. Jenny and the Pakistani operator became smiling buddies with Jenny inside our hotel room window not five feet from the back of his cupola in which he operated the crane each day. The young Singapore waiters, waitresses, and other personnel in the hotel became close friends of that little bundle of energy. Jane continued to suffer jet lag adjustment problems and slept a lot of the time.

Not to be thwarted, I even found Blair's and my former administrative assistant in the phone book, Doris Lim. I called her, and she and her wealthy "significant other" came in his BMW to the hotel to see Jenny. Then they took me out for a late, but elegant, Chinese dinner so we could catch up on eight years of mutual history. Doris was as bright as ever. I have mentioned the many languages she spoke back in 1972 as a twenty-three-year-old international secretary. She had added one or two since then, and, more importantly, had been traveling extensively and working all over the world in her boyfriend's businesses.

Charles Uphaus Meets Us at Colombo Airport at 2 a.m.

I had no idea who would be meeting us at the airport the night we arrived in Colombo, Sri Lanka, after quite a long trip from Singapore. It was Charles Uphaus, who was to be my superior and mentor at USAID/Sri Lanka for the next eighteen months. He ushered us through customs and had a USAID vehicle and driver to take us and our bags to the Galle Face Hotel on the Indian Ocean.

The Galle Face Hotel was as famous an old hotel at the edge of the old parade ground in downtown Colombo as was Raffles in Singapore. Even after thirty-four years of independence from Great Britain, Sri Lankan military forces still paraded on that large green frequently when we arrived in 1982, and one could imagine the grandeur of the Empire during Britain's 150 years of domination of old Ceylon, as it had been called.

This pear-shaped island off the southeast coast of India is about the size of West Virginia. It had about fifteen million inhabitants when we arrived there in 1982: 74 percent Sinhalese Buddhists, 18 percent Tamil Hindus, originally from the southeastern state of Tamil Nadu nearby in India, and the rest Muslims and various other nationalities and religions.

The Galle Face is Living on Its Past Reputation

Colombo's climate is one of the hottest, most humid, and uncomfortable of any place I have ever been. The temperature hovers between 90 and 100 degrees Fahrenheit daily. It rains nearly daily. "The World Factbook, 1993" describes the climate as "tropical monsoon, including a northeast monsoon (December to March) and a southwest monsoon (June to October)". This leads not only to personal discomfort, but to mildew and rotting of leather, fabrics, spoiling of food and other local phenomena. The Galle Face Hotel had suffered these maladies for at least 100 years and looked and smelled it. We decided we had to relocate as soon as possible.

I must say, however, that despite very poor service, plumbing probably installed in the late 1890s, air conditioners that pumped hot, stale air, and so on, the food in the seafront, open restaurant was very good, and quite popular. The major problem there, however, was the slowness of the service. Most of the waiters appeared to have been hired during Queen Victoria's reign—moved like snails. This was a bad situation for adults, an impossible one for adults with an active three-year-old constantly wanting to be on the go.

Rent Your Own House: Here's $10,000 to Furnish It

This was one of the strangest PASA contracts that USDA ever entered: certainly the most unusual I ever served under. While in Latin America and the Caribbean, where all my other resident assignments were held under USAID funding, the USDA technician was either given a house leased by the U.S. embassy (as in Bolivia), or was told ex ante what the housing costs/allowances were per month and was also permitted to ship his or her own furniture at U.S. government expense. We were not allowed to do either under the terms of the PASA with USDA in Sri Lanka. Later I understood the background of this strange arrangement.

The "hypothesis" here was that because Sri Lanka had a new, official "duty free" store, $10,000 would be sufficient to get us a whole household of furnishings, including appliances and air conditioning units. Not necessarily. Apparently nobody at the USAID executive office had checked the inflated prices at the "duty free" emporium in many months. And those prices had risen dramatically. For example, a 12-pound-capacity washing machine imported from Scandinavia cost $700—in 1982 U.S. dollars. That machine was big enough to wash a single Swedish lady's dainties once a week in an efficiency apartment.

The refrigerator was about a four-cubic-foot dandy with a two-tray icemaker: price? $900! I was outraged, but powerless to do anything except decide to try to find a furnished or semi-furnished house for us.

So we started the hunt with real estate agents recommended by the U.S. embassy. Wife Jane was in her normal jet lag syndrome. The first few houses shown us were real dogs. Jane, I think, wanted to go back to the United States and call this a bad deal. But I insisted that we keep trying. We were finally shown something fairly new, and a bit contemporary, for Sri Lanka.

It had an open atrium with a fishpond and tiny water falls off the dining and living rooms, and a winding staircase to the upper floor. A small yard and garden in front, with a high wall all around the property. It had a carport from the main street, Jawata Road, and another entrance and parking space from the side street. The rent was outrageous, but there were beds, a dining table with seating for 10, and other chairs and sofas, which made it "semi-furnished."

I signed the lease after getting permission from the owners to close in all the open spaces and vents with glass, cover the atrium with screening to keep out mosquitoes, cats, birds, and other critters, install another hot water heater, and air condition the whole place with window machines.

Then the fun began: contracting with Sri Lankan remodelers. Carpenters, electricians, installers, and others came by bus, by jitney (a three-wheel device run by an engine we would use for a gasoline-powered lawn mower), or by taxi. Since this construction was poured concrete walls (a fairly new house by Colombo standards), the electricians, by Sri Lankan custom, had to chisel a channel in each wall of concrete in order to install hot and cold water pipes and electrical conduits for our newly installed hot water tank and system, and power for the five air conditioning units I was about to buy.

Fitting fixed glass to all the opened orifices throughout the house so that window air conditioning machines would cool the inside of the house and not Jawata Road was another challenge. But our ace Sri Lankan carpenters were up to it. We bought three 18,000 BTU window air conditioners and one 12,000 BTU unit. The latter was for the pantry to keep boxed foods, shoes and other leather goods mildew-free. The three larger units went into the "communication room" (where we had our shortwave radio, stereo/hi-fi system and "liquid libation" preparation area) and one each to the master bedroom and to Jenny's bedroom.

We left the living/dining room closed, thinking that the ceiling fans would pull cooler air from the upstairs down to sufficiently cool the living room, the dining room, and the kitchen area. This was a major miscalculation.

Howard: Get Another Air Conditioner in the House

One afternoon I came back from my office in the Agricultural Research and Training Institute (ARTI) about 5 p.m. to find Jane in the kitchen in a pair of shorts and halter with our maid Jenita. Jane said: "Look at me; I'm making soup for all of us, but the sweat is running off my forehead, down my nose, across my chest and into the soup; now will you get another air conditioning unit installed before I die from heat exhaustion?"

So this time I bought a 24,000 BTU unit to be installed in the upstairs window at the head of the staircase, the cold air to be pulled down by the ceiling fans in the dining and living rooms. This did the trick. Jane's discomfort ceased and we were actually quite comfortable indoors from that point on. But you, the taxpayer, suffered; our electric bills were outrageous, and the embassy paid for them. Colombo was considered a "hardship post," and to temperate climate people like us, it was! The other benefit for us was it reduced the level of noise from busy Jawata Road, and the pollution from the diesel trucks and buses constantly passing the front of the house.

Teaching Young Agricultural Research and Training Officers

That was my project in Sri Lanka at the Agricultural Research and Training Institute (ARTI), a branch of the ministry of agriculture. Specifically, I was to help establish an agricultural marketing information system with uniform grades and standards for the basic food products. The young ARTI officers, most in their twenties and thirties, were to be trained in basic marketing grades and standards establishment, methods used by the USDA to gather and report representative prices for basic food commodities, and eventually adapt such a system to the Sri Lanka Ministry of Agriculture's needs.

English Was Not Taught to a Generation of Sri Lankans

The young officers, male and female, I was working with were all bright, pleasant and eager to learn. A problem rose: communicating in the English language. You see, the Bandaranaike governments in power from 1948 until 1977—first husband, then wife (following his assassination in 1959) forbade the teaching of English in the schools. The two Bandaranaikes moved Sri Lanka into the Soviet orbit and ran the country's economy into ruin. So for most of the fine young officers I was working with, English was a new, second language to their native tongues, either Sinhalese or Tamil.

Normally we could communicate quite well, but if the discussion between the officers became excited, if an embarrassing matter occurred, or if the issue was in any way sensitive, the young officers immediately switched to their native language, and I would be lost. This is a distinct disadvantage when working in a country other than your own in which a different language, or in this case languages, are spoken. You are either left outside the conversation, or you miss its nuances.

What Is Samba Rice? What Is Samba Grade One?

Let me illustrate with a frustrating example. Rice is the staple in the Sri Lankan diet; in fact, Sri Lankans' per capita rice consumption is among the highest in the world, nearly 100 kilograms per year. One day, with about a dozen of the ARTI officers in tow, I went to the major central market for rice in Colombo. I asked them to show me the best Samba rice (a variety of rice that has been partially cooked or steamed and partially fermented—it is the favorite of the typical Sri Lankan family). They all pointed to a display of rice in a basket on top of many 50-kilogram bags at a rice merchant's warehouse. I asked: "How do you know that is Samba rice? Why do you say it is the best? Would you consider it Grade One? Grade A? The highest quality? Why?"

Well this really started the emotional conversations going, in both Sinhalese and in Tamil, between men and women, between men and men, and between women and women. The final answer to all my questioning, baiting, disagreeing, and discussing with them was: "Well, Dr. Steele, we just know Samba Number One rice when we see it!"

But my point was made as became clear in the near future; scientifically, you must have measurable parameters of quality that are replicable before you can establish uniform grades that will be acceptable to all trading entities. Only then can you have a market information reporting system with prices that are meaningful, accepted, and transmittable.

For example, good grade standards specify the percentage of broken grains that may be in a volume of rice, the percentage of foreign material such as chaff, may specify the average length of a grain of the rice, may specify the amount of moisture allowed in the grain, etc., etc. But the ARTI officers had never been exposed to these variables before. So in effect, I was challenging their knowledge of the basic staple food all of them had been eating since childhood: that raised emotions, and the native languages dominated the arguments. But we were soon joking about the incident, and the young officers were helping me to challenge the "state of the art" in the marketplace. We were making progress.

How Best to Escape Colombo's Heat and Congestion

We tried a number of escape strategies including trips to (1) the Royal Ceylon Motor-Yacht Club; (2) the Colombo Swim Club; (3) oceanfront hotels, the mountains at Kandy, and the highest mountains at Nuwara Eliya; (4) the Maldives for snorkeling in the reefs. All of them worked!

The island of Sri Lanka has an interesting rib of mountains in its middle that rises to about 8,000 feet near the former British imperial vacation town of Nuwara Eliya in the south central. From Kandy on up, one passes through gorgeous tea plantations and can see the former British tea planters' "cottages"—mansions by any standard. Those former empire barons had a great thing going for them.

At Nuwara Eliya, approximately 6,000–7,000 feet above sea level, the climate is marvelous; quite chilly at night, and fire in the fireplaces and blankets on the beds feel wonderful. The British had their horse races here when on "holiday" from their businesses in Colombo or elsewhere on the island, had golf clubs, dining clubs, and a very good life. They even had mountain trout fishing at Horton Plains.

One of the most incredible experiences in my life was catching lovely twenty-inch rainbow trout on my fly line at 8,000 feet while

Rhesus monkeys were chattering at me from the trees overhanging the river.

It seems a Scotsman by the name of Horton discovered the high plain in the late 1800s, and it reminded him so much of his home in the Scottish highlands that on his next trip home he procured a supply of rainbow trout fingerlings. But, can you imagine keeping those fingerlings alive during a thirty-day ocean boat trip halfway around the world?

Much of that trip would have been in the broiling tropics, then Horton had to have the trout carried up the mountains from Colombo, another long journey in those days, and finally released them at 8,000 feet above sea level. Now that is a dedicated trout fisherman! The man must have been quite a famous ecologist and conservationist, since they named the area after him, "Horton Plains."

No Children under Twelve in the Dining Room after 8 p.m.

That was the sign outside the main dining room of The Hill Club, a famous old British club in a beautiful mansion overlooking Nuwara Eliya. To enter the club, one must wear "Proper Attire," as the sign on the door demanded. The head steward would open the door, and if a gentleman did not have a suit coat and tie on, he would usher the gentleman into a cloak room to select from a closet full of various sport coats and ties to choose from, at a small rental fee. All guests gathered in the Trophy Room where stuffed wild animal heads were mounted on the walls and over a gigantic fireplace, always with roaring fire, to await the head steward's arrival to usher the party to its table—"only accepting prior reservations, please." Of course the waiters were all dressed in white tuxedos and wore white gloves while serving. Sterling silver, polished to a mirror-like glaze, and linen table service was the standard. One could quickly imagine being a part of the old empire, and I often thought at times like these how unsettling it must have been for our British colleagues to hear Americans talk about them giving independence to all their colonies.

Of course that is exactly what they, the French, Belgians, Italians and Dutch, did following World War II. Obviously it was a political necessity whose time had come. But I do have news for some who have not had the privilege to observe reality in former colonies such as Sri Lanka as I have been fortunate to have done. The British, at least, remained very active behind the scenes.

I believe they were still the subtle directors of many, many enterprises in their former colonies. True, local people fronted the organizations, but funding and capital, voting power on boards of directors in such organizations as the local banks, in the tea enterprises, in real estate, in these clubs, etc., were still controlled by expatriates. It was a revelation to me! The ongoing civil war between the majority Sinhalese and the minority Tamils in Sri Lanka has confounded old loyalties somewhat.

For example, radical Indian politicians first supported the Tamils while the British supported the Sinhalese. Later, the government of India supported the Sinhalese government and India's President, Sanjay Ghandi, was assassinated by a Sri Lankan Tamil suicide-bomber. Many British thought the Sinhalese government ought to give the Tamils in the north of the country more autonomy and stop the bloodshed. Unfortunately, the killing and civil war go on.

We Join the Swim Club and Royal Motor Yacht Club

In addition to taking as many trips to the mountains to escape Colombo's heat and congestion as possible, we joined the Colombo Swim Club for swimming, sunning and weekend lunches in the sun. Jenny and her little friends were all signed up to take swimming lessons at the club under excellent coaches. I could not believe my eyes the first day I saw her dive off the low diving board into 9 feet of water and quickly surface and swim back to her Sri Lankan swim coach as fast as she could paddle. That Sri Lankan coach could get those little kids to do anything he asked; things we parents could not get them to do in the water no matter how hard we tried.

But the Royal Ceylon Motor Yacht Club was the most relaxing of all the spots around Colombo. It was on an inland bay of the Indian Ocean—fed by fresh water but also affected by the salt ocean tides—yet appeared to be a lake. The facility, probably 60 years old, had a lovely dining room, bar, and lounge for rainy weather. But for us the nicely landscaped picnic area under the coconut palm trees lining the lakeshore, where there was always a breeze from the ocean, was our favorite spot on many Saturdays and Sundays.

I stopped flying light airplanes in Sri Lanka once I found out how expensive and scarce general aviation airplanes were to rent. Also, I observed the maintenance techniques practiced by the local mechanics at the airport and said to the family: "I think I'll take up sailing at the Yacht Club and postpone my flying!"

So an American colleague, an English friend, a Scottish friend, and I each invested $200 in a 15-foot sloop that was for sale at the club. The Englishman and the Scotsman were accomplished sailors and raced our sloop in the club's weekly competitions. Of course we would also be there to cheer them on. On Saturdays they, or other American friends, would teach us how to sail. Jane and Jenny were not too excited about sailing, especially the part about tacking into the wind at an angle and having to lean out the side of the sloop to help keep it from capsizing! But they did love the picnics there in the breeze and having fun with other international friends. We also had friends with wind surfers, and we tried our hands at that exciting sport.

Keep Left: Cars on Right in Roundabouts Have Right of Way

We bought a right-side steering Datsun 140-J, four-door sedan from the departing political officer at the embassy. It was a fine little car, just right for our small family. Learning to drive on the left-hand side of the road and understand who had the right-of-way at crossroads and in roundabouts gave us some trouble at first. But soon we became accustomed to it and became mobile!

The first Sunday in Sri Lanka, before we bought the car, we took a jitney up to the Colombo zoo. Jenny really wanted to see the elephants and giraffes. The big elephants were chained to the ground and separated from each other. Soon I learned why our orientation leader at the embassy had told us when we started to drive to avoid elephant "scat" on the roads by driving around and not over it at all times! The keepers brought a large coconut palm tree trunk and put it down between two large male elephants. I thought: "Gee, they use tree trunks to help separate these gigantic beasts from each other." But after I turned my back on the scene, I heard a ripping sound. I looked back, and the elephants were tearing off the bark from the trunks of the tree, and chewing it as if it were grass. Now I understood why not to run over elephant droppings—they are tree cellulose, and probably as hard as rock, and would break your steering mechanism, or other car parts.

Again, Blond Americans Are an Attraction for Natives

The first Saturday we had our car and decided to venture out on the Sri Lanka highways, we took a ride up into the hills to a town we were told specialized in making wicker furniture, which we needed in our house. Now elephant "scat" is not the only thing that must be avoided on the Sri Lankan highways. Bullock carts, bicycles, jitneys, people walking hand-in-hand, trucks, live elephants with mahouts (the elephant's rider and master) riding on their necks, water buffalo and buses, all behave as if they have the right-of-way at all times. If one is smart, one drives with one hand on the horn, one foot poised over the brake for immediate action, and the other on the accelerator—a motoring challenge.

We soon found the town and were amazed to see that the main highway was lined on both sides for about a mile with hundreds of small artisan shops busy as beehives making wicker furniture. It was a bright, sunny day.

"Over there is a nice looking shop with pretty wicker outside— pull over and stop Howard," Jane said. Jenny held our attention about something momentarily, then all of a sudden it grew dark inside the car. Imagine our surprise to look up from Jenny to see nothing but Sri Lankan faces peering in at us from every available spot of window glass. They "oohed and aahed" at Jenny's blond pigtails.

When we exited the car, the most brazen of the younger children came up to feel Jenny's hair. She was scared, but we assured her that they meant no harm. They would say in their best Sri Lankan English, "What a preeety leetle girl!" Jenny soon began to relax and smile and say "thank you very much." Of course nearly all Sri Lankans have dark brown skin and masses of very straight, black hair. We went on, after ordering some furniture built to our specifications for later pickup, to a baby elephant orphanage run by the government. There it was a thrill to see the little ones led down to the river for their daily baths. That was a sight I will never forget, nor will Jenny and Jane.

The Brewing Political Storm in Sri Lanka

I mentioned above that we bought the Datsun car from the departing political officer at the embassy. Actually, we bought it from his wife, because he had been asked by the Sri Lankan government to leave the country within forty-eight hours the week before our arrival, and our ambassador had to comply. It seems that the political officer was the only American official in either the embassy or in USAID in Colombo who spoke Tamil, the language of 18 percent of the population. He had reported the Tamils were getting restless at their treatment by the Sinhalese majority.

The political officer commented at a diplomatic function, we were told, that the Sinhalese majority was going to have to give some suffrage and authority to the Tamils, at least in the north around Jaffna where they were in the majority. The government in power in Sri Lanka at the time did not want to hear this kind of "advice" from an American; he had "gone from being a diplomat to a preacher or meddler."

But, he was right, as we found out in July 1983 the weekend we returned from vacation in the States. A bloody civil war started, which, unfortunately, continues today, more than twenty-four years later. The political officer had heard it straight from his Tamil-speaking friends. They could no longer mollify the young Tamil Tigers (revolutionaries) who wanted to take over and form Tamil Eelam, a separate country in the north and northeast where they were in the majority. Guerrilla warfare was soon upon the country.

The most incredible thing about the whole situation was that: 1) the British had brought Tamils to Sri Lanka from India many years before to work in the tea plantations. They found them to be very hard-working people and also bright. The British used them fully in the civil service system, in the army, and in police. Many Tamils went on to university and became professionals. The native Sinhalese grew jealous of their accomplishments. 2) Sri Lanka is a small island the size of West Virginia with a population of some fifteen million people at that time, 18 percent of whom (three million) were Tamil and twelve million Sinhalese. But across the very narrow Palk Straits live 60 million Tamils in Tamil Nadu State of India. Who might survive best if an ethnic war is pursued over the long run? — the Tamils, of course. And that seems to be what is happening; twenty-four years after it began, the "civil disturbances" in Sri Lanka make the headlines every day. Tens of thousands have been murdered, killed in bombings and raids, and hundreds of thousands made homeless, fatherless, or seriously maimed or wounded.

One wonders if the slaughter will ever end. And it has other serious dislocations and negative economic repercussions. I personally thought that the departed political officer, whose car I bought and drove for two years, was right: give the Tamils voting rights at the local level — let them have their own mayors, police officers, school leaders, and fully assimilate them into the society. Then the radicals have no cause. (Nobody asked me for my candid opinion when I was there, either.)

Peter Joseph Cooks "Mild" Curry for Master

We heard about Peter Joseph, a Tamil jack-of-all-trades, from people in Honduras who had been stationed in Sri Lanka working for CARE, the feeding program for very low income people in developing countries. Peter had been their "houseboy/driver" for a couple of years, and they arranged for a job with CARE for him before leaving Sri Lanka for Honduras.

We looked him up, and he was available part-time to work for us. Peter was unique. He was an outstanding cook. He had trained himself and had become one of the best mechanics in the CARE motor pool. He was an excellent driver. Peter could fix anything, and he had a marvelous way of directing other people—he was a take-charge individual.

So soon he was coming in the evenings to teach Jane how to cook many unique Sri Lanka curry dishes, string noodles, poppadans, fresh pepper crab (the crab man came to the door carrying a burlap bag full of snapping crabs on ice, and you picked them out fresh, shoved them into the freezer, and they "calmed down" until you were ready to drop them into boiling, seasoned water) and many more. But talk about hot and spicy —the farther south one goes on the Indian continent, the more hot peppers are used. Sri Lankan is the hottest food I have ever eaten. With me it starts on the tongue and lips—that really burning sensation—then I break out in a sweat on my forehead, soon the sweat forms on my nose, and I m really uncomfortable clear to my stomach and then down to my toes. How Sri Lankans can get used to eating that hot food I will never understand.

I thought it was an unfortunate thing also because if you could get them to hold half the hot peppers they normally use, the food was very tasty. They use a lot of coconut milk in their cooking, and this adds a most delightful flavor. Well, Peter would make special recipes, holding the peppers and making it "mild for master." I am sure glad he did not make his dishes "hotter for master."

When traveling with my ARTI colleagues, eating at ministry of agriculture facilities, they would go to the kitchen, explain that an American "with a tender stomach" was traveling with them, and ask to have a "mild curry" prepared for him (me). Then they would get bowls of yogurt and special bread for me; those were the only things that would put out the fire in my mouth and stomach when I ate those "special curries."

Peter Joseph Organizes Our Household Staff

Sri Lanka differs culturally from Latin America in many ways. For example, domestic help is very specialized. We hired Jenita, a wisp of a little Sinhalese who probably did not weigh 85 pounds, and stood about 4 feet 10 inches tall. She was a live-in lady's maid. We had a servant's room and bath/shower outside the kitchen, so she had privacy. We did not have privacy. In Sri Lanka the lady's maid, especially where there are small children, is also the nanny and does not ever go to bed until the child, the master and the madam have gone to bed.

In the morning the lady's maid is first up, making coffee or tea and hovering outside the child's door, or waiting outside the master's/ madam's bedroom for early morning instruction about delivering the coffee, tea, or breakfast to their bedroom. One long weekend (Sri Lanka has so many holidays we used to lose count; every full or new moon, for example, is called Poya, and is a national holiday in Buddhist Sri Lanka) Jenita had to go to her village because a relative was sick. Jane's reaction? "Thank God she's going to be gone for three days; now I can run nude through the house in the morning if I want to. There won't be somebody hiding behind the wall waiting to jump out to help!"

Jenita was the kindest, most agreeable person one could ever want to find. She was marvelous with Jenny and with Jane, was very respectful with me, and never caused any trouble. But she was "always there"—you could not get away from her presence. But Jenita would not do any heavy work. Assisting as a nanny with Jenny, with the madam's laundry, assisting in the kitchen, setting the table, doing dishes, that was it. Cleaning floors? Cleaning windows? Waxing floors (done every other day)? Cleaning and polishing furniture? Vacuuming? Never. Those were houseboy chores.

In our case, it was a young Sinhalese man about twenty years old (I think Jenita was about twenty-eight years old) named Wickremasinga, who came three days per week. Wickremasinga was also the gardener. Even though the U.S. Embassy insisted that we have uniformed guards inside the gates and fence of our property twenty-four hours per day (two men performed this function on 12-hour shifts each), and there was little work for them to do, and they most often were "bored stiff," they dare not—when Wickremasinga was there—do any gardening work, such as water the plants and flowers.

This "specialization of domestic labor" in Sri Lanka did not exist where we were in Latin America. Gertrudes in Bolivia, or Norma in Honduras, would do any jobs they were asked to do. It did not make any difference to them; they wanted to be of help and earn their money however we asked them to. I think what we were seeing was a bit of the caste system, so prevalent still in India, that the British used to their own purposes when Sri Lanka was Ceylon and part of the empire.

On weekends when Peter Joseph was there all day, everything "jingled"—was letter perfect. He had those people all working like an assembly line in a factory. Peter would find jobs, assign tasks, and work really would be accomplished. I had a strange experience one of those days: I caused a bit of "losing face" among the staff—inadvertently, of course—and got my comeuppance.

I was in the communications room on a Saturday afternoon listening to shortwave radio—probably a Voice of America replay of a college football game with one of my favorite teams. Suddenly there was a "thump" in the sound, and the radio went dead. I had no idea what had happened outside because the air conditioning units—always on—blocked any outside noise.

So I went out to the front yard. The day guard came up to me in uniform, saluted me and said: "Master—crows up on roof broke radio wire!" I looked up to where Peter Joseph and I had strung the thin copper wire between two poles attached to the ends of the peaked roof with insulators to form my radio antenna, with a lead wire into the window of the communications room, and sure enough, only saw two dangling wires lying on the corrugated roof.

I went back to the adjoining neighbor's yard, asked to borrow a ladder and carried the ladder back to my upper balcony where I started to climb up to the roof to splice the two pieces of antenna wire back together. Such a commotion you have never seen. Jenita, the day guard and Wickremasinga the gardener, all three were shouting for Peter Joseph, who came running in his bare feet, jumped up on the bottom rung of the ladder shouting "No master—I will climb up and fix it! Down master! Master cannot go on the roof without Peter"!

Apparently I had broken a taboo—doing work that was to be done only by hired servants. No normal, properly thinking master, would move to take the place of a hired servant and do manual labor he or she would ordinarily do. I would have caused them to lose face with each other. Now that really is specialization of labor in a country that still has a bit of the caste system left over from bygone years.

Master's House Caught on Fire—but It Is Out Now

One of the watchmen we hired at embassy insistence, and who worked the 6 p.m. until 6 a.m. shift, unfortunately had a drinking problem, as we found out later. We were away one weekend and I had asked him to burn all the cardboard boxes and papers that our sea freight had been wrapped in when the lift-van containing it was finally unloaded.

Imagine our concern when arriving back Sunday after dark to see scads of people, including Peter Joseph whom we had given the weekend off, milling around our house. The roof had caught on fire from burning ashes blown up by the wind, and the guard had paid little or no attention to what was happening. Fortunately a boy servant across the street saw the smoke coming from the roof and called his employer who called the fire department.

A Christmas Surprise from the Night Guard

Now the night guard apparently heard the details from one of our employees, and so for Christmas, to make up for two goofs, he had a surprise for us. He hired a cobra snake charmer to come to our house with his cobras and put on a show for us. We did watch and were polite, but could hardly wait until "the show" was over, and the cobras were safely back in their wicker baskets with the lids securely fastened. The cobra owner took his baskets under his arm and hopped the next bus that came by on Jawata Road in front of our house. I still imagine a fellow passenger asking the charmer: "Say, what do you have in those baskets? May I see? ..."

The next time we went on a trip up to Kandy we took Peter along to drive. We also passed by his boyhood home in the tea country. I found out on this trip that Peter could not see at night to drive; we nearly missed a couple of sharp curves, and I made him turn the wheel over to me when the truth was finally admitted. After we returned to our house in Colombo, we found the night guard replaced by his company; it had checked up on him one night and found him drinking again.

Some Magnificent Scenery and History in Sri Lanka

Before the "civil disturbances" broke out in Colombo during July 1983, we did quite a bit of touring on the island to look at historic places. Some of this was done in connection with my work, Jane and Jenny traveling with me. Everywhere one goes in Sri Lanka, one sees: 1) Elephants and 2) "Tanks." The elephants are still beasts of burden, trained to carry and haul logs and do timbering in the jungles, and are dressed nearly every full moon, or Poya, to parade in torch light parades. There were still quite a few herds of wild elephants in Sri Lanka, which caused problems for the government as jungles were cleared and more farmland brought into cultivation.

"Tanks" are an interesting phenomenon; they are really man-made reservoirs, some dating back hundreds of years, and many several miles in length and width. These are used to store water for use in irrigating rice and other crops during drought conditions.

And the tanks are everywhere in the country. The more ancient ones are at the sites of Buddhist shrines and temples. I have never seen so many statues of Buddha—all different sizes, shapes, and adornments.

Anuradhapura Has the Most Buddhas

Anuradhapura, which lies on the northern plain, was the ancient capital of Ceylon, probably founded in the fifth century B.C. It is beastly hot there—and the food is even hotter! But the area contains many beautiful tanks from ancient days, and *dagobas*, or shrines to Buddha, of simple but elegant design line many of these tanks or reservoirs. At Anuradhapura the greatest of the Sinhalese Buddhist architecture was achieved. The lotus flower is sacred to Buddhists, and it is delicately carved in many of the architectural forms, along with elephants, tigers, and sensuous human forms in dance, in romance, and other poses. Procreation and love were obviously high in Buddhist values.

Sigirya—the Mountain Fortress

Sigirya is a paradox. This gigantic mountain of granite rises alone out of the northern plain and has a strange history. An ancient king, Kasyapa, murdered his father, seized the throne and then sought refuge from the realization of the horrors of his deeds and the vengeance of his brother by constructing an impenetrable fortress on this rocky mountain. But he also imported Indian painters to adorn the fortress. The famous bare-breasted courtesans of Kasyapa's court still adorn the walls of a winding gallery high in the rock. I passed all twenty-one of them as I climbed up the narrow passage to the top one very hot day.

The paradox about the "fortress" is that to capture and punish Kasyapa, the brother only had to surround the mountain in a siege and starve the king and his followers into surrendering. This he did, according to Sri Lankan historians, but now all that is left from this fascinating period in the country's ancient past are the beautiful paintings of the courtesans!

Trincomalee Was a Favorite Tranquil Spot

Trincomalee, on the far northeastern part of the island, perhaps 160 miles from Colombo as the crow flies, was a beautiful port on the Bay of Bengal of the Indian Ocean. It is the second most important seaport in Sri Lanka after Colombo. A Sri Lankan businessman who was trying to return purebred horses onto the island from India introduced us to the area. Jane learned about him from her equestrian friends, and we were even shown the first breeding stallion and mares that he had in quarantine in Colombo.

The gentleman, his wife and family owned a motel/resort on the Bay of Bengal and invited us to visit them. We drove in two cars, since each family had brought a maid along, but encountered a monsoon rain on a road pocked with potholes. These were full of water, and not knowing how deep they were, and fearful of breaking down in the jungle far from any mechanics or service people, we had to come to nearly a complete stop at each one. The trip took forever, but the breath-taking scenery and tranquility when we arrived was well worth the long journey. We stayed several days with this lovely family.

By the time we made the trip, he had all his horses at the farm adjoining his motel and resort at Trincomalee. We enjoyed sleeping in air conditioned splendor as he had his own generator for electricity. Most places on the plains—where it was so hot —had only ceiling fans, if they had electricity at all. Because of all the tanks, mosquitoes—including those that spread malaria and other fevers—were a constant concern. Thus we normally slept under mosquito netting during the nights.

I believe it safe to say that other than the high mountain country around Nuwara Eliya, Trincomolee was our favorite tourist attraction. I am sad to report that during the height of the civil war in the late 1980s, we heard that our friend's motel was burned to the ground, and all his purebred horses killed. The Tamil extremists controlled large parts of this area in the northeast of the island.

The Maldives Have the Most Beautiful Reefs I Have Seen

The Maldives consist of about 1,200 coral islands in nineteen atolls some 600 miles from Sri Lanka off the southwestern coast of India. Many have said that the Maldives have the most beautiful coral and reefs of anyplace but Australia. To me, never having been to the Great Barrier Reefs of Australia, these are the most beautiful I have seen and are a bit more enchanting than those we learned to love in the Caribbean.

This is an interesting Islamic republic, very conservative in many ways, but which earns much of its income from foreign tourism. We were told how beautiful and peaceful the islands were, and how beautiful were the sand beaches, coral, flora, and fauna under the sea. So three families got reservations through Air Lanka (the Sri

Lankan national airline) and took a Lanka scheduled jet flight to the Maldives to spend a long holiday weekend.

Evidence of the dichotomy between the Islamic nature of the country and its interest in earning foreign exchange from tourists soon became evident. As soon as we landed at the jet airport on Male, the capital of the Maldives, and were shuttled through customs, our boat (for a particular island hotel where we had reservations) was waiting for us, as were about thirty other hotel-resort boats. The authorities do not particularly want tourists, of which there were many from Europe, roaming around the city of Male.

As long as the tourists stay on the island or atoll where their hotel-resort is located, all is well. The conservative Islamic republic has no alcohol or gambling in its capital city, or elsewhere. Native women wear the sari, and many also wear veils; no shorts or skimpy bathing suits allowed. However, the hotels and resorts on the isolated atolls have "special license," and have very complete bars, casinos, discotheques and dancing, topless bathing (a favorite of the European tourists from Italy, Germany, France and Scandinavia) and other "liberties."

Each family had a cabana right on the beach, with palm trees giving shade. The sand was a pristine white and fine as silk. The coral was right there not 15 feet from the edge of the beach, and the water was warm and calm. We wasted no time donning snorkels and exploring. I must tell you the colors of the coral and sea life were exquisite.

Whale-Watching and Sea Turtle Egg-Laying

We also made great trips to see the impressive gray whales off the coast of Batticaloa, and the giant sea turtle *aribada* beaching to lay eggs off the west coast of the island. Again, colleagues had gone great gray whale searching in small ocean-going launches off the east coast of the island from the port of Batticaloa. They came back to Colombo with stories of touching, snoozing whales on the surface as the small launches quietly and slowly closed on the giant mammals, much bigger by far than the boats! So we went and got probably to within 25 feet of a couple of giants, but were never able to get close enough to touch one. That was fine with me. Twenty feet was close enough. One swipe of the boat by one of those whales' giant flukes would smash the vessel to smithereens, and me with it.

An interesting side note on the great gray whales of the Indian Ocean: They are captive, we were told, since they will not cross the equator. Thus, they spend half the year off the west coast of Sri

Lanka, since the southwest monsoon (June to October) carries cool mountain rivers through the plains to the sea, where the nutrients washed from the land result in growth of billions of krill, the food of the baleen whales (i.e., those that have no teeth, but giant strainers for capturing krill, small shrimp and other morsels of tiny sea animals that make up their diet). During the northeast monsoon (December to March) the whales have swum around the island to the northeast coast where the monsoon rains have washed nutrients to feed the minuscule sea life, which then feed the whales.

My PASA Difficulties with the Embassy and USAID Are Clarified

Thanks to a fine USAID controller and an embassy executive officer, I finally found out why we were kept "cooling our heels" in Washington, D.C. for more than a month before the PASA contract was signed between my agency, USDA, and the USAID Mission to Sri Lanka. This also explained why I had so much trouble getting access to the benefits we were entitled to, such as commissary privileges, NPO (Navy Post Office mail), embassy medical, and others.

One officer in the USAID Mission did not want a USDA specialist, but wanted a university professor instead. Not only that, but the officer specified one of the finest from two of the best universities in the country, either Iowa State or Cornell. So the officer was assigned this "clod" from USDA—from Pennsylvania, no less.

The first few weeks we were in Sri Lanka, trying to adjust to a new culture, home, climate, etc., I would go to the commissary to pick up some American "necessities," and the foreign service national manager, who daily run most American facilities overseas for our embassies, would take me aside and say something like: "Oh sir, I am told you are a 'contractor' and not entitled to use our commissary—so sorry

So I would go to the proper American authority, in this case whoever was chair person of the commissary committee, with my PASA contract in hand, pointing out the clause granting me commissary privileges, and state that "I'm a federal employee just like you, pay income taxes on my whole salary, just like you!" (Private sector "contractors" had income tax exclusion on the first $70,000 of income earned overseas then, and this was a bone of contention with many Foreign Service officers from the State Department).

An "official memo" would be drafted, go through the normal, lengthy U.S. government clearance procedure, and eventually get to the manager of the commissary, or the military post office (Navy, in Sri Lanka), and finally after days and days of hassling, we would be permitted to do that which we were entitled to.

One day the then-executive officer of the embassy called me and asked me to come by. The individual was packing up to leave Sri Lanka and wanted to give me my personnel file. Give me my personnel file? In all my work overseas for the U.S. government, nobody had ever wanted to give me—even show me—my personnel file in the embassy. But dutifully I went to the individual's office, because I respected and admired that person. I remarked when my file was handed to me: "Nobody has ever shown me this information—what gives?" The executive officer said: "Don't ask questions, Howard—take the file and read. I do not want it back, so destroy it when you've finished reading!"

Well, it soon became obvious why I had so much trouble. The officer, who did not want me, or any USDA person, tried every way possible to stop the PASA contract. But the USAID Mission Director, Ms. Sarah Jane Littlefield, overruled the officer. It was Sarah Jane who also made it possible for me, Jane, and Jenny to return to the United States in the summer of 1983 for a vacation, "Rest and Recuperation Leave" (R&R) in this case, because the officer denied permission for us to have "home leave" to which we would normally be entitled. Because of the glitch in getting the PASA contract signed in Washington, my office put me on a non-overseas payroll for thirty days, and that, technically, wiped out my eligibility for the midterm transfer to Sri Lanka, and a normal midtour home leave, after one year at the second overseas post.

I noticed in early 1983 that Sarah Jane Littlefield would go out of her way, when seeing me at a distance around the embassy, to call me over and introduce me to whatever VIP was visiting from Washington, D.C. She also would describe in glowing detail the success of my teaching and technical assistance work at ARTI with the young Sri Lankan officers. Where she got her information I do not know, but she gave Jane, Jenny, and me a waiver to go on R&R Leave to New York City, rather than to the normal R&R post of Bangkok. That kind gesture saved us a bundle of money. God rest her soul; she passed away several years after we left Sri Lanka. I also must say: God bless the USAID Controller, Art Schantz, who is now deceased, and also the embassy executive officer, who is still living, but who gave me private access to the information that explained some causes of frustration!!

The "Civil Disturbances" Were Frightening

Our servants told us about the deteriorating circumstances in Colombo when we returned on July 22, 1983, from our R&R trip to the United States. They claimed that goon squads were burning Tamils' houses, arresting Tamil professionals, and harassing Tamil families all over the island.

The next Monday when I went to work, there were fires burning all over the city of Colombo. All the foreign national employees at USAID and the embassy—both Sinhalese and Tamils—were very frightened. We got the word about 11 a.m. that the embassy and USAID offices would probably close at 3 p.m. I arranged for a ride to our house on Jawata Road—about four-and-a-half miles away from the embassy and USAID.

I was late returning to the USAID offices from my office at ARTI (about four miles in a different direction from my house) and went into the Oberoi Hotel for lunch. When I came out after lunch about 1 p.m., there were thousands of Sri Lankans running down the main road away from the city. I managed to cross the street to the USAID office, and the English-speaking guard there yelled: "GO home—offices all closed—soldiers may come and shoot anybody on the street in an hour!"

I took off running with the crowd. At a major crossroad I saw a group of armed men in civilian clothes quizzing children in a Volkswagen microbus. They let the Sinhalese kids out (later I heard they asked the children to pronounce certain words, which Sinhalese pronounced differently than Tamils), then wired the door shut, poured kerosene on the bus, and set it afire.

I made a quick detour and started running through back alleys. I reached my house in forty-five minutes. I was never that afraid of being shot at in South Vietnam (after all it was in a war, and we knew where not to go from careful intelligence briefings) or being held up by guerrillas in Bolivia. There was no predicting or understanding what was happening in Sri Lanka; it was anarchy and genocide!

We always had the drapes drawn in our house on Jawata Road, to keep the hot sun out, and for privacy at night, so when I banged on the door Jane came and cracked it a bit, and was I ever glad to be home! Inside were our Tamil servants and their families. Later that night another Tamil woman, who worked for the Overs (an American family who were away on home leave) came with her children. Before morning we had eleven adults and children, including Jane, Jenny and me, sleeping fearfully in various rooms in our house.

We were fortunate. Our Sinhalese neighbors up the street lied for us. Apparently the goons, searching for Tamils to capture or kill, stopped at several Sinhalese homes and asked if the Americans down on the corner had Tamil or Sinhalese servants. Well, we did have Jenita living in—she was Sinhalese—so the neighbors said: "Oh they have Sinhalese servants and guards!" The goons never came to our door, or we would have been in deep trouble.

Three days later we got a visit from a security guard from the American embassy announcing that they had permission for us to go to the commissary—that we would be escorted by convoy. We cleaned out the food in the commissary in about half an hour. The following week the Sri Lankan army had taken the city over from the civilian police (who I believe were involved in anarchy, perhaps with the army turning its back and staying in the barracks).

Telephone service was restored (although we were warned by a visit from our American block captain not to say anything confidential on the phone because they believed all American calls were being monitored), and the word was that on the following Monday chickens and eggs would be available—to go to our regular chicken/egg retailer where we were known. Only the men were to be out on the street. I went. I stood in an unruly line, watched over by an army soldier, for three hours, and came away with two scrawny chickens and ten eggs!

By this time, with all the people we were feeding in the house, those chickens and eggs were most welcome. We had about exhausted the American canned meats, cereals, flour, rice, instant potatoes, and so on, and were ready for some fresh protein in the form of chicken and eggs.

President Junawardena named a new prime minister and peace— of a sort—returned to the country. I was told that tens of thousands of Tamils—mostly professionals, civil servants, businessmen, retailers, teachers, wholesalers, university professors and the like—fled the country during this period. Most by boat across the Palk Strait to India, others by international flights, other than Air Lanka—if they could afford it.

Unfortunately, the civil war continues today. Some estimates put the number of dead, or missing and presumed dead, at more than 100,000 people. Some of these may have successfully fled to other countries but have not contacted relatives for fear of reprisals. What a pity for such a beautiful country with a rich heritage and culture.

Charlie Porter Comes to Help Me Train ARTI Officers

My Sri Lanka experience would not have been complete without Charlie Porter's contribution to our work with the Sri Lankan ARTI officers. Charlie came to me from the USDA's Agricultural Marketing Service (AMS) where he had been a grades and standards and agricultural marketing information specialist for many years.

Charlie had also worked for the State Cooperative Extension Services in both Pennsylvania and Maryland and knew how to get along with all kinds of people and also how to motivate them to change their way of doing things too. Interestingly, this was Charlie's first working experience in a developing country. He had been in the U.S. Army during World War II, so knew about the differences between American culture and that of other countries, principally European. But Charlie was not aware of what he would see in Sri Lanka.

However he quickly adjusted to the work at hand. He was instrumental in moving quickly to incorporate the two major assembly markets "up country" into our price reporting plan for the major market of Colombo. We were developing a daily price reporting system for eight basic food commodities, including the ubiquitous "Samba rice," and some other popular vegetables and fruits. We avoided the early problem of no scientifically based valuation criteria, in order to get some reporting system in place that would be useful, by having the young officers evaluate and quote prices for: "above average, average and other quality" daily.

This would work to get the system started. ARTI officers telephoned the prices each morning to radio stations, and the only television station, which was government-owned. Now it was time to build a database for future use in analyzing trends. The U.S. government had bought ARTI a state-of-the-art small mainframe computer. We planned to use it at night to analyze the prices arriving from the two assembly markets in the interior, plus Colombo's for that day. But the ARTI employee whose area of responsibility included data processing and analysis exercised a personal ownership responsibility for the very expensive computer that we Americans had donated to ARTI. Every night when she left to go home from work, she locked the computer in with two large, industrial locks, to which she was the only one who had keys.

Neither Charlie, nor I for that matter, liked this monopolization. We certainly could not do anything about it either, since we were guests in the woman's country. We burned slowly. I learned that the situation did not get rectified until that particular individual retired several years later. I hope the market news and price reporting system Charlie and I started—elementary as it was—is up and running. Charlie did a great job training and motivating those ARTI officers. But at night over drinks at my house, we shook our heads in disbelief many, many times.

In early 1998 the minister of defense of Sri Lanka had to resign when suicide bombers of the radical Tamil Tigers blew up the sacred Buddhist Tooth Temple in the city of Kandy. That was the most sacred of all the Buddhist temples in the country, said to contain a partial fragment of Buddha's tooth. The civil war goes on today as the Tamil extremists try to form a separate Tamil state in the north and northeast of this picturesque island in the Indian Ocean.

Peter Joseph Visits Us in Northern Virginia

Imagine my surprise one morning at about 4:00 a.m. when my telephone rang on the nightstand next to my bed. I answered, and it was Peter Joseph calling from South Korea. He did not talk very long but indicated he will see us in northern Virginia on December 18, 2004. I have no idea what this meant, but prepared myself for whatever Peter came up with. Sure enough, on December 18 in the evening he called and we had an animated conversation. Seems that his sister Rita Joseph, who also emigrated to South Korea from Sri Lanka during the "civil disturbances", is a "nanny" for a Korean/American family temporarily in Reston, Virginia. Peter has come to visit his sister and to see America for the first time.

We had several nice visits with Peter and his sister Rita at our home. Typical Peter: the first evening he arrived before Christmas, he brought me gifts: four pairs of socks and four neckties. He also brought wife Elaine some appropriate gifts. Peter has not changed at all in the twenty years since we were in Sri Lanka together. Peter returned to South Korea soon after the first of 2005 and resumed his career as headwaiter at the Spanish embassy in Seoul, South Korea. Peter is one fine friend, and all of us, including Jen, who did remember him from Sri Lanka days, were truly glad to see him again.

16

Back to Virginia

We returned to Washington, D.C., and our home in Fairfax, Virginia, in the summer of 1984 after spending about a week in Greece touring historic spots and taking a boat trip to the Greek islands in the Aegean Sea. The boat trip was a favorite of Jenny's. We stopped on one island for a few hours, and I hired a horse-drawn two-wheel open cart for a ride up the mountain overlooking the sea.

The Greek driver insisted that Jenny sit up front on the driver's seat with him! They made quite a pair; we have a picture of her long blond pigtails flying straight out in the breeze as the little horse took us at "flank speed" down the road. Both Jenny and the driver are grinning from ear to ear.

We toured the Acropolis and the Parthenon in Athens. But it was the fresh Greek fruits and vegetables, like fresh figs and sweet tangerines, and the fresh grape leaves wrapped with various Greek cheeses that really impressed us. Baklava, that exotic Middle Eastern pastry, is worth a stop-off in Athens all by itself! But, oh the calories!

The Greek people were friendly everywhere we went. I would go back in a minute for an extended tour of the country and its many islands and history.

Readjusting to American Life and Culture after Eight Years

The readjustment after eight years overseas in residence for me, and seven for Jane, was amazing. One does not realize how different our culture really is, especially when compared with cultures of the developing world. Even though we had been back to the United States on home leaves and on R&R, the total immersion when finally returning permanently was a real shock. One example: We were going to the farm up in Somerset County, Pennsylvania, one home-leave trip directly by rental car from the Pittsburgh airport. We stopped to get some groceries because I knew that there would be no fresh cereal, milk, eggs, margarine, and so on, at the farmhouse, as my mother was at her retirement home near Johnstown, Pennsylvania. Jane said: "I'll get some bacon and eggs and milk, you get some breakfast cereal and bread."

I turned around the end of the cereal aisle, and there in front of me were hundreds of boxes, different brands, different sizes, different flavors, sugared, non-sugared, with fruit, without fruit, and so on, as far as the eye could see to the end of the aisle. At the commissary in Tegucigalpa, whence we had just come, it was a choice of one of three: Rice Krispies, Corn Flakes or Raisin Bran—and all the same size! Then I went through the same frustration all over again trying to decide about bread. Welcome home, Americans!

One Has Time and Help When "Settling In" Overseas: Not Here

My second son, David, and his wife Meg, had rented an efficiency apartment for us near the metro bus line in Arlington County. They knew that we had renters in our townhouse, and we would have to wait for them to move, then probably repaint, re-carpet and do other repair work to the house before moving in; it had been rented for seven years. I figured I would have a couple of weeks to get lots of things done.

Overseas the U.S. Embassy and USAID mission people are pretty laid back with newcomers as they deal with getting established, especially in developing countries where things just do not get done in a timely manner. We ordered a telephone connection in one country and they said: "Oh fine—we're so glad you've come to our country; you are number 160 on the waiting list. It's a pleasure to serve you!" I then asked when the phone would probably be installed, and they said something like "You will know when the installer comes to your house." Overseas, you also have good hired help to run errands for you, help with heavy labor, installing, painting and so on.

But back in the States, we were fully into "readjustment shock." My office said that I could have two days administrative leave to get unpacked and do whatever I had to do. The first day of those two days, I got a call from the branch chief under whom I had worked in Latin America asking if I could come to work the next day. I demurred. He said, "But the chief of the rural development division of the Latin America and Caribbean Bureau of USAID/ Washington needs your expertise in agricultural marketing now and insists that you come to work immediately, if you want to help him for a couple of years!"

This is an assignment I would like very much, back in Latin America and Caribbean affairs, with which I felt comfortable because of my knowledge of the languages and cultures. I negotiated by saying I wanted to work for him, but had to shop for and buy a new car, look at our townhouse, unpack unaccompanied air freight, etc. He called back later and asked if I could go for an interview with the chief on Wednesday, then start work on Monday. I said, OK. After all, I was lucky to have a job—and a potentially good one too!

Back to Work at USAID: Paint the House at Night

Albert Brown, my new boss at USAID, was known affectionately as "Scaff," short for Scaffold, all around the world because of his height. He was a former basketball player from the Midwest, about six feet four inches tall at a time when anyone over six feet was considered tall—thus earning him the nickname. Scaff was one of the finest men I have ever worked for; smart as a whip, friendly with everyone, seldom losing his temper, and patient with all kinds of people, especially economists like me.

My first day at USAID/LA& C, he asked me if I could type. "Yes, why?" I replied.

"Because," he said, "we have only one and a quarter secretaries for thirteen professionals, and you are going to have to master using the Wang personal computer."

I said: "Alright, send me for training; how long will it take?"

He said: "Training! Heck, we'll have Yvonne work with you an hour, then you're on your own. But, we'll be here to help answer your questions and get you out of trouble." That, indeed, was my introduction to the powerful new PCs. At first I was afraid to touch the keys for fear of blowing the machine up.

I had experience with mainframe computers, having worked on one for my Ph.D. dissertation research years before. But overseas in the embassies and USAID missions, we had lots of local hires— bilingual secretaries to do our typing on Wang PCs—so I had never touched one before. I soon lost my fear, even invested in a used Commodore 60 system for personal use and to teach myself the modern methodologies. The Commodore 60 was as slow as molasses in January, but just the right speed for my rattletrap PC-mind at that time.

Son David Steele and I Paint until the "Wee Hours"

The only way I could get our town house in Comstock Homes repainted was to do it after hours, way after hours. Fortunately, second son David and his wife were living in an apartment complex right next door to Comstock in Fairfax City. I would drive from the efficiency apartment we were renting near Interstate 395 to meet David after supper, and he and I would scrape and paint until we could no longer see straight—midnight, one a.m., or whenever. I paid David for his time, as he needed the money, and he was also saving me a lot. We had fun together, talking about old times and new experiences.

Then we replaced all the carpeting in the place and made some basic overdue repairs. A part of the patio fence in the back had rotted and fallen, and the front stoop was settling at a precarious angle. Finally, we moved in with what we had—slept on the floor for a few nights until the arrival of our sea freight from Sri Lanka, our stored freight from Johnstown (mostly my mother's and dad's furniture put in storage after Mom's death in 1982), and the stored junk I had been using before Jane and I were married.

Jane described what happened one day when three vans with all these belongings of Clan Steele had the whole cul-de-sac blocked. Most people in the complex did not know who we were yet. It surely must have seemed that about three families of hillbillies were moving into that little townhouse, what with that mass of furniture of various sizes, in various states of repair or disrepair, filling up the cul-de-sac. We heard later all about the gossip that flew around the neighborhood. David also recovered some of our old chairs and a sofa for us. His stepfather, Cy Farren, who had married Sally two years after our divorce, had a slip-covering business and trained David in how to do it. David needed the work, as he could not find a job in dairy technology up in Somerset County, as he had hoped. So the new trade Cy taught him helped keep the wolf from the door. He did excellent work too, as he is quite a craftsman.

Scaff Brown Puts Me on the Road

Scaff Brown did not waste any time getting me out to the USAID missions in Latin America and the Caribbean. Together he and I went to Costa Rica to help put together a project paper about the Caribbean Basin Initiative for the USAID Regional Office, Central American Programs (ROCAP). Then my old friend Bill Baucom, rural development officer for USAID in the regional office for the Caribbean, asked me to come to Barbados to present a paper on agricultural export marketing to a regional agricultural marketing workshop at the Wendt Center.

In both instances I was quite excited because I had never been to either country. David Joslyn was the ROCAP agricultural and rural development officer we worked with in Costa Rica. He had established his office in Costa Rica, while headquarters for ROCAP was in Guatemala, to be closer to development institutes he worked with most. These included the Inter-American Institute for Cooperation on Agriculture (IICA) in Coronado, a suburb of San Jose, with which I would work closely during my last six years at USDA, the Tropical Institute for Agricultural Research and Training (CATIE) at Turrialba, and INCAE, the business management institute which was temporarily in San Jose while the Sandanista communists ruled Nicaragua.

Costa Rica, a Jewel in Central America

Everyone I talked with in the mid-1980s said that if I liked Guatemala and Honduras, I would love Costa Rica, called by some "the diamond of Central America." So when I made that first trip to the capital city of San Jose with "Scaff" Brown in 1985 to work with David Joslyn at the Rural Development office of ROCAP there, I was excited. I was not disappointed either. My former brother-in-law Steve Cornelius, who had lived in Costa Rica off and on each year since his Peace Corps days, had moved his family from Missouri to a home up the inactive volcano near the town of Heredia. He and his wife Brigitte and their three children had me to their home on several occasions on my trips to San Jose on this assignment. I should explain that Steve was gathering ten years of data about Pacific Ocean sea turtles and their laying of eggs in the sands of Costa Rica's northwestern beaches as a professional world wildlife specialist concerned about the endangered species status of these magnificent sea creatures.

Steve loved Costa Rica and its people and was very helpful in teaching me the nuances of the country and its culture. Other Central Americans call Costa Rican men *Ticos* and the women *Ticas*. The country advanced ahead of the others in the region economically, culturally, and educationally, I was told. It is probably true to say that Ticos and Ticas had a lot of pride in their accomplishments. Costa Rica is the only country in Central America that does not have a standing army. While they do have a very large and active national police force to keep law and order, they have, as a nation, rejected war as a way to settle international differences. It is very true that they have developed a cadre of well-trained diplomats and participate in international fora in an outstanding way. There is, however, as in all Latin American countries, some corruption. Steve's wife Brigitte, of German ancestry, was particularly incensed with the corruption and bribery she saw in the process of getting the family's household goods and automobile through Costa Rican customs. Attempts to "soak Americans and other foreigners with undeclared 'taxes' and license fees" also disgusted both Steve and Brigitte.

Howard Commits a Social Blunder at a Costa Rican Dinner

In Honduras where I had last lived in residence in Central America (1980–1982) before that first trip to Costa Rica with "Scaff" Brown in 1985, evening dress in the tropics was quite casual, even for "formal invitations". The men wore their best Guayabera shirts to such an occasion and it was considered "the fashionable 'in thing' to do". So when David Joslyn and his wife Ximena (pronounced "Heemena" in English) invited "Scaff" Brown and me to their home in San Jose for dinner one Friday evening, I put on my best white Guayabera, as I would have done in Tegucigalpa, Honduras. No way Jose! Scaff and all the invited male guests were in their best business suits. Now the invited guests were the newly elected Director of the Inter-American Institute for Cooperation on Agriculture (IICA) — a man I later had real difficulty with in 1993, as related in *Food Soldier*, the newly elected director of the Center for Tropical Research and Training (CATIE), their deputies, and wives. A VERY FORMAL OCCASION in San Jose!

I was "saved" by the deputy director general of IICA, my old friend from USAID/Washington days, Dr. Harlan Davis. He kept introducing me to the men and their wives (the wives' dresses looked like they had all been bought at Nordstroms or Neiman Marcus) as Dr. Howard Steele, *un professor de economía rural magnífico y bien, bien Hondureño!* (Dr. Howard Steele, a magnificent professor of agricultural economics and very, very Honduran!) Everyone laughed, but I was most embarrassed. Again, little cultural nuances often mean a lot. The Costa Ricans and other Latin Americans serving in Costa Rica turned out to be very formal people, as well as nice ones. I adjusted quite quickly!

A new political appointee was soon installed as ROCAP mission director in Guatemala City, and she asked David Joslyn to move his agriculture and rural development office back there. David resisted, explaining why he had worked so hard to move the ROCAP office to Costa Rica in the first place, and the ease with which he could work with the institutes located in Costa Rica. Having seen David's beautiful home and fine family (he married a lovely Chilean woman, and his two teenagers were well established in Costa Rican schools, which were quite good), I knew he also had a personal reason to want to finish his tour in San Jose.

In a matter of months, the ROCAP mission director insisted that David either move to Guatemala City or go back to Washington, D.C. In the meantime, David and I witnessed the first truly democratic election in Guatemala in many years. He and I just happened to be finishing editing the new project paper I mentioned above, parts of which had been done by a private consulting firm (we called them "Beltway Bandits," but most of them had a cadre of talented specialists who were good at putting government projects together).

We were staying near the famous Camino Real-Biltmore Hotel in a pension (like bed and breakfast lodging in the States), and David had been invited to celebrate the election with the U.S. staff members of the Democratic Election Monitoring Team. The election monitoring was sponsored by the Organization of American States for the first free, civilian election in Guatemala in many years, that is, one not controlled completely by the Guatemala military. The staffers had a hospitality room in the hotel with all kinds of goodies for American politicians who were helping to monitor the precinct voting in various places throughout the country, and for the ever-present American news media representatives.

This was before satellite and cable TV were installed throughout Guatemala, but the U.S. Embassy had made a hookup, and we were watching a National Football League game, enjoying the refreshments, while waiting for the U.S. observers to arrive back from monitoring precinct voting. I was sitting on a couch, and a man I thought looked familiar, but whom I did not immediately recognize, sat down next to me with a soft drink, and we began to cheer for the same team. David came in from downstairs in the hotel and sat on my other side. He whispered into my ear: "Do you know who you are talking with next to you?"

I said, "No."

He said: "Be careful what you say; that's Senator Mark Hatfield from Oregon!"

I said to David: "He seems like a pretty regular guy to me; he sure knows his pro football—and I'll bet he puts his pants on one leg at a time, just like I do!" Dave laughed, and we had a good time with Senator Hatfield and the various media members.

The following day, Dave and I were eating in the Camino Real-Biltmore outdoor cafe around the pool, when the apparent president-elect of Guatemala and his entourage entered and sat at the large tables next to us. As the television and other cameras started clicking, David said: "I think we had better move before we end up in the pictures and have a lot of explaining to do." Move we did.

Later that year David got into a real argument with his new ROCAP mission director about resisting the order to move to Guatemala City from San José, Costa Rica. Earlier he had hypothesized to me that the mission director did not like him, and his tenure was precarious. I said that our new chief at LAC/USAID/Washington, Steve Wingert, was looking for a deputy chief, and I thought David would be a great candidate.

David picked up on the suggestion immediately, and we went to the U.S. Embassy in San José, where another mutual friend, Dan Chaij, was the USAID mission director for the U.S. bilateral program with Costa Rica, and David went in to ask him about the idea. They called Steve Wingert right then.

The bottom line here was that a couple of months later several of us were standing in the outer office of LAC/USAID/Washington at the Department of State with our coffee, as was our custom, when David Joslyn appeared in the doorway, attaché case in hand, and asked loud and clear: "Does anyone know where a Foreign Service officer with USAID can find political asylum in this building?" He was soon named deputy chief of the Rural Development Division, LAC/USAID/Washington. David did a good job in that position, too.

Earlier I mentioned going to Barbados to present a paper to an Agricultural Export Marketing Workshop at the Wendt Center in the capital city of Bridgetown. Bill Baucom, USAID agricultural and rural development officer in the Caribbean island countries, had his headquarters in Bridgetown. He and his wife, Ann, lived north of the city on the Caribbean side on the beach. Bill had invited me to be a key speaker and resource person for a number of breakout groups at the workshop.

Bill and Ann were from North Carolina, and Bill had been on a USDA RSSA contract like I was then serving on before he went direct hire with USAID's Foreign Service. In fact while I was project manager of Diversification in Coca Zones in Bolivia, we contracted Bill through USDA to come and head up a team of experts on spices and cacao production and marketing technologies. Bill was, and is, an outstanding leader.

Howard: What the Devil Is USDA Trying to Do to Me

That—in even stronger terms—was what Bill asked me in a telephone call, pulling me out of a small group session one afternoon at the Wendt Center. He had received a call from the minister of agriculture of Barbados who wanted Bill to commit $67,000 from his USAID funds to another Caribbean Basin Export Marketing

Workshop that my USDA group wanted the minister to sponsor. Apparently the minister had recently visited my organization, then called The Office of International Cooperation and Development (OICD) of USDA, and OICD's administrator had said that USAID was keenly interested in the Caribbean Basin Initiative and that the minister should contact Mr. Baucom to see if he could co-finance the workshop.

Unfortunately, nobody from OICD's Private Sector Relations Group (OICD/PSR), which wanted to organize and manage the workshop for the minister, thought to check the idea with Bill Baucom or USAID first! Bill Baucom was livid with rage—and he had sound reasons too!

Why have a second workshop on the same subject in Barbados within a matter of weeks?

Even though the USAID/Caribbean Offices were in Barbados, the country's per capita income had increased sufficiently so that the U.S. government no longer had a bilateral development assistance program with the country.

Bill Baucom knew that the minister was running for prime minister; by inviting all the other ministers of agriculture and prime ministers from the twelve other island countries, the minister hoped to advance his candidacy.

All of Bill's USAID funds for that year were already committed to sound projects in the other twelve nations.

So I was on the hot seat. I got on the phone to Washington, D.C., to inform my director of the situation. And, I asked for guidance on how to respond to our good friend and former colleague Bill Baucom—whom our administrator had compromised with her cavalier statement to the minister from Barbados. My director, Bill Hoofnagle, was livid about the action of our administrator, and of OICD/PSR. He said: "Support Bill Baucom and USAID/ Caribbean in whatever action he decides to take with the minister of agriculture. I'll read the riot act to those people in OICD/PSR and to the administrator here!"

I got a car and went to Bill's office. He had calmed down somewhat by the time I got there. Then he said: "We have a meeting with the minister in an hour—I'd sure like for you to come with me"! I told him about my director's instruction to me. He said "great—I'm going to tell the minister to postpone the proposed dates your private sector relations people suggested for about six months. And, ask him to solicit all the ministers of agriculture in the countries I serve to find out how interested they are—meaning, how much money they're willing to kick in for the workshop. Then, and only then, will I try to get USAID/Washington to match it with travel money for their specialists to come to Barbados. What do you think?"

I said: "Bill, now I know why you are in charge of this program." It was a smart, diplomatic way to save face with—and for—the minister and to avoid conflict with my administrator and OICD/PSR.

In our meeting with the minister of agriculture Bill was all sweetness and light. He deferred to me as an expert whom he had invited to give an export marketing lecture at the Wendt Center for the current workshop, and one who knew all about OICD's private sector relations group. Further, he said that he and I had discussed the minister's interesting idea to help promote the Caribbean Basin Initiative and export enhancement possibilities in the region. "What would the minister think of this strategy to fulfill his idea?"

The minister beamed all over with "his" new idea, as articulated by one very smart Bill Baucom. After we left the minister's office, Bill said: "Howard, we're going to my house on the beach, have a big, tall glass of liquid refreshment and go snorkeling on the reef just off my back porch, OK? Then Ann and I are going to grill a barbecue for us in the backyard. Howard, I sure am glad you came to visit us!"

Baucom was USAID/Washington's representative to the Food and Agriculture Organization of the United Nations in Rome when I wrote this and was undoubtedly every bit as effective there as he was in Barbados.

Belize Gains Independence: USAID Helps Its Development

In 1981 British Honduras gained its independence from the United Kingdom and became Belize. This small country, about the size of Massachusetts, is bordered by the Caribbean on the East, Mexico on the north, and Guatemala on the south and west. It has a mixed culture of Mestiza, Creole, and Mayan, with that group of Keyans (Quayans) from old England in the islands off the east coast as mentioned before regarding Honduras.

Belize had a long history of colonial domination, first by the Spanish, then by the British. In fact, Guatemala claimed Belize as one of its departments until recently (and a border dispute has still not been resolved), a legacy of colonial Spanish days. Britain, however, controlled the country for more than 175 years and used it as one source of valuable tropical hardwood timber. British merchants cut and shipped timber to the motherland, and their ships returned with agricultural staples to feed the natives, with other essentials such as salt, coffee, tea, and needed manufactured goods such as clothing, furniture, shoes, hardware, and the like.

We were told during our orientation before departing to work with the government and private sector that in fact natives were not allowed to show any entrepreneurial initiatives under the tight British domination. Prison—and at times worse—was the reward for showing an interest in private enterprise, especially in trying to compete with imported goods from Mother England. So there was a dearth of capital and capital enterprises in little British Honduras, now independent Belize, right up until British colonial rule ended and the country gained independence in 1981.

Howard: Take a Good Look at the Belize Food Marketing Company

That was my assignment from USAID/Washington. I was to go to Belize, meet the new USAID mission director for Belize, Ned Brashish, and his rural development officer, and make an economic analysis of the basic foods marketing monopoly run by a subsidiary of the Belize government. After the government-run electric utility company, the Belize Food Marketing Company was alleged to be the second biggest money loser of the treasury.

Since much of the technical side of this type of analysis would involve looking at how efficiently rice, corn, sorghum and edible beans (all staples in the economy) were being produced, stored, marketed and handled, I suggested that we subcontract with the Food and Feed Grains Institute of Kansas State University to help us with the analyses and study. Brashish strongly endorsed my suggestion, and I soon met Dr. Dick Phillips from Kansas State. I knew that Dick had done similar, outstanding work elsewhere in the developing world. We met in Washington, D.C., and began to outline our approach to the research problem. Then we journeyed to Belize City, met Ned Brashish and Steve Zaydek, the deputy agricultural development officer, with whom we would be working day-to-day. They in turn made arrangements for us to travel to the new capital city of Belmopan to meet the minister of agriculture, Dean Lindo, his permanent secretary, Rodney Neal, and Mrs. Sandra Bedran, the pleasant and capable new president of the Belize Food Marketing Company.

Belize Carves a Capital Out of the Jungle, and England Defends Belize for Fifteen Years

Why do I include these two diverse items on the same line? We were touring the new capital Belize was creating as it carved Belmopan out of the higher mountainous plain inland from the Caribbean Sea when I thought I was a "dead man." Four Royal Air Force Harrier jet airplanes, traveling at a speed that must have been Mach .8 (.8 the speed of sound at sea level), buzzed the city and blew my hat off (as I hit the ground) and nearly burst my eardrums. Part of the agreement for Belize's independence was that the British Army, the Royal Air Force and the Royal Navy would help defend the tiny country for fifteen years.

This was no idle diplomatic nicety, as Guatemala had been claiming British Honduras as its sovereign territory for hundreds of years. Who knows what other enemies the fledgling country might discover? So the United Kingdom agreed to protect Belize and train its new armed forces for that period of time. Belmopan was patterned after the very successful Brasilia, Brazil—only in miniature. After all, Belize claims a population of only about 210,000, while Brazil—at the time it started its new federal capital in the jungle—probably had ninety million inhabitants.

Belmopan has a lovely, nearly temperate climate, unlike Belize City, which is low, hot and humid on the Caribbean Sea. While the mountains in the interior of Belize are not very high—perhaps 3,000 feet above sea level—the lush jungle foliage and altitude result in cool, drier breezes as the tropical air rises and has dropped its moisture along the coast. We found Belmopan quite delightful. However, much of the action, both commercial and political, is still in hot, humid Belize City on the coast. Later I was to work and temporarily live also in Punta Gorda in the south of the country, and in Orange Walk, in the north.

Everybody Stops at "Ted's Place"

The new capital Belmopan, some 70 miles to the southwest, was being carved out of the Belize mountain forests. Anybody traveling from Belize City to Belmopan usually stops at "Ted's Place," about halfway between the two cities. This is more a cultural requirement than a physical or other necessity. For many years, there was nothing between Belize City and Belmopan—now connected by a reasonably good blacktop, two-lane highway—except Ted's Place. So it is customary for everyone to stop there. It was a watering stop, a pit stop, a news exchange stop, a gasoline and car repair stop, and a fun stop, all in one, back when the road from Belize City to the southwest was muddy or dusty, depending on the season, and horrible regardless.

Ted's Place is really not much more than an open wooden pavilion, with a gas station in front, truck and car repair facilities in the rear, and a well-stocked bar and grill in the middle. Supposedly the original owner, Ted, was a retired British Army Sergeant who drove and repaired all kinds of road vehicles in a long career in far out of the way places.

Dick Phillips and I tried to visit all of the major Belize Food Marketing Company's buying, storage, processing and sales facilities. We flew to the Punta Gorda region in the south, where a large rice purchasing and storage center was located. We looked at facilities near Belmopan, in Belize City, at a large Mennonite land development concession south of Orange Walk City. We also inspected some directed colonization projects being carved out of the jungles southwest of Belmopan. Here the Hershey Chocolate Company, operating in Belize as Hershey Hummingbird Company had built a large cacao bean fermenting and drying facility.

Hershey-Hummingbird also had a nursery where Witches Broom Disease (a kind of devastating plant virus/cancer) resistant nursery stock was being raised for sale and distribution to the new colonists. The company also had trained agronomists, horticulturists, entomologists and plant pathologists to help establish the new cacao culture and guide the peasant farmers with technical assistance. Most of the peasant colonists were Mestizos of Mayan Indian backgrounds.

Dick and I saw some exciting new citrus plantings, lots of new and renovated mango plantations, bananas, and other tropical vegetable and fruit cultivations. Unfortunately, the basic food and feed grains cultures and marketing systems were in the worst shape.

But Dick Phillips was astute at suggesting remedial, and not too costly, solutions. I believe that the permanent secretary, the minister of agriculture and the president of the Belize Food Marketing Company were all impressed with our report and its suggestions for change. At least both Kansas State University specialists, and I—along with teams we organized at USDA to serve with me—were invited back frequently in the 1984 to 1990 period.

Steve Zadek Takes Us Snorkeling at "Two-Palms Key"

Sometime in 1987 I was asked to put a team of specialists together to evaluate the effectiveness of an export development project from the former sugarcane-producing region of north-central Belize. This project involved studying the production and exportation of passion fruit, chyote (a type of popular Latin American squash), star fruit (Carambola), spices and other specialized tropical fruits and vegetables for the Latin niche markets in North America.

I recruited two faculty members whom I knew to the program: Dr. David Hahn, professor of agribusiness management at Ohio State University, and Dr. George Wilson, professor of horticulture extension at North Carolina State University. These experts in their respective fields, having both domestic and developing country expertise, were joined by Belizean expert Agripino Cawich.

Steve Zadek had become the agricultural and rural development officer for the USAID Mission in Belize and was our host and mentor. He arranged for us to stay at the USAID Guest House in Belize City, a lovely former home and office of a minister counsel from another country who had vacated. It was a comfortable two-story house with a kitchen and living room on the second floor. It came with a maid/cum cook (if you wanted to hire her for her culinary services), but we opted only for her cleaning and maid service (paid for by the USAID Mission) and prepared our breakfasts and lunches, when in town, ourselves. There was a nice small supermarket within walking distance and some fresh produce stores also.

I had talked longingly about the great snorkeling to be done in the Caribbean and had yet, despite about five previous trips to Belize, to test the Caribbean reefs off its coast. Steve Zadek told me before departing from Washington, during one of our many telephone conversations, to be sure to bring my snorkeling gear, as he had a Boston Whaler-type boat and motor, and knew where the good reefs were. Neither Dave Hahn nor George Wilson had snorkeled before.

So near the end of our study time there, after traveling and staying at some interesting USAID contractor facilities at Orange Walk Town in the north-central part of the country and returning to Belize City to finish making our report, Steve arranged a full day out of sun and fun for us with his charming wife to guide us. We put all our gear, plus the cookout grill, a gigantic cooler with liquid refreshments, another cooler with food, charcoal, and other goodies in his boat, and headed out for Two-Palms Reef, (we American experts knew not where).

After about an hour of open Caribbean Sea wave smashing, we arrived at the lovely reef/island. Properly named, the island had two tall, spindly coconut palm trees in its middle. I swear, the island was about as big as two or three suburban front yards in Fairfax, Virginia—maybe an acre in size. There were about half a dozen people spread out swimming and sun bathing when we arrived. I threw on my mask, flippers and tube and went out to the reef after helping to unload the Boston Whaler. Such magnificent coral, fish and other sea life! I had not seen anything this beautiful since Barbados or the Maldives.

I urged Dave Hahn to come out and take a look. It took a bit of coaxing and training on the sandy shore of the island until Dave got the hang of it and felt comfortable to follow me out to the reef in shallow water. Once Dave saw that beauty, he was hooked! He and I had our backs to the sea and were really enjoying the scenery (I had borrowed one of Steve Zadek's masks), when I heard a boat horn—very loud. I came up out of the water, turned toward the sea, and was staring into the bow of a giant Royal Navy Landing Ship bearing down on Dave and me! What a shock.

Dave and I scrambled out of the way. The ship crunched up on the sandy beach, the bow opened and out came about fifty Royal Navy, Royal Air Force, and Her Majesty's Army Troops. Each serviceman was carrying something: food, refreshments, cookers, volleyball posts and net, beach chairs, and various other picnic supplies. Her Majesty's servicemen had also arrived for a Sunday picnic. With their loud boom boxes and music, Two-Palms Island really swung that day.

Some Interesting Contrasts in Belize

For such a small country, Belize encompassed significant cultural contrasts. In the north around Orange Walk Town, center of the former sugar cane producing region, but now depressed as many of the sugar mills had ceased operations, were many Belizeans of Mexican and Guatemalan ancestry and many blacks from the days of African immigration and, at one period, slave labor.

In the south, however, were many direct descendants of the Mayan tribes and culture. That part of Belize reminded me of the various Mayan tribes in the villages of the highlands of Guatemala. In fact, it is obvious that many of the tribes in southern Belize were indeed related in ancestry to villagers and tribes in adjoining Guatemala, including speaking a variance of the Quiche language.

In the middle of the country are many Carib people, mixed with Spanish, African-Caribbean, and native Central American Indian, and there are still many Belizeans of English, Scotch and Irish ancestry who stayed after independence. Quite often these are the businessmen, bankers, plantation owners and other types of entrepreneurs. Some of the best citrus groves and mango groves I have seen anywhere are owned and operated by these businessmen in Belize.

Howard, David, and George Go from Preaching to Meddling

After living in a former plantation experiment station housing complex near Orange Walk Town and interviewing many former sugar cane growers now converting to export crops, and the many technicians hired by an American consulting firm to help train the former sugar cane farmers, truckers, middlemen, and so on, we concluded our report and recommendations to USAID/Belize. It was not very favorable. We found some significant deficiencies in the way the program was being run, a lot of dissension among team members, and some questionable practices. We reported these in draft to the USAID mission director, with a list of recommendations for change and improvement.

When the draft report got back to the consulting firm's management in Washington, D.C., the "fir hit the fan." David, George and I were vilified, castigated, ridiculed, and opposed. But we stuck to our guns and had the data to back up our concerns and proposals for change. Primarily, we asked for a new chief of party for the project in residence and called for a complete reorganization of the project for the remaining five years.

About a year later we were proven correct and exonerated within the USAID bureaucracy. The chief of party, whom the consulting firm had steadfastly refused to remove despite our strongest recommendation in the report, was found to have a conflict of interest, and the American ambassador removed him and made him leave Belize. He and his wife were accused of having established their own export/import business while he was supposed to have been a "neutral" negotiator and mediator.

Little Belize Suffers Many Growing Pains

Not the least of these was the evidence that the international narcotics mafia was using sparsely populated Belize to transship various controlled substances to the United States and Canada. We were shown open, flat gravel highways that locals told us at times were closed to vehicles.

"Why?"

"So small aircraft could land to pick up loads of marijuana or cocaine brought in by the local farmers, or the Colombian cocaine mafia, for reshipment to the United States or Canada," we were told.

This has turned out to be a serious problem for the Belize government. The money available to corrupt local officials in countries in the hemisphere, including sheriffs in our own country now, —especially when civil servants are so poorly paid—is an insidious temptation used very effectively by the international mafia. Eventually, if not already, the average Belizean will suffer.

Howard: Are U.S. Bankers Going to Wipe Out Belize's Jungles?

My former brother-in-law, Steve Cornelius, asked me this question after my return from one long stay in Belize. Steve is a dedicated naturalist and conservationist. At the time he was working for the World Wildlife Federation, helping countries—especially the tropical ones—establish wildlife preserves and trying to protect endangered species.

Steve had heard through the rumor mill that a group of bankers from Houston had cut a deal with the Belize government to purchase up to 100,000 acres of choice land in Belize's northwestern area. Since much of this area is heavy, tropical jungle, Steve was concerned that it would be clear-cut for agricultural or oil exploration and well digging, and another natural habitat for the Central American leopards and ocelots would be lost.

As a matter of fact the Belize government announced a land contract with a financial group, eventually identified with the Minute Maid Corporation. But, it was for a much smaller area (I believe about 30,000 acres eventually, if all options were taken), but in a rich plain in north-central Belize formerly in sugar cane. Of course the Minute Maid people intended to plant citrus trees, oranges, grapefruit and tangerines. I put Steve's mind at some ease with these facts.

In fact, I recently opened a can of concentrated orange juice processed and packed by a Florida cooperative whose label read: "Made from concentrate from Florida, Brazil and Belize oranges." I knew that fruit from the beautiful citrus groves I saw in various areas of Belize in the mid-1980s, and the ones I saw in Brazil many years before, when they were not permitted to export any products to the United States, would someday find its way to our retail food stores and to our homes and kitchens.

I had many arguments with my Florida colleagues in the 1970s when I took the position that Florida, California, Arizona and Texas collectively could not meet the growing year-round demand for citrus juices from their domestic production in the future. It was obvious to me when projecting the growing per capita demand, coupled with our growing total population, and seeing how rapidly those Sunbelt areas were being covered with concrete and asphalt—houses, shopping centers, highways and factories.

Andeans are "Cerrados," Central Americans are "Abiertos"

I do not mean to be negative here, but rather to point out differences in cultural comportment as I observed it. The typical Paceino, or citizen of the La Paz area, was very closed in his or her comportment during office or work hours. It was hard to tell what their true thoughts were in response to a given situation or conversation. Not so the Central American in the same situation, who seemed more like the Brazilians I knew— not exactly the same, mind you, but much more *abierto*—more open, animated, and willing to discuss, argue, laugh, or get a bit mad in everyday conversations and situations. Not so the Paceino from the Alto Plano in Bolivia and, as I later learned, the same type of personal conservatism exists in the Andean countries of Peru and Ecuador.

But let me tell you something else I found out. When the sun goes down those Paceinos like to dance, drink, party, and raise heck like nobody else I had ever seen. Apparently they hold their feelings in are *cerrado*, until after work or official time, then, in the modern terminology, "they let it all hang out"! Some of the Bolivians I got to know could even make the Brazilians look tame, and that's saying something. These were all lovely people I was privileged to work with, no matter what the cultural differences, whether in the Andes, in Central American countries, in Brazil, or elsewhere.

Other Assignments in the Caribbean Basin

While seconded from USDA to the Latin America and Caribbean Bureau of USAID from 1984 to 1988, I was the Rural Development Division's agricultural marketing specialist. About 1986 I was also given the agribusiness advisor responsibility, so was "wearing two hats". These two positions working out of Washington, D.C. kept me on the road to the region quite a lot. Any USAID mission in the hemisphere could call for assistance in evaluating their projects, in putting together new ones, or in helping look at how contractors they had hired were performing. My assignments, of course, were to look at the agricultural marketing and/or agribusiness aspects of them for an agricultural or rural development officer at the mission.

I had a good experience working for Bill Baucom in Bridgetown, Barbados. He was Chief of the USAID/Regional Office of the Caribbean (USAID/OC), and had invited me to be a guest speaker and group "break out" leader at the Caribbean Regional Agricultural Marketing Intelligence Seminar from January 6–11, 1985. The Windward and Leeward Island Republics of the Caribbean, who had recently received their independence, all sent representatives to the Seminar. Soon Bill Baucom called me from Barbados and asked if I could come back down, join a German marketing economist from the European Union (EU) and an economist from the University of the West Indies (UWI), and evaluate the Caribbean Agriculture Trading Company's (CATCO) performance. I was pleased to be asked by my friend to be of help, but pleaded ignorance of the situation and asked him to send me some briefing materials before I headed to Barbados again and met my coworkers. I really did not want to show up and start asking stupid questions about the company to be evaluated, the small republics and their commodity marketing problems and so on.

A little background is germane here. Great Britain had granted independence to a number of these small republics in recent years and although they were still participating members of the commonwealth group of nations with certain agricultural advantages, principally quotas and favorable prices for their banana exports, it was anticipated that these trade advantages would soon end. Although there were no "cut off" dates for the privileges, all of the small republics were getting nervous. Should they try to diversify their agricultural bases? What alternative export crops might yield significant foreign exchange in place of banana exports? Where would these markets be?

USAID/OC was also suggesting to them that the U.S. Caribbean Basin Initiative was available to them for agricultural commodity exports and that they should be taking better advantage of its duty-free provisions and begin to export to the United States.

The nine countries with special concerns, all former colonies of Great Britain, were: Anguilla, Antigua, Barbuda, St. Kitts and Nevis, Montserrat, Dominica, St. Lucia, St. Vincent and the Grenadines, and Grenada. These countries had received their independence from Britain in the 1970s and 1980s. In 1966 Barbados and in 1962 Trinidad and Tobago had received their freedom from Britain as republics, but were the subject of special interest with the others in CATCO's export proposals and activities. So it was particularly important to include their export history and agricultural diversification plans in our study. Another factor was that CATCO had offices and warehouse facilities in both countries.

Of particular concern to USAID/OC and the EU development program was that both entities had given development grants to CATCO to help the emerging democracies expand their nontraditional exports. The objective was to see if CATCO could help private sector agribusiness firms and cooperatives on these relatively small islands find viable markets for nontraditional commodities in export to help replace their dependence on exports of bananas to Europe under subsidized terms, expected to expire in some unknown future time period.

It was a noble objective. However, what new agricultural commodities were being cultivated? Where would the new export markets be for these commodities? Were they competitive in international trade? If new agribusiness exporters of these new nontraditional commodities were not known in either North America or in the EU countries, how was CATCO trying to inform the importers about the commodities and exporting firms and what efforts was CATCO making to "penetrate" the new markets? What were CATCO's successes and failures?

These were not simple questions to be answered. We consultants had to do a lot of interviewing, had to study detailed statistics and reports, and craft well conceived evaluations. The most serious problem of all, we concluded, was that historically "hucksters", not entrepreneurs, headed the agribusinesses on these small islands. Now hucksters have a place in any agricultural marketing system. Hucksters buy or contract for a supply of goods for their own account at a given price, hoping to resell those same goods at a higher price quickly somewhere and make a profit. Usually their risk is low, i.e., no storage, no processing, minimum financing. This is not the kind of practice that entrepreneurs engage in with international trade. International trade involves assuming more significant risks on the part of the entrepreneur, including providing significant amounts of working capital for specific periods of time. The hope is that the entrepreneur will be rewarded with appropriate profits for assuming these risks and that the business initiated will continue to grow with his or her inputs of managerial skills, capital, expanded production and marketing services.

CATCO was trying very hard to educate the agricultural leaders on each of the islands on how to cooperate with each other, how to combine financial assets for mutual benefit, and appealing to the governments of each of the new republics to improve the infrastructure for future trading. It is true that the islands were providing large quantities of bananas for the British Commonwealth countries, and for some others in the EU. A large European conglomerate, which controlled much of the perishable shipping to Europe with its refrigerated boats (or its "reefers"), and had a very tight control on the export of bananas, would have to be dealt with by CATCO if it was to be successful. CATCO was providing a fairly new export market for tropical vegetables and fruits that West Indians living in Europe loved.

We are talking about commodities such as cocoa yams, yucca, passion fruit, mangos, avocados, sweet potatoes, squashes and *carimbola* (star fruit), for example. CATCO was also encouraging the growing and processing of black pepper, first processed hot peppers for sauces, and other spices of various types. Spices are small volume, high value and can be air freighted easily to Europe, or to the United States and Canada. Cocoa yams, yucca, passion fruit, carimbola, mangos and so on are high volume and weight per unit of value and are not conducive to airfreight shipping, which is expensive. Therefore, they are usually shipped in ocean freighters.

We "experts" inquired of CATCO if they had considered promoting the production and export of processed tropical fruit products. We were thinking of processed mango concentrate, a very valuable product used in ice creams, in baking and in other deserts. There were, we thought, also opportunities to produce jellies and jams from the tropical fruits. We pointed out two advantages in considering these types of alternatives. 1) Processing concentrates of the product significantly raises its value per unit of weight (permitting it to "absorb" more transportation cost without unduly harming profits), and 2) it permits storage of the product and extends its useful life until export sales of sufficient volume have been contracted. CATCO had not developed plans for this concept, but eagerly accepted the idea and intended to develop strategies to promote it.

Another factor that concerned our team was that the islands had done a fine job promoting tourism, especially in the winter months in northern climes. They had built jet airports on a number of the islands that would accommodate the jumbo jets from Europe and North America. A number of five star hotels were built on the islands to host these travelers. Barbados and Trinidad had many of these fine hotels for tourists. St. Lucia, St. Vincent, Granada and the other island republics were also building the tourism business at a fast pace. But the thing that boggled our minds was that the resort hotels imported vast quantities of fresh and processed fruits, vegetables, juices, meats, poultry, and so on from Miami, Florida, or New York, London, and other cities. Why was an entrepreneurial effort not being made by the native agribusiness men to supply a significant portion of this high value market? Why were they not trying to produce high quality things for the hotels such as lettuce, cherry tomatoes, chives, onions, oranges, and orange juice and on and on? Again we concluded that it was a "huckster" mentality that CATCO would have to reeducate for this to happen.

Another factor we pointed out was that although the new jet airports on the islands had excellent facilities for passengers and tourists, including duty free stores selling liquors, cigarettes, imported perfumes and so on, they had no refrigerated and/or protected storage for quantities of perishable fruits and vegetables. These facilities would be absolutely essential for assembling and exporting products originating on the various islands to Europe or North America. Certainly air freighting whole cargo loads of the bulky West Indian fruits and vegetables would be much more efficient than trying to ship in small batches. CATCO agreed to take all of our recommendations as things to develop in the five years remaining on their contract with USAID/CO and the EU. So we recommended that the contract continue and successes and failures be evaluated in four more years.

Trying to Merge Agricultural Packing Facilities with Volume Producers

This was one of the most frustrating experiences we consultants had in evaluating the agricultural marketing and export situation in the Leeward and Windward Islands of the Caribbean. For example, one minister of agriculture complained that his agribusinesses were not building grading and packing facilities required to export to Europe and North America for their growing mango production. They could not get loans from the local banks or the government for this construction purpose. Yet, as we consultants explained, on the adjoining Island Republic a farmers' cooperative had a marvelous, modern grading and packing facility that could be used for mangoes, other tropical fruits and vegetables, but did not have sufficient volume of product to run the facility profitably. Why did the two governments and producers' associations not get together and make a contract? Both countries, their farmers, and their middlemen would benefit. This type of marketing cooperation had not been tried before and there was a great reluctance to move toward mutual cooperation to take advantage of the Caribbean Basin "no tariff" Initiative of the United States with this type of cooperation. We put it in the final report. I hope it is being done now!

On to Haiti, The Hemisphere's Poorest Country

If one wishes to see abject poverty on a colossal scale, go to Haiti. In all my travels around the developing countries of the world, Haiti was the poorest I had seen. It certainly is the poorest in the western hemisphere by whatever criterion you use. It has the lowest per capita income (45 percent of the population live in abject poverty according to United Nations statistics), the most erosion of soils, the highest rate of infant mortality, one of the lowest life expectancies in the world, high unemployment and underemployment, lowest level of education and on and on. Yet the educated Haitians are trying to reverse these statistics and bring higher levels of living to the masses of the population. This has not been easy, especially given the corrupt and unenlightened governments the country has had for too many decades.

So I was invited by USAID/Haiti to participate in a Haiti Agribusiness Workshop in Port-au-Prince, a city of perhaps a million people and the country's capital, during the last week of August 1985. To help us expatriate participants get some orientation about the various sections of the country and its agriculture, a number of trips were scheduled into the provinces before the workshop began. Here was where the very negative statistics about the country and its economy were confirmed by observation. People were trying to scrabble out food production up the sides of Haiti's steep mountains devoid of most vegetation and subjected to horrible erosion of the existing soils. All the trees and shrubs on most of these mountainsides had been cut for firewood.

Passing the pregnant women and small children with distended stomachs walking barefoot on the dirt country roads carrying bundles of firewood on their heads brought painful emotions. There was much evidence of serious illness and malnutrition everywhere. Even the livestock and poultry that we saw in the villages or countryside were underfed, emaciated or showed signs of disease.

Despite these signs of mass poverty, we were taken to several well-run agricultural enterprises. We saw some modern dairy farms with healthy cows and calves, some nice groves of mango trees which were well kept and appeared properly fertilized. We also saw some of USAID/Haiti's erosion control demonstration projects on specific hillsides in the middle of seriously eroded land. The use of tree crops and reforestation will be critical to Haiti's future well being. One very positive aspect of USAID/Haiti's development program related to the export of beautiful Haitian mangoes to the United States, Canada and Europe. One of the very serious problems with the cultivation of mangoes in the Caribbean, as well as in Central America, is the prevalence of the Mediterranean fruit fly. This serious pest cannot be allowed to enter the United States, Canada, or other Southern European countries where it has been exterminated or controlled.

As I understand it, the Mediterranean fruit fly has unique metamorphoses, which can be extremely harmful to a number of fruit crops, but is particularly feared by the citrus industry. The adult fly lays eggs in fruit like the mango, then the larva hatch and somehow find their way to oranges, grapefruit, lemons or limes and there the pupa form. These pupa hatch and devoir the flesh of the host fruit leading to the hatching of the adult flies, and the cycle starts all over again. Since these cycles can lead to the complete ruin of a marketable crop of citrus in U.S. citrus orchards, no fruit that is a host for the Mediterranean fruit fly, such as mango fruit, may be imported into the United States unless treated.

Fortunately the Animal and Plant Health Inspection Service (APHIS) of the USDA had perfected a hot water dip treatment for mangoes that will destroy eggs and larva, which might have been introduced into the fruit. This hot water treatment and inspection program had been successfully implemented in Haiti, and beautiful Haitian mangoes were being exported to the United States and other northern climate countries in the late winter and early spring months. The protection program, heavily financed by USAID/ Haiti, had been a very successful pest control program advertised throughout the developing world. At the time we were in Haiti at the agribusiness workshop there were APHIS technicians stationed in Haiti who were supervising the training of Haitian personnel to carry on the hot water dip program, and were also taking regular samples of the mangoes which had been treated to verify the success of the program.

It is a fact that without a successful control program such as that being carried out in Haiti, the lobbyists for the U.S. citrus industry, representing citrus farmers and marketers in Florida, Arizona, Texas, New Mexico and California, would see that no mangoes from Haiti could enter the United States. The American citrus growers were insisting that their orchards be protected from infestation by this very serious insect pest.

In my formal remarks to the participants at the workshop I made the following points, which I hoped they would take very seriously. "Your country is facing a very competitive and sophisticated market for the products you would like to grow and export....Many other producers and countries in the Caribbean Basin (and elsewhere in Latin America) either are supplying or want to supply the same products to the same markets as you do. And they are working hard at the task every day. Thus your farmers, fishermen, middlemen, traders and exporters all must become more knowledgeable and more productive before you can hope to penetrate the extra-regional markets you are contemplating....It is still a basic economic question of who has the greatest comparative advantage in selling to the United States, Canada, or European markets. Whoever can supply the highest quality product in a timely, reliable manner and at the best price gets the business."[12] I continued. "Here are the important components that are prerequisites to achieving a comparative advantage in producing and marketing a product anywhere at a profit: (1) produce and deliver a quality product that meets consumer wants; (2) obtain yields in the production of that quality product such that average cost per unit is as low as possible (certainly equal to or lower than your biggest competitor country growers, unless you have an offsetting transportation cost advantage); (3) deliver the quantity and quality of products at the times your marketing firms need them to fulfill their delivery commitments in the importing country; (4) pack, store, and ship your products in the types of containers that are convenient for ultimate retailers and that help maintain the high quality of your product through the channels of distribution to final sale points; and (5) maintain flexibility in your production, grading, and packing operation so that you can keep abreast of changing consumer or market demands and ahead of your competition."[13]

I wish I could say categorically that Haiti has made significant strides to eliminate its abject poverty, to begin serious control of its terrible soil erosion problems, its health problems, its unemployment, and underemployment problems. Sadly I cannot. One of the most intractable problems has been the continuation of corrupt and incapable government and public institutions. Even the support of a populist presidential candidate by the Organization of American States and its members, including the United States, has turned out to be fruitless. There seems to be an institutional and individual mind-set left over from the decades of dictatorships of the Duvalier family members. There is also the mystic of the leaders who practice and frighten individual Haitians with the "curse of voodoo." It is stated that although the country is said to be 90 percent Roman Catholic, 80 percent of these practice voodoo or one of its many branches. There are still secret society members left over from the days of the dictatorships who control the minds of the uneducated masses. Haiti has much background misery and many cultural adjustments to make if it is to overcome its present poverty condition.

John O'Donnell and USAID Invite Me to Work in Ecuador

Ecuador had a new government in 1986, much friendlier to the United States than its predecessor, and USAID cranked up its technical assistance and development program in that lovely Andean country. I had never worked there before but had been impressed with the Ecuadorian people whom I had met.

So, in the winter of 1986 the assistant mission director for rural development for USAID/Ecuador, my old friend John O'Donnell, invited me down to give him and the USAID Mission some help. John had been my USAID boss in Guatemala. He had also been in Peru with USAID while we were in Bolivia, and we visited him and his wife, Sharon, in Lima in the winter of 1978.

I did a number of analyses for the rural development division of USAID/Ecuador, including working with Dr. Dale Colyer, on leave from the University of West Virginia as professor of resource economics. In effect we were taking a hard look at Ecuador's agricultural economy and how it was influencing, or inhibiting, farm income, rural development and levels of living. Of course a part of this analysis, of necessity, yielded information about the country's domestic food production system, its costs, prices, and marketing efficiencies—or inefficiencies. Dale and I did some interesting forecasting and also looked at future export potentials.

Apparently I did a good enough job that the USAID Mission asked me to look at an interesting microeconomic project in the early spring of 1987. This was a calf milk replacement project, using surplus U.S. government nonfat dry milk in USDA bonded warehouses, and a formula developed by Land O'Lakes Cooperative of St. Paul, Minn. The objective was to get more nutritious milk and dairy products produced for the benefit of Ecuador's children, and at lower prices and costs. The benefits of the project were hypothesized thus:

1. Ecuador dairy farmers (we were working with a dairy producers' cooperative in the Machachi Valley several hours south of Quito by car) had good Holstein-Friesian and other high-producing breeds of dairy cattle but were letting the cows' calves nurse on the mothers far too long after birth until weaning them. This meant that months of rich milk from each cow each year of birth went to feed calves instead of to market to feed Ecuador children.

2. After the calves were weaned at about three months, they were turned out on pastures until they put on enough weight on grass to breed, drop their first calf, and begin producing milk for market. A very long, slow process, and more months of needed milk production were lost.

3. Land O'Lakes had good information from the United States and other developing countries on the system of weaning dairy calves on commercial milk starter within a few days after their

birth and freeing their mother's milk for delivery to the domestic consumers who needed it—especially city children.

4. Not only was the rich calf milk replacement food, made with surplus nonfat dry milk powder, butterfat, and other vegetable fats, more nutritious for the calves when combined with a calf growth supplement of commercial grains, vitamins, and minerals (to be made out of local grains by the cooperative under technical assistance of the Land O'Lakes people for a year), but it put weight on them much quicker than their mother's milk plus grass. Installing and using this new system entailed costs quite unfamiliar to the average Ecuador dairy farmer. But we showed each dairy farmer the significant additional returns possible by using the system, based on the actual prices of raw milk in the country. The government of Ecuador was impressed with our economic data for the dairy farmers and their incomes. It was even more impressed about the social benefit data we showed of having so much more milk being delivered from the existing dairy herd in the country each year. We were given the full speed ahead signal.

On my next trip to Ecuador I brought down Raul Hinojosa, a Mexican-American livestock and dairy production specialist who worked for my unit at USDA and had spent a lot of time in Latin America working with cattlemen. Raul quickly analyzed the situation in Ecuador from an independent perspective and enthusiastically endorsed the calf-milk-replacer program being proposed. Raul also made some important modifications based on his knowledge of Latin American farmers' practices.

By the spring of 1987 we had the project off and running. Land O'Lakes put a lot of effort behind it, and sent down some well-trained technicians who also spoke Spanish and had worked in various countries in Latin America with "dirt farmers." Things were going vary well. The cooperative of Ecuador farmers, with their government's help, built a small calf-milk-replacer mixing plant and also installed grinding and bagging equipment for the calf starter grain rations, which were essential as follow-up to the calf milk replacer concentrate. After a year, this program was both a technical and economic success. Then a major problem developed.

The U.S. Government Reneges on Its Promises

Somewhat later, after the Calf Milk Replacer Project was going great guns, I got a call from the USAID Mission in Quito. This time John

O'Donnell had moved on to a new assignment, and Dick Peters (another old friend and colleague from our working days in Bolivia) was the agricultural and rural development officer in Ecuador. "What's the USDA trying to do Howard, sabotage our milk replacer project and our relationship with dairy farmers here in Ecuador?" I asked him what he was talking about. He said that the USDA had informed the Ecuador Dairy Producers' Cooperative, Land O'Lakes Cooperative in Minnesota, and the Ministry of Agriculture in Quito that it was out of surplus nonfat dried milk powder, and couldn't deliver the 100 tons agreed to in the Public Law 480 (PL-480), Title I agreement with Ecuador.

I immediately got on the phone to the Food for Peace Office of USAID/Washington and to the Office of the General Sales Manager of USDA! It was true, to an extent. USAID and USDA had committed themselves to send more nonfat dry milk powder to countries around the world than was in their bonded warehouses. Normally that would not have been a problem as they would have bought enough on the open market to cover their contracts under the PL-480 program and would have stopped committing more in new agreements.

But because of the Chernobyl nuclear disaster in the then Soviet Ukraine, and the drifting of nuclear cloud radiation and rain all over Western Europe, milk produced by dairy cows there was suspect. So vast quantities of European milk were dumped, and European dairy marketing cooperatives and dairy products processors had come into the U.S. and Canadian markets and quietly bought up all the commercial stocks of butter, cheese, and whole and nonfat dry milk powder. There was none in commercial stocks for the U.S. government to buy. So programs, including that in Ecuador, were cut.

I spent a lot of time on the phone with Land O'Lakes executives, one of whom had been a graduate student with me at Penn State in the early 1950s and was now a vice president. It soon became evident that Land O'Lakes had a substitute for the dry milk powder that they could use in the calf milk replacer formula, if the Ecuadorian Ministry of Agriculture and the Dairy Producers' Cooperative would agree in its use. This was to cover the short run and to keep the program going, until dairy stocks again reached normal sizes in the United States. The program was designed to move to a commercial basis in the future anyway, and the U.S. government's participation with PL-480 surplus milk powder was to jump start the development process.

The reader may have guessed what the proposal was, and thus why it required formal approval. The substitute components in the calf "milk" replacer starter, replacing the necessary fat (butterfat) and protein (nonfat dry milk powder) were to be made out of soybeans and pork fat!

Earlier because I liked Ecuador so much, and the USAID Mission felt positive about my work, John O'Donnell pushed through a resident assignment offer for me. So, during Jenny's spring break from Layton Hall Elementary School's 2nd grade in April 1987, I persuaded Jane to take a trip with me to Quito to have a look at Ecuador, the job, and the country. Jenny was easy to convince. I knew that Jane had a great deal of respect for John O'Donnell's wife, Sharon, and her judgment, so off we went.

Eastern Airlines on Its Last Legs

First, however, I have an observation to make about the decline of Eastern Airlines, the brainchild of World War I flying ace and American hero, Capt. Eddie Rickenbacker. I had been flying Eastern Airlines up and down the East Coast of the United States since the mid-1950s. As long as Captain Eddie was at the helm, that airline was pretty darn successful. But then he retired and Wall Street financial wizards took control. When I had to fly "American carrier" as an employee of the U.S. government, Eastern was the one that had most of the routes to Central and Western Latin America out of Miami. I had no choice but to fly Eastern, and it was having serious labor problems with flight attendants, pilots, and, worst of all, mechanics!

Any pilot who knows that an airplane is an engineering miracle that routinely "almost doesn't work" does not care to attempt any flight when unhappy, angry mechanics have been working on the plane. Time after time, I had been caught inside an Eastern Airline's jet sitting on the tarmac at Miami International Airport for interminable delays, hearing, "Good evening folks; sorry about the delay in our takeoff here in Miami, but we have a small mechanical problem up here in the cockpit, which will be fixed any moment now!" Read that as labor union featherbedding and slowdown; fighting for more wages, work rules changes, and so on.

On my trip to Quito in April 1987 with Jane and Jenny, it happened again. In Miami, we entered our Eastern Airlines DC-10 Jumbo Jet right on time for the nonstop flight to Guayaquil, Ecuador, with a quick stop there before the short flight up into the Andes Mountains to our final destination, Quito. This Eastern DC-10 airliner had been in service for an eternity. I noticed as soon as we entered that it had a skin on the outside showing long age and serious wear. Dents, flaking paint, and other quick observations told me we were entering a tired, old bird.

But, right on time (this was a shock to me), they started up the right outboard engine, then the middle engine, just below the vertical stabilizer (or rudder to some), then the left engine on our side of the plane. They had one terrible time with it. It would start, then stop. They would start it again, then shut it down. I whispered to Jane: "I don't think this plane will be flying to Quito. They have a problem with the left outboard engine. I know."

This did not make Jane feel very comfortable. But after about a half hour, and five or six mechanics outside our window on the ground under that engine, they all left, and sure enough, the captain came on, welcomed us, apologized for the delay, and we started to taxi. Then we took off from Miami, had a great lunch, and tooled down to Guayaquil nonstop.

Before landing in Guayaquil, the captain came on the intercom and said: "Folks, I'm sorry to announce to our Quito passengers that we won't be going up there this evening. I've had to shut down our left outboard engine some time ago as it was overheating. No worry; we are able to fly well in this DC-10 on only two engines, but we cannot climb up safely, with spare power if needed, on only two engines, from sea level here in Guayaquil up over the Andes Mountains into Quito at about 8,000 feet above sea level. You Quito passengers will be given hotel accommodations and dinner tonight, and another plane will fly you to Quito early in the morning!" I knew that DC-10 was an old dog. So we spent the evening and night in hot Guayaquil.

The next morning we flew Fawcett Airlines, a domestic Ecuadorian carrier, and arrived safely in Quito. John and Sharon O'Donnell knew all about our aborted trip and were waiting for us at the airport when we arrived. Unsurprisingly, our baggage did not arrive with us until later that night—a typical Eastern Airlines story.

VIP Treatment in Quito

John and Sharon O'Donnell treated us royally, and Sharon showed Jane and Jenny everything they wanted to see. We also visited with my old friend and colleague from Bolivia and the University of Florida team, Dr. Larry Janicki and his family. Larry was now the chief of party of the combined University of Florida/ Utah State University development team in Ecuador, sponsored again by USAID.

Jane had been quite incensed in Bolivia and Honduras about the condescending way she felt the Department of State still treated spouses. I can remember when she first got her official passport back with the Official Visa from Bolivia stamped in it that read: "Dependent Of A Person." This made the Iowa German blood in Jane really boil! Now she asked Sharon O'Donnell again if the U.S. government still had that silly protocol with the host country that said spouses of American officials could not take jobs away from Ecuador citizens, therefore they could only work for the U.S. government offices or teach in the English language school.

Sharon said yes, the protocol was still in place, but that nobody paid any attention to it anymore. "Anyway," she continued, "the skills you have do not exist here in Ecuador, so you will not be taking a job away from an Ecuador woman. They do not have therapeutic horseback riding programs for the handicapped here, so you would be making a new contribution—and a lasting one—to the society."

Jane was not buying. She then asked me if she and Jenny could make a trip to the Galapagos Islands to see the strange flora and fauna Darwin had described and cataloged in his *Origin of the Species*. She said, "Ecuador is a lovely Andean country; the people are very nice; I'm sure your work here would be rewarding. But I want to go back to northern Virginia, keep Jenny in American schools, and reestablish my career. Let's go back, sell our town house, and find a single family dwelling to buy, O.K.?"

I finally agreed. Overseas life was not for Jane. I got them airplane and boat passage to the Galapagos Islands, and they had an interesting visit while I finished my work assignment for that trip. Little did I realize this signaled what would be the end of our marriage.[14]

17

Some African Adventures

I resisted taking work assignments in developing countries in Africa for many years. My rationale was that the development problems were either too detailed or that there were so many tribal languages and cultural differences that I would never learn what was happening or what to do.

But Cathy Watkins of our organization, who had sent me to South Vietnam many times when she was our administrative assistant in Asia Programs back in the early to mid-1970s, was very persuasive. She was now a program officer in the Africa Programs Branch and had many successful projects in Africa funded by USAID for our Office of International Cooperation and Development (OICD) at USDA. She said I would love Kenya and asked me to head a short-time research project there.

This, by the way, was after the USAID/Latin America and Caribbean Bureau in Washington, D.C., had cancelled most of the Resource Services Supply Agreements (RSSAs) with the OICD/USDA, including mine as an agricultural marketing/agribusiness management specialist, in the fall of 1988. USAID/Washington decided to bid this type of work out to the private sector "for profit" consulting companies — "the beltway bandits".

The Associate Administrator of NASS and I Look at Kenya's Data

USDA's National Agricultural Statistics Service (NASS) is world-renowned for its ability to accurately forecast crop production and other agricultural statistics. USDA is also a leader in gathering and reporting meaningful agricultural prices and other important market information helpful to farmers, middlemen and consumers. We were asked by USAID/Kenya to come and evaluate Kenya's system of developing and disseminating agricultural data such as those used in the United States and described above.

The associate administrator of NASS, Raymond Hancock, who had never been on an international development assignment before, although he was very supportive of and knowledgeable about the work NASS did internationally, decided he wanted to take this assignment with me. All the "working stiffs" I knew in NASS said that he was a good man and fun to work with. We started to plan our strategy and itinerary together with Cathy Watkins, who would handle the logistics for us with USAID.

I began to worry a bit when he asked if I played golf and wouldn't it be logical to take our golf clubs along. He had heard that there were great golf courses in Kenya left over from British colonial days, and golf was one of his recently acquired passions. I wondered—"will this turn out that Howard does the work while Raymond plays golf?" In retrospect, I did not have a thing to worry about. Ray worked mightily with me all week, days and nights if necessary, and exercised his golf passion only on weekends.

Kenya Is a Rich Country

Ray and I were immediately struck by the many resources that we observed in Kenya. First and foremost were the Kenyan people themselves: hard working, pleasant, intelligent, and so friendly and willing to please. Too bad that they have had to suffer through some corrupt and inefficient governments, as have so many of the newly independent African countries. People are Kenya's greatest resource, followed by the rich and varied soils, climate and topography. I cannot fully describe the richness of Kenya's Rift Valley. And despite significant plantation agricultural development, wildlife flourishes in most of Kenya's protected areas and natural preserves, which are extensive.

One of the cultural factors I feared, because I did not understand it, was the still-powerful influence of tribes and tribal chiefs in Kenya society. Tribes are one of the reasons that wildlife and natural preserves, established as tribal hunting reservations, are so extensive in the country. There are so many tribes and ethnic groups, none of which makes up a majority, that each had to be satisfied to avoid constant warring and bloodshed, even in colonial times.

Ray and I were soon impressed with the level of education of the Kenyans we came in contact with daily in Nairobi. Some 80 percent of the male population over age fifteen is literate; while the literacy rate for the female population is only 60 percent, the women are catching up fast.

In fact, a well-educated extension specialist working for the USAID Mission in Kenya, Jennifer Gachagua, was assigned to help us locate information, interview government officials and travel to various parts of the country. Jennifer, a native Kenyan, held a master of science degree in agricultural economics and was planning to study for her Ph.D. at one of the best land-grant universities in the United States the following year. She was an outstanding resource person. She also possessed the gifts of a great sense of humor and a positive, "can do" philosophy. We were so fortunate that they assigned Jennifer to help us.

It was crucial to Ray and me to have Jennifer as our leader as we traveled to various provinces to conduct our research with the locals. Although English is one of Kenya's two official languages (the other being Swahili), there are numerous local languages and dialects that Jennifer either knew, or had friends in the local extension service who knew. Jennifer's many friends from the agricultural college, now working at the provincial level, made our trips pleasant and our information gathering easier.

Ray and Howard Eat with the Locals

Eating with my hands was not a new experience for me, having eaten without utensils in a number of countries. But it was definitely a new experience for Ray Hancock. We arrived with Jennifer at a small town in one province near the Rift Valley one day and were met by the local home economics extension friend of Jennifer's who would help us interview some farm women. There seemed to be a lot of widows in Kenya who were farming small plots of land they had inherited from deceased husbands.

Jennifer's friend first took us to a small farm plot owned by a woman whom she greeted lovingly and introduced as her mother. Later Jennifer explained to us that the woman was not her friend's natural mother but one of her deceased father's many wives and thus her "adopted mother," all wives normally sharing equal status.

We found the woman in her plot, with machete in hand, cutting some sugar cane for "squeezing some sweet sap," as she said. After politely answering our several questions about where and how she marketed her cash crops, we were invited back to her small house up the hill for "sweet cakes and tea". Ray and I were reluctant to accept treats from this poor rural lady, but Jennifer took us aside and said it was custom and she would be offended if we did not accept. In the car as we drove away from "Mother's house," Jennifer and her extension friend started discussing something excitedly in Swahili. Ray and I asked what they were discussing and reminded them that they had promised to speak only English in our presence. The

Kenyan driver got a big bang out of their conversation in Swahili and laughed and laughed.

The problem was that they had a favorite restaurant in the little local village on the main highway about fifteen minutes away but did not know if they should take us there. We asked why. They got embarrassed, and started to laugh. "Because, you would have to eat with your hands," they said. "The favorite meal there is goat meat with rice and vegetables, cooked over a gigantic charcoal and wood fire," they continued, "and you probably wouldn't want that" But Ray and I replied, "Take us to it—we know how to eat with our hands!"

Ray and I got one heck of a lot of attention in that restaurant. There were probably forty Kenyan men eating there, maybe a dozen Kenyan women and our party of four. All eyes were on Ray and me to see if we took the pita-type bread and ate directly with it and our hands out of the big, round, steaming pan of goat, rice, tomatoes, onions, and other unknown (to us) Kenyan vegetables in the middle of our table. We soon satisfied the curious—especially when we ordered another round of giant bottles of Tusker beer for the four of us. This made Jennifer and her friend laugh hugely. "Ray and Howard are regular guys!" they concluded.

Kenyan Women Control Many Resources and Businesses

Later that same day we were visiting trucking companies in some of the larger towns. The Kenyan government had a law, left over from socialistic days, that made it a crime to sell basic grains to anybody but the Kenyan Cereal Grains Marketing Board buying station in any county. In other words, grain could not be moved across counties unless it was hauled by the Kenyan Cereal Grains Marketing Board. Ray and I heard that this monopolistic and monopsonistic set of laws was being violated and so we wanted to check out the situation in the interior of the country. Certainly the law was in conflict with the new President Daniel Arap Moi's stated belief in the free market and free enterprise system.

We met one owner of a large trucking company, a very impressive Kenyan woman, most intelligent, loaded with facts and information. She was very candid with us. Again, I give Jennifer credit for convincing the interviewees to tell us anything we wanted to know, as we had promised to group information and not reveal or compromise a named source.

The Kenyan woman owned a large fleet of trucks and said with a grin: "Oh sometimes the Grain Board's buying station gets the price all wrong, and we can buy there, pay a 'tax' [I think this was her term for a bribe], haul the grain across country to a buying station that pays a much higher guaranteed price and make some nice profit after all expenses, including the tax!" Now that's "free enterprise" at work in a developing country! The speculation equalizes prices too.

Ray and I were such curious devils that we asked her what would happen if some higher official in the Grains Board heard about her enterprise and cited her for violating the Grains Board's laws. She smiled and said: "Another risk we have to take, just like accidents on the highway and robbery of our drivers by bandits. I have some pretty good lawyers on my payroll, who are there to help me if I get into trouble of any kind. These are calculated business risks we all take."

Too Many Cooks in the Kenya Statistics Kitchen

Some weeks later after many, many interviews with government, university and private sector business people, Ray and I concluded that there were too many organizations collecting and publishing statistics about agricultural crop production, harvesting, prices, movements and forecasting. For example, we discovered five different sets of crop production data, none of which agreed with any other. The policymakers, to make matters even worse, made up their own set of statistics, which became the official ones for the country. Ray and I proposed legislation to make one entity in the ministry of agriculture the coordinator of all agricultural statistics and professional arbiter of differences in agricultural statistical methodology.

Population data in rural areas, market prices, inventory data, movements of commodities and other statistics related to agriculture we assigned to other entities, thus saving institutional face, yet making the ministry of agriculture the "czar of last resort" for the prime minister and his cabinet, vis-à-vis agricultural information. We think it worked. Kenya seems to be the leader in methodology relating to agricultural and other statistical series in eastern Africa. Ray and I cannot take credit for this—the educated Kenyans are responsible. We just legitimized some needed changes in their institutional structure and responsibilities.

Richard and Sharon Edwards Take Us under Their Wing

I had worked with Dr. Richard Edwards in OICD at USDA a number of years before. He had been a branch chief in economics and agribusiness training affairs for international students in our shop. Then he accepted overseas assignments in residence in Africa, as I had in Latin America. USAID missions liked him so much that they suggested he go "direct hire" with USAID and join the Foreign Service of the Department of State. This he and Sharon decided to do, and he ended up in Kenya coordinating the economic analyses of development programs of USAID in eastern Africa.[15]

Ray Hancock and I were the beneficiaries of their kindness. Dick arranged some golf games for Ray on weekends at some of Nairobi's great country clubs. Then he and Sharon introduced us to a number of fine restaurants, or "clubs" as they are called, left over from colonial days. A high point of our stay in Kenya was a Sunday with Dick and Sharon in their Land Rover in the middle of the Nairobi Wild Life Preserve. This is no small "park"—it must cover hundreds of thousands of acres. We saw nearly every wild animal that exists in Africa—all in the wild; all unfearful, but wary, of man. I have three strong memories I will carry with me the rest of my life from that lovely day.

We saw a large female cheetah—probably with kittens hidden somewhere near—stalking one of the many antelope herds there on the open savannah. She tried to ignore us as Dick slowly drove his Land Rover closer to where she crouched in the high grass. Ray, Dick and Sharon got out slowly to try and take pictures. The cheetah looked disdainfully at us, then at the antelope she chose, lagging behind the herd, probably 100 yards away.

One out of our party made a noise that attracted the attention of the antelope, and off it ran. This disturbed the cheetah and she immediately started toward us—perhaps as her substitute meal. We scrambled back into the Land Rover, wound up all the windows, and waited to see what she did. She circled us. If looks could kill, we would all be dead. Her expression of anger was so evident; I did not even feel completely safe inside that Rover. Then she slowly walked off into the grass over a knoll, temporarily defeated by our thoughtless enthusiasm in wanting to get close-up photos.

Dick suggested that we have our picnic supper at a lake within the wildlife preserve that they knew of. We arrived on the shore, and he said he was disappointed because there were usually a number of adult hippopotamuses there. So we got out our portable folding card table, camp chairs, grill, food and beverages. The sun was about to set, and the sky was gorgeous. Cameras were again out and snapping, when all of a sudden not 20 feet from where Ray was standing on the shore, one giant hippo surfaced, having been completely submerged in the water, and "blew" spray all over, scaring the heck out of Ray and me. Dick and Sharon roared with laughter; they had expected this, but did not want to tell us.

Apparently the hippos submerge for long periods under water during the heat of the tropic day to keep cool, only coming up to breathe when necessary. Then three more giant hippos came up for air. The commotion disturbed a group of crocodiles, also submerged, not far enough away (for me) around a bend in the lakeshore. That was enough "close action" for this Western Pennsylvanian that day.

Earlier that afternoon we had driven up to a high promontory overlooking the valley where Sharon and Dick knew a picnic kiosk and tables were located. This was where they planned to have our "sack lunch." But, a family with three kids, all under age ten, had beaten us to the location. We stayed a few minutes, looking with binoculars out over the valley at the wildlife below and talking with the children's parents. Then Dick suggested we get back into his Land Rover and head for another spot he knew for our sandwiches.

As we drove out the dirt road, not 100 yards from the kiosk, three furry lion cubs came running down the road toward us. Dick stopped immediately, and the cubs darted into the tall grass. "We must turn around and go back to the kiosk and warn the parents of those kids to get them into their car," said Dick. "The mother of those cubs is hunting food, and it has happened quite often here in Kenya—you read about it in the Nairobi papers often—that mother lions attack and kill children! If nothing else, they are protecting their cubs." So we drove back and warned the parents, and they got their kids into their station wagon in a hurry.

I Try My Portuguese in Mozambique

The United Nations Development Program (UNDP) in New York City was looking for a Portuguese-speaking economist to go to Mozambique to evaluate and possibly rewrite a reorganization plan for Mozambique's ministry of agriculture, which had been developed by a Food and Agriculture Organization (FAO) team sometime earlier. UNDP, which had financed the FAO team's work, rejected it upon close inspection. This time they wanted a USDA economist, with Portuguese credentials, to head up the rewrite team. I was selected.

Mozambique, on the southeast tip of Africa, was for many years a colony of Portugal. In fact, it did not receive its independence from Portugal until June 1975, and a devastating civil war had been fought since then. A peace agreement had been arranged between the warring factions, but there was little evidence of it when I was there in 1990, other than news media hyperbole. Our travel was limited to not more than 20 miles outside the capital city of Maputo. However, a new constitution, which would allow multiple political parties, was being written.

My team consisted of Mr. E.L.K. Bubelwa, from the ministry of agriculture of Tanzania (and an FAO consultant), Mr. M. Santos, FAO agricultural officer resident in Mozambique, and myself. Bubelwa spoke only Swahili and English; Santos, mostly Portuguese. I did a lot of translating.

It had been twenty years since I had spoken Portuguese daily, although I had a good speaking knowledge of Spanish from frequent use over that period. But there are significant differences between the languages, as I have addressed in earlier chapters, and one must be very careful. What to do? I decided to take my twenty-four-hour rest stop in Lisbon, the capital of Portugal, add a couple of days' annual leave to it, find a small hotel off the beaten path where nobody spoke English, and immerse myself back in the language.

A small hotel in a suburb away from the tourist area was recommended to me. The only person who spoke English there—the owner—fortunately was away in England on holiday when I arrived, so I was really on my own. The first evening there, walking the back streets looking for a local restaurant, I stumbled on a bonanza. It was a small, family-owned local restaurant in the basement of a small building run by a brother and sister. And, they had only recently arrived from Mozambique, where they had been born and raised.

When they found out that I was on my way there to work in Maputo for a couple of months, I could have had anything I wanted in that restaurant. I soon became "one of their family," and ate all my meals there, chatting in Portuguese with them and all their friendly customers and neighbors. I got a quick education on what had been going on in Mozambique for the past twenty years, and a good feel for the country's many problems, all supplementing my verbal briefings and written material in Washington.

However, I had to swear to return to their restaurant on my way back to the United States at the end of my tour to bring them up to date. Otherwise, they threatened, they would send the "American Portuguese mafia to Fairfax, Virginia, to capture me and return me to Lisbon" They were a fun couple and extremely helpful to me.

Where Is Our Air Mozambique DC-10?

When the day came for me to join about 300 others in the DC-10 flight from Lisboa to Madrid, Spain, then from there to Maputo,

Mozambique, heading nonstop all the way across Africa from northwest to southeast, I was excited. The flight was to leave the airport at 8 p.m., flying all night and arriving at Maputo the next morning.

Naturally, you are supposed to arrive for check-in two hours before flight time. I did and never have I seen so much passenger freight being lifted, dragged, carried and hauled before in my life! Television sets, computers, radios, baby carriages, boxes and boxes of clothing, every kind of gadget and widget those people going to Mozambique could take. This told me a lot about the economy in the newly independent, but warring country.

By 8 p.m. there still were no Air Mozambique personnel anywhere to be seen at the air counter. People were beginning to get very testy (all in Portuguese, of course). Finally at about 8:30 p.m. a woman in a uniform of the ground personnel arrived and put up a notice, "Flight 101 to Maputo has been delayed," and disappeared before answering a single question. No expected departure time; no explanations. At about 9:30 p.m. the woman returned with several baggage men and announced that they were going to check in all the baggage. Still no explanation about intended departure, nor any discussion about the cause of the delay.

Then we had mass confusion as people tried to mark very large packages as carryon; I imagined that the aisles would be full of boxes as there was no way those big crates could "stow completely away in the overhead bins or under the seat in front of you."

At about 11 p.m. an important-looking man arrived with a bullhorn and announced that Air Mozambique Flight 101 would not fly to Maputo tonight. After loud booing and groaning died down, he said in Portuguese that we all would be bused to a hotel, each given dinner and breakfast chits, and bused back to the airport promptly at 8:30 a.m. for our trip to Maputo the next morning. Now more pandemonium, as everyone who had checked their baggage wanted it back because it contained their sleeping clothes, toiletries, and so on.

We did not get to the hotel until after midnight, but I was up at 6:30 the next morning ready to do battle again. This time, after a hearty breakfast, we sat all day in the hotel waiting for the buses to come and take us to the airport. They arrived at about 6 p.m., and we went all through the baggage check-in routine again at the airport.

On board, I was anxious to know what happened to our flight and why the ground personnel did not tell us honestly what was going on for twenty-four hours. So I gave the head steward my pilot's license and passport and asked to see the captain. Soon he returned to my seat and said that Captain Santos would be honored if I would come up to the flight deck.

Captain Santos was, it turned out, the senior captain and head pilot for Air Mozambique. He was in his early forties, very pleasant, with a good command of American English. He introduced me to the first and second officers, both clean-cut young Mozambique pilots. Captain Santos was obviously pure Portuguese but explained that he was born, raised, and schooled in Mozambique before going to Europe to college. He also quickly told me he was on the Boeing Aircraft Company's "board of advisors" in Seattle, Washington. And, Air Mozambique had a new Boeing 767 intercontinental jumbo jet on order. He was quite proud.

"What happened to this flight yesterday?" I asked.

"Didn't our ground personnel tell you?"

"Tell us what?" I asked.

"That we had to fly to Madrid and get the middle motor replaced," he continued.

I said no, they kept us cooling our heels until about 11 p.m. when they finally told us we were going to a hotel. Even then they did not tell us the truth.

Captain Santos was furious with his ground personnel. He called the head steward in and asked him what he knew. The steward confirmed what I had said, and Captain Santos got on the radio phone to operations and his Lisbon manager immediately and read the riot act to him. Later, on the plane's intercom to the passengers, following a very special meal that somebody in Air Mozambique had enough sense to provide a bunch of irate passengers, Captain Santos gave a thorough apology and explanation.

I got to ride in the jump seat behind the captain on the flight deck all the way to Maputo and had a ball. I must say that it is lonely flying diagonally across Africa at night. Only a few planes were using those jet routes. We talked to some British Airways, Air France, and KLM Royal Dutch crews as they passed overhead going in the opposite direction to Europe. Other than an occasional check-in with air traffic controllers in various countries we were crossing, all was quiet.

But we discussed aviation, air travel, airplanes, and politics all night—while drinking copious cups of steaming, hot coffee, eating cookies, ice cream, and whatever else the flight attendants brought us. It turned out, after a very nasty start, to be a great flight for me. As I have said before in these chapters, there is a great deal of camaraderie among pilots, and this proved it again. We became friends, and Captain Santos even looked me up at my hotel in Maputo one weekend and came by for a drink. He was not flying again for at least eight hours as per standard practice — "eight hours between bottle and throttle."

Elisha Bubelwa and I Had Never Met

It may seem strange to the reader that I was named chief of party to work with people I did not know, nor had even met until we were at the site of our project in the country. However, that was the way UNDP organized this team. We were actually supposed to meet for briefings in New York, then in Rome, but that never happened. I received a telephone call at my offices in Washington, D.C., stating that my trips to New York and Rome were cancelled since Mr. Bubelwa was already en route to Mozambique, and Mr. Santos had already been to Rome and was back in Maputo!

This kept me tossing in my sleep for a couple of nights. Will the three of us be compatible? Are they professionals, or just political hacks being given a job by friends (or relatives—nepotism is not unheard of in international organizations!)? Will we be able to do an objective analysis, or will I have to fight for honesty and objectivity?

Within fifteen minutes of meeting Elisha Bubelwa in Maputo, my fears were gone. He and I had exactly the same development philosophies. He believed sincerely in the market mechanism as the best engine for development, with applied research and extension education and training for farmers and cooperatives as a serious responsibility of government. Best of all, he believed, as I did, that government should get out of trying to run agricultural businesses and promote growth of the free enterprise system for that purpose. Competition should be encouraged, with government as an enforcer of fair competitive rules and mediator/arbitrator when things do not function.

Santos had been brought up in the days when Mozambique was a Portuguese colony, with the state monopolies in charge of everything and plantation agriculture dominated by absentee landlords. So Elisha and I had many long hours of discussions with him trying to sell our points of view. But Santos did show some flexibility later in our work together; fortunately, we kept him so busy with the logistics of our visits and interviews, his major responsibility, that he did not interfere in the philosophy of our ideas for reorganizing the Ministry of Agriculture.

The local offices of UNDP and FAO had reserved rooms for us in a famous old hotel within walking distance of the UNDP offices on the Indian Ocean. Our rooms were not air conditioned, and it was hotter than blue blazes, humid, and noisy. The service and food were bad, and the cost was outrageous for what we got. We started looking for a better deal.

We found a family-run hotel in the heart of Maputo, the Cardoso, owned and managed by a Portuguese widow and her daughter. The hotel had its own power generation equipment and air conditioning. Further, it was off the heavy traffic routes in a quiet residential area with a swimming pool overlooking the protected bay and former port of Maputo. The port, unfortunately, was then nearly abandoned and rusting from lack of use since the railroad from the interior had been cut by the rebels for the previous ten years. There was a good restaurant on the top floor with a great view of the city and the sea. The price was right, and we were happy as larks!

However, we now had to find transportation. I asked UNDP to loan me a car for driving within Maputo only. This would facilitate our moving from one side of the city, where our offices in the National Directorate of Agriculture (DINA) were located, to various other ministry of agriculture, other government and private sector offices. The FAO offices were in the middle of the city, and we went frequently to the UNDP offices, up the coast of the Indian Ocean. The U.S. embassy was also close to the UNDP offices, and I spent some profitable time there with the Director of USAID/ Mozambique, my old friend Jules Schlotthauer from our Honduran days together. "Julio," as he was called there, provided Elisha and me with some urgently needed, and verified, data that we could not get from the Mozambique government.

Julio was the capital development officer in Honduras who first labeled my cucumber export project "The Golden Cucumber Project," as mentioned earlier. However, we had always been able to work together as colleagues. In Maputo, Mozambique, eating delicious Indian Ocean prawns, washed down with good Mozambique beer, we became friends as well as colleagues. Julio also gave Elisha and me some badly needed insights into personalities and people to be wary of while we were in the country.

Elisha and I wanted a chance to see the rich natural resources by flying over the rural areas, then visiting supposedly secure government areas in the north. Goodness knows we did not need to interview any more people from all sectors than we had because most of the future—and past—private sector and government leaders were in and around Maputo, and we had already interviewed them. But one wants to get a better feel for the natural resources and topography of the country when possible.

We scheduled a flying trip to the northern provincial city of Tete, between Zimbabwe and Malawi, but the trip was cancelled at the last minute for "security reasons." So we settled for a conducted trip to a ministry of agriculture experiment station and field day, with armed security troops as our escorts along with about twenty other vehicles full of international consultants and private sector people. This was a most educational trip, perhaps 50 miles from Maputo into the agricultural area around Manhica.

We not only saw diversified agricultural enterprises on the way to Manhica, we were also amazed at the sophistication of the basic agricultural, varietal research trials underway at the experiment station and at their results. This was in spite of the prolonged civil war. Elisha and I became convinced that Mozambique had great potential, if and when it resolved its political situation.

I cannot leave this discussion about Mozambique without mentioning the impressive work being done by Ulf Aversson and his team of plant breeders and certified seed specialists at SEMOC. A large Swedish agricultural company trying to improve Mozambique's seed quality, certification and crop productivity, SEMOC was being funded in its pioneering efforts in the country by the Swedish Development Agency. Ulf Aversson had recently retired as executive vice president of SEMOC, Sweden.

When we asked why he had moved to Mozambique in retirement, Ulf told us that he and his wife wanted to do something for the developing world and to help increase food production in sub Saharan Africa while they were still in good health. Apparently the opportunity came to help establish a private sector operation in Mozambique that would conduct research, do propagation trials, and distribute certified seed. SEMOC also had a history operating in developing countries and establishing technical assistance and training programs of agricultural extension specialists whose career was helping small farmers. It was also willing to transfer this technology to Mozambique as a part of a total developmental package.

SEMOC Criticizes U.S. Imports of Common Seeds

Ulf Aversson was candidly critical of the U.S. government's Public Law 480 program in Mozambique, which was designed basically to help feed starving refugees displaced by the civil war. The refugees were given small plots of land by the Mozambique government outside of "secure refugee camps" to produce some food.

Ulf claimed that a lot of the imported corn, rice, sorghum, and legumes obtained by the U.S. government elsewhere in Africa was being used to plant crops—not to feed starving families. There was, I assumed, a black market in these commodities for both purposes. Ulf's position was that without closer controls by our embassy and

USAID mission, the United States was undercutting his carefully orchestrated certified seed production and distribution program designed for the longer-run benefit of the country.

We discussed this with Julio Schlotthauer, and he said he thought Ulf, whom he knew and whose program he admired, was exaggerating a bit. Julio thought the U.S. program was being monitored better than Ulf believed but admitted there might still be as yet uncontrolled corruption by old socialists and military officers in the government. He promised to call for an accelerated U.S. Inspector General's audit and investigation, ahead of its regular schedule, to look into the uses made of the PL-480 imported grains program

I Give My Final Briefing to the Minister in Portuguese

Elisha had to leave Mozambique to fulfill a commitment to his country while I cleaned up the final rewrite of our report before giving a final briefing to the vice minister of agriculture and returning to Lisbon and the States.

Friday afternoon Santos came into my office at DINA quite emotional. He said the minister himself had read a summary of our recommendations in Portuguese and wanted to meet me and discuss them with Santos and me. I was a bit nervous about this possibility, but after all, I was the chief of the UNDP party in his country, making long-term reorganization recommendations that would be reported back to UNDP/New York and FAO/Rome. So be it. Santos wondered if he could translate from my American English into Mozambiquean- Portuguese well enough for the minister to understand. I said: "Well, if you want, let me try to do it in Portuguese, and if he doesn't understand, then you come in and together we'll get our points across." He agreed.

As Santos and I waited in the minister's reception area the next morning, I asked him how long we were scheduled to be with the minister. He said he thought no more than a half hour, as he was a busy man. That pleased me. The minister, a very young man, in my opinion, for such a difficult job (funny, in recent years, how men and women in high places seem to be so young, while I have not changed at all), was keenly interested in what I had to say.

Apparently in responding to his questions, I was "rushing my answers" in the interest of time. At one point, probably fifteen minutes into the debriefing, he stopped me and said: "*Devagar, por favor, devagar Dr. Steele: quero saber tudo—quero entender todas suas recomendações! Tem tempo para isto!*" (Slower, please, slower Dr.

Steele: I want to know all about this—I want to understand all your recommendations! We have time for this!")

The debriefing lasted for nearly an hour and a half. After we left the minister, as we walked out through the reception area, Santos said in Portuguese: "That was really great; and, your Portuguese was really great—congratulations! The minister is really impressed with the work that you and Elisha Bubelwa did for him and his country!"

Then, and only then did I realize, that not one word of English had been spoken during that meeting! I certainly wish I still could speak Portuguese like that. On the way back to the States I stopped again for my twenty-four-hour rest stop in Lisbon and visited my "family," the brother and sister restaurateurs who had grown up in Mozambique, to report on the great progress in their home country. We had half a day together, and they were pleased to hear that things were truly improving. It was a great experience in my career. Media reports indicate that peace is gradually coming to the country, and its people are slowly beginning to use their resources to produce a much better level of living. There remains much untapped potential in that lovely part of southeastern Africa.

On to Tanzania—Another African Country in Reform

This time Cathy Watkins asked me if I would be willing to join another one of her specialists, Gene Peuse, who had lived in Tanzania for more than six years and was married to a Tanzanian woman. Gene and I would look at the private sector agricultural marketing possibilities in Tanzania, now endorsing private sector capitalism after several decades of socialist government. I agreed. She informed us that there would be a World Bank team in the country at the same time, trying to help the new government develop a bona fide private sector commercial banking system, including agricultural credit for small farmers.

We were booked into the Kilimanjaro Hotel, the best hotel in the capital city of Dar-es-Salaam. Gene Peuse had arrived the day before I did and had visited his wife's relatives and other friends. He was absolutely floored at the political and cultural changes that had taken place in six short years. "Private sector" money changers had approached him in the street at the hotel—something that would have garnered them long-term prison sentences when Gene had lived there before free enterprise had been turned loose. When Gene lived there the socialist government controlled all retailing, and especially food sales. Everything had been rationed—one way or another — and it was a grim existence. Now there were basic food sellers everywhere.

One of our jobs in the country was to work with the World Bank team and the ministry of agriculture to help the government of Tanzania organize flexible agricultural credit windows in both commercial banks, and in a new agricultural development bank. Both these concepts were unheard of in the previous government, which had moved Tanzania close to the Soviet orbit, and government ran (or, mis-ran) state farms and cooperatives where "socialist planning committees" made all the decisions. Peasant farmers merely had provided backbreaking labor, perhaps some tools and a beast of burden, and took what the managers gave them for their labor.

Gene was a training specialist. He developed a comprehensive training proposal for the midlevel agribusiness managers and young ministry of agriculture specialists who would be helping develop cooperatives. Such institutions were owned and controlled by farmer members and made agribusiness development loans, among other things. We chose two emerging agricultural commodity industries likely to have the most immediate needs for technical assistance and showing the most promise for significant near-term profits, job and income opportunities, and foreign currency earnings from potential exports. These were the horticultural and oilseeds industries.

Commodities that we analyzed and made recommendations for included, in the horticultural industry, mangoes, avocados, pineapples, potatoes, some vegetables, and cut flowers. Oilseeds suggested were sunflower, simsim, soybeans, castor beans, and various pulses and lentils. In the case of the oilseeds, growing poultry and livestock industries could use the cake and meal for nutritious animal feeds, byproducts of the oil extraction process.

The fruits and vegetables we selected could be exported fresh to northern markets in the Middle East and Europe, when market "niches" had been developed, and also processed into storable byproducts such as purees, jams, jellies, and other products for storage and later sale. All of the newer, nontraditional products can be marketed profitably in local markets, both in fresh and processed forms, as the country experiences a growing middle class and/or increasing per capita incomes. The commodities diversify and enhance the population's level of living and nutritional well being.

We also included in our recommendations ways for the Tanzanian government to encourage the development of joint capital ventures, management contracts, and specialized sales contracts. These are excellent ways for developing countries to "jump start" their agribusinesses by providing expatriate experienced management, with its technical assistance programs and badly needed capital too.

Local Police Try to "Shake Us Down" and Fail

One evening Gene suggested that, for a change of scenery, we go to an Indian restaurant he was familiar with for some good curry. He thought it would still be in business because it had been popular and had great food. Further, he said, it was within walking distance of the Kilimanjaro Hotel, and we really had not been getting enough good exercise. So off we went.

The restaurant was indeed still in business, and we enjoyed a great meal, at a leisurely pace. We left the restaurant to walk back to the hotel, perhaps a mile distant, as the sun was setting and dusk coming on. The most direct route took us past the tip of the port area, not a good place to be at night. But we kept up a good pace, talking as we walked.

I thought I heard somebody behind us saying: "Misters. Stop, misters!" I asked Gene if somebody was calling us to stop.

Gene whispered to me: "Just keep on walking—I'll handle this; you do not need to say a word!" Finally he stopped, we turned around and there were three Tanzanian men following us, one telling us to stop. Two of the men were in the standard military dress of the country; one was wearing a cap with a visor, the other had a beret. The third man was not in uniform.

"What is the problem gentlemen?" Gene asked in perfect English, though he spoke excellent Swahili.

The policeman (or civil guardsman) with the visor cap, who obviously outranked the one in the beret, said: "Let us see your passports, please."

Gene responded that, oh yes, they could see our passports; we had them, they were in our rooms at the Kilimanjaro Hotel just up ahead there. "Come on with us and we'll show them to you."

"Oh no," said Mr. Visor Cap, "you must not be out in the streets at night without them. We must see them, or we will have to take you in!"

Again Gene took the offensive and said in English: "I have never heard of that law and I've been living here in Tanzania for more than six years" (A bit of a falsehood, since he had been out of the country six years, even though he had lived there with his Tanzanian wife the six years prior to that). Again the three men were insisting that we must go with them.

Suddenly Gene switched to Swahili, and the three men looked scared to death. Gene kept interrogating each man in Swahili quite forcefully, and the man in the flowering shirt and civilian clothes started a hasty retreat saying "Come on boys —let's go," then some more words in Swahili. The other two men soon started backing away from us, then turned and, in a run, joined their civilian buddy!!

I said to Gene: "What happened? Why did you start in English, then switch to Swahili in the middle of the conversation?"

He explained that he was stalling in English while checking the men out to see if they had any weapons. Not seeing any, he "lowered the boom" on them in Swahili, asking each one for his name, his superior officer's name, his native village, and the name of each man's tribal chief and father. Gene scared the hell out of them, and they left the scene of their proposed shakedown of two tourists running for safety. We laughed all the way to the hotel. It could have been serious had they had weapons; but Gene knew the play in Tanzania.

Just as in Kenya and Mozambique, and I feel quite certain in many other countries in Africa, Tanzania has rich resources, including its people. I hope that this time the move to open, free democracy really takes, and that those wonderful Tanzanian people have the freedoms they deserve.

Perhaps the free market democracy they are experimenting with will be successful—I certainly hope so. Unfortunately, I have heard that there has been a regression in Tanzania's march toward a market economy and additional government barriers have been put in the path of free enterprise firms. Old socialist patterns often die lingering deaths!

When honest, facilitating governments help their people to help themselves, democracy, freedom, free enterprise, and growth in both incomes and levels of living will take place in these African countries. I hope I live to see a lot of it.

18

Diplomacy in Action

Sometime in 1991 the Office of International Cooperation and Development (OICD) combined two divisions into one, and I was moved from the External Affairs Division to the newly combined group labeled the International Organization Affairs Division. The acting administrator of OICD, John Miranda, soon began calling me into his office to discuss affairs of the Inter-American Institute for Cooperation on Agriculture (IICA). He was then serving as the head of the U.S. delegation to IICA and attended its annual executive committee meetings. He also attended the biannual Inter-American Board of Agriculture (IABA) meeting, IICA's governing body, along with State Department representatives. The IABA consisted of the thirty-four hemisphere ministers and secretaries of agriculture, or their representatives.

Since IICA was a technical agency, although a dependency of the Organization of American States (OAS), USDA provided technical leadership in U.S. government policy formulation about its technical matters. However, the State Department gave leadership on financial matters, since U.S. funding for IICA came out of State's foreign affairs appropriation. In 1992, of the thirty-four Western hemisphere countries making up IICA's board of directors (only Cuba did not participate), the U.S. government contributed 60 percent of IICA's operational budget on an annual basis. This amounted to approximately $16 million that year. While small by comparison with the U.S. contributions to the United Nations agencies—such as the Food and Agriculture Organization (FAO), to which we contributed $90 million annually (25 percent of FAO's total budget) —our financial contribution (and our stance on issues) greatly influenced IICA's programs and activities.

John Miranda wanted me to take responsibility for IICA's activities within USDA on a daily basis, under his review of course, and also suggested that I begin attending the United Nations

Economic Commission for Europe (ECE) Agriculture Committee meetings in Geneva, Switzerland. These were exciting experiences for me. I had never had direct responsibility in diplomatic circles before, even though I had been a staff person "looking on" many times.

IICA's headquarters is in a suburb of San Jose, Costa Rica, called Coronado. The institute had been founded in 1942 under the old Pan American Union and was dedicated by Secretary of Agriculture Henry A. Wallace at a beautiful agricultural valley southeast of San Jose called Turrialba. That location now houses the agricultural experiment station and graduate school of The Tropical Agricultural Research and Training Center (CATIE). As their names imply, IICA is the technology institute, CATIE the research and training center.

IICA had offices in thirty-four of the thirty-five countries in the Western hemisphere and also had five regional centers at that tine. The thirty-four country technical programs were directed from the regional centers of the Southern, Andean, Central American, Caribbean, and Northern regions.

"What's the United States doing in the ECE?" was my first question when my attending the next meeting of the Agriculture Committee of the ECE in Geneva, Switzerland, was brought up at staff. The history was quite simple. (1) This was one of the first subsidiary bodies of the United Nations in which the Soviet Union participated and U.S. representatives could meet directly with the Soviets and watch their actions and gather information about their crucial food supply-and-demand problems; and (2) this was also one of the few bodies in which we met as equal voting members with the European Community and Common Market countries, both growing in importance.

By the time I made my first ECE Agriculture Committee meeting as head of the United States delegation, the Soviet Union had broken up. But, Russia, the Ukraine, and a number of the former communist Warsaw Pact countries were all active in the ECE. Ironically, I soon found that I could often count on support from the Polish and Russian delegations, even when our European "allies," except the United Kingdom, all but abandoned me!

The United States Pushes a New Agenda at IICA

For many years before the 1990s, U.S. involvement in the IICA was limited. U.S. delegations had attended IICA's annual executive committee meetings in Costa Rica, participated in the IABA and election of the director general every four years, paid the U.S. financial assessment (whose percentage of IICA's operational budget was established by the OAS), and returned home. The deputy director general (DDG), or number two position in IICA, was established as "an American position" sometime in the early 1970s, so the United States was content to nominate a DDG candidate to the director general then rely on his advice following the quadrennial election. The DDG did, however, serve at the pleasure of the director general, and several Americans were asked to leave by their directors general.

Under Acting Administrator of OICD John Miranda's, leadership beginning with the Bush administration in 1992, USDA and the Department of State decided to exercise more influence on IICA's policies. The U.S. bilateral development program in Latin America and the Caribbean, through the U.S. Agency for International Development (USAID), was being cut back drastically, causing closure of many of the program's offices and reductions in staff both at home and overseas.

Thus, the U.S. government was looking to the international agencies, to which we also contributed significant funding, to carry out geopolitical, humanitarian, and development/trade programs and activities. Of course in these organizations there were conflicting country interests, and influencing programs required a lot of negotiation and compromise. IICA in 1992–1993, when I became active in its programs and projects, was dominated by a director general and a number of key officers all from Argentina or the "southern cone" countries, namely, Argentina, Brazil, Paraguay, Uruguay, and Chile. The director general's cabinet also had a strong Colombian contingent.

A special committee was developing a new five-year Medium Term Plan (MTP) for IICA's program and activities, to run from 1994 to 1999. At the time, IICA's total budget included the $27 million core or operation part, and another $28 million from contracted funds. The core or operational budget was made up of the member country assessments, including 60 percent for the United States. — more than $16 million—Canada with 15 percent, Brazil 10 percent, and Venezuela and Argentina each about 5 percent. Thus the five largest countries contributed nearly 95 percent of the total, with the other twenty-nine countries combined contributing 5 percent.

The $28 million of contracted funds came from various sources such as the Inter-American Development Bank (IDB), the World Bank, FAO, UNDP, the German Development Agency, USAID, and so on. Most of this money came in the form of directed technical assistance or specific grants for agricultural or rural development, and was managed in a particular country by IICA. Unfortunately, many of the member countries were in arrears in paying their annual assessments to IICA. At the time I became active, Brazil was six years in arrears, about $15 million, and the total arrearage from all countries amounted to nearly $30 million. So, one of the first policy statements the United States insisted be in the MTP was tough language demanding that member countries pay their arrearages and meet their annual assessment payments to keep IICA financially sound. The United States, Canada, and a number of the smaller countries had always paid their assessments within the year.

A second factor the United States insisted on was that it and Canada become partners with IICA and not merely donors. In other words, the days of U.S. delegates taking a "fun trip" to attend an annual meeting of IICA and then doing some tourist and shopping bits were over. We wanted to have a bigger say in how IICA spent its assessed contributions from member countries, especially our $16 million annually. We were tasked by the Bush administration and by Congress to find IICA activities that would benefit U.S. agriculture and to help make them a success.

Later, in June 1996, when IICA and USDA signed an extension of their longstanding Technical Cooperation Agreement for an additional five years, we added a new clause that permitted "personnel exchanges for scientific and technical cooperation" between IICA and USDA. This idea met with some skepticism in both organizations, especially from the old guard in each.

A third point we insisted on, and negotiated into the MTP, was recognition by IICA that member countries were nearly all confronting serious budgetary constraints domestically. Canada, for example, was threatening to pull out of IICA and stop its financial contribution unless made a full partner and able to demonstrate some benefits to Canadian agriculture from IICA membership. We promoted the need for IICA to "seek more contracts from outside sources and rely less on member country assessed contributions." This could be a double-edged sword if not monitored carefully. The institute could become just another consulting firm if member countries completely lost their roles and IICA lost its status as an "intergovernmental body."

Later the U.S. delegation established a marker in its own policy within the U.S. governmental departments, suggesting that outside contracting at IICA generally should not exceed 80 percent of the institute's total budget.

Diplomatic Trial by Fire

In June 1993, just as IICA was preparing for the crucial September election in Mexico City for director general, IICA's Argentine administration called for a special mini-executive committee meeting in San Jose, Costa Rica. We in the United States believed this was an attempt to railroad the eighth and last budget of that administration through the annual executive committee scheduled for the following week.

As luck would have it, the United States held the chairmanship of the executive committee, but our administrator—John Miranda, who would not relinquish that role until the regularly scheduled meeting the week following the "mini-meeting"—could not attend because of prior commitments. I was soon certified by State Department cable to be the head of the U.S. Delegation. Fortunately for me, I would be assisted at the "mini meeting" by experienced IICA hand and Foreign Affairs Officer Roger Lewis. I had to do a lot of homework before getting on that American Airlines jet for San Jose.

My job was complicated by four factors: (1) I had never participated before at this level in IICA matters, with thirty-three other member countries represented, nor did I know the personalities. It was difficult getting an approved set of U.S. government strategies for this meeting on such short notice through the normal policy clearance procedures through the State Department and USDA agencies.(2) There was a nasty pre-election campaign for the next director general position going on behind the scenes between a Mexican, supported by the IICA administration; a Guatemalan employee of IICA at headquarters, supported solidly by the Central American countries; and a candidate from the Dominican Republic, who had strong support from the Caribbean countries. (3) The IICA administration had taken issue with many of the special drafting committee's MTP recommendations, especially those that the United States had proposed and which had been incorporated into the final report. (4) As chairman of the special meeting of the executive committee, I would have to remain as neutral as possible in dealing with the delegates, thus negating my ability to help Roger Lewis lobby the other delegates before votes were taken. The outgoing IICA administration thought it had the U.S. delegation right where it wanted us! It got a surprise.

"Howard: Here is the way we'll run the meeting. Here are the desired outcomes we hope for" Those were the "instructions" given me by the then-director general the morning before the first plenary session! I took all the materials he handed me and went back to the Hotel Palacio with Roger Lewis. We began to plow through the documents to find the strategies IICA planned to use to force its ideas through the full executive committee the following week.

Roger and I also ran up a large telephone bill to Washington, D.C., as we cleared points and strategies. We sought to delay votes on the IICA administration's attempts to railroad its desired agenda, budget, and program through and to make sure all participants had plenty of time to talk—even to the point of talking to death many published agenda items. Roger spent most of those two days standing just inside the Canada Room door with a telephone sticking out of one ear (talking to Washington, D.C.) while listening to my decisions as chairman with the other ear.

Canada and the United States alternately held what was called "the North American seat" on IICA's executive committee. That is, the countries took turns serving for two years on the executive committee with voting rights and then acting as observer for two years without voting rights. In 1993, Canada was serving its second year as observer, so it had no voting rights. It could, however, as could all observer countries, speak to any agenda item. In fact, the IICA executive committee at any one time was made up of twelve member countries, rotated on a geographic basis. The system guaranteed that all five regions in the hemisphere—with their very different perspectives and needs —could be heard.

But Canada's interventions at the special meeting of the executive committee in June 1993 angered IICA's "Southern Cone" leadership. At one point in the two days of plenary sessions, the director general threatened the Canadian delegation chief with expulsion if he continued to speak out against many of the IICA reports and recommendations. I was "happy as a clam" because my Canadian colleague was, in effect, doing what I would have been doing had I not been in the chairman's seat. Roger Lewis and the Canadians caucused constantly. Both groups contributed a lot of money to the Costa Rican Telephone Company's revenue during that two-day period, as they stayed in touch with Ottawa and Washington.

The United States had made a strong effort to show the smaller countries of the Caribbean area that we were sympathetic to their needs and concerns. These island nations felt that they had not had much help from the IICA leadership in recent years and were looking for more major countries to support them. We did so, and were leaning toward supporting the candidate for director general from their area, Carlos E. Aquino Gonzalez from the Dominican Republic.

The United States had not yet endorsed anybody formally, but we had many concerns about the other two candidates, and we shared those concerns with our colleagues from the thirteen Caribbean countries who were members of the Caribbean Common Market (CARICOM). They told us that they intended to vote as a bloc of thirteen countries for Mr. Aquino at the IABA election in Mexico City in September 1993.

Roger Lewis and I met informally with the representatives of CARICOM and in so doing, we were able to gain their support for many of the comments made by our Canadian colleagues in the plenary sessions. We were able to forestall any significant agenda votes that would be binding on the executive committee regular meeting the following week. The director general was so upset at this outcome and so mad at the U.S. delegation and me personally that he would not speak to Roger Lewis or me for two days.

We in the U.S. delegation, and Canada and the other large countries in the hemisphere, gave the director high marks for improving IICA's finances and professionalism during the eight years of his administration. We simply disagreed with him about IICA's future direction. We also questioned the qualifications of the person he had endorsed as his successor.

The IABA meeting and election of the director general to guide IICA for the period 1994–1998 was held in Mexico City during the third week of September 1993. Mexico's secretary of agriculture and water, Carlos Hank Gonzalez, a powerful member of the Institutional Revolutionary Party (PRI), hosted the meeting for the thirty-three other ministers and secretaries of agriculture and was also chairman of the IABA. This turned out to be a bit of an embarrassment for the secretary.

IICA's leaders from the Southern Cone countries had selected a Mexican, who was serving as Mexico's ambassador to South Korea, as their candidate for director general. The United States wanted to meet all of the candidates, including the Mexican, the Guatemalan, and the Dominican, as soon as possible and to quiz them about their proposed program for IICA.

We found it strange that the Mexican embassy in Washington did not seem to know anything about the upcoming IICA election, nor about the Mexican candidate selected by the IICA leadership to run for director general. The other embassies were making arrangements for their candidates to meet high-level American government officials and fully supported and accompanied them.

Then we began to get a barrage of "negative information" about both the Guatemalan and Dominican candidates. In the case of Carlos Aquino, a Dominican minister of agriculture on two different occasions and an active participant in the Dominican Republic's export industry, we were told (1) that he could not speak English,

(2) that he did not have any support in countries outside the tiny Caribbean ones and his own, and (3) that he was an intellectual "lightweight."

We managed to get a meeting with Aquino onto the already full agenda of U.S. Under Secretary of Agriculture Eugene Moos. We also helped arrange a similar meeting for him with the State Department's permanent representative to the Organization of American States, Ambassador Harriet Babbitt, newly appointed by the Clinton administration.

Carlos Aquino "wowed" all of us who heard him! In his clear and well-organized presentation to Under Secretary Moos, Aquino thoroughly explained his recommended changes to IICA's program and activities and demonstrated a good command of the issues and of English. He spoke English with a "Texas A&M accent"—quite logical since that was where he had done his graduate work. I heard him make the same presentation at the State Department, and it was every bit as good in Spanish!

Something did not ring true in early summer of 1993 as the campaign warmed up. We finally had a chance to interview the Mexican and the Guatemalan candidates at the IICA executive committee meeting in June. Both men gave good responses to the U.S. questions and points of view. But, as always, words are cheap. The United States decided at the executive committee meeting that we had better return home to Washington and engage in some serious research about each candidate. We had quite a fight about the medium-term plan and IICA's next annual budget before the executive committee meeting was over, but we persevered—and won our points. I was vindicated, in my positions taken the week before, not to give in to IICA's outgoing administration.

The United States Does Its Research before Going to Mexico City

We soon learned from confidential sources why the Mexican embassy and government were vague about the Mexican candidate that the outgoing IICA administration had selected to succeed it. He had been an employee of that same IICA administration some years before and had been in some trouble within the Mexican government's Portillo administration. There were rumors of contracting violations under his direction. But, PRI politics being what they were in Mexico, he was never indicted or tried, only accused, and banished to Seoul as ambassador—moved "out of the way" by the Salinas administration.

Our confidential sources also indicated that Carlos Aquino had been a fine minister of agriculture for the Dominican Republic and was well liked and respected. A former U.S. ambassador and two USAID mission directors in the Dominican Republic gave him high marks. They also said he was above reproach and one of the most honest men they had ever dealt with in Latin America.

The United States finally endorsed Carlos Aquino "at the eleventh hour," after one heck of a battle within the U.S. government. A member of the National Security Council, a friend of the Mexican candidate from university days, tried to hold up the cable to all U.S. embassies announcing our support. A number of countries, waiting to know the U.S. position, thus felt constrained to make an endorsement. Consequently, the election was a very close contest.

The Guatemalan candidate had the five Central American countries and Panama committed on the first ballot. Carlos Aquino had the thirteen countries of the Caribbean region, his own Dominican Republic, and the United States, or fifteen votes. The Mexican candidate apparently had the other thirteen countries. It required eighteen votes of the thirty-four member countries participating to win. So the election required a second ballot.

The IABA meetings were held in Mexico's historic and beautifully renovated Ministry of Foreign Relations. The thirty-four delegations and their staffs stayed at the elegant Fiesta Americana Hotel on Avenida Reforma in the center of Mexico City. Buses took us back and forth to the ministry for plenary, voting, and other sessions.

It was my responsibility to try to convince the Guatemalan candidate that he could not win the election and to throw his support to Carlos Aquino. I was also tasked with ensuring that the ministers from the thirteen Caribbean countries held their support for Aquino as a bloc. Then I worked with my old friend and former graduate student (also the coauthor of my first textbook in Portuguese), Francisco Vera-Filho, a member of the Brazilian delegation, to try to get Brazil to vote for Aquino on the second ballot, if one were required (Brazil was committed to vote for the Mexican on the first ballot.)

I failed to convince the Guatemalan to withdraw. The thirteen CARICOM countries, however, assured me that they would stay solid for their Dominican colleague; in the end only Surinam switched its vote from Aquino. Brazil switched to Aquino after we agreed to nominate Brazil to the board of CATIE as the country representing the IABA on CATIE's Board.

The second ballot was a cliffhanger. Aquino picked up Brazil, lost Surinam, but gained three of the Central American countries and Canada and ended up with nineteen votes. The Mexican had fifteen votes, and Secretary Hank declared Aquino the winner. It was a bitter election. I thought the United States had done a good job with the representation funds the State Department gave us to use in meeting and dining with other delegates to advance our positions. But our dinner for the outgoing director general, nice as it was—and expensive as it was—at the Fiesta Americana, and our breakfasts with the CARICOM ministers, were surely modest by comparison with the gala Secretary Hank threw for all delegations the last night in Mexico City. That affair was held at a large hacienda owned by the Mexican government on the outskirts of the city. What a feast! The ten-course dinner for 400 was most elegant, served as Mariachi musicians strolled from table to table. A full show with dancers, singers, an orchestra, actors, and Mexican celebrities followed the banquet. Finally, at about 1 a.m., Secretary Hank thanked everyone for coming and introduced a special "goodbye" presentation for us—a fireworks display that lasted about half an hour. Some show!

We left Mexico City exhausted but happy to have successfully "turned IICA away from the Southern Cone mafia" toward more help for the smaller countries in the hemisphere. I must say that our confidential research also paid off in our selection of Carlos Aquino. He has turned out to be an innovative director general of IICA, has increased outside contracts for development work to nearly $115 million (from $28 million when he took over in 1994), and easily won reelection for a second term as director general in 1998. We heard from other sources that had the Mexican candidate won, the former "Southern Cone mafia" had a private consulting firm established in Argentina which, the sources alleged, would have been given many lucrative IICA contracts. Hard to prove, but not surprising, knowing how money was thrown around in the last years of the previous IICA administration, especially by the institute's outgoing director of external relations.

President Clinton and Congress Close the Government, and I Am Caught in Europe

I was head of the U.S. delegation to the agriculture committee of the U.N.'s European Economic Commission over Thanksgiving 1995 when the U.S. government shut down operations! I had come home in late October and had a telephone conversation with Jennifer, my youngest daughter who was living nearby in an apartment with her mother, Jane, and complained, "Europeans never recognize American holidays."

Cable traffic from the ECE Secretariat summoned me to a postponed, but regular, meeting of the ECE's agriculture committee in Geneva, Switzerland, for the week of Thanksgiving (here in the United States). Jenny asked where and when I was going. I explained: "To Geneva, Switzerland, to a meeting of the ECE the week of Thanksgiving."

"Please Daddy, take me along!" she pleaded. She was out of high school that week for the holiday, so I agreed. This turned out to be a most pleasant experience, and she inadvertently helped me with a diplomatic problem.

Jenny's mother, Jane, agreed with me that we could use some of her college savings for this trip, since it certainly could be a good educational experience for her. So I bought her tickets and reserved a small suite at the Mon Repose family hotel, overlooking Lake Geneva but within walking distance of the UN Palace of Nations, the former League of Nations headquarters.

Jenny and I arrived in Geneva Saturday morning before Thanksgiving after flying all night. We quickly checked out the possibility of going into the Alps by train. With help from the hotel staff, we obtained reservations on an early Sunday morning train (the European train system is fabulous—frequent, punctual service, reasonably inexpensive, and so many travel options) to the end of Lake Geneva. There we transferred to a narrow-gauge train. Narrow gauge, yes, but with first-class plush seating, a stewardess, beverages served in each car, and a snack lunch as well.

We climbed up the Alps ever so slowly, through tunnels, through the snow-covered conifer trees, a truly "Christmas-like fairyland," toward our destination—Interlaken, a lovely city between two gorgeous Alpine lakes in the shadow of the Jungfrau, one of the highest peaks in the Swiss Alps.

We had a great time together touring the many shops in Interlaken, then a great Swiss lunch, and more touring between the lakes. The clouds finally parted a bit, and Jenny got to see the Jungfrau. We took a different set of trains back to Geneva through Bern, arriving at our hotel quite late but very relaxed. Jenny snapped interesting pictures there and later all over Geneva.

"The U.N. is going broke and it is all the Americans' fault!" Those were the "kind words" of the acting executive secretary of the ECE at our first plenary session on Monday morning. I had requested that Jenny accompany me and sit behind my delegation spot at the conference table. I felt it would be good for her to see the kind of diplomatic activity that we get involved with. I never expected to be baited by the ECE acting executive secretary, a professional woman and long-time U.N. functionary named Carolyn Cosgrove-Sachs. She looked at me the whole time she was blaming the United States for the ECE's and the U.N.'s financial problems.

Now this bit of verbal tongue-lashing in public—there were twenty-two countries represented, and also full press coverage—was not called for, and, as head of the U.S. delegation, I could not ignore it either. What to do? I kept my patience as I saw a number of delegations with their signs up wanting to speak. First Sweden, then Russia, then Poland and Switzerland, all telling the chair and madam that they too, like the U.S. government, as they understood it, had domestic monetary problems.

I put up my sign indicating a desire to speak and was recognized by the chair following Switzerland's comments. I said: "Mrs. Cosgrove-Sachs, acting executive secretary, you spoke truthfully about the serious financial and budget condition the U.N., my country, and government find themselves facing. And, although painful to hear, I was appreciative of the words of my fellow delegates describing budgetary difficulties in their countries. But, madam executive secretary, you have no idea how very true were your words about my government's impasse and crisis. If you saw BBC or CNN on your television, or read your local newspapers this morning, you would know that for the first time any of us can remember—if not the only time—the U.S. government is closed today! Shut down; locked up for lack of money!

"I wish to tell you that sitting behind me is my sixteen-year-old daughter Jennifer. The monetary crisis my government faces is so serious that I do not know what we will be doing in the next few days or weeks. Goodness gracious, come to think of it, I may have to borrow money from her college education fund—that which we are using so she could make this educational trip with me—to get back home to Washington, D.C.!"

The whole plenary session roared with laughter once the translators had translated all I had said into the various official languages conveyed through delegates' earphones. In one sense I hated to use my daughter to make a point, but the ruse worked. The laughter defused the session, and soon we all got down to the work of trying to figure out where the ECE agriculture committee was going to go between 1995 and the year 2000.

USDA's Agricultural Marketing Service had participated in working groups of experts and technical committees of the ECE's agriculture committee for many years. These met frequently with colleagues from the European Community, Israel, the Soviet Union, and other countries, under sponsorship and funding of the ECE, to establish and monitor quality grade standards for perishable agricultural commodities. They sought to facilitate trade between nations and regions and to eliminate trade barriers not based on scientific principles.

Until the World Trade Organization was established, following the Uruguay Round of the General Agreement on Trade and Tariffs (GATT), the ECE grade standards for perishable agricultural commodities were the generally accepted ones around the world for negotiation and adjudication purposes. Thus, it was in the interest of the United States and its agricultural industry to participate in all meetings—self-interest dictated it as well as policy negotiations based on scientific principles.

As mentioned above, the United States also used this forum to find out what the Soviet Union was doing during the Cold War, and it gave us a seat to negotiate directly with the European Community member nations. One can gain much useful information from colleagues from other countries when directly involved with them as equal partners.

While I continued the diplomatic chores inside the Palace of Nations for the next couple of days, Jenny quickly learned her way around the Geneva rapid transit system and traveled all over the region with her cameras taking most interesting pictures. At night she introduced me to some very exciting restaurants and historic places of interest—in both old and new Geneva.

The last afternoon in Geneva, following closure of the ECE meetings, Jenny asked me if we could go into France. She had found a Geneva rapid transit bus that would take us to the border of France. Since France surrounds Geneva on three sides, this is not a long trip—perhaps forty-five minutes. I agreed.

Jenny was quite anxious to have her passport stamped with entrance and exit stamps from France, to go with those in her passport for Switzerland; I suspected this would be a real conversation item when she got back to school after Thanksgiving vacation!

We got off the bus and started to walk toward the customs/emigration hut on the border of the two countries. There were two uniformed Swiss guards at their end of the hut watching cars enter from France. No one was in the office on the French side. Curious! So I approached the Swiss guards and asked them if my daughter could have her passport stamped. They said they did not know where the French officials were.

Being young soldiers, and very accommodating, they asked if Jenny would like them to stamp her passport. She smiled from ear to ear and nodded her head up and down with enthusiasm. The Swiss guards hunted through all the drawers in the desks in the little hut trying to find a passport stamp. These stamps are seldom used anymore in Europe; they just gather dust. They finally found one, stamped her passport with quite a flourish and wished us a pleasant walk inside France. This we did for the next couple of hours, and then bused back to Geneva, took the rapid transit to our hotel and started to pack for the trip home. We had enjoyed a great trip together.

For about six years previous to our trip together to Geneva that Thanksgiving of 1995, Jenny had been talking and investigating a career in graphic arts. She is, indeed, a gifted artist—photography, sculpture, drawing, painting—all done with much talent and enthusiasm. Can you imagine my surprise on the airplane when she said: "Daddy, what would you think of my majoring in college in international relations? I don't think I have enough skills to make a career out of art. I'm not a gifted artist!"

Surprisingly, I had never once suggested that she pursue a career path similar to mine. So we discussed the pros and cons. I had to agree with her that I felt there might be more options in international relations including international business, government, foundations, international organizations, and so on. I did point out, however, that there is also strong competition in the field.

Then she asked: "What about trying to combine the two fields, Daddy?" After a little reflection, I had to admit my daughter was a little ahead of me. No matter what organization she might find herself employed by in the international arena, all of them have serious public relations needs. And, public relations media need good graphic artists. So I gave her full encouragement.

19

Challenges at the Roundtable

In 1994 Attorney James W. Schroeder, deputy under secretary of agriculture for farm and international services, began an active interest and role in IICA affairs. He took over as head of the U.S. delegations to all executive committee and IABA meetings. John Miranda and I found ourselves in many interesting conferences with Jim Schroeder and found him a fine man to work with

It was my responsibility to read all the IICA papers presented for each official agenda item at every meeting and then start the process of drafting U.S. government position papers. These drafts would then be reviewed by individual agency members of the Inter-Agency Working Group on IICA Matters, some twenty-one persons within the USDA, the Department of State, and USAID. Quite often we would meet as a committee of the whole. At other times, subcommittees would be appointed to handle specific IICA policy matters.

My responsibility also involved obtaining agency clearances for each position paper and then putting official briefing books together for the U.S. delegations. The most interesting part of this task was to draft intervention statements for Schroeder's use regarding what the Working Group regarded as critical agenda items. These usually related to budgets, arrearages of other countries in paying dues, overhead rates being charged by IICA for contract work, policy changes, and/or operational and administrative matters of concern to the United States.

I related above the hard work involved in IICA's election process. Every bit as complicated, and quite often as frustrating was the task of nominating American technicians to fill positions within IICA. We were always trying to get the institute to hire more American citizens; the other thirty-three countries were doing the same regarding their own citizens. We felt—and the State Department kept score on this matter—that supporting IICA's operations budget

382 Bushels and Bales

to the tune of 60 percent ought to get us more than the 11 percent to 13 percent of the professional positions we then had within IICA. We were pushing for 20 percent. As mentioned earlier, the deputy director general position was considered an "American position." So after Carlos Aquino's election as director general of IICA in September 1993, we went through a complicated search process through the interagency working group to locate the best possible candidates for him to choose from.

We used, as required by law, full advertising about the position among many media and contact points, objective criteria in evaluating each applicant's resume, with a scaling device established for that purpose, winnowing down to the three to five top candidates to interview. Then came the interview process and final formal submission of the successful candidates by letter from the secretary of agriculture to Mr. Aquino.

We had three top candidates for the position of deputy director general. Aquino selected one of the three as his new deputy director and offered one of the others a position in IICA's program in El Salvador. One never knows about "the chemistry" between people. Within the year Carlos Aquino had dismissed the man he selected as his deputy. The two just did not get along.

So we went through the whole process again. This time Aquino also selected two of the three candidates we nominated, one to be his deputy director and the other to be IICA's representative in Aquino's home country of the Dominican Republic—quite an honor. In the interim we had to replace the American director of human resources with another American, and also the director of agricultural health, both having resigned to take other positions.

Then the second deputy director had to resign over a serious diplomatic error he made. This time Aquino asked us to let him transfer the American he had hired as IICA's representative in the Dominican Republic to be his deputy director. The third time seemed to be the charm, as this American stayed six years until DG Aquino's maximum second term ended. The two men were quite compatible.

I must say that I got a few more gray hairs over all these gyrations involving American hiring problems. In addition, the Clinton administration in Washington seemed to think that all IICA positions should be filled with its political friends and I resisted that until the bitter end. I will say that the administration's amateurish behavior and attempts to politicize all IICA hiring hastened my decision to retire in August 1997.

Deputy Under Secretary of Agriculture, Full American Airlines Plane Prohibited Takeoff

Every morning between 8 and 9 a.m. there were, in this era, four major U.S. airlines that left San Jose for major American airports of entry, usually a 2 ½ hour flight to Miami, Houston, New Orleans, and others. In the 1990s these were American, Delta, Continental, and United. Deputy Under Secretary of Agriculture James Schroeder, my Acting Administrator John Miranda, and I from USDA, and several State Department representatives had been attending an annual meeting of the Executive Committee of IICA, representing the United States. Schroeder and Miranda wanted to get back to Washington by midafternoon for some commitments they had and booked passages on the first flight out, on American Airlines. An item in the San Jose newspapers had reported that the single jet runway at the international airport would be closed for repaving at 8:30 a.m. the morning after conclusion of our IICA Executive Committee meeting, but Secretary Schroeder and Administrator Miranda paid it no attention. That situation was the responsibility of the captain and crew of American Airlines, right? Well, yes and no.

I had to stay an extra day to rewrite some of the U.S. position papers for inclusion in the official proceedings of the Executive Committee. This was a time when I appreciated the value of portable laptop PC computers. I had booked my return flight from San Jose to Miami for the following day. Imagine my surprise when the two distinguished gentlemen called IICA offices late in the morning, around 10 a.m., after having been escorted through the diplomatic departure process by the IICA protocol team at about 7:45 a.m. for entry into their waiting American Airlines jet for its scheduled departure. They were still at the San Jose International Airport!

The deputy director general asked them: "What in the world happened gentlemen? Why are you still in San Jose? Didn't your American Airlines flight leave?" Apparently the captain and crew of the American flight were a bit blasé about the announced closing of the airport at 8:30 a.m. for repaving the main runway. Perhaps the airline crew had a very late/early morning party at their hotel. Only they know why they did not show up at the airport until close to the 8:30 a.m. announced closing time. As Schroeder and Miranda explained it, all passengers were on board, strapped into their seats, and the plane left the gate and started taxiing toward the active runway when it stopped on the taxiway for what seemed a very long time. Apparently the captain and operations personnel were trying to negotiate approval for departure from the San Jose airport authorities. No such luck!

The jet had to return to the gate and all passengers were told to disembark. No airplanes would be permitted to depart on the main runway at San Jose International Airport until late that afternoon. The new asphalt cap being laid on the runway as the American Airlines jet returned to the departure gate could not be used until it hardened in place in about six hours. So sorry, Americans and other passengers; the 8:30 a.m. closing was announced in the newspapers in San Jose the day before. And when Ticos say they intend to close the main runway at San Jose International Airport at 8:30 a.m. for repaving, by darn, it will be closed, and any airline, domestic or foreign, had better be rolling on takeoff before that minute, or they will wait the six hours until granted permission to take off again! All civil aviation authorities in every country have the power to remove your license to pilot an airplane if you do not obey their instructions—they are the "monopoly police of the air"!

Modern Cybertechnology Makes Its Debut

Early in the 1990s, not many other countries in the hemisphere were using portable computers. I would take my place at the large U-shaped table for the thirty-four official delegates and their assistants. If near an outlet, I would either plug in my laptop's power transformer or use the charged battery pack inside the machine. I would rewrite our position statements when they had been modified or draft a tentative reporting cable to be sent to Washington from our U.S. embassy in San Jose or Mexico City. This made me a "small hero" with the marvelous IICA staff of secretaries and clericals. Why? Well, I was the only delegate that did not yell at them to translate and type this or that scribbled handwritten statement in a native language into the four official languages immediately and run off forty copies for use as soon as possible! I had the U.S. statement typed out in English on a diskette for them to use at their convenience. They loved it! In San Jose I would take my typed diskette to Carmen, the deputy director general's very efficient secretary, who would see that the talented staff translated it into Spanish, Portuguese, and French, the other official languages of IICA, then distributed it to all the delegates.

Here again I must congratulate the IICA administration for providing those marvelous Tica secretaries and translators, as well as the simultaneous interpreters working in the soundproof booths who provided instantaneous translations of every delegate's comments. Not only were they fun to work with all day long, but when many of the delegations had drop-ins, cocktail parties, and buffets in the evenings, they were always invited and provided a lot of spice to the conversations. They had some very funny translation stories to tell. For some reason I have not yet figured out, some of the older linguists who had studied in the United States in their youths said that I reminded them of Walter Cronkite, the CBS television network anchor. I never saw the resemblance in the mirror—only that both of us had white mustaches. I was flattered nevertheless!

All Work and No Play Make Delegates Have a Dull Day

Many days at these important protocol meetings we worked until the "wee hours" and became dog tired. International negotiations can be tedious and exhausting. I was fortunate in that all of the heads of U.S. delegations I worked with were calm, laid-back, and fun to slave for. Since all the delegates from the thirty-four countries were in the same hard-working mode, the many dinners, drop-ins, and parties usually held near the end of each meeting were especially welcomed. One notable dinner party was hosted by DG Aquino at one of the five-star hotels in San José, in honor of his wife who had just been appointed ambassador to Costa Rica from their native Dominican Republic. What a blowout! The food was outstanding and the beverages "flowed like water"!

But the thing that impressed me most was the speed and enthusiasm DG Aquino, a robust and quite heavy gentleman, and his wife demonstrated dancing their favorite merengue and also the fandango. They must have had a lot of practice dancing those whirlwind steps together. Thank goodness nobody asked me to take a whirl with them on the dance floor. I surely would have ended up prone on that floor at the pace those Latinos danced. For some reason unknown to me, I was invited to sit at the table of the El Salvador delegation head, a most attractive young lady who just happened to be her country's new vice minister of agriculture. She had recently married (her husband had not accompanied her to Costa Rica as he was in Europe on business) and had been a graduate student completing an advanced degree in the United States.

She had worked closely with my friend Dr. Cornelius Hugo, IICA's technical representative in El Salvador, and also with the USAID mission there. She wanted to talk about the IICA and USAID programs in her country. All the attention she paid to me at her table made James Schroeder, our U.S. delegation head, and John Miranda, my administrator, very jealous. Our conversations were interrupted every few minutes by Latin men who invited her to dance. What really threw Schroeder and Miranda was when they saw the two of us having breakfast together the next morning in the hotel, at her invitation. She still had a lot of her questions that we did not get to discuss the evening before because of all the interruptions. Attorneys Schroeder and Miranda refused to believe this economist's innocence. My knowledge of Spanish was undoubtedly a factor for the vice minister.

EARTH, a New College and Learning Approach in Costa Rica

USAID/Costa Rica, with Dan Chaij as mission director in the 1980s, helped found a new college on the Caribbean Side of the country called EARTH. The Spanish acronym in English meant the Regional Agricultural College of the Humid Tropics. It took a new approach to research and training in the specialized agricultural crops, pest problems, and management and soil nutrition unique to lowland tropical agriculture. Of even more importance, the emphasis for students was on learning entrepreneurial and agribusiness management skills. As the final portion of an IICA executive committee meeting in the mid-1990s, DG Carlos Aquino arranged for a bus to take the delegates to visit EARTH.

The facilities were recently constructed and in fine shape. These included dormitories, dining facilities, a canteen, library, classrooms, laboratories, plots for crops, and small crop and food processing facilities. The faculty included specialists from many Latin American countries, from several tropical countries in Asia and Africa, and chemists and management specialists from North America and Europe. We were given overviews by a number of faculty and student speakers, then a tour of the facilities.

Students were required to join a hypothetical "company" with several other students and to develop a proposal for production and marketing of a final tropical agricultural product of some type. A special committee of the faculty carefully evaluated the students' technical, business and financial plans, including input costs, proposed revenues, and profits. When approved, often following modifications, the college would advance sufficient working capital to get the project started. One project we were shown will demonstrate the concept.

Banana production, packing, and exporting dominate a large segment of agricultural activity in the Caribbean coastal area of eastern Costa Rica. Recent changes in marketing procedures have "hands" of bananas removed from the large stalks on which they grow in the field, then packed in treated cardboard boxes for storage and export. But the process in the banana groves creates a lot of banana stalk and leaf frond waste on the ground. An EARTH student project was to determine if this waste had any commercial use. The project yielded a suggestion to gather the waste, to cook it at high heat in vats using controlled chemical digesters, then dry it and roll it into a heavy type of cardboard—banana refuse cellulose––to be used as packing material, in sheets, cut, or crimped. The project, with some modifications, was a profitable success, even on a small scale. One of the large banana-exporting companies was studying the feasibility of installing large processing equipment on a trial basis for this purpose at one of its large production areas. This was an exciting new approach for Latin American students learning agribusiness skills.

Sugar Cane Farmers Given Ownership of Their Mill

The most interesting finale to this trip to the Turrialba region occurred after we had done some whitewater rafting. The DG of CATIE asked us if we wanted to attend a pig roast and dinner in a nearby town where the former president of Costa Rica, Rafael Angel Calderon, was giving each member of the sugar cane cooperative certificates of ownership in a sugar-processing mill. The affair was held in the mill's empty warehouse. The previously private mill had fallen on hard management times. Calderon, who had been minister of agriculture before becoming president, was responsible for arranging bonds and financing for the farmer users. Transfering ownership was a well-conceived economic move to protect the farmers' market and also make them proud owners of the mill and its assets. Prudent managers had been hired, and a government oversight committee was to help the farmers' cooperative board of directors make sound business policies and support the new management.

I have seen a number of happy farmers' co-operative members at various times in my career, but I had never seen a group like this one, with all their family members present for the food, drink, music, and celebrations. What surprised Richard, John, and me was that the DG of CATIE introduced us to the former president, who then invited us to sit and eat with him on the raised dais prior to making his speech. Following his speech he handed out the certificates of ownership to each farmer-member and his family. Each was called to the dais alphabetically. We had plenty of time to savor all the Costa Rican foods prepared by many of the members' wives. The liquid refreshments also helped relax our weary bones and muscles from the rafting trip. It was a marvelous experience observing rural development activities at their finest. I hope those farmers are making good profits from the production and processing of their sugar cane.

"I'm Gonna Getcha One of These Days!"

I flew in and out of Miami International Airport so often for many years that several of the U.S. Customs Agents there recognized me. They would often say to me as I surrendered my Official Passport, "Well Mr. Steele, where have you been this trip, how long were you away, what were you doing, and are you glad to be back home?"— always accompanied by smiles. One very tall, thin agent with a bald rounded head and only a small fringe of hair at his temples had a great big smile for me every time I came in. We kidded each other. I kept saying to him: "What? You're still slaving away here, why haven't you retired yet?" His usual response was "I'm not retiring until I catch you. I'm gonna getcha!" all the while shaking his finger at me accusingly! I found over the years that those Customs Agents are good people. You treat them with respect and honesty and they will help you with the most favorable declaration, should you need to make one. He knew he would have no reason to ever "get me"!

An Interesting Assignment at FAO/Rome

Although I had worked with the Agricultural Committee of the Economic Commission for Europe, another UN dependency, I had never worked directly with FAO at its headquarters in Rome, Italy. The FAO is the largest nonprofit organization working with agricultural disciplines in developing countries. The United States contributes 25 percent of FAO's annual operational budget, between US $90 and $100 million annually in the mid 1990s. At the time the FAO's total operational budget was about US$400 million annually, representing the contributions of the member countries to FAO's programs and support. FAO also receives monies from the United Nations Development Program to administer and cooperates in other activities with the various development banks. It is one large bureaucracy. So although I had worked with various FAO missions in specific developing countries, I needed to go to Rome to meet some of the principal officers. The USDA attaché assigned to Rome to represent the USG with FAO was a colleague of mine with whom I had worked since 1971, Roberta van Haeften.

This was not just a pleasure trip for me. The director of our External Affairs Division was responsible for trying to pry money from Congress for International Development Interns (IDIs) to work with FAO either in Rome or in developing countries with FAO mission programs. The External Affairs Division worked closely with our agency's Development Resources Division, of which I had been a part for many years. The directors of the two divisions, along with Roberta van Haeften and me, all agreed that it would be helpful to U.S. agriculture and the USG if we could have more IDIs working with FAO. This was particularly true since the USAID missions and bilateral development programs with developing countries were being drastically reduced or eliminated. So in 1991 they sent me on a reconnaissance trip to Rome to work with Roberta and David Joslyn, the USAID representative to FAO, another acquaintance of mine from my many assignments with USAID.

Things did not start out smoothly. Roberta had made reservations for me at a small hotel used by many USG short-time consultants, close to the Coliseum and other historic Roman buildings that I could walk to. (Unfortunately, neither she nor David Joslyn gave me much time to do so!) But it was a long way from Rome's International Airport. So they cabled me to take the large limousine bus from the airport that goes to all the hotels and to specify which one I was staying at when I bought my ticket at the airport. Otherwise, they told me, a private taxi to the city from the airport would cost "an arm and a leg"! Typical of Italy, as I discovered on my several other trips through there, the bus and train drivers were on strike. So I had to hire a private cab. So did hundreds of others caught without bus or train service away from the airport. I did not speak Italian and the driver spoke no English. Things got a bit testy when we arrived at the hotel and I did not have enough Lira to pay him. But with the help of the hotel staff we soon made peace, and I could relax for the first time in many hours!

The next morning things got much better. After a fine breakfast in my small hotel, I taxied to the headquarters of FAO, a very large building, with many more in the complex. I met Roberta and David and they took me to pay a courtesy visit on FAO Deputy Director General Howard Hjort, a former under secretary of agriculture in the Carter administration. After a short and pleasant visit, he gave me "carte blanche" to visit all the FAO program directors who were in town.

The program directors head FAO's worldwide functional divisions such as forestry, agricultural research, agricultural marketing, plant physiology, entomology, and so on. All the directors I talked with said that they would welcome more young Americans in their programs. They pointed out that each member country paid the costs of the IDIs from their respective country. FAO only paid "in kind" costs such as office space at a mission or in Rome, use of library services, office electricity, and so on. The interns' modest salary costs, travel, and per diem subsistence costs were borne by the sponsoring country, as I knew. I was developing factual information for a reporting cable that I hoped would help persuade our congressional committees to put more funds into the IDI program.

One important set of facts I worked hard to obtain was the total number of IDIs each division had in its worldwide programs and from which countries they came. The results amazed me. The Scandinavian countries led the list, with Sweden, Norway, Denmark, and Finland having the most IDIs working for FAO. France, Belgium, Germany, Italy, and England were next. The United States was very close to the bottom; I believe we only supported six IDIs at that time. If my memory serves me correctly, Sweden had more than 200 working for FAO around the world.

Raw numbers tell only part of the story. A large percentage of the IDIs from the countries mentioned above worked at division headquarters in Rome, often on a rotating basis. How does a country make significant contributions to, or effectively influence new initiatives in, agricultural development under FAO-funded programs and projects? By being at headquarters and making inputs into the written proposals being developed for funding and implementation. If you are not involved in that process, significant intelligence can be gathered and reported to your home country about program and project proposals if you are at headquarters or in the field communicating with headquarters. In my reporting cable to Washington I made the analogy that the approach used by the other countries was exactly the one we had used to place our USDA specialists inside the U.S. Agency for International Development by seconding them under PASA or RSSA agreements. You can probably have more influence in helping "guide" or "influence" the direction of policies and programs when you are inside an agency or organization than outside it. Remember the Arab's analogy of the camel with his head inside the tent versus his relative whose head was outside and always surprised and shocked by events.

It took a lot of rewriting and modifying before we could get the embassy to approve our reporting cable and send it to Washington. The political officer at the embassy did not want to shock or offend the FAO administration, which would receive a copy of our observations and proposals in due course. Another factor was the sensitivity of allies who were sending large numbers of IDIs to the FAO offices. I was appealing to our Congress to obtain "a bigger piece of the action," which would have to come at the expense of the number of IDIs our allies were providing. FAO would only desire so many IDIs in any given year.

Postscript

I had no siblings growing up in Pittsburgh in the 1930s and early 1940s, although we had many cousins, aunts, and uncles living with us during the Great Depression from time to time when they were out of work, had health or other problems, and so on. So it really was not until I went away to college at Washington & Lee University in 1946 that I was immersed in cross-cultural living conditions. I quickly learned that one had to be tolerant of other people's values and life styles, if quite different from your own, and not be blatantly judgmental.

Graduate school at Penn State further honed this process for me. I discovered some unusual "intellectuals," whose values, life styles, and behavior—quite different from what I was used to in my family's protecting environment—I had to adjust to. I think these early life experiences at the universities, and especially in the dairy processing business later, helped train me to adjust to and address the interesting personalities I later met and had to work with in the developing countries.

The dairy processing business in western Pennsylvania, eastern Ohio, and West Virginia was very competitive, at times cutthroat. All the employees I had to lead in the latter years of my work there were loyal members of the International Brotherhood of Teamsters and Warehousemen, quite militant at that time. Unexpected competitive battles, finding ways to cut costs and make profits, money management such as cash flow problems, collecting accounts receivable, and dealing with bad debt problems were great educational experiences for me. I believe those experiences all helped me when it came time to budget for projects and programs in my development work, or in other instances to evaluate project and program performance for the funding agency.

Dealing with various personalities under stress or conditions of uncertainty, as I did at the universities for sixteen years, helped me greatly when assigned to work with proud counterparts in developing countries. As with undergraduate and graduate students at the universities, I was suggesting change, and people sometimes confronted change as something to be feared.

One of the most difficult practices for many development specialists from developed countries was not demanding credit for successes in their projects, but rather giving credit to counterparts for "their" idea and follow-up. Often we would plant a development seed with our counterparts and nothing would happen for what seemed an eternity. Then a planted idea would emerge in some form, not necessarily what we had hoped for; but this was the counterpart's idea, culture, and responsibility. "Water the idea: fertilize it; promote the idea and the counterpart with praise." I must admit that I found honing that skill difficult in my early development work. I was too anxious; wanted to see things happen faster. I finally learned patience and a calm way to work with my counterparts in the developing countries.

Did we have successes? Did we have failures? Yes, to both questions, as I have tried to point out in this book. I have no regrets in general about my three different career paths: private sector for-profit work, university teaching, and research and development work in less-than-developed countries. They really complemented one another and helped me have a satisfyingly successful career. Would I have done some things differently? Of course, as noted in the text, I hope that the reader of this book will recognize those mistakes, take them to heart, and not make the same ones I did!

I featured my youngest daughter Jennifer in a number of paragraphs above. In 2008 she is working in Ethiopia for the African Centre for Humanitarian Action. Occasionally I mentioned my three older children, as when we were in Brazil together. I am very proud of all of them. John, fifty-five in 2008, is one of three auditors for Somerset County, Pennsylvania. He and his wife Sue, along with her parents the Putmans, operate a successful truck farm near Bakersville in Somerset County. They produce and sell asparagus, rhubarb, blueberries, and cut flowers. They also produce greenhouse tomatoes, grapes, and wine and red wine vinegar, among other products.

Son David, fifty-three, who is the father of my two grandsons Eric (21) and Ryan (17), joined the U.S. Department of Agriculture's Natural Resources Conservation Service in 2004 after serving for fourteen years as general manager of the Somerset Conservation District. He still lives near the town of Somerset, but now covers six counties out of his Bedford, Pennsylvania, office managing a number of conservation and ecological projects.

Daughter Patricia married Ralph Moore in 2003, and they live with Pat's mother Sally in the town of Somerset. Ralph and his brother David operate a farm machinery business near Friedens, Pennsylvania, specializing in smaller farm machinery, keying to appropriate technology for the average to smaller farm sizes in the area. Much of their equipment is imported from Europe. Pat works for the business as needed. All three of the older offspring are successful in their chosen fields, the best of all worlds for a proud father. My stepsons Matthew and David Haddock, aged thirty-one and twenty-nine, are both artists. Matthew lives in Savannah, Georgia, doing theater set designs and construction, while Dave makes films in Los Angeles, California.

My wife Elaine and I were delighted when all four of my "kids," my two grandsons, and her two sons attended and participated in our wedding on August 23, 1997. Since then Elaine and I have done a lot of remodeling of the home I bought in Fairfax County, Virginia, in 1987. We have had some great trips together to Australia and New Zealand, to England and Ireland, to Alaska, and elsewhere around the United States. Elaine is still working full time at St. Matthews United Methodist Church in Annandale, Virginia, and I perform necessary chores here at home. We cook and garden together and are enjoying our marriage fully. Does it get any better than this? I do not think so!

Notes

[1] In some of the poorest developing countries, especially where rural birth rates are high and agricultural productivity increases lag significantly, there may be migration from the rural areas to the cities in hopes of finding higher incomes from the service and manufacturing sectors. Haiti and Bangladesh may be examples of this phenomenon.

[2] See *The Organization and Operation of Grade A Dairy Farms in South Carolina*, South Carolina Agricultural Experiment Station Bulletin 471, June 1959.

[3] See *Consumer Preference for Modified Whole Beverage Milks in S.C.*, South Carolina Agricultural Experiment station Bulletin 522, December 1965

[4] Eggs marked R had yolk color standardized at approximately 14 on the Hyman-Carver Yolk Color Rotor, while those marked S were very light in color, a 7 on the Rotor, and those marked T were a very dark 19.

[5] See *An Experimental Analysis of Market Potential for Shell Eggs Having Standardized Yolk Colors*, South Carolina Agricultural Experiment Station Bulletin 518, June 1965.

[6] See *Food Soldier* (Oakton, Va.: Ravens Yard, 2002). Chapter I, pp. 22–28.

[7] Ibid, pp 24–27.

[8] Ibid, p 27.

[9] My colleague and friend S. Blair Hutchison passed away peacefully in his sleep in August 1993. He was 83 years old. Blair taught me much about fly fishing for trout, at which he was a master, and about forestry economics, his career forte. His beloved Ellen moved to Albuquerque to be near her children Stephanie and Steven Lew.

[10] I am sorry to have to report that Ron died in December 2004 after a lengthy illness.

[11] I was sad to learn that Ed Watkins died in early May 2008. His many friends will miss his humor and kindness.

[12] See Howard L. Steele, PhD, RDD, *Haiti Agribusiness Workshop*, Port-au-Prince, August 29–30, 1985, Bureau for Latin America and the Caribbean, USAID, Washington, D.C., p.2.

[13] Ibid.

[14] My good friend and colleague John O'Donnell passed away in December 2003. We all miss his gentle being and very good humor.

[15] Dick Edwards passed away in January of 2007 after a long illness.

Glossary

Agricultural Attaché
A member of the Foreign Service of the U.S. Department of State but an employee of the U.S. Department of Agriculture, usually serving in a U.S. Embassy abroad. He or she promotes trade in U.S. agricultural commodities with the host country and provides agricultural facts about the host country's agricultural situation to the United States.

Agricultural Research and Training Institute (ARTI)
A division of the Sri Lanka Ministry of Agriculture in Colombo, where I served from 1982 to 1984.

Alliance for Progress
The program of technical assistance to Latin American countries by the U.S. government, as outlined in President John F. Kennedy's inaugural speech in 1961. Such technical assistance was to be coordinated and directed by the Agency for International Development (USAID), also formed in 1961 as a part of the U.S. Department of State. Congress funds USAID programs and projects through the Foreign Assistance Act on an annual basis.

Calacoto
The suburb of La Paz, Bolivia, 10,500 feet above sea level, where we lived on Calle Solidad from 1977 to mid-1980.

Caribbean Basin Initiative
A program enacted by the U.S. Congress and put into effect in 1983. The CBI removed all import tariffs on agricultural products produced and exported to the United States by the countries of Central America and the Caribbean, except for sugar, cotton, and related products. The purpose of the Initiative was to encourage

those countries to diversify their agricultural production away from monocultures, such as corn and beans, and take advantage of valuable exports of nontraditional crops to the United States, such as tropical fruits and vegetables, or temperate fruits and vegetables during the U.S. winter months.

"Clean Desked"
A bureaucratic punishment in which an employee's area of responsibility and work are taken away because of an infraction of rules or to encourage the employee to seek employment elsewhere. Sometimes the employee is recommended for employment in another agency. It is very difficult to "fire" a U.S. government employee, but it can be done for proven, blatant misconduct.

Colonia Los Angeles
The suburb of Tegucigalpa, Honduras, up the mountain from Toncontin International Airport, where we lived from 1980 to 1982.

Colombo
The capital and largest city in Sri Lanka. We lived on Jawata Road there from 1982 to 1984.

Consortium for International Development (CID)
A group of eleven western state universities from Alaska to Arizona that provided technical assistance in agricultural and rural development to many less-than-developed countries from the 1960s to the 1990s. CID's development funding came from various sources such as USAID, the Development Banks, the United Nations, and others.

Economic Commission for Europe (ECE)
An agency of the United Nations formed in 1961 as a part of the U.N.'s Economic and Social Council primarily to develop trade standards and adjudicate trade disagreements between countries. It originally comprised twenty-two developed country members and was the forerunner to the World Trade Organization. Its headquarters was in Geneva, Switzerland.

ESALQ
The Superior College of Agriculture "Luiz de Queiroz," Piracicaba, São Paulo, Brazil's oldest faculty of agronomy and

agricultural disciplines, where my family and I lived from 1964 to 1966 and where I taught economics in Portuguese.

Food and Agriculture Organization of the United Nations (FAO)
A U.N specialized agency formed in 1947 that provides research and technical assistance to developing countries in agriculture, fisheries, and rural development.

Foreign Economic Development Service
An agency of the U.S. Department of Agriculture (USDA) that provided technical assistance and training to other countries, with USAID, United Nations, or other sources of funding. In 1972 it became the Foreign Development Division of USDA's Economic Research Service. In 1976, under the Carter administration, it became the Office of International Cooperation and Development (OICD), then the International Cooperation Division of USDA's Foreign Agricultural Service in 1992.

Honduran Food Marketing Institute (IHMA)
The Honduran government agency originally responsible for the purchase, storage, sale, and export or import of all basic food grains, notably, corn, rice, beans, and sorghum. It became a research institute in 1985 to help guide food policy and price decisions by the Honduras Presidential Cabinet.

The Inter-American Development Bank (IDB)
Founded in 1959 by twenty-seven developed country governments to finance economic and social improvements in the thirty-five countries of the Western Hemisphere. It is the model on which the Asian Development Bank and the African Development Bank are patterned. These banks coordinate their projects and programs with the World Bank to avoid duplication.

Inter-American Institute for Cooperation on Agriculture (IICA)
An agency of the Organization of American States that provides technical assistance in agricultural and rural development in 34 of the 35 Western Hemisphere countries (excluding Cuba following Castro's takeover.)

The International Monetary Fund (IMF)
A specialized agency of the U.N. System founded in 1945 to help ensure the smooth international buying and selling of currency. It provides temporary financial assistance to countries with balance-of-payments problems, but it is not a bank.

Jardim Europa ("European Garden")
The suburb of Piracicaba, São Paulo State, Brazil where my family and I lived at 1195 Rua Dr. Alvin from 1964–1966.

Point IV Program
The fourth point in President Harry S. Truman's January 1949 inaugural address in which he promised the developing nations U.S. financial assistance to help in their development, to be provided by annual congressional appropriations to be administered by the U.S. Department of State.

PRODES
Project for the Development of the Yunges and Chapare regions of Bolivia, the Bolivian government project I managed with funding from USAID and the U.S. embassy from 1977 to mid-1980.

Public Law 480
A program enacted by the 83rd Congress in 1954 permitting the purchase in local currencies of surplus commodities owned by the U.S. government on favorable, easy, long-term repayment conditions to developing countries; it also permitted donations to countries suffering natural disasters, such as hurricanes, floods, and earthquakes.

Seconded
Describing the status of a government employee assigned from his home agency to another agency for a specified period of time and/or to perform a specific task, paid for by the requesting agency.

United Nations Development Program (UNDP)
The United Nations funding unit that provides, or funds, research and development expertise in many disciplines to developing countries. Such activity in the agriculture and rural sectors of those countries is a large part of the UNDP's portfolio.

United States Agency for International Development (USAID)
Originally founded as the Alliance for Progress in 1961 to provide technical assistance, humanitarian, and other assistance to developing countries, funded by tax dollars under the annual Foreign Assistance Act authorization administered by the U.S. Department of State.

United States Department of Agriculture (USDA)

The executive department that administers assistance to American farmers, cooperatives, and other agricultural businesses, promotes U.S. trade in American agricultural exports, establishes grades and standards to facilitate trade in agricultural commodities, engages in animal and plant safety regulations, provides food stamps and other food assistance to schools and lower income families, and carries out many more functions.

World Bank (formally, the International Bank for Reconstruction and Development)

The specialized agency of the United Nations system established at the 1944 Bretton Woods Conference in New Hampshire to fund postwar reconstruction. Following the reconstruction of facilities in Europe and Japan, the World Bank became, and still is, a significant source of funding for development projects in the developing countries.

The World Trade Organization (WTO)

The international organization founded by 104 countries in 1995 to replace the General Agreement on Tariffs and Trade (GATT). Like its predecessor, it aims to lower trade barriers and encourage multilateral trade, has wide authority to adjudicate unfair trade practices, and is located in Geneva, Switzerland.

Early Praise for
BUSHELS and BALES: A Food Soldier in the Cold War

"Here is one man's remarkable story of service to his government, fellow taxpayers, and yes, mankind's age-old struggle against hunger and backwardness. Howard Steele, a specialist in agricultural development and licensed pilot has been occasionally mistaken (not to his advantage) for a CIA operative; forced to flee from third world mobs bent on insurrection; an accidental close observer of a Viet Cong ambush; and at the controls of a small plane with a smaller margin of error maneuvering through the Himalayas.

"He advanced agrarian production and U.S. interests in dozens of countries for more than three decades. Along the way he made important agricultural findings, developed innumerable cross-cultural friendships, and met a few characters he can't forget – try as he might. *BUSHELS AND BALES* lets you accompany him on this amazing, entertaining journey."
—*Eric Rozenman, Editor, writer, and author of* Total Jihad

"Howard Steele has an enviable vivid, yet relaxed writing style that allows you to not merely read words on a page, but to become part of Howard's storytelling – the mundane, the life-threatening, and the hilarious, as he represented our country and applied his extensive technical expertise to better the lives of many people in the developing world."
—*Michael A. Boorstein, Director of Administration, Pan American Health Organization*

"I have admired Dr. Steele for many years. The integrity for which he is known in professional and academic circles shines through as he grapples with people and situations in foreign lands around the world. His book is recommended reading for anyone who has been in the U.S. Foreign Service, who is deep in the trenches today, or who is contemplating signing up for it. And, if you are none of these, read it for fun anyway."
—*Christine V. Emery, PhD, Vice President for Investment Policy, Overseas Private Investment Corporation.*

"The fifty years between 1950 and 2000 covered enormous technical and economic changes in our domestic and international food systems. With greatly increased information transfer, citizens of developing countries became increasingly aware of the lifestyle and cultural differences in developed societies. Howard Steele captures these changes from a unique perspective and rivets the reader's attention with anecdotes of his experiences. His lighthearted and informative writing style makes the material fascinating and easy to comprehend. The book should be required reading for students interested in international development and for career people planning to live in other countries."
—*David E. Hahn, PhD, Emeritus Professor of Agribusiness, Ohio State University*

"Howard Steele's *BUSHELS AND BALES* takes readers to many countries in various areas of the world in conditions not seen by people who enjoy Western lifestyles. His style is easily read and understood, enabling one to meet and enjoy many interesting people, places, processes, and events."

—*Louis S. Philhower, Founder-Partner, UBS, Macon, Georgia*

www.ingramcontent.com/pod-product-compliance
Lightning Source LLC
Chambersburg PA
CBHW020653270326
41928CB00005B/95